✔ KU-533-909

BRITISH ACADEMY
SHAKESPEARE LECTURES

d on z before

WITHDRAWN

822. 33 /BRI
College of.
St. Mark
& St. John
Library

BRITISH ACADEMY
SHAKESPEARE LECTURES
1980–89

INTRODUCED BY
E. A. J. HONIGMANN

Published for THE BRITISH ACADEMY
by OXFORD UNIVERSITY PRESS

Oxford University Press, Walton Street, Oxford OX2 6DP

Oxford New York Toronto
Delhi Bombay Calcutta Madras Karachi
Kuala Lumpur Singapore Hong Kong Tokyo
Nairobi Dar es Salaam Cape Town
Melbourne Auckland Madrid
and associated companies in
Berlin Ibadan

Published in the United States
by Oxford University Press Inc., New York

© *The British Academy 1993*

All rights reserved. No part of this publication may be reproduced,
stored in a retrieval system, or transmitted, in any form or by any means,
without the prior permission in writing of the British Academy.

The paperback edition of this book is sold subject to the condition that it shall not,
by way of trade or otherwise, be lent, re-sold, hired out or otherwise circulated
without the publisher's prior consent in any form of binding or cover
other than that in which it is published and without a similar condition
including this condition being imposed on the subsequent purchaser

British Library Cataloguing in Publication Data
Data available

ISBN 0-19-726139-6
ISBN 0-19-726133-7 (Pbk)

Printed in Great Britain
on acid-free paper by
The Cromwell Press Limited
Melksham, Wiltshire

CONTENTS

Notes on Contributors   vi

List of Plates   viii

Introduction   ix

'Forms to his Conceit': Shakespeare and the Uses of
Stage Illusion   1
R. A. FOAKES (1980)

Shakespeare's Mingled Yarn and *Measure for Measure*   19
E. A. J. HONIGMANN (1981)

The First West End Comedy   41
EMRYS JONES (1982)

Shakespeare's Liars   85
INGA-STINA EWBANK (1983)

The Dramatic Structure of Shakespeare's *King Henry the
Eighth:* An Essay in Rehabilitation   117
GLYNNE WICKHAM (1984)

The Reign of King Edward the Third (1596) and
Shakespeare   137
RICHARD PROUDFOOT (1985)

The Corridors of History: Shakespeare the Re-maker   165
GIORGIO MELCHIORI (1986)

Tales from Shakespeare   185
STANLEY WELLS (1987)

Hamlet: Conversations with the Dead   213
A. D. NUTTALL (1988)

Jacobean Playwrights and 'Judicious' Spectators   231
LEO SALINGAR (1989)

Index   255

NOTES ON THE CONTRIBUTORS

INGA-STINA EWBANK, Professor of English Literature, University of Leeds: joint editor of *Shakespeare's Styles* (1980), and author of many studies of the dramatic language of Shakespeare and his contemporaries, and of Ibsen and Strindberg; has translated (with Peter Hall) *John Gabriel Borkman* (1975) and other Ibsen plays.

R. A. FOAKES, Professor of English, University of California at Los Angeles (until 1992): recent books include an edition of *Lectures 1808–1819 On Literature* (2 vols, 1987) in *The Collected Works of S. T. Coleridge*, and *Hamlet versus Lear* (1993); editor of *Henry VIII* and *The Comedy of Errors* (Arden Shakespeare), of *The Revenger's Tragedy* (Revels Plays), and joint editor of *Henslowe's Diary* (1961).

E. A. J. HONIGMANN, Joseph Cowen Professor of English Literature, University of Newcastle upon Tyne (until 1989): joint general editor of The Revels Plays; author of *Shakespeare's Impact on his Contemporaries* (1982), *Shakespeare: the 'lost years'* (1985), *John Weever* (1987), *Myriad-Minded Shakespeare* (1989).

EMRYS JONES, Fellow of New College and Goldsmiths' Professor of English Literature, Oxford: author of *Scenic Form in Shakespeare* (1971) and *The Origins of Shakespeare* (1977); editor of *Antony and Cleopatra* (New Penguin Shakespeare) and of *The New Oxford Book of Sixteenth Century Verse* (1991).

GIORGIO MELCHIORI, Professor of English, University of Rome: author of *The whole Mystery of Art* (1960) and *Shakespeare's Dramatic Meditations* (1976); general editor of *Teatro Completo di William Shakespeare* (English and Italian, 9 vols); editor of *2 Henry IV* (Cambridge Shakespeare) and of *The Insatiate Countess* and (with V. Gabrieli) *Sir Thomas More* (Revels Plays).

A. D. NUTTALL, Professor of English and Fellow of New College, Oxford: author of many books and articles, including *Two Concepts of Allegory* (1967), *A New Mimesis* (1983), *The Stoic in Love* (1989) and *Openings* (1992).

RICHARD PROUDFOOT, Professor of English Literature, King's College, London: general editor of The Arden Shakespeare (1982–), formerly general editor of the Malone Society Reprints (1971–84); editor of *A Knack to know a Knave, Johan Johan, The Pardoner and the Friar*, and *Tom a Lincoln* (all M.S.R.).

LEO SALINGAR, Fellow of Trinity College and formerly Lecturer in English, Cambridge: author of articles in *Scrutiny* and other journals, and of *Shakespeare and the Traditions of Comedy* (1974) and *Dramatic Form in Shakespeare and the Jacobeans* (1986).

STANLEY WELLS, Professor of Shakespeare Studies and Director of the Shakespeare Institute, University of Birmingham: author of *Royal Shakespeare* (1977) and *Re-editing Shakespeare for the Modern Reader* (1984); general editor of the Oxford Shakespeare, joint general editor of the Oxford Complete Works, editor of *Shakespeare Survey* (since 1981).

GLYNNE WICKHAM, formerly Professor of Drama, University of Bristol: author of *Early English Stages 1300 to 1660* (3 vols, 1959–81), *The Medieval Theatre* (1974) and *A History of the Theatre* (1985).

LIST OF PLATES

I   *The Life and Death of Sir Henry Unton.* Anonymous
(*c.* 1596).   18

II   El Greco: *View and Plan of Toledo* (*c.* 1608).   31

III   Portrait of Katherine of Aragon by unknown
artist.   120

IV   Petruccio and Katherine: one of Frances Brundage's drawings for *The Children's Shakespeare* by E.
Nesbit (1897).   184

INTRODUCTION

THE annual Shakespeare Lecture of the British Academy has been published in the Academy's *Proceedings* from 1911; until 1986, lectures were also made available individually as pamphlets. In addition, three collections of lectures have been issued: *Aspects of Shakespeare*, with a preface by J. W. Mackail (1933); *Studies in Shakespeare* and *Interpretations of Shakespeare*, introduced by Peter Alexander (1964) and by Kenneth Muir (1985).[1] The first reprinted the nine lectures given in the years 1923–31; the second ranged more widely, with ten lectures selected from the years 1912 to 1961; the third offered ten lectures dating from 1942 to 1975.

In the present volume I have chosen to follow J. W. Mackail, reprinting ten consecutive lectures rather than a more personal 'selection'. Since the lectures are no longer issued as pamphlets, this will put them within reach of all those who do not have access to the *Proceedings*. The volume therefore lacks a 'theme', except that the lecturers observed the wishes of Mrs Frida Mond, who provided for the foundation of the series in 1910: Mrs Mond asked for an annual lecture 'on some Shakespearean subject, philosophical, historical, or philological, or some problem in English dramatic literature and histrionic art, or some study in literature of the age of Shakespeare.' As will be seen, the lecturers of the 1980s did not stray too far from the works of Shakespeare: their interest in Shakespeare and his immediate contemporaries holds the volume together.

The lecturers of course were aware of recent developments in their field, and some prepared lectures that grew out of debates then in progress. For this reason, and because the volume spans the 1980s, a brief survey of a few of the preoccupations and achievements of the decade may be helpful. It is necessarily selective, and makes no claims for the relative importance of different approaches.

(1) *Shakespeare's audience.* Two lectures (1980, 1989) deal with stage-illusion and with the audience's judgement, and several

---

[1] All three published by Oxford University Press, the first and third under The Clarendon Press imprint.

others touch on these and related topics. Such studies follow on from the work of Alfred Harbage;[2] Leo Salingar[3] mentions four widely discussed books published in the 1980s, by Ann Jennalie Cook, Michael Hattaway, Martin Butler and Andrew Gurr. See also Annabel Patterson, *Shakespeare and the Popular Voice* (Oxford: Basil Blackwell, 1989).

(2) *Authorship studies.* Two lectures (1984, 1985) analyse plays of disputed authorship. Although neither Glynne Wickham nor Richard Proudfoot is primarily concerned with 'the authorship question', they strengthen the case for Shakespeare's involvement in *Henry the Eighth* and *Edward the Third*. Other works attributed to Shakespeare in the 1980s include the poems 'Shall I die'[4] and *A Funerall Elegye* by W. S. (1612),[5] and the play *Edmund Ironside*.[6]

(3) *Revision theories.* A number of writers in the 1980s supported the case for Shakespeare as a reviser of his own plays, notably of *King Lear*.[7] The Oxford Shakespeare (1986) published both the 'first' and 'second' versions of the play, based on the Quarto and Folio texts. A less controversial play, *Sir Thomas More*, also attracted attention.[8] Giorgio Melchiori's lecture on 'Shakespeare the Re-maker' (1986) assumes an awareness of a general shift in thinking that includes many other plays.

(4) *Beginnings and endings.* Before 1980, several influential books had examined literary 'closure' and 'scenic form' (Frank Kermode, *The Sense of an Ending*, 1967; Emrys Jones, *Scenic Form in Shakespeare*, 1971; Walter C. Foreman, *The Music of the Close*, 1978). The last scene of *King Lear* probably received more attention than any other. In the 1980s criticism turned to opening scenes, as also in two Shakespeare Lectures (1982, 1988).

---

[2] Alfred Harbage: see especially *Shakespeare's Audience* (New York: Columbia U.P., 1941), *As They Liked It* (New York: Macmillan, 1947), *Shakespeare and the Rival Traditions* (Bloomington: Indiana U.P., 1952).

[3] Cf. p. 235.

[4] See Stanley Wells *et al.*, *William Shakespeare A Textual Companion* (Oxford, 1987), pp. 450–55.

[5] See Donald W. Foster, *Elegy by W. S. A Study in Attribution* (Newark: University of Delaware Press, 1989).

[6] See Eric Sams, *Shakespeare's Lost Play 'Edmund Ironside'* (1985).

[7] See particularly *The Division of the Kindoms Shakespeare's Two Versions of 'King Lear'*, ed. Gary Taylor and Michael Warren (Oxford, 1983).

[8] Scott McMillin, *The Elizabethan Theatre and 'The Book of Sir Thomas More'* (Ithaca: Cornell U.P., 1987); *Shakespeare and 'Sir Thomas More'*, ed. T. H. Howard-Hill (Cambridge, 1989); Anthony Munday and others, *Sir Thomas More*, ed. Vittorio Gabrieli and Giorgio Melchiori (Manchester, 1990).

(5) *Teaching Shakespeare.* Conferences in the 1980s produced many papers on the teaching of Shakespeare, especially in schools and in classes outside the English-speaking world.[9] Stanley Wells (1987) shows how earlier generations sought to prepare the young for Shakespeare. We may smile at their expurgated 'Tales': can we be certain, though, that more modern teaching methods (comic strips, plays compressed into thirty-minute videos) are more successful?

Most of the lectures of the 1980s pursued topics related to the general interests of the time. Inevitably some of the most discussed work of the decade is not represented at all. Many single plays were issued in new scholarly editions (in the Arden Shakespeare, the New Cambridge Shakespeare, the Oxford Shakespeare, etc.), and, a less commonplace event, the Complete Works were re-edited in old and in modern spelling (the Oxford Shakespeare). The social and political implications of the plays, and the theoretical assumptions of Shakespeare's critics, were re-examined, a debate that is not likely to die away for want of enthusiastic participants.[10] Although the lectures in this volume dwell on other topics, the 'Notes on Contributors' reveal that some of the lecturers also played a part in the re-thinking of editorial procedures (e.g. Stanley Wells) and of theory (A. D. Nuttall).

In addition to their awareness of other work produced in the 1980s, the lecturers pick up threads from earlier British Academy Shakespeare Lectures. R. A. Foakes on 'the Uses of Stage-illusion' (1980) may be compared with T. W. Craik, 'I know when one is dead, and when one lives' (1979), in so far as both attempt 'to understand the experience of audiences in theatres.' The lectures on 'Shakespeare's Mingled Yarn' and *Henry the Eighth* (1981, 1984) are concerned with genre and with the interconnections of different parts of a play, as was Harold F. Brooks in '*The Tempest* What sort of Play?' (1978). Giorgio Melchiori (1986) returns to questions that troubled E. K. Chambers in 'The Disintegration of Shakespeare' (1924); Leo Salingar's account of the social composition and intellectual

[9] See, for example, papers in *Images of Shakespeare*, ed. Werner Habicht (Newark: University of Delaware Press, 1988); *Shakespeare Survey 39* (1987); *Shakespeare Quarterly*, vol. 41 (1990), Summer issue (no. 2).

[10] See, for example, *Alternative Shakespeares*, ed. John Drakakis (1985); *Political Shakespeare*, ed. Jonathan Dollimore and Alan Sinfield (Manchester, 1985); *Shakespeare and the Question of Theory*, ed. Patricia Parker and Geoffrey Hartman (1985); Stephen Greenblatt, *Shakespearean Negotiations* (Berkeley: University of California Press, 1988).

attainments of Jacobean spectators may be compared with H. S. Bennett on 'Shakespeare's Audience' (1944).

All the contributors have taken the opportunity to correct misprints and to introduce a few minor improvements; one, Glynne Wickham, has added an important postscript. Otherwise we have left the lectures more or less as they were originally printed. This explains some perhaps puzzling inconsistencies— the fact that different lecturers chose to quote Shakespeare from different texts, and that consequently there are small surprises in the spelling of familiar names (for example, on p. 188) and in line numbering.

E. A. J. HONIGMANN

'FORMS TO HIS CONCEIT': SHAKESPEARE AND THE USES OF STAGE ILLUSION

By R. A. FOAKES

Read 23 April 1980

IN Shakespeare's age many seem to have taken it for granted that, in Roger Ascham's words, 'The whole doctrine of comedies and tragedies is a perfect imitation, or fair lively painted picture of the life of every degree of man'.[1] Sir Philip Sidney cited Aristotle as authority for defining poetry as an 'art of imitation', and then, alluding to Horace, rephrased it as 'a speaking picture'.[2] A third point of reference for this commonplace idea of poetry and drama was the phrase attributed to Cicero, but known only from Donatus, often quoted, as by Ben Jonson in *Every Man out of his Humour*,[3] and translated by Thomas Heywood in his *Apology for Actors*, where he wrote, 'Cicero saith a comedy is the imitation of life, the glass of custom, and the image of truth'.[4] Cicero's terms are not equivalent, but they tend to coalesce in Shakespeare's age in a common emphasis on imitation, picture, image of truth, reflection in a glass or mirror; the idea is expressed in various ways and crops up frequently in the drama itself, as for instance, in the prologue to Marlowe's *Tamburlaine*:

> View but his picture in this tragic glass ... (l. 7)

The most famous formulation occurs in Hamlet's advice to the players, where he rephrases Cicero's well-known formula in describing the purpose of playing as 'to hold, as 'twere, the mirror up to nature' (III. ii. 22) and goes on to condemn actors who 'imitated humanity' abominably.

[1] *The Schoolmaster* in ed. G. G. Smith, *Elizabethan Critical Essays* (2 vols., 1904), i. 7; see also Madeleine Doran, *Endeavors of Art* (Madison, Wisconsin, 1954, reprinted 1964), p. 71.

[2] *Defence of Poesie* in ed. A. H. Gilbert, *Literary Criticism from Plato to the Renaissance* (1940), p. 414.

[3] At III. vi. 206–7.

[4] *An Apology for Actors*, Sig. F1ᵛ; Gilbert, op. cit., p. 556; Doran, op. cit., p. 72.

It can readily be shown that Shakespeare did not simply accept the common equation of imitation and reflection in a mirror, as derived from Cicero. In various passages he seems to think of painting or art as mirroring nature, and providing 'a pretty mocking of the life' (*Timon of Athens*, I. i. 35), or 'the life as lively mock'd as ever' (*The Winter's Tale*, v. iii. 19), but he also envisaged the artist not merely rivalling but outdoing nature:

> Look when a painter would surpass the life
> In limning out a well-proportion'd steed,
> His art with nature's workmanship at strife,
> As if the dead the living should exceed . . .
>   (*Venus and Adonis* 289-92)

This surpassing of nature implies the possibility of idealization, as in the Painter's portrait of Timon:

> It tutors nature: artificial strife
> Lives in these touches, livelier than life
>   (*Timon* I. i. 37-8)

But the dramatist's idea of 'imitation' goes further, for Timon is depicted in the presence of the wholly imaginary goddess Fortune, so that the painting is doing something more than copy life, or improve on life.[1] Perhaps Shakespeare's most sophisticated conception of artistic possibilities occurs in *The Rape of Lucrece*, where Lucrece studies a painting of the Greeks and Trojans confronting each other before the walls of Troy, in which

> A thousand lamentable objects there
> In scorn of nature, art gave lifeless life.
>   (*The Rape of Lucrece* 1373-4)

In this 'skilful painting' it seems that the figures are brought to life, but not altogether,

> For much imaginary work was there, —
> Conceit deceitful, so compact, so kind,
> That for Achilles' image stood his spear
> Gripp'd in an armed hand: himself behind
> Was left unseen, save to the eye of mind:
>   A hand, a foot, a face, a leg, a head
>   Stood for the whole to be imagined.
>   (Ibid., 1422-8)

Here Shakespeare shows an understanding of the 'necessary incompleteness of all two-dimensional representation', and of the

---

[1] This point was developed by Madeleine Doran, op. cit., pp. 72 ff.

stimulus to the imagination to complete what is partially shown, a notable effect of illusion in art.[1]

At the same time, Shakespeare is of his age in thinking of the artist primarily as the ape of nature, and the performance of actors on the stage was regarded in the same way. Actors were praised for representing characters to the life, as in the well-known elegy on Richard Burbage:[2]

> Oft have I seen him leap into the grave
> Suiting the person which he seem'd to have . . .
> So lively, that spectators and the rest
> Of his sad crew, whil'st he but seem'd to bleed
> Amazed, thought even then he died indeed.

An actor's highest achievement was to play 'as if the Personator were the man personated',[3] and by the same token, the dramatist was applauded for achieving complete illusion, as in some prefatory verses addressed to John Fletcher in the 1647 Folio:[4]

> How didst thou Sway the Theatre! Make us feel
> The Players' wounds were true, and their swords steel!
> Nay, stranger yet, how often did I know
> When the Spectators ran to save the blow?
> Frozen with grief we could not stir away,
> Until the Epilogue told us 'twas a Play.

Passages such as this (which provides an early instance of the image of spectators intervening in a play, and confusing it with real life) reflect a common habit of taking imitation literally as a copying, or mirroring, of life. It informs not only the praise of actors and defences of the stage, but also, from the sixteenth century onwards, most attacks on the theatre as a source of corruption. In 1597 the Lord Mayor of London complained that plays corrupt young people by impressing on them[5] 'the very quality and corruption of manners which they represent . . . Whereby such as frequent them [are drawn] into imitation and not to avoiding the like vices'. In this he was echoing Stephen Gosson, and anticipating John Rainolds, who wrote of[6]

---

[1] E. H. Gombrich, *Art and Illusion* (second edition, 1962), p. 176.

[2] These anonymous lines, dating from about 1620 (Burbage died in 1619), may be found in E. K. Chambers, *The Elizabethan Stage* (4 vols., 1923), ii. 308-9.

[3] *An Apology for Actors*, Sig. B4r.

[4] By 'T. Palmer', in *The Works of Francis Beaumont and John Fletcher*, edited A. Glover (10 vols., 1905-12), I. xlviii.

[5] See E. K. Chambers, *The Elizabethan Stage*, iv. 321-2.

[6] *Th' Overthrow of Stage-Playes* (1599), p. 108.

The *actors*, in whom the earnest care of lively representing the lewd demeanour of bad persons doth work a great impression of waxing like unto them . . . the *spectators*, whose manners are corrupted by seeing and hearing such matters so expressed.

The circularity of such an argument passed unnoticed: plays imitate by copying life, and by representing vices (a part of life) players become corrupted; while by watching plays imitate life, the audience learn to imitate or copy the players, and are corrupted in turn.

In such attitudes to acting and the stage, the idea of imitation in the drama is taken literally as meaning to copy, picture or mirror life, and there is no room for a play of imagination, for the fantastic, or the exercise of what Shakespeare called the 'conceit deceitful'. Such attitudes imply a naïve or unthinking concept of stage-illusion, and assume that spectators are totally taken in by a spectacle which is a copy of real life; in other words, they imply that the illusion is complete. The notion that the drama holds the mirror up to life or nature, and that the audience is deluded into thinking what they see is real, has had a long life, and survives tenaciously in present-day criticism of the theatre. In the eighteenth century, a self-consciously neo-classical pursuit of correctness, stimulated by French theorizing, led to a long debate on the validity of the three unities. Imitation as a mirror of life was bound to seek to press the Unities into its service, but from about the same period perceptive critics began to recognize, even while condemning excessive irregularity or defiance of the rules, that all plays are likely to contain, in the words of Farquhar, 'several Improbabilities, nay, Impossibilities'.[1] His essay on comedy is especially interesting because of his defence of Shakespeare and his contemporaries, whose plots, he said, were 'only limited by the Convenience of Action'.[2] There were others who rejected a slavish attempt to obey the rules, but a major impetus to the argument was given by Dr Johnson's forthright treatment of the matter in his Preface to *The Plays of William Shakespeare* (1765).

He was particularly severe upon the unities of time and place,

[1] *A Discourse upon Comedy* (1702), in *The Complete Works of George Farquhar*, ed. Charles Stonehill (2 vols., 1930), ii. 341. Earlier still, Sir William Temple in 'Of Poetry', first published in his *Miscellanea* (1692), and reprinted in *Five Miscellaneous Essays by Sir William Temple*, ed. Samuel H. Monk (1963), pp. 173–203, had objected to the unities and 'rules' of drama, observing that no great writers among the ancients followed the rules.

[2] Farquhar, *Complete Works*, ii. 338.

recognizing the inadequacy of a naïve conception of imitation as a copy of life:[1]

The objection arising from the impossibility of passing the first hour at *Alexandria*, and the next at *Rome*, supposes, that when the play opens the spectator really imagines himself at *Alexandria*, and believes that his walk to the theatre has been a voyage to *Egypt*, and that he lives in the days of *Antony and Cleopatra*.

If the auditor is so deluded, then, Dr Johnson argued, he can accept anything, and this struck him as so implausible that he rejected altogether any possibility of stage-illusion:[2]

The truth is, that the spectators are always in their senses, and know, from the first act to the last, that the stage is only a stage, and that the players are only players.

This dogmatic position provoked an immediate response from William Kenrick, who saw the contradiction in Dr Johnson's argument that Shakespeare's drama is incredible, yet that he remains 'the poet of nature'. He tried to distinguish between delusion affecting our belief, and delusion affecting our emotions, and claimed that 'the deception goes no farther than the passions, it affects our sensibility, but not our understanding'. This was more subtle, but led him to conceive of the audience as merely passive, and to think that our 'convulsions of grief or laughter are purely involuntary'.[3]

Others attempted to work out a better understanding of stage-illusion, like Lord Kames, who thought of the audience in the theatre as in a 'waking dream',[4] but it may have been Erasmus Darwin, in the prose 'interludes' in his *The Botanic Garden* (1789), who took the debate an important stage further by introducing the idea of a voluntary participation by the audience; he wrote

if any distressful circumstance occur too forceable for our sensibility, we can voluntarily exert ourselves, and recollect, that the scenery is not real.

So he thought we 'alternately believe and disbelieve, almost every

---

[1] Ed. D. Nichol Smith, *Eighteenth Century Essays on Shakespeare* (revised edition, 1963), p. 118.

[2] Ibid., p. 119.

[3] His comments on Dr Johnson's *Preface* were published in the *Monthly Review* in October and November 1795; see ed. Brian Vickers, *Shakespeare The Critical Heritage*, vol. 5, 1765–1774 (1979), pp. 191–2.

[4] Henry Home, Lord Kames, *Elements of Criticism*, 6th edition, with the Author's last Corrections and Addition, 2 vols. (1785), ii. 418.

moment, the existence of the objects represented before us' on the stage.[1] It was left to Coleridge, who had read Kames and Darwin and many other authors who touched on the question of illusion in perception, to develop what remains perhaps the most searching analysis of the issue. In some elaborate draft notes for a lecture written probably in 1808, he rejected the common notion that the audience was in a state of 'actual Delusion', and Dr Johnson's idea that the audience is never deluded. He thought that 'Stage Presentations are to produce a sort of temporary Half-Faith, which the Spectator encourages himself and supports by a voluntary contribution on his own part, because he knows that it is at all times in his power to see the thing as it really is'; he went on to define this 'voluntary contribution' as a 'suspension of the Act of Comparison', permitting a kind of 'negative Belief', and suggested an image for the process in the dream or nightmare that 'takes place when the waking State of the Brain is re-commencing'.[2] These notes record the working out of ideas which were later summarized in a letter written in 1816:[3]

The truth is, that Images and Thoughts possess a power in and of themselves, independent of that act of the Judgement or Understanding by which we affirm or deny the existence of a reality correspondent to them. Such is the ordinary state of the mind in Dreams. It is not strictly accurate to say, that we believe our dreams to be actual while we are dreaming. We neither believe it or disbelieve it—with the will the comparing power is suspended, and without the comparing power any act of Judgement, whether affirmation or denial, is impossible. The Forms and Thoughts act merely by their own inherent power: and the strong feelings at times apparently connected with them are in point of fact bodily sensations, which are the causes or occasions of the Images, not (as when we are awake) the effects of them. Add to this a voluntary Lending of the Will to this suspension of one of it's own operations (i.e. that of comparison & consequent decision concerning the reality of any sensuous Impression) and you have the true Theory of Stage Illusion.

This fine conception of a temporary half-faith which the spectator

[1] *The Botanic Garden* (2 vols., 1789), ii. 87. The quotation comes from the second prose 'Interlude' on probability in art inserted in 'The Loves of the Plants'.

[2] See S. T. Coleridge, *Lectures 1808–1819: On Literature*, ed. R. A. Foakes (2 vols, Princeton, 1987), I. 134–6. The quotations have been checked against Coleridge's manuscript notes in the British Library.

[3] *Collected Letters of Samuel Taylor Coleridge*, ed. E. L. Griggs (6 vols., 1956–71), iv. 641–2. I am indebted to J. R. de J. Jackson's excellent account of 'Coleridge on Dramatic Illusion and Spectacle in the Performance of Shakespeare's Plays', *Modern Philology*, 62 (1964–5), 13–21.

encourages voluntarily by an act of will, suspending his powers of comparison and judgement, while he remains able to snap out of it and see the stage as a stage, explains the famous phrase in *Biographia Literaria*, 'that willing suspension of disbelief which constitutes poetic faith'. In stressing the spectator's voluntary participation and power of withdrawal, Coleridge formulated a concept of stage-illusion which allowed play for fantasy and the imagination, corresponding to something Shakespeare seems instinctively to have felt, as when he answered his own question in the Prologue to *Henry V*, 'Can this cockpit hold / The vasty fields of France?' with another image of the 'conceit deceitful': the obvious answer is 'no', but it is made 'yes' by the voluntary faith of the audience as the Chorus cries '*let* us . . . On your imaginary forces work'.

As in this passage, Shakespeare's comments in plays on the nature of his art often reflect upon its limitations,[1] but such remarks also reflect his confidence in the power of his art, and his instinctive grasp of the possibilities for stage-illusion. Behind Coleridge's analysis lies a very important distinction he made between an imitation and a copy, observing that our pleasure in an imitation, as in a landscape painting, comes from our consciousness of difference as well as likeness, whereas a copy strives to be identical with the original. Naïve theories of stage illusion start from a confusion between imitation and copy, as in the image of holding the 'mirror up to nature'. The confidence with which Shakespeare exploited this confusion from early on in his career is extraordinary, as is the subtlety with which he played variations on the uses of stage-illusion. In two plays he made it an issue in relation to the performances by companies of actors within the main action. In *A Midsummer Night's Dream* Bottom and the 'rude mechanicals' his companions spend the time when they might be rehearsing their play on 'Pyramus and Thisbe' for performance before Duke Theseus in anxious debate about problems of stage-illusion. They take for granted a naïve conception of illusion as copy, as Bottom as Pyramus must draw a sword to kill himself, which, he says, 'the ladies cannot abide'. His solution is to announce to the audience that he is not really Pyramus, but 'Bottom the weaver': he has made the common error of supposing the audience will be deluded into mistaking him for the real

---

[1] As Philip Edwards noticed in *Shakespeare and the Confines of Art* (1968); see also Anne Righter, *Shakespeare and the Idea of the Play* (1962). Both of these books have helped notably towards an understanding of Shakespeare's concern with the nature of his art.

Pyramus. The lion creates even more severe problems in Snout's
view: 'Will not the ladies be afeard of the lion?'. Again they assume
a total illusion, that the lion will be taken for real, and the only
way out is for Snug as lion to show his face, 'name his name, and
tell them plainly he is Snug the joiner'. The wall, on the other
hand, raises no problem; they realise they cannot build one, and
therefore must use an actor to represent it, who, in spite of having
'some plaster, or some loam, or some rough-cast about him to
signify Wall' is not likely to be mistaken for the real thing. Their
anxiety to prevent the audience being taken in, and their habit of
confusing their play with life, are funny because the scene exposes
how absurd it is to make that confusion, in a dramatic world
which begins, like Coleridge's theory of stage-illusion, from the
image of the dream, as opening vistas inaccessible to what Theseus
calls 'cool reason', and liberating the imagination of the audience
through the voluntary suspension of the powers of comparison.[1]

So this sequence continues with a rehearsal supervised by
Quince, but watched over also, as the audience knows, by Puck,
who does a little superior stage-managing on his own account in
sending back Bottom, when Thisbe's cue comes, 'with an ass-
head', as the stage-direction reads. Quince, Snout, Flute, and the
others run away at the sight of Bottom 'changed' or 'translated'
(Quince's word), whereas we in the audience see the actor playing
Bottom return disguised, to joke with the audience about it in a
brief soliloquy:

I see their knavery. This is to make an ass of me, to fright me, if they
could: but I will not stir from this place, do what they can. I will walk up
and down here and will sing, that they shall hear I am not afraid.   (III. i.
120)

Through all this scene Titania is on stage asleep, and Oberon has
applied the magic juice intending to 'make her full of hateful
fantasies' (II. i. 258) or delusions, but she wakes to see Bottom with
the ass-head and cry

    What angel wakes me from my flowery bed?   (III. i. 129)

Our pleasure in all this is related to our sense of the complex
variations Shakespeare is playing on the theme of stage-illusion.
The naïve realism of Quince and the 'hempen homespuns' causes

    [1] For an exploration of Shakespeare's use of the image of the dream, see
Marjorie Garber, *Dream in Shakespeare* (New Haven, 1974), and Jackson I.
Cope, *The Theatre and the Dream* (Baltimore, 1973), especially pp. 219–44, where
he relates the image of the dream to acting and illusion, with specific reference
to *A Midsummer Night's Dream* among other plays.

them to run away in fright from Bottom, for they see a monster; Titania wakes into a kind of dream to see Bottom as an angel, and fall in love with him; and we see him as the old Bottom, wearing an ass's head. Titania, as Queen of the Fairies, is no less incredible than Bottom transformed, and Shakespeare makes the most of the incongruities in this sexless encounter between embodiments of 'mortal grossness' and fairy grace. For each of them the experience is one of innocent delight. When Oberon releases her into the ordinary world of sight, she cries

> My Oberon, what visions have I seen!   (iv. i. 76)

So too Bottom wakes from sleep to exclaim, 'I have had a most rare vision. I have had a dream past the wit of man to say what dream it was'. Puck and Oberon do not share their illusion; Puck says, 'My mistress with a monster is in love' (iii. ii. 6), and Oberon, in releasing her, speaks of removing the 'hateful imperfection of her eyes' (iv. i. 63). Shakespeare exploits richly here the spectator's adaptability in response to forms of stage-illusion, his ability to yield to the play of imagination, and yet remain aware that he is watching a play in a theatre. The play brings together figures from classical legend in Theseus and Hippolyta, from fantasy and folklore in the Fairy King Oberon, his Queen Titania, and Puck, and from the peasantry of an English countryside in the working-men who rehearse their play in a hawthorn-brake. While Quince and Bottom seriously debate a naïve realism of stage-presentation, that debate is set against a dazzling proof of the possibilities of illusion in the visions Titania and Bottom have, visions which seem to them in some way better than the world of the play into which they awake. We both share in their visions of delight, and also, with Oberon, see this love of a fairy queen for an ass as a 'hateful imperfection'. The play exploits and exposes the naïve theory of stage-illusion, implying in the multiple levels of action here, and again in the play within the play in Act V, a recognition of the exciting possibilities the drama offers:

> Such tricks hath strong imagination
> That if it would but apprehend some joy
> It comprehends some bringer of that joy.
> Or in the night, imagining some fear,
> How easy is a bush suppos'd a bear.
>
> (v. i. 18)

How easily is an ass supposed a monster, an actress supposed a fairy-queen, or an actor supposed an Athenian Duke. Shakespeare maximises simultaneously our sense of the artifice of the stage, and the recognition that 'strong imagination' can make us 'suppose' anything. The play fittingly concludes with Puck speaking both in his role as a spirit, and out of it as an actor, reminding the audience at once of the way in which the play has shown them visions, inviting the imagination to suppose them for the moment in some sense real, and that Puck and his fellows are 'shadows', a term commonly applied to a semblance as opposed to the real substance,[1] and used here in the way Theseus had done earlier in this scene to refer to players, 'The best in this kind are but shadows' (v. i. 211). Shakespeare understood and relied upon that ability, identified by Coleridge, of the audience to yield to a half-faith and yet remain aware that they are watching actors on a stage, to believe anything while knowing all is make-believe.

Shakespeare returned to the issue of stage-illusion in *Hamlet*, which again incorporates theorizing about the nature of acting and drama, most notably in the form of Hamlet's advice to the players at Elsinore, which has often been taken as, in effect, the dramatist's own guidance to us all. Hamlet preaches moderation, from the point of view of a neo-classicist who despises the groundlings as 'capable of nothing but inexplicable dumb shows and noise' (III. ii. 11). His special recommendation is 'o'erstep not the modesty of nature' (III. ii. 19), since the purpose of playing has always been to 'hold as 'twere the mirror up to nature: to show virtue her feature, scorn her own image, and the very age and body of the time his form and pressure'; in this Hamlet offers a variant of the Ciceronian formula that defines drama as the imitation of life, the glass of custom and the image of truth.[2] Hamlet is offended by players who strut and bellow, and by clowns who speak more than is set down for them. All this commentary of his may be seen as deeply ironical in relation to his own performance. For on the one hand, he does not follow his own recommendations; if anyone in the play tears a passion to tatters it is Hamlet himself on those several occasions when he loses control over himself, as when he curses Claudius:

> Bloody, bawdy villain!
> Remorseless, treacherous, lecherous, kindless villain!
> Why what an ass am I! This is most brave,
> That I, the son of a dear father murder'd,

---

[1] See, for instance, *The Two Gentlemen of Verona*, IV. ii. 123–5:
> For since the substance of your perfect self
> Is else devoted, I am but a shadow;
> And to your shadow will I make true love.

[2] See above, p. 1.

> Prompted to my revenge by heaven and hell,
> Must like a whore unpack my heart with words,
> And fall a cursing like a very drab,
> A scullion.   (II. ii. 580)

Again, if anyone speaks more than is set down for him, it is Hamlet, who takes on himself a role like that of clown, and intervenes boisterously in the play within the play. On the other hand, there is nothing to indicate that the players performing 'The Mouse-trap' follow Hamlet's advice, and indeed Lucianus, making his 'damnable faces' (III. ii. 253) at the audience, evidently disregards it. In any case, Hamlet's neo-classical taste, perhaps fostered at Wittenberg, is hardly represented in the play within the play, which suggests, with its dumb-show and rhyming couplets, an old-fashioned play in the Senecan tradition written in a style reminiscent of that prevailing in the 1580s. The dialogue of the main action surrounding it is by contrast so much less formal that the play within the play evidently fails to 'hold . . . the mirror up to nature' and frighten Claudius, or 'catch the conscience of the King' (II. ii. 605). He watches the dumb-show and much of 'The Mouse-trap' with indifference, and is alarmed, it seems, not by the image it presents of the past, the murder of old Hamlet, but by the image it suggests of the future, when Hamlet identifies Lucianus as nephew to the Player King, and the play within the play suddenly seems to embody Hamlet's threat to kill his uncle Claudius.[1]

Hamlet's own taste seems to be for plays that are 'caviare to the general' (II. ii. 437), as suggested by his choice of 'Aeneas' tale to Dido' when he asks the players to show their quality. Yet this long descriptive speech, more in an epic than dramatic style, allows the First Player to enter imaginatively into the part, and become so absorbed in it that his face and body altogether express his feeling for Hecuba:

> Is it not monstrous that this player here,
> But in a fiction, in a dream of passion,
> Could force his soul so to his own conceit,
> That from her working all the visage wann'd
> Tears in his eyes, distraction in his aspect,
> A broken voice, and his whole function suiting
> With forms to his conceit?
>
>   (II. ii. 551)

[1] The debates about the staging and interpretation of this scene are summarized by M. R. Woodhead in 'Deep Plots and Indiscretions in "The Murder of Gonzago"', *Shakespeare Survey* 32 (1979), 151–61, an essay which is instructive on the various levels of irony at work.

The First Player here shows to Hamlet, and at the same time Shakespeare demonstrates to us, the inadequacy of a naïve realism that would tie drama to the image of the mirror of nature, an imitation or copy of reality; here the emotion is generated by an involvement of the imagination (or 'conceit') in 'a fiction, in a dream of passion', just as in the soliloquy that follows this Hamlet himself builds up a passion out of nothing and falls 'a-cursing like a very drab'. In his own actions Hamlet seems to contradict his theorizing, for as theorist he prefers neo-classical and formal modes of drama which have little to do with 'truth to life'.[1]

This is one of the ways in which Hamlet is 'placed' in the play, and it relates to Shakespeare's larger fascination with the nature of drama as fiction, dream, illusion. Perhaps the most daring feature of this play is the presentation of the Ghost in Act I, as a figure armed from head to toe. Whether audiences in Shakespeare's time had a greater readiness to believe in ghosts than theatregoers now do cannot be determined, but this Ghost does not wear conventional costume, and when he was poisoned old Hamlet was sleeping in his orchard, so that by the introduction of the Ghost in armour Shakespeare exploits not belief, but disbelief, or rather our willingness to yield a temporary half-faith to anything in the theatre. Perhaps it would be truer to say that with this startling and improbable apparition Shakespeare maximises both belief and disbelief. On its first two appearances the Ghost is merely seen and does not speak. At one point, according to the Quarto direction it 'spreads his arms', when Horatio accosts it, but, silent, it remains an apparition, to harrow with fear and wonder, as Horatio cries 'Stay, illusion'. If it is an illusion to him and Marcellus, what is it to the audience? When it next appears in I. iv, it speaks to Hamlet, and now is no longer an 'illusion', but becomes 'real'; for the moment it talks, the Ghost becomes Hamlet's father, as if he were alive,

A figure like your father,
Armed at point exactly,   (I. ii. 199)

as Horatio describes the 'apparition'. In I. iv the Ghost literally does 'assume' the 'noble person' of old Hamlet, as if he were brought back to life. When he speaks to Hamlet, we listen not to an

---

[1] And when occasion demands he can 'rant' as well as Laertes (v. i. 284), or any player who tears a passion to tatters. I have found very helpful Roy W. Battenhouse's discussion of 'The Significance of Hamlet's Advice to the Players', in *The Drama of the Renaissance: Essays for Leicester Bradner*, edited Elmer M. Blistein (1970), pp. 3–26.

'illusion' or 'apparition', but to a father admonishing his son, to an ordinary human being—for this ghost has a temper, has passions, thinks, is affected by a range of emotions, including horror and disgust. The Ghost abuses Claudius, reproves Gertrude, moralises on virtue and lust, describes the murder of old Hamlet as if he had been a spectator at it, and is especially outraged at the manner of his death:

> a most instant tetter bark'd about
> Most lazar-like, with vile and loathsome crust
> All my smooth body
>
> (I. v. 71)

The variety of his utterance registers a suffering, angry, and rather tedious figure, to whom most respond, like the Prince, as to old Hamlet indeed. Yet the whole thing is make-believe; Shakespeare challenges our incredulity by putting the Ghost in armour, yet paradoxically makes him more credible because he assumes the person of, and turns into, the old warrior King who smote the sledded Polack on the ice.

All fictions are possible on stage. The actor playing the Ghost playing old Hamlet is moved to anger and horror at the narration of his own death; the actor playing Hamlet is moved by the passion generated by the player in a play within the play, over Hecuba mourning for the death of Priam, to burst out, forcing his soul to his own (and Shakespeare's) imagination, with the passion of 'O what a rogue and peasant slave am I'. Shakespeare had a much more complex understanding of his art than Hamlet, and does not hold the mirror up to nature; he rather extends our capacity to give faith to anything, ghosts, fairies, witches, spirits, while playing upon our awareness of the make-believe of the theatre. At the very centre of emotion, the heart of a character's most powerful moment of dramatic life, he can pull us up short by this consciousness—as in *Macbeth*, for instance:

> Life's but a walking shadow, a poor player
> That struts and frets his hour upon the stage
> And then is heard no more
>
> (v. v. 24)

Through Shakespeare's exploitation of the audience's readiness to yield a temporary half-faith, and his simultaneous exploitation of their knowledge that they are in a theatre watching actors, there runs a deeper sense of the complex relation of life to drama, of the way we all play roles for our own audiences. Shakespeare's practice leaves room for and encourages the imaginations of the audience to collaborate with his 'conceits deceitful', and to animate by their own projective participation the dramatic world of his plays. In his mature plays Shakespeare seems to anticipate by two centuries that subtle understanding of the nature of dramatic illusion worked out by Coleridge.

I have been concerned with dramatic illusion as a concept refined during the eighteenth century by critics who were attempting to understand the experience of audiences in theatres without darkened auditoria, and to explain especially the working of illusion in relation to Shakespeare's plays. The trend towards realism in the nineteenth century was accompanied by refinements in theatre lighting and design which led to a kind of drama that attempted to mirror life, with the audience watching from the dark a brilliantly lit stage representing a room with the fourth wall removed. This led to the common use of the term 'illusion' to refer to stage-sets and plays which sought to copy real life, and to acting which pretended the audience was not there.[1] Effectively this produced a fundamental change in the implications of the word, for whereas Shakespearian uses of stage-illusion activated the imagination of the audience to share in relating and completing his dramatic images, the effort of scenic illusion was to deny participation by providing a stage-picture so 'real' and detailed that the audience would not need to use their imaginations at all. The reaction against this, which, as far as Shakespeare is concerned, was given an early impetus by Harley Granville-Barker,[2] was slow to take effect in the commercial theatre, and it is only with the new drama of the last twenty years that a sense of the possibilities of exploiting audience awareness in relation to stage-illusion has been recovered for serious drama. However, this recovery takes on a specific and limited character in relation to the two modes of drama which have most prominently been associated with it. One is the post-Brechtian drama of political commitment, as exemplified in the work of a dramatist such as John Arden, which has been seen as breaking away from a dominant nineteenth-century tradition of a drama of scenic illusion, a theatre of acceptance, persuading the audience to leave their 'critical, questioning faculties outside', into a new mode, a drama of

[1] The erosion of the Shakespearian or Coleridgean concept of the term is already to be seen in Charles Lamb's essay on 'Stage Illusion' (1825), which begins, 'A play is said to be well or ill acted in proportion to the scenical illusion produced. Whether such illusion can in any case be perfect, is not the question. The nearest approach to it, we are told, is when the actor appears wholly unconscious of the presence of spectators'.

[2] Notably in his British Academy Lecture of 1925, 'From *Henry V* to *Hamlet*'.

challenge, 'a theatre of scepticism and questioning'.[1] The second is absurdist drama, which tends to devalue language, and to emphasize the isolation of individuals who cannot readily communicate with one another. Such drama, with its 'indifference to the distinction between illusion and reality', is concerned with lonely figures preoccupied with appearances and role-playing; their only reality is the 'performing self', the self they create, since external reality presents itself as an inexplicable and impenetrable network of social and political relations.[2]

This concern with audience awareness and illusion in recent drama seems narrow in relation to Shakespeare's far more wide-ranging exploration of the uses of stage-illusion. This exploration culminates in the late plays in a demonstration of the power that the deceptions, metamorphoses, and illusions which are the stuff of art possess to enlarge our sympathies by giving life to images of coherence and reconciliation, as, for example, in the disguisings and tricks which run through the later part of The Winter's Tale, and lead to the final grand use of illusion in the play within the play, stage-managed by Paulina, in which Hermione appears as a statue, coming to life to be reunited with the penitent Leontes, who thought he was to be 'mock'd with art' (v. iii. 68).[3] The fact is that the word is often still, confusingly, used in its more limited sense, as if realism gave us 'a theatre of total illusion';[4] and a recent handbook on changes in the treatment of Shakespeare in the last hundred years concludes with the triumph of 'non-illusion', confusing stage-illusion with scenic illusion in pointing to Peter Brook's 1970 production of A Midsummer Night's Dream as an attempt to 'deny all stage-illusion, leaving a sufficient vacuum to be filled by the imagination of the spectator'.[5]

[1] Albert Hunt, Arden: A Study of his Plays (1974), pp. 24, 28. Hunt claims that Arden's drama is like both Brecht's and Shakespeare's in this 'scepticism and questioning', but he goes on to define it in ideological terms which illustrate rather how radically different it is from that of Shakespeare.

[2] See Christopher Lasch, The Culture of Narcissism (New York, 1878), pp. 86–7, 91–3, and Richard Poirier, The Performing Self (1971); cf. also Harold Pinter's comment on the characters in his plays: 'Obviously, they are scared of what is outside the room. Outside the room is a world bearing up on them, which is frightening . . . we are all in this, in a room, and outside is a world . . . which is most inexplicable and frightening' (quoted in Martin Esslin, The Peopled Wound, 1970, p. 35).

[3] See N. S. Brooke, 'Shakespeare and Baroque Art', Proceedings of the British Academy, lxiii (1977), 66–8, for further comments on illusion in this play and The Tempest.   [4] J. L. Styan, Drama, Stage and Audience (1975), p. 170.

[5] Id., The Shakespeare Revolution (1977), Chapter 11, 'Shakespeare, Peter Brook and Non-Illusion'; the quotation is from p. 230.

All productions tend to fix a play in the images imposed by the director, but by the same token none completely restricts the imagination of the spectator. There can be no such thing as a theatre of 'total illusion'. At the height of naturalism, Strindberg understood this, when he wrote in his preface to *Miss Julie*:[1]

As far as the scenery is concerned, I have borrowed from impressionistic painting its asymmetry, its quality of abruptness, and have thereby in my opinion strengthened the illusion. Because the whole room and all its contents are not shown, there is a chance to guess at things—that is, our imagination is stirred into complementing our vision.

The notion of a theatre of non-illusion is as misleading as the idea of a theatre of total illusion, and both reflect a simplistic and crude concept of the way illusion works. It is strange that criticism of the drama and of Shakespeare especially should suffer from such misconceptions, for recent studies of the uses of illusion in painting, and in relation to reading literature, especially the novel, have provided a basis for recovering a much subtler understanding of the way it works. These have been concerned in particular to emphasize the complex nature of the illusions by means of which all art functions, exploiting the 'power of expectation, rather than the power of conceptual knowledge' in the viewer or reader, his readiness to project and complete images in accordance with his own 'mental set'.[2] So Wolfgang Iser argues that in reading novels, illusion in effect means

our own projections, which are our share in gestalten which we produce and in which we are entangled. This entanglement, however, is never total, because the gestalten remain at least potentially under attack from those possibilities which they have excluded but dragged along in their wake. Indeed, the latent disturbance of the reader's involvement produces a specific form of tension that leaves him suspended, as it were, between total entanglement and latent detachment. The result is a dialectic—brought about by the reader himself—between illusion-forming and illusion-breaking.[3]

If in reading fiction our involvement is potentially under attack from excluded possibilities, so that there is a dialectic between

---

[1] This is reprinted in A. M. Nagler, *Sources of Theatrical History* (New York, 1952), reissued as *A Source Book in Theatrical History* (New York, 1959), p. 583.

[2] E. H. Gombrich, *Art and Illusion*, pp. 188–90.

[3] *The Act of Reading* (1976; translated into English 1978), p. 127. In relation to illusion in the novel, see also Robert Alter, *Partial Magic* (1975), and Michael Irwin, *Picturing: Description and Illusion in the Nineteenth Century Novel* (1979).

'illusion-forming and illusion-breaking', then this is more vividly true of the theatre, where the audience is conscious of watching a performance by actors playing roles. The most naturalistic drama cannot do away with that dialectic, however much it may seek to minimize it; perhaps the most exciting aspect of Shakespeare's extraordinary achievement as a dramatist is that he realized the rich possibilities that lay in maximizing it, and playing upon his audience's consciousness of being in a theatre. If we are to appreciate fully the uses of stage-illusion in Shakespeare's plays, as distinct from scenic illusion, we would do well to bring to bear on them that exploration of the concept that began in the eighteenth-century, led to the fine perceptions of Coleridge, and has been revived in recent analysis of the visual arts and of the novel.[1]

[1] Line references are to the Riverside Shakespeare (ed. G. Blakemore Evans, 1974).

PLATE I

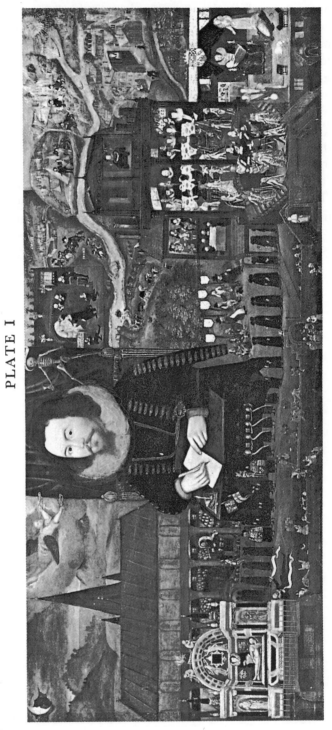

The Life and Death of Sir Henry Unton. Anonymous (*c.* 1596)
National Portrait Gallery, London.

SHAKESPEARE'S MINGLED YARN AND *MEASURE FOR MEASURE*

By E. A. J. HONIGMANN

Read 23 April 1981

THIS will not be a lecture for purists. I propose to examine a trend
that troubled Sir Philip Sidney when he lamented the fashion for
'mongrel tragi-comedy'—a shift in literary taste that owed much
to the genius of William Shakespeare. It started, perhaps, with the
mixing of comic and more serious matter in medieval drama; Kyd
and Marlowe gave it a new impetus; and it had certainly arrived
by the time of *Measure for Measure*, Shakespeare's darkest comedy.
But I have in mind something more far-reaching than the
hybridization of kinds, or the doctrine of purity of genre. As
Elizabethan drama moved towards realism, and simultaneously
lurched in several other directions as well, many kinds of 'mixing'
were developed—prose and verse; natural and stylized language,
and stage behaviour, and acting; Elizabethan and 'historical'
costume, as in the Peacham sketch of *Titus Andronicus*; plot and
sub-plot—to name just a few 'mixings' that must have been in
general use by the 1580s. Then Shakespeare appeared on the
scene, pressed a button, and the mixer-speed accelerated remarkably, much to the disgust of purists (like Ben Jonson). Shakespeare
delighted in mixed metaphor; Jonson reputedly said of some of the
grandest speeches in *Macbeth*, which 'are not to be understood',
that 'it was horror'. Shakespeare specialized in crazily complicated plots, cross-wooing comedies, plays with time-jumps, plays
that zigzag between different countries—disgraceful 'mixings'
that Jonson castigated publicly. More modern critics discover the
same tendency wherever they look: Shakespeare's expert inter-
weaving of different views of the same person, of past, present, and
future, of slow time and fast time, of conflicting motives, or the
interplay of many emotions in a single phrase—'Pray you, undo
this button'; 'Kill Claudio'. If, as I shall argue, Shakespeare's
mixing skills were of the essence, as indispensable to his success as
his inventiveness in metaphor, it may be no accident that he so
often peaks as a poet in scenes of intense emotion or madness

(Hamlet's, King Lear's), where a 'mixer' mechanism in the play triggers off his own special talent. I believe that these mixing skills are conscious artistry, not inspired fumbling, if only because the dramatist so often draws attention to them:

> You have seen
> Sunshine and rain at once: her smiles and tears
> Were like, a better way.   (*King Lear*, IV. iii. 16 ff.).

We need not doubt that a writer who said that 'the web of our life is of a mingled yarn' would know, even without Ben Jonson's unnecessary help, that he himself was a purveyor of intricately mingled yarns.

The 'mixing' principle in Shakespeare is my subject today. Ben Jonson was merely the first of many good critics who could not come to terms with it, and one or two other examples will illustrate the range of problems. Dr Johnson, though he defended tragicomedy, thought that 'the poet's matter failed him' in the fifth act of *Henry V*, 'and he was glad to fill it up with whatever he could get'; in Johnson's view, Act V did not mix with the rest. Coleridge repudiated the 'low' porter-speech in *Macbeth*, which reminds us that bawdy, once removed by editors as intrusive dirt, is now praised as an integral part of the Shakespearian 'mix' in both comedy and tragedy. T. S. Eliot faulted Shakespeare's 'mixing' even more ingeniously, arguing that it is

strictly an error, although an error which is condoned by the success of each passage in itself, that Shakespeare should have introduced into the same play ghosts belonging to such different categories as the three sisters and the ghost of Banquo.[1]

These are all 'mixing' problems, and they warn us that Shakespeare's imagination scrambled the ingredients of a play in so many new ways that even the very best critics 'hoppe alwey bihinde'.

Examples of supposedly bad 'mixing' are alleged, and have to be endured, in almost every book on Shakespeare. Yet the mixing principle itself has not had the attention it deserves. This may be because criticism finds it convenient to deal with detachable units—imagery, character, genre, scene-by-scene analysis—rather than with the intermeshing of such units, which I consider the heart of the mystery. After four centuries criticism is still largely defeated by a procedural problem, how to grapple with the play as a whole: I suggest that we may solve this problem by focusing on

[1] T. S. Eliot, *Selected Essays* (ed. 1953), p. 116.

the mixing principle, searching for its unique functioning in each text. Not only Shakespeare criticism could benefit: we do not have to look far to discover similar needs elsewhere. Let me illustrate, tactfully, from *Juno and the Paycock*, where, it has been said, the tragic element 'occupies at the most some twenty minutes . . . for the remaining two hours and a half this piece is given up to gorgeous and incredible fooling'.[1] Who has not heard that *The Winter's Tale* consists of three acts of tragedy followed by two of comedy? Or that some scenes in *Measure for Measure* are 'tragic', others 'comic'? It is the interpenetration of comedy and tragedy that now needs our attention—or, more exactly, the interaction of everything with everything else, in these unfathomably rich plays.

O'Casey once remarked: 'I never make a scenario, depending on the natural growth of a play rather than on any method of joinery.'[2] Shakespeare criticism, when it attempts to explain the mixing principle, still tends to think too much in terms of joinery—as in a brilliant paper on *The Winter's Tale* in which Nevill Coghill showed that the bear, the famous bear, 'was calculated to create a unique and particular effect, at that point demanded by the narrative mood and line of the play. It is at the moment when the tale, hitherto wholly and deeply tragic, turns suddenly and triumphantly to comedy.'[3] Much that Coghill said about the bear seems to me perceptive, yet his is largely an explanation of joinery. Looking at the play as an organic growth, I am struck by the fact that each of its two movements ends with an addition to the story by Shakespeare—the bear, and the statue. In each case the bystanders, astounded, react aesthetically, as if the bear and statue are merely a thrilling spectacle, then struggle comically to adjust their bewildered feelings—and thus lift the scene, emotionally, in a very similar way. If the bear and statue are connected, as I think, then the mixing principle works not only in local joinery but also, more elusively, in shaping dramatic units that are far apart.

I am going to assume, in what follows, that in 'organic' drama everything joins on to everything else; that bears and statues can shake hands, as over a vast, and embrace as it were from the ends of opposed winds. The logic of our bread-and-butter world need not apply; the linear structure of events, and of cause and effect, is

[1] James Agate, quoted from *Sean O'Casey Modern Judgements*, ed. Ronald Ayling (1969), p. 76.

[2] Sean O'Casey, *Blasts and Benedictions* (1967), p. 97.

[3] Nevill Coghill, 'Six Points of Stage-Craft in *The Winter's Tale*', *Shakespeare Survey XI* (1958), pp. 31–41.

not the only structure that concerns us. Although we are sometimes told that a literary work grows in the reader's mind as does a musical composition, being a process experienced in time, and should not be compared to a painting, which is frozen in time, a play that lasts two to three hours differs from longer literary works, such as an epic or a novel, in so far as its process can be held in the mind as a single experience, somewhat like a painting. Aided by memorable dialogue and good acting a poetic drama will not pass away from us while we surrender to its magic, as do the trivia of day-to-day existence: such a play grows in the beholder's mind in a present continuous, partly insulated from time, a single shared experience framed by the stage, one that remains present, like a painting, even as it unfolds, challenging us to connect the ends of opposed winds, a bear and a statue, Claudio's guilt and Angelo's, Angelo's ignorance of the world and Isabella's and the Duke's. 'Only connect' is the dramatist's command, and the more unexpectedly he mixes the play's ingredients the bigger the challenge.

I would like to illustrate the 'present continuous' of drama from a soliloquy that some of you may remember—'To be or not to be, that is the question'. I find it surprising that, according to some competent editors, Hamlet here talks not of his own suicide but only of the general problem of life after death. Dr Johnson paraphrased the opening line succinctly, as follows: 'Before I can form any rational scheme of action under this pressure of distress, it is necessary to decide whether, after our present state, we are to be or not to be. That is the question . . .' Another editor soon offered a different interpretation, 'To live or to put an end to my life', which, he thought, was confirmed by the following words. Johnson had his supporters, and I find this surprising not because of the following words but because of preceding speeches that prepare us for 'To be or not to be'. Hadn't Hamlet wished that 'this too too solid flesh would melt'? (Knowing what we know about the frauds and stealths of injurious imposters, I had better say firmly that 'solid flesh' is the reading of the only authorized text . . . of this lecture.) 'You cannot, sir, take from me anything that I will more willingly part withal—except my life, except my life, except my life.' These and other passages determine our immediate impression that in 'To be or not to be' Hamlet meditates upon his own suicide; the soliloquy is not a detachable unit, it throbs with implications planted in our minds in earlier scenes.

If my example seems fanciful, let us take two that are more

straightforward. Let us take the one sentence that occurs in both *Othello* and *Macbeth*. Lady Macbeth waits for Macbeth; he appears, the daggers in his hands, blood on the daggers; the deed is done, and wrings from her a terrible, gloating cry—'My husband!' Othello explains to Emilia that the murder of Desdemona proceeded upon just grounds ('Thy husband knew it all'), and she reacts in shocked surprise—'My husband!' The same words, but the effect is totally different, because the words mingle with previous impressions, there is an inflow of power from very different sources. Lady Macbeth had taunted her husband that he was not man enough to commit the murder; when he has proved himself she cries, in effect, 'My true husband, at last!' Emilia had suspected that Desdemona had been slandered by 'some cogging, cozening slave, to get some office'; as soon as Othello names Iago it dawns on her what has happened, and she feels that she has come to a crossroad in her life. Her exclamation marks the end of a marriage, Lady Macbeth's a new beginning (as she thinks) of hers. The words that are spoken out loud are only a small part of the complex communication that goes on at the same time; whether we are conscious of it or not, these words mix with other impressions—are, indeed, completely dwarfed by momentous implications that immediately rush in upon us.

So far I have concentrated on the play's organic growth, indicating how important lines or episodes grow out of others, mixing with what we may have heard or seen much earlier in the play's 'present continuous'. The mixing principle can also be illustrated from 'joinery', as O'Casey called it—an unkind word that refers, presumably, to the way one episode is cobbled on to the next. Such local joinery, in the hands of a Shakespeare, can serve to illustrate the highest skills, where the craftsman's conscious mixing and the play's organic growth are indistinguishable. We can observe how felicitously each episode joins on to its neighbour and fits the needs of its individual play by comparing three with very similar functions—the grave-digger episode in *Hamlet*, the porter-scene in *Macbeth*, and Cleopatra's interview with the clown who brings the asp. In each case a clown's 'low' humour precedes and follows scenes of high tension, or of tragic seriousness, yet each of the three has unique features determined by its play. In *Hamlet*, where there had been much talk of suicide and the hereafter, the two clowns pick up these themes and fool around with them as naturally as grave-diggers pick up bones. Hamlet's interest in the question, 'How long will a man lie i'th'earth ere he rot?' is related to an earlier topic, how long will a man's memory outlive his life (two hours? twice two months?) — two kinds of survival after death. The play being filled with mock-interviews, in which the prince pretends to misunderstand a questioner (Rosencrantz and Guildenstern; Claudius; Osric), first grave-digger turns the tables on him, answering knavishly — so the shape of their exchanges is another thread that hooks into a larger design. 'Alas, poor Yorick' mysteriously echoes 'Alas, poor ghost'; and so on. The grave-digger episode, in short, mixes with the rest of the play in its larger themes, in specific questions, in verbal echoes, and in using a special dialogue-device, the mock-interview; and no doubt in other ways too.

A word will suffice for *Macbeth*. The dramatic irony in the porter's soliloquy is familiar: it is Macbeth who is an equivocator, who has 'hang'd himself on th'expectation of plenty'. True. I am equally struck by the porter's exchanges with Macduff — for the porter, in the delightful afterglow of his carousing, also resembles Macbeth in the previous scene in being present and not present; his tipsiness has the same effect as Macbeth's imagination — he only gives half his mind to the matter in hand. And in each case there is a cool observer and questioner, Lady Macbeth and Macduff, whose presence measures the distance of Macbeth and the porter from normality. Just as the knocking in the porter-scene spills over from the previous scene, the porter's tipsiness grew out of Macbeth's intoxicated imagination and his slowness in answering the call of the here and now and his psychic distance from Macduff were also influenced by the previous scene. It should be noted in passing that alcohol plays a part in the grave-digger *and* porter scenes, yet its effect is adapted to the needs of the play no less than is each clown's distinctive way of speaking and relating to others.

Next, Cleopatra's clown. Plutarch mentions a 'countryman', who brings the asp in a basket of figs, but not a word about his interview with Cleopatra, which is pure Shakespeare — perhaps his most daring 'mingle' in the tragedies, because here comedy modulates immediately into the tragic climax. Appropriately, it is comedy shot through with sexual innuendo, and even the chastest ears cannot miss it.

You must not think I am so simple but I know the devil himself will not eat a woman. I know that a woman is a dish for the gods, if the devil dress her not.

The richest insinuation and 'mingle' in the clown-scene, however, grows out of one keyword, repeated eight times — 'Hast thou the pretty worm of Nilus there?', 'I wish you all joy of the worm'. It's a word not used by Plutarch at this point, and conjures up a very different image from Plutarch's one specific description of the asp: Cleopatra pricked the creature with a spindle, so that, 'being angered withal,' said Plutarch, 'it leapt out with great fury, and bit her in the arm'—not really what one expects from a bona fide worm. In Elizabethan English, of course, *worm* could mean reptile, or serpent, or other things—and, since no one in the play's first audience is likely ever to have seen an Egyptian asp, the uncertain meaning of *worm* was particularly useful. We are made to wonder exactly what this hidden worm may be. 'The worm will do his kind', the clown explains, helpfully. 'The worm's an odd worm.'

I have dwelt on the spectator's inability to imagine exactly what to expect because there must have been a reason for the dramatist's teasing vagueness. I am reminded of another teasing device in the play—its concealed penis imagery, a joke repeated several times, in different ways, by different characters. Since learned editors don't feel obliged to explain what can't be seen, I had better give some examples. (1) The soothsayer tells Cleopatra's ladies that their future fortunes are alike. 'Well,' says Charmian to Iras, 'if you were but an inch of fortune better than I, where would you choose it?' Reply?—'Not in my husband's nose'. (2) Cleopatra, bored, asks Charmian to play billiards; Charmian suggests Mardian the eunuch instead, and Cleopatra quips 'As well a woman with an eunuch play'd / As with a woman'. (3) A third concealed image is given to Agrippa:

> Royal wench!
> She made great Caesar lay his sword to bed.
> He plough'd her, and she cropp'd.

The wicked word is not mentioned—indeed, was not known yet, though the English language was rich in alternatives. Here, then, are three examples of concealed penis imagery—a distinctive series in the play that puts us in a state of readiness for the clown's *worm*. We have to remember at this point the infinite variety of Shakespeare's sexual imagery, and that he had used the same image before, when Lucrece exclaims against rape—'Why should the worm intrude the maiden bud?' (a traditional image long before Blake's *The Sick Rose*). Recalling also how tirelessly the Elizabethans punned on the sexual sense of *lie* and *die*, we observe that the general context also nudges us towards concealed imagery. 'I would not desire you to touch him', the clown tells Cleopatra,

for his biting is immortal; those that do *die* of it do seldom or never recover.

Cleopatra. Remember'st thou any that have *died* on't?

Clown. Very many, men and women too. I heard of one of them no longer than yesterday: a very honest woman, but something given to *lie*, as a woman should not do but in the way of honesty; how she *died* of the biting of it, what pain she felt—truly, she makes a very good report o'th'worm.

The extraordinary power and flavour of this clown-scene partly depends on concealed imagery, imagery reactivated by the puns on *lie* and *die*, by 'a woman is a dish for the gods, if the devil dress her not', by the clown's winking knowingness and by Shakespeare's teasing vagueness as to what the worm might be. At one and the same time the worm refers to the asp (a word carefully excluded until the clown has gone), to the worm in the grave, and to the sex-worm whose 'biting' is also immortal—hence the pungent rightness of the clown's parting shot to sex-obsessed Cleopatra, 'I wish you joy o'th'worm!' Here, marvelling at a treble pun that has its tentacular roots in other local puns, and in concealed imagery that acts upon us subliminally, one is tempted to cry, with Cleopatra, 'O heavenly mingle!'—for what more is possible? Yet the mingling continues:

> Give me my robe, put on my crown; I have
> Immortal longings in me.

'Longings for immortality', thought the New Arden editor. Perhaps; but, after 'I wish you joy o'th'worm' she also means 'immortal longings' as opposed to 'mortal longings'—a higher form of sexuality, a kiss from the curled Antony 'which is my heaven to have'. The sublime 'Give me my robe', a speech structured round the idea of 'immortal longings', grew out of the largely latent sexuality and low comedy of the clown-scene.

The three clown-scenes, possibly written for the same actor, have been thought to have a similar function in three of the greatest tragedies. Yet they are not merely 'comic relief', since each one builds upon ideas, images, mental states, or relationships from previous scenes—that is, flashes back to more serious concerns, mingling seriousness with laughter. (Meredith's phrase, 'thoughtful laughter', is peculiarly apt: an awareness that the clown-scene somehow mingles with what has gone before pulls us back from surrendering wholly to laughter, even though we cannot stop the play to trace all the connections.) More important for my purposes: not only are the clown-scenes sewn into the fabric of the play in so many ways—each one is sewn in in its own distinctive way. There may be superficial resemblances, but we fail to appreciate the dramatist's skill unless we see that seemingly similar devices always 'mingle' quite uniquely with their dramatic surroundings.

That brings me to the notorious 'bed-trick' in *Measure for Measure*. It was Shakespeare's error, we have been told often enough, that he chose to solve the problems of a realistic plot by resorting to pure folk-tale. After the 'realism' of the early scenes, of Angelo's passion for Isabella and of his demand that she buy her brother's life by yielding her virginity, comes the bed-trick— Angelo's betrothed, Mariana, takes Isabella's place in his bed—a hangover from folk-tale or romance, it is said, quite out of keeping with what has gone before. This account of the play assumes that Shakespeare had got into trouble with his plotting, and that the bed-trick was an attempt to slither round a difficulty. Shakespeare had departed from his sources in making Isabella a novice in an order of nuns, and in giving her a passionately virginal nature; unlike her prototype in the sources, therefore, she could not comply with Angelo's demand—so we have the bed-trick instead, a desperate expedient.

Before I argue that, on the contrary, the bed-trick is beautifully right where it is placed, no less than the bear in *The Winter's Tale*, a multiple 'mingle' in a self-consciously mingled yarn, let us examine our terminology—realism and folk-tale. So-called realistic scenes in the play do employ non-realistic devices: the low-life characters meticulously finish their sentences; Angelo soliloquises —in verse. Realism is adjustable; so, too, folk-tale episodes can be presented more or less plausibly. Much can be done to bring realism and folk-tale together, to make them tone in with one another; before we denounce the bed-trick as a desperate expedient it is our duty to ask how it mingles with its surroundings.

First, though, I must correct a common misrepresentation of the bed-trick in literature. Bed-tricks, though familiar in folk-tale and romance, were not restricted to one or two *kinds* of literature: we have all read Genesis 19: 33, and *The Escapes of Jupiter*, and *The Magus*. Next: a bed-trick story can be told in the spirit of the *Reeve's Tale* or of the *Knight's Tale* or—somewhere in between. The use of significant detail will sharply differentiate one bed-trick story from another.

We can learn what Shakespeare might have done, had he thought a bed-trick too 'unrealistic' after his play's earlier scenes, by glancing at some other literary versions. Even Malory, not the most realistic of writers, felt that a drugged drink was needed to trick Lancelot into sleeping with the fair Elaine—'as soon as he had drunk that wine he was so assotted that he wened that maiden Elaine had been queen Guinever' (xi, 2); later Elaine's lady-in-waiting 'took him by the finger' (there's realistic detail!) 'and led him unto her lady'. Deloney's *Jack of Newberry*, a rip-roaring narrative, provides a more representative example of bed-trick realism. An English girl, Joan, had an importunate Italian lover, who became a nuisance until Joan's kinsman taught him a lesson. The kinsman gave a 'sleepy drench' to a young sow, put the sleeping sow in Joan's bed, 'drawing the curtains round about', and told the lover that his opportunity had arrived. But, he warned, 'you must not . . . have a candle when you go into the chamber, for . . . dark places fits best lovers' desires'. The Italian knelt down by the bedside, saluted the invisible sow with a love-speech, slipped into bed, ardently embraced her, and only discovered his mistake from her non-human grunting.[1] I hesitate to call this realism, but we may say that Deloney made room for more 'realistic' touches than Malory. In Marston's *The Insatiate Countess*, which is close to *Measure for Measure* in genre and date, two ladies plot to sleep with their own husbands (the husbands each having importuned the other's wife), 'and the better to avoid suspicion', one wife explains, 'thus we must insist: they must come up darkling'. 'But,' says the second wife, 'is my husband content to come darkling?' This problem solved, she thinks of another difficulty. 'I am afraid my voice will discover me.' 'Why, then you're best say nothing . . .' 'Ay, but you know a woman cannot choose but speak in these cases.'[2] The dramatist positively delights in applying a 'realistic' imagination to the bed-trick, without damaging his play.

It appears, then, that you can choose between comedy and seriousness, between more and less realism. In bed-trick scenes you can adopt almost any position, as it were. This is hard for us to grasp today, because we have been taught to think of the bed-trick as a purely literary device, one that belongs to literature at its furthest possible remove from life. Before the invention of electricity, however, the night-life of Europe must have been much more tricky than now, and there is plenty of evidence that strange things happened in the dark.

> Now 'tis full sea a-bed over the world,
> There's juggling of all sides . . .
> This woman, in immodest thin apparel

[1] *The Works of Thomas Deloney*, ed. F. O. Mann (Oxford, 1912), pp. 51–2.
[2] *The Plays of John Marston*, ed. H. Harvey Wood (3 vols., 1939), iii. 29.

Lets in her friend by water. Here a dame
Cunning, nails leather hinges to a door
To avoid proclamation.
Now cuckolds are a-coining, apace, apace, apace, apace!

I have laboured the point that Shakespeare did not have to fall
back on a 'ready-made' bed-trick, the figmentary bed-trick of
folk-tale and romance, simply to suggest that he was free to devise
his own. The stark contrast that so many critics have disliked in
Measure for Measure as 'realism' is succeeded by the bed-trick,
I conclude, was entirely of his own choosing. The play was written
when he was at the height of his powers, when he had fully
mastered the art of mingling one episode with another, yet this
bed-trick jars all expectation. Why did Shakespeare choose it, in
this form, when there were other options open to him?

As I mentioned at the outset, drama in the later sixteenth
century introduced many new kinds of 'mingling'. Some of the
dramatists no doubt did so unconsciously. By the turn of the
century, however, the mingled yarn of literature was a matter of
public debate. Italian critics defended tragicomedy; Sidney
moved with the times in defending pastoral, where some 'have
mingled prose and verse . . . Some have mingled matters heroical
and pastoral', though he was not happy about 'mingling kings and
clowns'.[1] In *The Faerie Queene* Spenser aimed at variety, copying
the artful confusion of Italian epic so that, as he put it, many things
are 'intermedled' with one another—again, the mingling principle, artful combination. Metaphysical poetry, said Dr Johnson,
experimented with the 'combination of dissimilar images . . . the
most heterogeneous ideas are yoked by violence together'.[2]

Similar experiments took place at the same time in the visual
arts, and they also have a bearing on *Measure for Measure*.
Mannerist painters of the later sixteenth century sought out new
combinations, mingling realistic detail in a recognizably non-
realistic ensemble, as in Arcimboldo's *Librarian*, a deplorably
bookish gentleman, or his *Autumn*, a jolly old Bacchus made out of
fruit and veg whose features are recognizably those of the Emperor
Rudolph II. Sometimes the Mannerists even mingled different
levels of realism: Pontormo's *Joseph in Egypt* in the National
Gallery playfully distorts scale and perspective, and includes
clothed figures standing on pedestals like statues, wholly fanciful
architecture with stairways leading nowhere—an imagined world,

[1] Sir Philip Sidney, *An Apology for Poetry*, ed. Geoffrey Shepherd (1965),
p. 116.
[2] Johnson's *Life of Abraham Cowley*.

consciously deviating from nature, in no sense intended as a copy of nature.

Whether such Mannerist experiments of the late sixteenth century were influential in England is difficult to determine. We do know, however, that illustrations in sixteenth-century English books often depicted mingled scenes: a single crude woodcut may combine the creation of Eve, the Temptation, and the Expulsion from Paradise. This is a tradition that goes back to medieval art; inevitably, it appealed to later book illustrators, and English readers would know it from Harington's *Orlando Furioso* of 1591, where the engravings are copied from an Italian edition. One unusual painting of the late Elizabethan age also belongs to this tradition— *The Life and Death of Sir Henry Unton* (it hangs in the National Portrait Gallery), an attempt to bring together many scenes from the life of one of Queen Elizabeth's ambassadors: his arrival at Oriel College, Oxford; his wedding-masque; his diplomatic missions; his funeral procession and burial. Although not strictly a Mannerist painting, it mingles different scales and different degrees of realism, and each scene mingles differently with its neighbours. The artist or artists may not have been of the highest quality (some of the detail is most delicately finished), but there can be no doubt that the 'mingling principle' is consciously employed. Remember, please, how the half-length figure of Sir Henry Unton holds the whole composition together. For there is a similar centre-piece in one of the greatest Mannerist compositions, El Greco's *View and Plan of Toledo*, which belongs to the same decade as *Measure for Measure* and deserves our closer attention. According to one admirer, El Greco here did his utmost

to prevent the actual view of Toledo from dominating the picture. He put the figure of the river god of the Tagus in the left foreground. He also removed the monastery, which lay outside the town and for which he presumably painted the view of the town, from reality by transferring it from *terra firma* to a bright airy cloud. Above it he painted the vision of Mary borne high over the town by angels. . . . The painter further distorted the view of Toledo . . . by the addition of the half-length figure of a boy holding out the plan of Toledo to the spectator.[1]

Unlike the allegories of the High Renaissance, such as Botticelli's *Primavera*, El Greco's composition reassembles matter in jarringly new ways; his centre-piece, the monastery in the clouds, asserts the artist's right to make the most unexpected combinations, where heterogeneous ideas and images are yoked by violence together.

[1] F. Würtenberger, *Mannerism* (1963), p. 239.

PLATE II

El Greco: *View and Plan of Toledo* (c. 1608)
Museos de las Fundaciones Vega-Inclán

I have digressed in order to suggest that discussions of 'mingling' problems in tragicomedy and pastoral, of 'intermeddling' in Italian epic and its derivatives, the self-conscious mingling of heterogeneous ideas and images in metaphysical poetry, and the radical rethinking of compositional norms by the Mannerists, all reflect the spirit of the age, no less than Guarini's *Compendio* of 1602, which Shakespeare could scarcely have seen, and all point forward to *Measure for Measure*. While we cannot demonstrate Shakespeare's knowledge of Italian and Spanish Mannerists, there are signs of similar experiments in England, and we can claim that he was aware of the new trends in literature. Polonius announces the actors in Elsinore—the best actors in the world for 'tragedy, comedy, history, pastoral, pastoral-comical, historical-pastoral, tragical-historical, tragical-comical-historical-pastoral, scene individable, or poem unlimited'. If even Polonius grasps that the dramatic poem no longer conforms to the traditional limits of genre, we may take it that Shakespeare and his public must have been interested in such technical developments as well.

In *Measure for Measure* Shakespeare went one step beyond any he had previously taken, not merely mingling the play's ingredients surprisingly, as often before, but making an issue of it, challenging the audience to put the pieces together and to think critically about a 'poem unlimited'. The notorious bed-trick comes at the point of no return, when a spectator *must* ask himself, even if he has previously failed to do so, 'What kind of play is this?' Terms such as 'problem play' and 'dark comedy' had not yet been invented; 'tragi-comedy' was sometimes discussed, but there was no agreed definition—in England there had been no serious attempt at definition. Up to Act III it would be reasonable to see *Measure for Measure* as a tragedy that includes a good deal of low comedy (like *Romeo and Juliet*), or as a new-formula play such as the 'tragical-comical-historical-pastoral' of Polonius, or as tragi-comedy. Whichever one favours, the important thing is that one can't be certain—and, consequently, that one keeps returning to the question, 'What kind of play is it?' Even the modern spectator can't avoid this question, since he still has to fit all the bits and pieces together. 'Is Angelo's self-accusing honesty, or Isabella's torment, too life-like, placed beside a disguised duke and a comic constable, in *this kind of play*?' The question has already nagged us for a while when suddenly Shakespeare introduces the bed-trick, a twist so unexpected that now we can no longer escape our dilemma—'What kind of play?' Observe that the bed-trick, Shakespeare's addition to the story, whatever it may achieve in simplifying Isabella's problems, notably complicates the play's genre problems and the spectator's genre expectations.

The bed-trick resembles the bear in *The Winter's Tale*, and the 'Cinna the poet' scene in *Julius Caesar*, and the porter-scene in *Macbeth*, in coming at the point where the play modulates from one mood into another. It is done differently in each one, of course, but nowhere more self-advertisingly than in *Measure for Measure*. For, just at this point, the play's style joltingly changes gear several times. The Duke soliloquises in rhyming tetrameters, a new voice for him—

> He who the sword of heaven will bear
> Should be as holy as severe,
> Pattern in himself to know
> Grace to stand, and virtue go;
> More nor less to others paying
> Than by self-offences weighing. . . .

Then follows the play's only song, and shortly thereafter the Duke switches in mid-speech from verse to prose—all warning signals that the play is about to change direction. Then follows the play's most arresting modulation, Isabella's speech about the proposed midnight meeting with Angelo, a speech that the dramatist could easily have left to the audience's imagination. Shakespeare chose to give Isabella this speech, I think, because it allows him to suggest, in passing, a unique mingling of realism and romance, and the unique nature of his play: the speech combines a romantic sense of mystery, as in Mariana's song, with an insistent factualness.

> He hath a garden circummur'd with brick,
> Whose western side is with a vineyard back'd;
> And to that vineyard is a planched gate
> That makes his opening with this bigger key;
> This other doth command a little door
> Which from the vineyard to the garden leads.
> There have I made my promise
> Upon the heavy middle of the night
> To call upon him.

Despite its factualness (the garden, brick wall, vineyard on the western side, the gate, the smaller door, the two keys), this speech cannot be called 'realism'; a garden *circummured* with brick and a vineyard with a *planched* gate also carry overtones from another world, the world of Mariana of the *moated grange*, the world of *The Romance of the Rose*. The mingle, and the sense of a special creative pressure, is supported by out-of-the-way words (*circummured* and *planched*, like *moated*, occur nowhere else in Shakespeare; *circummured* was his coinage); and it is all bonded together by a concealed image—the Freudian slip when Isabella's imagination dimly anticipates sexual contact ('Upon the heavy middle of the night', an unusual turn of phrase that stamps her personal feeling upon this special bed-trick).

In this speech, neither realism nor romance, we are asked to give a willing suspension of disbelief to an experience as strange as the coming to life of the statue at the end of *The Winter's Tale*—a bed-trick as peculiar to this play as Hermione's statue is different from all the other statues that return to life in romances before Shakespeare. It is a far cry from Deloney's passionate Italian and his drugged sow, and from all other bed-tricks in literature, because Shakespeare (like El Greco in *The View and Plan of Toledo*) has reassembled and mingled his material in new ways. Instead of the 'clever wench' or 'clever wife' who wishes to reclaim her husband (as represented by Helena in *All's Well*) he gives us Mariana, a mere pawn in someone else's clever game; and he changed the man, a mere sex-object for the traditional 'clever wife', into the brooding, vulnerable Angelo. The bed of the 'bed-trick' disappears from view, and Shakespeare eliminates the snigger found in other plays (including *All's Well* and *The Changeling*) when one of the principals goes to or returns from copulation: instead we are asked to apply our imagination to a garden, a vineyard, a planched gate. The actors, the moral implications of the action, the feelings involved, our sense of place, our awareness of a containing society—all are changed for the specific needs of *Measure for Measure*.

Shakespeare's immense care in fitting the bed-trick into his story is also evident in his handling of Mariana. It may seem, to those who believe that the dramatist snatched the bed-trick out of the air to solve an unforeseen plot problem, that Mariana accepts it too readily. That is to presuppose that her character is reflected in the hauntingly romantic song sung for her when she first appears at the moated grange—'Take, O, take those lips away'. Producers usually cast her thus, as a dreamy romantic, for which we must partly blame Tennyson's poem *Mariana*.

> She only said, 'My life is dreary,
>   He cometh not,' she said;
> She said 'I am aweary, aweary,
>   I would that I were dead!'

Yet Shakespeare's pure and romantic maiden jumps without

hesitation at the offer of a place in Angelo's bed; the whole complicated story is explained to her by Isabella while the Duke speaks a short soliloquy, and Mariana is ready. Out of character? No: Tennyson misrepresented her. Shakespeare had previously stressed that, when Angelo rejected Mariana's love, this, 'like an impediment in the current, made it more violent and unruly' (III. i. 237 ff.). She suffers from an overmastering passion—easily conveyed to us if she has a picture or keepsake of her lover, kissing it passionately as the boy sings, 'But my kisses bring again, bring again'. Mariana's willingness to undertake the bed-trick is prepared for by what we are told about her 'violent and unruly' affection, and probably by her 'body-language' as she listens to the song; instead of being just a romantic dummy in the plot, she has character—sufficient character—to tone in with the near-realism of adjacent scenes. And she also tones in with all the other characters in the play who suffer from irresistible sexual impulses —Claudio and Juliet, Lucio, Mrs Overdone, Angelo.

To argue that Shakespeare by no means lost sight of the demands of realism, or near-realism, when he decided to introduce the bed-trick, may seem unwise. I would like to pursue this possibility for a moment, since the entire second half of the play appears to pull away from realism, and indeed to pull away from the first half, and this requires some explanation. The sense that the play modulates into a new mood, or changes direction, comes in Act III Scene 1, where the bed-trick is announced. Just before we hear of the bed-trick, it is important to notice, Shakespeare jolts our trust in the Duke, who proposes the bed-trick. How can the Duke say so confidently to Claudio, 'Son, I have overheard what hath pass'd between you and your sister. Angelo had never the purpose to corrupt her; only he hath made an assay of her virtue . . .'? We *know* this to be false, since we overheard Angelo's soliloquies, whereas the Duke didn't. He continues 'I am confessor to Angelo, and I know this to be true . . .'. Some critics have wondered whether the disguised Duke could be, or could ever have been, confessor to Angelo, and one has even expressed indignation that the secrets of the confessional should be revealed, contrary to the rules of the Church. The ordinary theatre-goer, however, is unlikely to encumber himself with such idle fancies: aware that the Duke's assertion, 'I know this to be true', is a fabrication, he is cued to regard 'I am confessor to Angelo' as another fabrication. Whatever his motives, the Duke appears to snatch arguments out of the air, and Shakespeare invites us to note his dexterity, and inventiveness. Then, within a few lines, the

conjurer-duke produces from his hat the bed-trick—snatches it
out of nothing, another brilliant improvisation, again one that he
has scarcely had time to think through, any more than his right to
say 'I am confessor to Angelo'.

Just as Angelo tangles himself in one deception after another,
and Lucio, the comic foil, in one lie after another, the disguised
Duke finds himself obliged to improvise more and more desperately—inventing the future, as it were, and becoming more and
more unable to control it. We already feel uneasy about his
reading of the future, I think, when he explains to Friar Thomas
that he needs a disguise because he wants Angelo to clean up
Vienna, and immediately adds that he half-mistrusts Angelo—

> Hence shall we see,
> If power change purpose, what our seemers be.

At this stage the Duke sees his own future role as that of an
observer:

> And to behold his sway
> I will, as 'twere a brother of your order,
> Visit both prince and people.

When he reappears, however, the observer feels impelled to throw
himself fully into his new role as a friar, interrogates Juliet
('Repent you, fair one, of the sin you carry?'), and then improvises
impressively as he lectures Claudio on death. Has an observer the
right to impose thus on another human being, merely by virtue of
his disguise? The moral authority of his speech, 'Be absolute for
death', is undercut by our awareness that he is playing a part—a
growing uncertainty about him, corresponding to our uncertainty
about the nature of the play. More unmistakably disturbing is the
Duke's sudden expedient that Barnardine's head should be sub-
stituted for Claudio's; the Provost's amazement, and reluctance
to comply, inform the audience, if ordinary human instincts fail to
do so, that to play with life in this way is presumptuous. What, we
ask ourselves, is he up to?

Everything said and done by the Duke, from his initial decision
to appoint Angelo as his deputy and to look on as a 'friar', can be
read as improvisation, usually as hurried improvisation. We are
therefore prompted to think of the bed-trick not as an 'archaic
device' placed in uncomfortable proximity to psychological
realism by a fatigued dramatist, but as the Duke's device, just as
much an expression of his character as his disguise-trick, and his
other surprising and whimsical expedients. As the second half of
the play pulls away from realism, and the question 'what *kind* of

play?' grows more urgent, we look to the Duke to solve our prob-lems, while at the same time we half suspect that the dithering Duke merely improvises irresponsibly. His awareness of Angelo's intentions, and of all that happens, serves as a hint to the audience that a tragic outcome may be prevented; yet the Duke's sheer inefficiency, highlighted by his failure to control Lucio, by no means guarantees a happy ending. Our uncertainty about the nature of this mingled yarn therefore continues—augmented, I think, by our uncertainty about the Duke's double image (as duke and friar), and about his motives and his control.

In the second half of *Measure for Measure*, as we wonder whether the Duke and the dramatist know where they are going, we are teased with several possibilities. The shape of the play begins to resemble a familiar Elizabethan stereotype—the story of the clever man who overreaches himself, who initiates a dangerous action, and has to improvise more and more frantically to hold off disaster (Marlowe's Barabas, Shakespeare's Richard III and Iago). But, if we sense this kinship, Shakespeare refuses to conform to his model, for in this version of 'the sorcerer's apprentice' the fumbling friar reassumes control at the end, as the Duke, and the stereotype is shattered.

Another possibility is that the ending will be like that of *The Malcontent*, where a disguised duke resumes his ducal authority, forgives his enemies, and only one, the wicked Mendoza, is punished by being ceremonially kicked out of court. Yet Shake-speare also includes intimations of a tragic outcome—a possi-bility that remains open, even though neither of Angelo's intended crimes (the rape of Isabella, and the judicial murder of her brother) has been committed. The deputy's abuse of power deserves to be punished with death, as he himself recognizes:

> When I, that censure him, do so offend
> Let mine own judgment pattern out my death . . .

And later:

> let my trial be mine own confession;
> Immediate sentence then, and sequent death,
> Is all the grace I beg.

Angelo's death, or tragic humiliation, must be what Isabella intends when she denounces the 'pernicious caitiff deputy' and clamours to the Duke for 'justice, justice, justice, justice!' This echo of *The Spanish Tragedy*, of Hieronimo's cry to his king—

> Justice, O justice, justice, gentle king! . . .
> Justice, O justice!   (III. xii. 63, 65)

—brings to *Measure for Measure* a similar tragic intensity. There are even moments when we are reminded of a play performed by the King's Men shortly before *Measure for Measure*, another play in which a ruler withdraws from his responsibilities, leaving, in effect, a deputy, whom he has raised but distrusts, a man whose abuses are closely watched by the ruler's spies, who is at last trapped and exposed as theatrically as Angelo. And in the case of *Sejanus* the outcome is tragedy.

It appears to have been Shakespeare's strategy to leave open his play's outcome and genre to the very end. We recognize several possible models, including *The Malcontent* and *Sejanus*, but not one that really answers our question, 'What kind of play is it?' Until the very last minutes the execution of Angelo remains a possibility —all the more so since some spectators would know that in some versions of this widely dispersed story Angelo did lose his head. Then, just as we think we know where we are, Shakespeare springs two more surprises. The play seems to turn into a comedy of forgiveness—until the Duke remembers Lucio, and hacks at him with unforgiving vindictiveness. In addition, we have the Duke's proposal to Isabella, which invariably comes as a surprise, despite all the efforts of producers to prepare us for it—and surely was meant to be one, the 'happy ending' of another kind of comedy grafted on here with the same careful tissue matching as we found in the bed-trick. Is a disturbing proposal not appropriate at the end of a deeply disturbing play?

It is particularly in the second half of the play that its genre is brought into question—and here Shakespeare protects himself, and teases the audience, by making it more emphatically the Duke's play. The Duke, of course, was given the role of inventor of the plot, and stage-manager, from the beginning. In the second half of the play he has to interfere more and more decisively, to resume the active responsibility that he had found so irksome, and becomes more completely the play's dramatist. After the bed-trick—*his* bed-trick, as I have said—there follows a little scene of comic misunderstanding, modelled on *The Spanish Tragedy*, that demonstrates exactly how far he may be trusted as a dramatist. Angelo's messenger arrives with a strict order that Claudio is to be executed punctually, and the Duke, all at sea, declares, preposterously, 'here comes Claudio's pardon', and again

> This is his pardon, purchas'd by such sin
> For which the pardoner himself is in.

He's wrong, and Shakespeare wants us to notice it. The dramatist-duke has lost control of his play—and as he hurriedly attempts to reorganize his plot, he, almost as much as Shakespeare, becomes responsible for its genre, and for our genre expectations. Knowing him as we do, we cannot expect artistic tidiness. He, the Duke of dark corners, is the inventor of almost all the improbable, 'non-realistic' twists of the story that make *Measure for Measure* Shakespeare's most challengingly mingled yarn before *The Winter's Tale*—his disguise as a friar; the bed-trick; the substitution of another head for Claudio's; the concealment of Claudio's escape from Isabella; the unexpected proposal of marriage. All these improbabilities, dreamed up by one man, are therefore rooted in psychological realism, being all expressions of the Duke's imagination, which is as individual as Hamlet's or Prospero's. Duke Vincentio's imagination, like that of a Mannerist painter, delighting in unexpected combinations, makes his bed-trick as necessary a centre-piece to the play's design as El Greco's monastery, which sits so solidly and improbably in a cloud of cotton wool. The Duke, in short, with his love of mystification and ingenious twists and turns, forever revising his options, was the ideal dramatist to put into this mingled yarn—the distinctive feature of which is that it mystifies and keeps changing direction, both at the level of story and of seriousness, insisting on our revising our expectations to the very last.

And what have the Duke and the bed-trick to do with all my other examples—the bear and the statue in *The Winter's Tale*; 'To be or not to be'; the cry 'my husband!' in *Othello* and *Macbeth*; the grave-diggers in *Hamlet*, the porter in *Macbeth*, and Cleopatra's clown? Only this: they demonstrate, together, how variously the 'mingling principle' works. Each example connects with its immediate context and with the present continuous of its play, but no two are the same. Isolated examples illustrate Shakespeare's habitual 'mingling' under the microscope, as it were, but of course each play consists of an infinite number of examples—reaching out in all directions, interpenetrating one another, enriching one another. *Measure for Measure* affords a different kind of example, in so far as Shakespeare also asks us to observe a violently 'mingling' dramatist, in the person of the Duke, and also a more efficient dramatist who tidies up, so to say, behind the Duke and ensures that all of the play's bits and pieces combine plausibly together.

My argument draws to its conclusion, and a scandalous conclusion it is. I have argued that in *Measure for Measure*, one of his most puzzling plays, Shakespeare wants the audience to take an

interest not merely in the story but also in the nature of the play—
an idea that we have all encountered before, in studies of other
plays and of the novel. Having bowed politely to Mannerism and
Structuralism and all things fashionable, the besotted lecturer
drags in Metadrama as well. Is it really necessary? If I am told that
a packed Bankside audience of prentices and prostitutes would be
less alert to such questions than their distinguished descendants,
whose haunt is Piccadilly,[1] I need only remind you that *The Old
Wive's Tale* and *A Midsummer Night's Dream* also required the
audience to ponder the nature of the play, and that the same
challenge is built into the early plays of Marston and Jonson. In
Measure for Measure Shakespeare addressed an audience already
trained to query genre boundaries, and to expect the forms of
things unknown.

> And as imagination bodies forth
> The forms of things unknown, the poet's pen
> Turns them to shapes, and gives to airy nothing
> A local habitation and a name.
> Such tricks hath strong imagination.

The time has come for me to sum up, and I can do it in a single
line from Shakespeare, slightly improved:

> Such *bed-tricks* hath strong imagination.

Quotations from Shakespeare are taken from *The Complete Works* (1951),
ed. Peter Alexander. I have changed some other quotations from Elizabethan
to modern spelling.

[1] In 1981, when this lecture was delivered, the British Academy was located
in Burlington House, near Piccadilly Circus.

THE FIRST WEST END COMEDY

By EMRYS JONES

Read 22 April 1982

I

MOST people, I imagine, would agree that West End comedy has become a thing of the past, perhaps not wholly extinct, but coming to seem somewhat antiquated.[1] It is no longer contemporary with ourselves, so that even the latest specimens of the kind now strike us as period-pieces. They are the products of an age whose social assumptions we can more and more easily regard with detachment. For several months last year Noel Coward's *Present Laughter* was running at the Vaudeville Theatre in the Strand. This play (written in 1939 but not acted until 1943) is not perhaps one of his best, and I am not claiming for it any special distinction. But one feature seemed to me of interest from the point of view of dramatic history. This is its opening scene. The action is set in the London home—the 'studio'—of a successful West End actor, a matinée idol in his early forties, someone whose public image was not (when it was first acted) too far removed from that of the play's author. The play opens at morning ('about 10.30 a.m.', says the stage direction in the published text), with the famous actor still in bed offstage. The members of his household arrive one by one and prepare for the day's business—his housekeeper-cook, his valet, his loyal secretary, and later his still friendly former wife. And then finally, from his bedroom, wearing a flamboyant Chinese-looking dressing-gown, the actor himself emerges—to have breakfast, to engage in non-stop conversation, and to get on with the play.

The scene belongs to a familiar prototype. One might call it the levee of the man of fashion. It has a certain classic formality; it makes a variation on a well-known theme, and as such seems to echo any number of such scenes from earlier plays, so that when we see it we instantly know where we are. And indeed Noel

---

[1] In this 'Shakespeare Lecture' I am taking advantage of the terms laid down by the founder, which allow the lecturer to speak either on Shakespeare or on 'some problem in English dramatic literature and histrionic art'.

Coward's scene comes at the end of a long line of such scenes, and
it is these that I want to use as a way of designating a whole tradition of English stage comedy.

Essential to this morning situation is the young, or at any rate
not elderly, hero, who lives in a fashionable part of London. He is
attended by servants and sought after by persons of his own class,
so that the scene invariably develops into a succession of visits. He
is not burdened with responsibilities; he is not subject to the
harsher forms of economic pressure (though he may often be in
need of ready cash); he lives largely for his own pleasure. For us
probably, such a scene will have Edwardian or late Victorian
associations: we think of Somerset Maugham or, earlier, Wilde.
But I want to suggest that the form of the scene, as well as the social
way of life it dramatizes, can be traced back much further. They
can be traced back to Victorian novels of fashionable life which
exploited the forms of stage comedy (Thackeray, Bulwer-Lytton),
and back further still to Georgian and Restoration comedy, in the
last of which such opening morning scenes receive their fullest
development: as, notably, in Congreve's *Love for Love* (1695) and
Etherege's *Man of Mode* (1676). The first act of *The Man of Mode* is
without doubt the most resplendent and charismatic instance of
the kind in English drama. But Dorimant's levee, first staged over
three hundred years ago, is still not the first of the line. We can go
even further back, over sixty years before. And it is with its chief
Jacobean forerunner that the line we have traced back from *Present
Laughter* comes to an end. Ben Jonson's *Epicoene, or The Silent
Woman*, first acted in 1609, is the earliest English play to open with
a London levee scene of the kind I have described. More significantly, we can say of it, in retrospect, that it inaugurated a tradition of comedy which, in terms of historical duration, has been
overwhelmingly the dominant one until recent years.

Epicoene was the first of Jonson's plays to be set throughout in
London. Of course there had been earlier London comedies. But
such plays as Dekker's *Shoemaker's Holiday* (written ten years
before, in 1599) were set in the City of London and celebrated the
City within the walls, the City of the Livery Companies and the
craftsmen. *Epicoene*, on the other hand, opens in the fashionable
lodging of a young gallant called Clerimont. The first stage direction indicates the time of day: '*He comes out making himself ready*' (i.e.
dressing himself).[1] But it does more than that: it signals that we are
in a certain social world, a world of confident privacy and leisure.

---

[1] Quotations from *Epicoene* are from the New Mermaids edition (1979) by
R. V. Holdsworth.

Clerimont is attended by a servant, and is no doubt dressing himself in an appropriately fashionable style. Everything that he says, does, and looks proclaims his social position. He is completely free and idle, a gentleman who can afford to do nothing but pursue his own pleasure. He speaks with what is presumably the Jacobean equivalent of a fashionable drawl; and Jonson's text is careful to make him slur his words for this his first utterance: 'Ha' you got the song I ga' you, boy?' The boy warns him not to let anyone else hear the song he has composed. 'Why, I pray?' 'It will get you the dangerous name of a poet in town, sir.' The precocious boy speaks in his master's modish voice: to make a distinction that was already becoming well established, we are not in the city, we are 'in town'.

For its date, this opening scene of *Epicoene* will now strike anyone as startlingly modern. It seems to anticipate by half a century Restoration comedy. Of course to say that the whole play anticipates Restoration comedy is a cliché of literary history, but if it is a truth, then this opening scene must be largely responsible. There are other 'Restoration' features in *Epicoene*; but given no more than this witty, stylish opening, one can see why this play should have been the first to be acted after the Restoration and why Dryden should have chosen it as the subject of his 'Examen' in his *Essay of Dramatic Poesy*. From a post-Restoration point of view, *Epicoene* stood out as showing what 'the former age' could achieve in comedy, and in a mode moreover which seemed peculiarly congenial to a fashionable audience over fifty years after it was written.

If we ourselves find the opening of *Epicoene* surprisingly modern for its period, then it must be in part because our sense of that period is at fault. However novel some of the play's features were at the time, the play itself cannot be anachronistic; what is mistaken is the concept, the half-conscious picture, of the Jacobean age which perhaps most of us carry in our heads. In what follows I shall be looking first at some of the play's historical contexts, social and theatrical, before returning to *Epicoene* and the tradition which it helped to bring into being. Indeed I shall be as much concerned with the idea of the West End and the tradition of West End comedy as with the play *Epicoene* itself.

II

Of course the term 'West End' is, strictly speaking, itself anachronistic when applied to a play written only half a dozen years after the death of Queen Elizabeth. The West End as we know it had not yet come into being. Apart from St. James's Palace and a sprinkling of other buildings, the area to the west and north of Charing Cross that we now think of as the West End was still open fields. Looking at a map of the area drawn in the mid seventeenth century, we can pick out one or two anticipations of what was to come. The name 'Piccadilly' itself is Jacobean, though the earliest recorded instances are a little later than *Epicoene*; but Jonson may well have known the name. An even earlier plan of the Piccadilly area, drawn in 1585, shows the actual windmill on the site of what later became Windmill Street, later still (much later) to be associated with the Windmill Theatre, whose proud motto during the Second World War blitz was 'We never closed'.[1] But our West End is essentially a product of the Restoration.

Nonetheless there was of course an extensive and, in terms of its impact on London life, immensely important development west of the City during the half-century before the Civil War. The Elizabethan City of London was grossly over-populated for its geographical size, despite the efforts of successive governments to check its growth; it was bursting out in all directions. Like all medieval cities, London until the sixteenth century did not enforce any clear segregation of the social classes: rich and poor, courtiers and tradesmen, lived in what would later have been thought unseemly proximity.[2] Yet the signs of social segregation were already there in the late sixteenth century, and were to become more and more clear during the century that followed. 'The dominant fact in the development of London, from the time of Elizabeth', says one historian, 'has been the cleavage between the East and West.'[3] Certainly, the westward movement of the fashionable classes, already perceptible in the last decade of Elizabeth's reign, was acquiring more momentum throughout the reign of her successor. The magnetic force which decided that this movement was to be westward and not in any other direction was primarily the presence of the Court in Westminster—for the fact that the country's capital was not one city but two (with trade and wealth in the City of London, law and government in Westminster)

[1] C. L. Kingsford, *The Early History of Piccadilly, Leicester Square and Soho* (Cambridge, 1925).

[2] Valerie Pearl, 'Change and Stability in Seventeenth-Century London', *London Journal* v (1979), 7.

[3] M. Dorothy George, *London Life in the Eighteenth Century* (1925; 1966 reprint), p. 75. See also M. J. Power, 'The East and West in Early-Modern London', in *Wealth and Power in Tudor England* (1978), ed. E. W. Ives, R. J. Knecht, and J. J. Scarisbrick.

was from at least the fourteenth century fundamental to life in London.[1] The City had no choice but to grow in that direction, since it was from there that power and influence emanated. But as well as the Court, the presence of so many great palaces on the south side of the Strand was a strong incentive to the ambitious to live close at hand. It helped too that legal business was centred on the west side of the City, where the Inns of Court were, within easy reach of Westminster Hall, where cases were heard. Indeed from at least the 1590s onwards, and no doubt from some time previously, the Strand was the most sought-after address in the whole of London. And since the Strand will figure prominently in what follows, I must say something about this once celebrated thoroughfare.

With the exception of its two beautiful island-sited churches (and perhaps Somerset House), the Strand today is no longer an exceptionally distinguished street, and has little in it to detain anyone. Despite the resonance which still clings to its name, few people will now think of it as London's main street. It is becoming just a characterless urban chasm, a mere link-road between West End and City. Yet something survives—its geographical place-ment, its length, its width—even if hardly a single building known to Ben Jonson still stands. Cities are to some extent a matter of psychic space, of distances and directions, the lay-out intimately known through the effort needed to traverse it on foot and through the vistas registered repeatedly by the eye. In this sense something important of Jonson's London remains. And for my purposes it is essential to insist that our London grew by degrees out of his and that his London persists—perceptibly, if not wholly visibly—into ours.

Unfortunately we have no pictorial record of the Jacobean Strand. Perhaps the closest we can get is a print of Wenceslaus Hollar's of about 1660 or just before, too late to convey the authentic Jacobean feeling, but giving some sense of what the area was like in late Caroline and Commonwealth times.[2] We can peer down, at a steep angle, as if from a helicopter, into the quite wide

[1] T. F. Tout, 'The Beginnings of a Modern Capital—London and Westminster in the Fourteenth Century', *Proceedings of the British Academy*, 1923.

[2] I am grateful to Mr. H. M. Colvin for drawing my attention to this print. A detail of it is reproduced in *The History of the King's Works* (General Editor, H. M. Colvin), iii, *1485–1660 (Part 1)* (1975), pl. 12. There are some evocative nineteenth-century photographs of streets and houses dating from early Stuart times (mostly demolished before 1900) in Graham Bush's *Old London: Photo-graphed by Henry Dixon and Alfred and John Bool* (1975); see especially pl. 110, 'Old houses in the Strand'.

street, noting the tall gabled buildings on the north side, three or
four storeys high. On the south side are the great palaces, over on
the right Arundel House (a recent addition), then Somerset
House, and then the Savoy, laid out like Oxbridge colleges, with
gatehouses fronting the Strand and, within, buildings disposed
round quadrangles or courts, and parterred gardens running
down to the Thames.

From the Elizabethan to the Caroline period, the Strand and
its immediate environs were subjected to an intense pressure
from those seeking accommodation. To judge from the writings
of the time, everyone of standing, and anyone ambitious for
standing, wanted to live in the Strand. So in his prose work *Father
Hubburd's Tale* (1604), Middleton tells the story of the young
student coming up to London: 'The Lawyer . . . embraced our
young gentleman (I think, for a fool), and gave him many riotous
instructions how to carry himself . . . told him he must acquaint
himself with many gallants of the Inns-of-Court, and keep rank
with those that spend most, always wearing a bountiful disposition about him, lofty and liberal; his lodging must be about the
Strand, in any case, being remote from the handicraft scent of
the city . . .' The 'handicraft scent' was on the other side of the
City of London, towards the east. He goes on later: '. . . up again
we trotted to London, in a great frost, I remember, for the ground
was as hard as a lawyer's conscience; and arriving at the luxurious
Strand, some three days before the term, we inquired for our
bountiful landlord, or the fool in the full, at his neat and curious
lodging . . .'[1] As this and other such passages suggest, part of the
pressure for lodgings came from the floating student population
of the Inns of Court, all of which were near the Strand. John
Donne, for example, was at Lincoln's Inn in the 1590s; when a
few years later, in February 1602, he wrote a letter to his new
and outraged father-in-law shortly after he had eloped with his
daughter, he was careful to add his unimpeachable west London
address: 'From my lodging by the Savoy'. Naturally the best-
appointed and best-positioned lodgings went to those most able
to pay for them, and some were willing to pay a lot. In Brome's
comedy *The Court Beggar* (1632), a knight is scolded by his
daughter for having sold his entire country estate: '. . . a fair
mansion house, / Large fruitful fields, rich meadows and sweet
pastures, / Well cropp'd with corn and stock'd as well with

[1] *Works* (1886), ed. A. H. Bullen, viii. pp. 76–7, 81. See Ann Jennalie Cook,
The Privileged Playgoers of Shakespeare's London 1576–1642 (Princeton, 1981),
pp. 81–6, for a brief account of lodgings in London in this period.

cattle, / A park well stor'd with deer, too, and fish ponds in't, / And all this for a lodging in the Strand. . . .'[1] No doubt Brome is exaggerating, but his satire must have had some point. One catches glimpses not only of the scramble for rooms but of the lodgings trade from the point of view of the landladies. When Middleton's unscrupulous couple the Allwits (in *A Chaste Maid in Cheapside*) come into some unexpected money, Mrs Allwit at once knows what to do with it: 'Let's let out lodgings then, / And take a house in the Strand'. It was not until the troubles of the forties that these prosperous room-letters met their downfall: 'In 1642 the people in the Strand, who chiefly lived by letting lodgings, were in despair, having to pawn their furniture in order to pay the rent, their lodgings being all empty.'[2] For the first time in over fifty years perhaps, it was easy to get a lodging in the Strand. After the Civil War, the Strand was never to recover its social pre-eminence.[3]

Clerimont's lodging in *Epicoene* is not actually in the Strand, although Sir Amorous La Foole pronounces it 'a fine lodging, almost as delicate a lodging as mine.' 'Not so, sir', protests Clerimont. 'Excuse me', Sir Amorous insists, 'if it were i' the Strand, I assure you.' Precisely where Clerimont lives we are not told; but it is clearly not far from the most desired thoroughfare, where Sir Amorous himself lives. Indeed just before Sir Amorous makes his first appearance, Clerimont describes him in terms of his town address: 'He does give plays and suppers, and invites his guests to 'em aloud out of his window as they ride by in coaches. He has a lodging in the Strand for the purpose, or to watch when ladies are gone to the china-houses or the Exchange, that he may meet 'em by chance and give 'em presents . . .' In fact Sir Amorous is a typical Strand character, just as *Epicoene* itself is the first play to deal directly with the Strand social world.[4]

[1] Quoted by C. V. Wedgwood, 'Comedy in the Reign of Charles I', in *Studies in Social History* (1955), ed. J. H. Plumb, p. 129; reprinted in C. V. Wedgwood, *Truth and Opinion* (1960).

[2] Sir Walter Besant, *London in the Time of the Stuarts* (1903), p. 55.

[3] Lawrence Stone, 'The Residential Development of the West End of London in the Seventeenth Century', in *After the Reformation* (Manchester, 1980), ed. Barbara C. Malament, p. 194: 'The combination of a rush of nobles, courtiers, and officials back to the revived Restoration Court, and the decay of the old residential area in or near the Strand created an acute shortage of upper-class housing in the early 1660s.'

[4] Cf. Shirley's comedy *The Lady of Pleasure* (acted 1635). Whereas *Epicoene* gave its scene as 'London', Shirley's play states 'Scene: The Strand'. In the

Given this pressure for fashionable accommodation, the moment was more than ripe when the Earl of Bedford made his decisive move to employ Inigo Jones to lay out the Piazza at Covent Garden with fashionable houses of an altogether new neoclassical design. This was the moment (in the 1630s) which marks the creation of the 'inner West End'—to borrow a phrase from Sir John Summerson.[1] This is not the Piccadilly and St. James's Square West End but the West End which centred on the Strand and the new district now to be known as Covent Garden. (Even today, when we go to the Royal Opera House and the theatres in and around Drury Lane, the Aldwych, and the Strand, we still think of this area as being in some sense 'West End', despite its isolation from the more obviously fashionable residential parts of the other 'outer' West End of St. James's and Mayfair.) Indeed one might trace back the beginnings of this 'inner West End' further still, to 1609, when the Earl of Salisbury founded the New Exchange on the south side of the Strand. The New Exchange was an upper-class shopping centre, which set out deliberately to compete with the older-established shopping centres in the City— and as such it epitomizes the incipient West End movement already well under way during the opening years of James I's reign.[2] This very year—1609—that saw the New Exchange founded also saw *Epicoene* performed.

In some ways perhaps we need to revise our mental picture of the Jacobean period. Literary and dramatic historians still see the seventeenth century too much in terms of contrasts and discontinuities, of before and after the Civil War. And one tendency

opening scene Celestina announces 'I live i'th' Strand', and elaborates a fantasy of what she will see from her window:

> 'The horses shall be taught with frequent waiting
> Upon my gates to stop in their career
> Toward Charing Cross, spite of the coachman's fury;
> And not a tilter but shall strike his plume
> When he sails by my window. My balcony
> Shall be the courtier's idol, and more gaz'd at
> Than all the pageantry at Temple Bar
> By country clients . . .'

(*Six Caroline Plays* (Oxford, 1962), ed. A. S. Knowland, p. 18).

[1] *Georgian London* (1945), p. 5.

[2] For the New Exchange, see Lawrence Stone, *Family and Fortune* (Oxford, 1973), pp. 95–109. A design for the New Exchange by Inigo Jones has survived, though whether, or to what extent, the builders actually made use of it is not known. See Sir John Summerson, *Architecture in Britain 1530–1830* (Harmondsworth, 1953; 1970 reprint), p. 115.

especially prevalent is to postdate the occurrence of what are thought of as 'Restoration' developments and so to under-estimate the extent to which some practices usually associated with the age of Charles II were already flourishing in late or even early Jacobean society. As far as the fashionable life of London is concerned, an essay by the economic historian F. J. Fisher, published in the 1940s, remains of fundamental importance.[1] Professor Fisher makes it clear that, during the late sixteenth and early seventeenth centuries, there was a large influx into London of landed gentlemen and their families, partly in order to supervise more closely their legal business, partly to live more cheaply in lodgings than they could on their country estates, and partly simply to enjoy a more interesting, or more exciting, certainly less tedious, social round than they would at home. 'By the early seventeenth century, there had developed a clearly defined London season which began in the autumn, reached its climax at Christmas, and was over by June.' This 'seasonal influx of thousands of visitors' put an unprecedented strain on London's accommodation and transport, as well as on the catering trades:

By the early seventeenth century, therefore, the economy of London and its suburbs was called upon to adapt itself to a substantial seasonal immigration of rural landowners, many of them accompanied by their families. It had to accommodate itself to an ever-changing and steadily growing student body which had already, under Elizabeth, exceeded a thousand. It had to absorb an uncertain but not inconsiderable number who, from either poverty or choice, from either boredom or ambition, had abandoned their country seats for permanent residence in town. The incomes of those immigrants no doubt varied, but their total revenues must have been considerable. The result of their expenditure was to create a series of demands which it became an important function of the metropolis to fulfil. . . . From that tendency towards conspicuous consumption the luxury trades of the city waxed fat. As in all ages, the gentleman come to town required transport, and it was during the early seventeenth century that the coach became a familiar part of the London scene. By the reign of Charles I, not only were hackney coaches to be found in their hundreds, but the cab rank had become an institution and the sedan chair was ceasing to be a curiosity.[2]

[1] 'The Development of London as a Centre of Conspicuous Consumption in the Sixteenth and Seventeenth Centuries', *Transactions of the Royal Historical Society*, Fourth Series, xxx (1948), reprinted in *Essays in Economic History*, ed. E. M. Carus-Wilson (1962), ii. 197–207, to which references are given. See also Lawrence Stone, *The Crisis of the Aristocracy 1558–1641* (Oxford, 1965), pp. 547–86.
[2] Fisher, p. 204. Cf. Brome's comedy *The Sparagus Garden* (1633) for its

These wealthy, eager-to-spend newcomers to the fashionable London scene wanted not only accommodation, eating and drinking places, transport; they also wanted recreation, amusement, formal entertainments. Clubs were already being formed in this early period; and by the reign of James I, observes Fisher, 'the gentry were already manifesting that taste for parks and pleasure-gardens that one normally associates with a later age.' Taking coach-rides in Hyde Park was a fashionable diversion by the second half of James I's reign. And above all, says Fisher, 'there was the theatre. Lord Keynes is reported once to have said that England obtained Shakespeare when she could afford him. Presumably his meaning was that Shakespeare could flourish only in a commercial theatre, and that a commercial theatre could flourish only when there was sufficient surplus wealth to pay for it. If that argument is valid, then perhaps the urbanised and semi-urbanised gentry of Elizabeth and the early Stuarts may claim at least some share of reflected glory, for it was their demand for entertainment that helped to bring the commercial theatre into being.' The way of life which these pleasure-seeking visitors, or rather immigrants, to London adopted would, says Professor Fisher, 'have seemed familiar to the eighteenth century. It would have been incomprehensible to the fifteenth.'[1]

There is one further aspect of London's transformation into the city known to Dryden, Pope, and Dr Johnson, and with it I return to what I was saying earlier. This is the new style in English, and more particularly London's, architecture as we see it embodied in the work of Inigo Jones. We think of Inigo Jones as Ben Jonson's personal rival and even enemy; but in a longer perspective we should perhaps see him as also his ally in the task of heaving England into a new cultural era. Inigo Jones's contribution to the physical fabric of the West End consisted of two major undertakings. The first was the Covent Garden Piazza and his magnificent church of St. Paul's—the first West End square and the first West End church. The other was the terrace of houses in the

reference to litters with clearly marked numbers on them like modern buses: *Brittleware*: 'I pray gentlemen which way took she.' *Samuel*: 'Downe towards the Strand I tell you, in a new Litter, with the number one and twenty in the breech on't.' (*Dramatic Works* (1873), iii. 197).

[1] Fisher, p. 204. Cf. Peter Clark and Paul Slack, *English Towns in Transition 1500–1700* (Oxford, 1976), p. 74: 'From the 1650's the old respectable drinking establishments, inns and taverns, faced competition from new houses selling cocoa, tea, and above all coffee ... but not less important was the social pressure for more exclusive meeting places for the greater merchants and landed classes. Here the élite might talk business and politics, and read the latest newspapers.'

Italian taste he designed for Lincoln's Inn Fields. This row of houses has a peculiar importance, for in it he established the prototype of what was to become the London town house.[1] The pattern fixed by Inigo Jones—town house, terrace, and square—was to last for more than two centuries. In this respect Inigo Jones and Ben Jonson both inaugurated extraordinarily long-lasting traditions—in the one case of the gentleman's town house, in the other of what one might call the gentleman's town comedy. For West End comedy—that is to say, Jacobean West End comedy—came into being just as the West End was itself coming into being. They are both aspects of the same comprehensive social process. Jonson, like Inigo Jones, stands at the beginning of the new age.

III

A certain degree of social exclusiveness was common to both these developments, architectural and dramatic. But the full extent of the movement was not to be seen until after the Restoration. It was to result in a rift dividing the city which from then until the mid twentieth century was to be central to the way Londoners themselves regarded London. From the seventeenth century onwards London was to be divided into two social worlds.

In 1662 Henry Jermyn, Earl of St. Albans, obtained from Charles II a lease of Pall Mall Field, and he soon planned to build houses there 'fit for the dwellings of noblemen and gentlemen of quality'. 'In laying out his estate the founder of the West End of London, for so Henry Jermyn deserves to be designated, reserved a central site for the great piazza.'[2] This square—St. James's Square—was the first of the great West End squares west of Charing Cross, and was even more socially exclusive than Inigo Jones's Piazza. And with it the West End, in the full modern sense of the term, comes into existence.[3]

Not only the locality came into existence at about this time but the name. The *OED* does not record 'West End' before 1807; according to this authority, the term belongs to the age of Byron. But this is very misleading. The term 'West End' is undoubtedly seventeenth-century in origin, although it is found at first only in what might be called technical contexts. A rate book of 1667 refers to a house in 'Jarman Street, West End, North Side'.[4] Though the

---

[1] Summerson, *Georgian London*, pp. 17-19.
[2] A. I. Dasent, *The History of St. James's Square and the Foundation of the West End of London* (1895), p. 5.
[3] Norman G. Brett-James, *The Growth of Stuart London* (1935), pp. 366-99.
[4] Dasent, p. 8.

exact meaning of the term here is not clear, it evidently refers to a part of the St. James's locality. There is an even earlier usage. In Sir William Petty's influential *Treatise of Taxation* (1662) occurs a passage in which he mentions the movement west of London's inhabitants: 'I say in the case of *London* it must be Westward, because the Winds blowing near 3 fourths of the year from the West, the dwellings of the West end are so much more free from the fumes, steams & stinks of the whole Easterly Pyle; which when Sea coal is burnt is a great matter' (1689 edn., p. 22).[1] If Petty could casually use the term in 1662, it is probably pre-Restoration in origin. Once the term 'West End' became established, whenever that was, 'East End' must eventually have followed. For 'East End' the *OED* records no instance earlier than 1883, yet the following passage was translated into English in the 1790s: 'the east end, especially along the shore of the Thames, consists of old houses, the streets there are narrow, dark and ill-paved; . . . The Contrast between this and the West end is astonishing: the houses here are mostly new and elegant; the squares are superb, the streets straight and open . . .'[2] Both these passages, but especially the second, testify to the growing sense of contrast between east and west London. As the West End became more splendid, so the East End became more wretched and sordid. Certainly by the time Archenholz wrote his book, the principle of social segregation had been fully accepted and, as his words suggest, even shockingly so. Two recent urban historians sum up the continuing situation: 'The development of the West End for the nation's ruling élite underlined the great extremes of wealth and the growing social segregation within greater London. Complementing the great

[1] This shows that the term 'West End' precedes the St. James's Square project, contrary to what Dasent seems to have thought. Petty's sentence is quoted in Charles Wilson, *England's Apprenticeship 1603–1763* (1965; 1975 reprint), p. 47, where it is attributed, without a precise reference given, to Evelyn. I am grateful to Dr E. S. de Beer for answering queries about Evelyn and to Dr Paul Slack for correctly locating the sentence for me.

[2] J. W. von Archenholz, *A Picture of England* (1797); quoted by M. Dorothy George, *London Life in the Eighteenth Century*, p. 76. Another passage from Archenholz brings out a different kind of London contrast: 'The shops are open by eight o'clock every morning in the city; all is then in motion, every body is at work; while on the other hand, at the *court end* of the town, the streets are empty, the houses shut, and even the very domestics are asleep; the sound of coaches is not heard, and one seems to walk about in a place that has been deserted. . . . Those in the city charge the people who live at the west end of the town with luxury, idleness, effeminacy, and an attachment to French fashions; while the others speak of a citizen as a dull, fat animal, who places all his merits in his strong box.' (I quote this from the Dublin 1791 edition, p. 79.)

households with their income of three thousand pounds a year or more were the migrant labourers and sea-men concentrated in the East End, living on a few shillings a month.'[1] The process which was decisively begun in Charles I's reign was to continue for the following two hundred years, culminating in the building of Belgravia, the grandest and most palatial of all London's residential areas, and undertaken as the immediate consequence of the conversion in the 1820s of Buckingham House into Buckingham Palace.

Despite a few scattered pre-nineteenth-century occurrences of 'West End', it is undeniable that most people in the seventeenth and early eighteenth centuries used other terms to express their strong sense of London's east–west axis. The terms most often favoured were simple directional ones—'this end of the town', 'the further end of the town', 'the other end of the town'. (The last mentioned has persisted until the present day: East End people still use the phrase 'the other end' for the West End: 'I'm going up the other end' is still a common expression.) Such expressions are frequent in Restoration comedy: Wycherley uses 'this end of the town' twice in the opening twenty lines of *The Country Wife*, while Aphra Behn even uses such a phrase adjectivally: '[She] is grown a very t'other-end-of-the-Town Creature'.[2] In his description of London, Defoe more than once refers to 'the Court end of the town', and variants on this, like 'the fashionable end of the town', are common.[3] The point to be made is that in the course of the seventeenth century Londoners became highly conscious of this polarity, and while expressions of this east–west sense are much more frequent after the Restoration, instances can also be found much earlier in Jacobean writing. This east–west opposition is not to be confused with the more overtly political opposition which was traditional between Court and City. It is much more a matter of social topography, of what recent geographers call 'mental mapping', which involves the highly subjective ways in which people may experience in their own minds the shapes of the public places they inhabit.[4] In the early seventeenth century, before even the Covent Garden 'inner West End' had been laid out, this east–

---

[1] Clark and Slack, *English Towns in Transition*, p. 69.

[2] Quoted by David Cook and John Swannell in their Revels edition of *The Country Wife* (1975), p. 9.

[3] Daniel Defoe, *A Tour Through the Whole Island of Great Britain* (Harmondsworth, 1971), ed. Pat Rogers, pp. 308, 323.

[4] See Peter Gould and Rodney White, *Mental Maps* (Harmondsworth, 1974).

west sense was no doubt by later standards only incipient, though it was already there—as, for example, in the passage already quoted from Middleton, with its reference to the Strand's being 'remote from the handicraft scent of the city'.

For the following three hundred years, however, the two Londons were something which ordinary Londoners must have taken utterly for granted. Certainly by the late nineteenth century it was a natural fact of life, reinforced by subliminal notions of ascent and descent which are still operative, perhaps on the analogy of such expressions as 'going up to town' and 'down to the country': hence colloquialisms like 'going up the West End', 'going down the East End'. The modern growth of Greater London into the western suburbs has not obliterated the old directional expressions so that even those who live west of Hyde Park and who therefore have to travel in an easterly direction to get to the centre still talk of 'going up into the West End'. The dramatist John Osborne, destined himself to be the scourge of West End comedy, provides an example from his recent autobiography: 'Kensington High Street was the Appian Way to the West End. The border ended at Barker's Store and we rarely ventured beyond it except for visits to Woolworth's in Cork Street, which was scarcely going Up West. Going Up West was something we didn't do until the later years of the war. . . . Up West in the 1940s was a very different affair from Kensington High Street in the thirties.'[1]

In the seventeenth and early eighteenth centuries people of fashion availed themselves of yet another way of marking the social distinction between where they lived and where their social inferiors lived, whether in the City of London and its eastward developments or in the poorer parts of Westminster. (Westminster contained, as it still does, extensive working-class areas, and is therefore not to be identified with the West End, even though administratively the West End was part of the sprawling City of Westminster.) The expression they often used for the fashionable area was simply 'the Town' (with or without the capital 'T'). And this term was naturally opposed to 'the City'. But in any historical period the term 'Town' has several senses (as it still does), and it is often difficult, in seventeenth-century usage, to decide which particular sense is being used. It is often synonymous with 'city', especially in Jacobean English, as it may still be in such phrases as 'town and country'. At other times, however, 'town' or 'Town' is used to designate a specifically fashionable part of a city, and

[1] *A Better Class of Person* (1981), p. 35.

particularly of London. Such a usage can of course occur only when cities have outgrown or are outgrowing their socially unsegregated lay-out and assumed the more familiar modern arrangement whereby certain areas are set apart for the more or less exclusive use of the rich and powerful.

In post-Restoration and early eighteenth-century England, the term 'Town' becomes fully established as the name for the capital within the capital, the part of London where, fashionably speaking, 'everyone' lived. Some of the social assumptions behind this understanding of 'Town' are explained by Steele in his periodical *Town-Talk* (1715–16). He writes in the form of a 'letter to a Lady in the Country':

But when I tell you I will give you only the Talk of the Town, it is necessary that I explain what I understand you expect by that Description of the sort of Intelligence you would have. It is ordinary to say the City, Town and Country: This takes in the residence of all the Inhabitants of this Great and Virtuous Island: But the Word Town implies the best People in the whole, wherever they are pleased, or are disposed, or able to live. The Town is the upper part of the World, or rather the fashionable People, those who are distinguished from the rest by some Eminence. These compose what we call the Town, and the Intelligent very well know, that many have got Estates both in *London* and *Westminster*, and dy'd in those Cities, that could never get into Town. As the Exchange is the Heart of *London*; the great Hall, and all under the contiguous Roofs, the Heart of *Westminster*, so is *Covent Garden* the Heart of the Town. What happens to be in Discourse or Agitation among the Pleasurable and Reasonable People is what shall make up the *Town-Talk*.[1]

Making allowances for the arch emphases of Steele's humorous-didactic manner, one must assume that he is caricaturing a situation actually existing. He goes on to say: 'The Idle, and the Lazy are equally out of Town, if nothing arises from their Sloth or Employment worth preferring them to the Notice of the Elegant. It is in this Spirit, that when the Streets and Houses are full, it is often very justly said there is no Body in Town.' Steele's 'Town' is what in the following century was to be called 'Society'.

When we go back a hundred years or so earlier than Steele, however, it is not easy to know to what extent 'Town' has acquired this Society connotation. 'Town' is certainly often used merely as a synonym for 'city'; nevertheless there are, in Jacobean literature and drama, enough instances where the context requires a

---

[1] *Richard Steele's Periodical Journalism 1714–16* (Oxford, 1959), ed. Rae Blanchard, p. 191.

fashion-conscious sense to make it probable that the word had already extended itself into what one might call its West End viewpoint. So, for example, we catch this intonation in a letter written in 1618 by the court-gossip John Chamberlain: 'The Lord Digbie made a great supper and a play at White-hall to the best part of the great Lords and Ladies about this towne'.[1] The word 'city' would not, one feels, be quite right in this context. More clearly, the poem by Francis Beaumont, 'Letter from the Country to Jonson', written some time between 1610 and 1613, is surprisingly 'Restoration' in feeling, contrasting the dullness of the country to the brilliant wit and stimulus of 'the Towne' and contrasting that in turn to the witlessness of the City: 'witt able enough to iustifie the Towne / for three dayes past; witt yt might warrant bee / for the whole Citty to talk foolishly / Till that were Cancell'd . . .'[2] Here, in a poem contemporary with *Epicoene*, we have 'Towne' and 'Citty' clearly distinguished and opposed to each other. In *Epicoene* itself, especially in its first act, we have, I believe, a very early instance of 'town' comedy, so that when Truewit uses the expression 'here i' the town' (I. i. 71), he is not just referring to the whole of London (what Beaumont calls 'the whole Citty') but only to a special part of it, the fashionable part, where Clerimont among others has his lodging.[3]

IV

Those who lived in 'the Town' were, almost by definition, ladies and gentlemen, members of the nobility and gentry. In a period of such profound social readjustment as the early seventeenth century, the qualities and duties of gentlemen especially were much discussed. Gentlemen feature with quite exceptional prominence among the *dramatis personae* of West End comedy—so much so that one might be tempted to rename the genre 'gentry comedy' (and in fact Horace Walpole did call it 'genteel comedy')[4] were it not that 'West End' seems preferable in insisting on the importance of the fashionable London scene. Given the dominance

---

[1] *Letters* (Philadelphia, 1939), ed. N. E. McClure, ii. 193.

[2] *Ben Jonson* (ed. Herford and Simpson), x. 374–6.

[3] For the phrase 'here i' the town', cf. Jonson's Epigram 12, 'On lieutenant Shift', which begins: 'Shift, here in town not meanest among squires'; in *Poems* (Oxford, 1975), ed. Ian Donaldson, p. 11.

[4] Horace Walpole, 'Thoughts on Comedy', written in 1775 and 1776; in *Works* (1798). It has been reprinted in *Essays in Criticism* 15 (1965): 'The Man of Mode shines as our first genteel comedy . . .' By 'genteel comedy' Walpole means 'comedy of fashionable life' or 'upper-class comedy'.

of gentlemen in this tradition of comedy, its social temper will be clarified a little by a glance at current notions of what gentlemen were in actual life.

The essential social mark of a gentleman was his freedom from the need to labour for his subsistence. In Elizabethan and Jacobean society, rural labourers, tradesmen and shopkeepers, artisans, and the enormous class of persons who must be called servants of one kind or another, all helped to define by contrast what gentlemen (aristocracy and gentry) were not. As Sir Thomas Smith put it in a much-quoted phrase: 'whosoever studieth the lawes of the realme, who studieth in the universities, who professeth liberall sciences, and to be shorte, who can live idly and without manuall labour, and will beare the port, charge and countenaunce of a gentleman, he shall be called master, for that is the title which men give to esquires and other gentlemen, and shall be taken for a gentleman.'[1] Lawyers, university graduates, and the rest, had earned through their studies the right to be called gentlemen, but the idea of a gentleman in its unqualified purity is always linked with his freedom not to work, his not having to get up early in the morning to earn his bread. Henry Peacham, in his *Complete Gentleman* (1622), puts it more caustically, though he is describing the same social phenomenon of the man of means who does not need to work: '. . . to be drunk, swear, wench, follow the fashion, and to do just nothing are the attributes and marks nowadays of a great part of our gentry.'[2] Viscount Conway, speaking as a gentleman himself, and not merely describing one from the outside, puts it in his own way: 'We eat and drink and rise up to play and this is to live like a gentleman; for what is a gentleman but his pleasure?'[3]

The implications of these remarks, and others like them, might be summed up as saying that gentlemen were not only free, but were positively entitled, to do nothing with their time if they chose. Expressions such as 'living like a lord', or 'like a gentleman', 'the idle rich', etc., though later than the Jacobean period, epitomize the views of the common people. That a gentleman was

---

[1] *De Republica Anglorum*, repr. 1906, pp. 39–40; quoted in Ruth Kelso, *The Doctrine of the English Gentleman* (Urbana, 1929), p. 26.

[2] *The Complete Gentleman* (Ithaca, 1962), ed. Virgil B. Heltzel, p. 19.

[3] Quoted by Maurice Ashley, *England in the Seventeenth Century* (Harmondsworth, 1952), p. 18; and by Ann Jennalie Cook, *The Privileged Playgoers of Shakespeare's London*, p. 79. Neither Ashley nor Cook notes that Conway's final phrase is a proverbial expression. See M. J. Tilley, *The Proverbs of England in the Sixteenth and Seventeenth Centuries* (Ann Arbor, 1950), p. 253. Tilley cites examples of 'What is a Gentleman but his pleasure?' from 1573 to 1732.

seriously to be defined in terms not only of his pleasure but of his sense of honour as well as of his willingness to assume unpaid public responsibilities is equally true, though satirists and writers of comedies were naturally not so interested in saying so. For them, conspicuous leisure and conspicuous waste not only of time but of other commodities were the obvious badges of the town gentleman.

The king might create a duke, but not even he could create a gentleman. This was a fact that contributed to the mystique of gentlemanliness, and enhanced the independence and pride of rank of especially the old-established gentry. Such men owed their gentility to no one, and nothing could take it away from them. Birth and breeding, property and wealth, education, all contributed to but did not finally explain the gentlemanly ethos. Webster's definition (cited by Tilley as proverbial) probably represents the prevailing view: 'What tell you me of Gentrie? — 'tis nought else . . . But ancient riches.' (*The Devil's Law-Case*, I. i. 40-3).

In London, for reasons already touched upon, the young gentlemen who were to be seen in the fashionable centres of amusement and entertainment were early associated with the Inns of Court. Membership of the Inns of Court was expensive; most places were filled by the gentry. As Ruth Kelso put it in her treatise on the Gentleman over fifty years ago: 'Of all professions . . . the fittest for a gentleman and those aspiring to become gentlemen was the law.'[1] This was the period when landed gentlemen in the country assumed the role that was to be theirs for the next three hundred years: local administrators and justices of the peace. They sent their sons to the Inns of Court to acquire the rudiments of law and to meet others of the same age, class, and mentality. 'Young men reading law in order to become justices of the peace mixed with other young men studying to become professional lawyers; the latter may themselves have been sons of the landed gentry, or they may have belonged to landless, professional or commercial families. Thus, lawyers, regardless of their family background, came even more to be thought of as gentlemen.'[2] Jonson's *Epicoene*, with its comic use of law-Latin and its protracted 'divorce' proceedings in the fifth act, is not only a comedy for gentlemen but a comedy for lawyers. And there was

[1] Kelso, p. 51.
[2] Mark Bence-Jones and Hugh Montgomery-Massingberd, *The British Aristocracy* (1979), pp. 45-6. See also Wilfrid R. Prest, *The Inns of Court under Elizabeth I and the Early Stuarts 1590-1640* (1972).

a strong chance that many of the gentlemen and lawyers, or rather law students, in Jonson's audience were the same people. In a word, the Inns of Court were an integral part of the Jacobean West End.

V

I have nominated *Epicoene* as the first West End comedy, and it is undeniably in many ways an innovative work. But it would be a mistake to suppose that those features in it which seem to us to look forward to Restoration comedy were all original with Jonson. *Epicoene* has its own specific theatrical and literary context; for Jonson, in so many respects a leader, sometimes naturally followed others. It would be truer to see *Epicoene* as the most distinguished of a whole group of plays, some of which were written before it. This is not of course to deny Jonson a fundamental originality; and in any case, as I shall argue in a moment, he was in some ways building upon what he himself had achieved in his earlier satirical comedies and these preceded most of the plays I am about to refer to. Nonetheless, in this time of radical readjustment of dramatic forms, the new subjects, the new treatments, and the new scenic structures which result, are all to some extent a co-operative venture, more the shared work of a group of dramatists closely inter-acting with each other than the sudden creation of a single genius. This is the justification for glancing at the work of one or two of Jonson's contemporaries.

The plays I have in mind were mostly written for the Boys' companies of actors, which had resumed activity in 1599. From the start this turn-of-the-century movement of highly professional boy-actors' drama was imbued with the spirit of the new satire. No doubt the rigorously trained boys were especially good at holding up precociously knowing mirror-images of social types actually to be found in their audiences. At any rate the years following James I's accession see the crystallization of a new theatrical formula. The plays in question are comedies, usually set in some fictitious vaguely foreign court, often with a double-plot of which one part may be romantic and the other more frankly comic. The comic action often involves the exhibition of an eccentric, which sometimes takes the form of a comic persecution, a 'baiting' extended through several episodes. A notable instance of this type of comedy is Beaumont's *The Woman Hater*. Others are the series written by Chapman, *Monsieur d'Olive*, *The Gentleman Usher*, and *Sir Giles Goosecap*. All these plays, written like *Epicoene* for one of the Boys' companies, preceded *Epicoene* on the stage.

Despite the fact that they are usually set in a foreign country, often in a notional ducal court, these plays sometimes adumbrate features from the immediate London scene. Indeed they represent a curious intermediate phase in the process which was to establish as a convention the setting of polite comedies in fashionable London. Of course *city* comedies were already being set in the City of London: Dekker's *Shoemaker's Holiday* is the obvious case. But Jacobean comedies of fashionable life—comedies of the incipient 'town'—at first preferred to distance their satirical actions by using the fiction of an exotic setting. Some plays use an odd half-way procedure, as Jonson himself did in *Every Man Out of His Humour* (1599), in which the characters are given Italianate names, while the manners and even at moments the settings are plainly English. Indeed one episode here is explicitly set in London's St. Paul's.[1] Jonson's earlier *Every Man In His Humour*, which we now think of as a triumph of London comedy, was of course first written (in 1598) with an Italian setting, and was re-cast in its London form only some years later (exactly when is not known; though 1612 or thereabouts seems to be the favourite present conjecture).[2] However, most plays of fashionable life before *Epicoene* used a foreign setting, so that London is glimpsed, if at all, only through a thin veil of romantic fiction.

The Woman Hater (first acted in 1606, published in 1607; according to Cyrus Hoy 'substantially Beaumont's', though 'with at least five scenes revised by Fletcher')[3] is, I think, important for the composition of *Epicoene*. The play is set at the faintly sketched court of the Duke of Milan, but the atmosphere throughout is one of topical immediacy, and it soon emerges that what we are seeing is a play about fashionable London. (The dialogue frequently incorporates burlesque and parody, with more than one joke at the expense of Shakespeare: his recent big success, *Hamlet*, for instance, is 'taken off' in a fast allusive exchange: *Lazarello*. '. . . speake I am bound to heare.' *Count.* 'So art thou to revenge, when thou shalt heare . . .'). The young Count Valore,

[1] Jonson's scene clearly caught the attention of Wycherley, who modelled on it the ambitiously constructed episode set in Westminster Hall in *The Plain Dealer* (1676). *Every Man Out of His Humour* was given a single isolated stage revival in 1675. See R. G. Noyes, *Ben Jonson on the English Stage 1660–1776* (Cambridge, Mass., 1935), p. 297.

[2] See Gabriele B. Jackson (ed.), *Every Man in His Humour* (New Haven and London, 1969), pp. 221–39.

[3] *The Dramatic Works in the Beaumont and Fletcher Canon*, general editor Fredson Bowers (Cambridge, 1966), i. 150. Quotations from *The Woman Hater* are from this edition.

whose sister eventually marries the Duke, is really a London gallant, a gentleman of means with plenty of time on his hands. Early in the play he soliloquizes: 'Now am I idle. I would I had bin a Scholler, that I might a studied now: the punishment of meaner men is, they have too much to doe; our onely miserie is, that without company we know not what to doe . . .' (I. iii. 54–7). His gentlemanliness is shown in his being 'idle', in his ostentatiously belonging to the *non*-working class. He goes on to say that he ought to act like others of his class ('I must take some of the common courses of our Nobilitie'): walk about the town in such a way as to attract attention, after dinner go to the theatre and attract more attention, and if possible find someone he can laugh at. What he needs above all is 'sport': amusement of any kind, preferably at the expense of someone else. At least he would do all this if he did in fact follow 'the common courses of our Nobilitie'; actually he is both more honourable and more subtle than that. But we are made to register some of the attitudes of the idle town gentry, as later when the Count says to Lazarillo, a courtier whose highest pleasure is eating rare dishes: 'hast thou not beene held to have some wit in the Court, and to make fine jests upon country people in progresse time, and wilt thou loose this opinion . . .?' (III. ii. 56–8). And we are made to notice too that the town-setting in some sense adumbrates London, as when the Count, musing about his sister, remarks that 'she did not pretend going to any sermon in the further end of the Cittie', for since the scene takes place in a fashionable courtier's lodging, the implication is that 'the further end' would be on the City's other, unfashionable, eastward side. In another scene a reference is made even to the Inns of Court (III. ii. 46).

The courtier in question is the Woman Hater himself, Gondarino. A widower, he hates women with an uncontrollable ferocity. One of the strongest scenes in the play is set in his town lodging, and shows him trying—unsuccessfully—to prevent the visit of a woman. What is at once striking about this scene is its strong sense of interiority: we are inside an upstairs room, with only one means of entry and exit:

Servant. My lord, the Counts sister beeing overtaken in the streets, with a great haile-storme, is light at your gate, and desires Roome till the storme be overpast.
Gondarino. Is shee a woman?
Servant. I my lord, I thinke so.
Gondarino. I have none for her then: bid her get her gone, tel her shee is not welcome.

Servant. My lord, shee is now comming up.

Gondarino. Shee shall not come up, tell her any thing, tell her I have but one great roome in my house, and I am now in it at the close stoole.

Servant. Shee's here my lord. (*Exit*).

Gondarino. O impudence of women, I can keepe dogs out of my house, or I can defend my house against theeves, but I cannot keep out women.

(II. i. 19–33)

Beaumont establishes not only a world of polite social constraints but also Gondarino's outrageous violation of them. And the enclosed upstairs setting, of a kind evidently very familiar to Beaumont's audience, sharpens the sense of social conflict. The upstairs first-floor apartment (the *piano nobile* a later age might have called it) was the most sought-after position; something of its social connotations of privilege and affluence are inherent in the scene's conception. For although the town outside is called Milan, Gondarino's windows might as well be opening on to the Strand. This is an early occurrence of a setting that is to become much more common in later Jacobean and Caroline comedy; the first act of *Epicoene* is one such instance.

Beaumont's misogynist has an obvious kinship with Jonson's misanthropic Morose. And later scenes in *The Woman Hater* show the Jonsonian affinity more clearly. In one scene Gondarino is subjected to further unwanted female company: he is talked to endlessly by a deaf old woman from the country who is under the impression that he is listening sympathetically to her suit. All he can say is: 'why should women only above all other creatures that were created for the benefit of man, have the use of speech?' (IV. i. 90–2). And in the final scene, as a last refinement of torment, he is tied to a chair and forced to listen to the endearments of women who in turn sit on his knee, stroke his hair, and even kiss him.

Beaumont's play seems to have failed when it was first acted, and critics since have not had much to say on its behalf. It is usually said to be raw and tentative; a bit stiff in the sinews. It is also said to be clearly derivative from Jonson's earlier humour plays. That there is an indebtedness need not be disputed; but I would want to claim that there is also something new in Beaumont's approach and that, in his turn, Jonson may have owed his friend a debt. The nature of this debt is to be found in the nature of Beaumont's subject. An intransigent woman-hater who is brought to heel by the concerted efforts of others, men and women, is a topic which will arouse complex and involuntary emotional responses. The punishment of an outsider by a group serves to dramatise in a rudimentary but oddly powerful way the workings of human societies, bringing to mind while being performed the instinctual societal bonds that both keep human beings together and hold them frustratingly apart. In short, *The Woman Hater* is peculiarly social in its field of discourse. One might perhaps say something similar of Jonson's earlier humour plays (or even of Shakespeare's treatments of Malvolio and Parolles). But where Beaumont marks an advance on Jonson is in focusing attention on the single extended Gondarino action: the opposition between outsider and group is simplified, so that the stage is not over-crowded as it tends to be in, say, *Every Man Out of His Humour*. The gain in unity and coherence is important. And quite as important, Beaumont brings to the stage a relaxed, unaffected upper-class tone and point of view. He writes as a gentleman. He was himself a member of the landed gentry, and retired early from writing plays to take up his country estate; it is possible that the lower-born Jonson could acquire from him some useful hints of a social nature.[1]

I have taken *The Woman Hater* as an instance of the incipient 'town' comedy of the first decade of the seventeenth century. But Beaumont was not alone in exploring the new area: he may him-self have been following Chapman, some of whose sporadically interesting but hopelessly uneven comedies show a parallel development. Another original Inns-of-Court voice, similar to Beaumont's in social class, was Marston's, who also wrote comedies for the Boys. In all these plays a new concept of social comedy is emerging. And one sign of this development is the dramatist's new sense of interiority: his imaginative evocation of the private room.

Of course earlier Elizabethan drama has the occasional indoor scene, and in some of these scenes the sense of indoors is rendered with some distinctness. One might instance the opening scenes of Marlowe's *Jew of Malta* and *Dr Faustus*. But what is noticeable about these and others is that the interior setting is usually of either a professional or a public nature.[2] So in Marlowe's plays

---

[1] Beaumont could give Jonson hints of another kind. Dryden says of Beaumont that he was 'so accurate a judge of plays that Ben Jonson, while he lived, submitted all his writing to his censure, and, 'tis thought, used his judgment in correcting, if not contriving, all his plots'. (*'Of Dramatic Poesy' and Other Critical Essays* (1962), ed. George Watson, i. 68).

[2] An exception is *Arden of Feversham* (*c.*1588–91), which has several strongly rendered interior domestic scenes, notably that of Arden's murder. In addi-tion the tavern scene in 2 *Henry IV* (II. iv), unlike the corresponding scene in 1 *Henry IV*, is set in an upstairs room, and is much less public in atmosphere. Shakespeare seems to have imagined the setting as a private room or 'chamber' to which Falstaff and Dol Tearsheet could retire after supper. After Pistol has

we have the counting-house of the merchant Barabas or the even
more stereotyped scholar's study of Dr Faustus (the kind of setting
which had already been given numerous pictorial representations,
as in portrayals of St. Jerome in his study or the various portraits
of Erasmus). As for indoor public settings, one might instance
the great Boar's Head tavern scene in 1 *Henry IV*, with its
precursors in Tudor morality plays, or else the many court scenes
which showed the king enthroned. In such scenes the setting may
be indoors, but the space evoked is essentially public space.

In the incipient 'town' plays which I am now considering space
becomes not only more interiorized but more private. Scenes may
now be set not only in professional and public places but in the
places where people merely live, the rooms where they retire from
the public domain to be themselves, to talk to friends, to make
love, to sleep, even—as Gondarino reminds us—to use the close-
stool. It is this sense of the inviolably private that we do not find in
most earlier Elizabethan drama. Shakespeare's *Two Gentlemen of
Verona*, for example, opens with the two friends talking together,
yet there is not the slightest indication where the exchange is
taking place. It could be indoors or outdoors; it is simply not
specified—and it does not matter. Only with Ben Jonson, no more
than nine years younger than Shakespeare yet of a quite different
outlook, do we find the dramatist taking a positive interest in
private space. In perhaps his earliest surviving play, *Every Man In
His Humour*, we first meet Bobadil (to give him his later English
name) in his lodging. His visitor Mathew finds him at his
extremely unfashionable address ('lie in a water-bearer's house!
a gentleman of his havings!') and proceeds upstairs to his room,
where he finds him lying not in a bed but on a bench. 'Now, trust
me', says Mathew sarcastically, 'you have an exceeding fine
lodging here, very neat, and private.' The joke arises from the
social pretentiousness of Bobadil and the sordidness of his actual
surroundings: Bobadil's embarrassment is acute, and social
embarrassment—a sense of confusion arising from the invasion of
the private by the public—is something of a new emotion for the
drama. Yet the scene is in its way a levee scene, or a parody of one,
as the stage direction makes clear: '*While Master Mathew reads,
Bobadill makes himself ready*' (the usual phrase for 'gets dressed').
Jonson may have taken over something from Shakespeare here:
Falstaff (at least in Dover Wilson's plausible interpretation) is

misbehaved, he is driven downstairs, the term 'downstairs' receiving repeated
emphasis. Shakespeare's scene may have suggested the choice of an upstairs
private setting in later dramatists like Jonson and Beaumont.

also first revealed lying on a bench. But one difference is crucial: Falstaff, who is in any case imperturbable and unembarrassable, is shown in an unspecified setting, certainly not specifically private, whereas Bobadil wakes up in a room definitely private, and it is the shift to a specifically private place that marks a new viewpoint and a new sensibility.

The dramatist's new sense of the enclosed private room should not be seen in isolation from developments in European society at large. In his wide-ranging book *The City in History* (1961), Lewis Mumford traces the process whereby the place of business or work becomes separated from the house of residence, so that 'the "private house" comes into existence: private from business'. In due course 'Every part of life came increasingly to share this privacy.' 'A new type of housework was invented . . . : the care of furniture. The fixtures of the medieval household were equipment: chairs to sit on, beds to sleep in . . . so much and no more. Furniture is really a reinvention of the baroque period: for by furniture one means useless or super-refined equipment, delicate vases to dust, inlays and precious woods to polish . . .' In short, 'Display outstripped use.' And inevitably with the accumulation of new kinds of commodities developed a new sense of space: 'Up to the seventeenth century, at least in the North, building and heating had hardly advanced far enough to permit the arrangement of a series of private rooms in the dwelling. But now a separation of functions took place within the house as well as within the city as a whole. Space became specialised, room by room.' This new form of space, however, was not for everyone; it was expensive. 'Privacy was the new luxury of the well-to-do. . . . The lady's chamber became a boudoir, literally a "sulking place". . . . For the first time not merely a curtain but a door separated each individual member of the household from every other member.'[1]

The complex social processes impressionistically evoked here can be corroborated from dozens of places in seventeenth-century English writing. As Mumford notes, the separation of functions proceeded both outside the house and within it. Outside the house,

[1] Mumford, pp. 383-4. Cf. Barbara Everett, 'The Shooting of the Bears: Poetry and Politics in Andrew Marvell', in *Andrew Marvell: Essays on the tercentenary of his death* (Oxford, 1979), ed. R. L. Brett, p. 61: 'Post-Tudor England saw the discovery of the formal private life. . . . England becomes a country of high-walled gardens and collectors' cabinets. Its gentlemen hang their houses with muffling silk and with silencing Turkey carpets; its ladies read romances and write letters.'

different parts of the city became devoted to specific purposes; efforts were made to rationalize the urban environment, to put things in their proper places. A small but significant incident will illustrate this development. In the middle of the most fashionable of streets, the Strand, there was a fish market. But as Howes notes, in his continuation of Stow's *Chronicle*, it was objected to: 'For divers yeares of late certain fishmongers have erected and set up fish stalles in the middle of the street in the Strand, almost over against Denmark House, all of which were broken down by speciall Commission, this moneth of May 1630, least in short space they might grow from stalles to sheddes, and then to dwelling houses, as the like was in former times in Old Fishe Streete . . .'[1] Denmark House was now a royal palace, named after Anne of Denmark; but in the London of Queen Henrietta Maria it was clearly felt to be intolerable to have a fish market outside the palace gates. (As a matter of fact, Howes was wrong in supposing the fish stalls to have been set up only a few years before. The recently published *Lisle Letters* show that fish was being bought in the Strand at least as early as the 1530s, and probably even earlier.)[2] The point to emerge is that in pre-modern London palaces and fish-stalls could share the same street; public decorum was not affronted. But segregation was now the order of the day. As we have noted already, the West End was purposefully pushing away from the City in one direction while the East End, badly laid-out, badly built, overcrowded, helplessly expanded in the other.

Inside the house, as Mumford observes, there were more walls and partitions, and more doors. There was a sharper sense of domestic demarcation. By the end of the century, when Congreve's Millamant lays down her conditions for marriage, she demands something, with complete seriousness, which none of Shakespeare's heroines would have thought of: 'And lastly, wherever I am, you shall always knock at the door before you come in.'

VI

I have been saying that from the late 1590s on, dramatists begin expressing a new sense of interior space and personal privacy. But before I return to the opening of *Epicoene*, I must raise a further

[1] Howes, *Annales*, 1631, p. 1045; quoted by Peter Cunningham, *Handbook for London* (1849), ii. 785.
[2] *The Lisle Letters* (Chicago and London, 1981), ed. Muriel St. Clare Byrne, v. 407.

question about the literary provenance of this type of levee scene. We should look for it, I think, in the direction of classical satire.

The satirical comedies of the ten years or so before *Epicoene* took much of their imaginative impulse from the non-dramatic satires of the 1590s. It was the verse satirists such as Donne, Hall, Marston and the rest—with Donne in the lead—who first began anatomizing contemporary society by hitting off the latest fashions in affectations and vices. They collected them into versified portrait-galleries; and they were enabled to do so by imitating classical Roman satire. By the late sixteenth century London had become, like early imperial Rome, a true metropolis, and for the first time English writers could view their own urban society through the spectacles of Horace, Persius, and Juvenal.

Jonson's comic-satiric play *Poetaster* (1602) is an upper-class drama of morals and manners set in Augustan Rome, with Ovid, Virgil, Horace, and Augustus himself as leading characters. In this play classical Rome and contemporary London have merged into each other, at least in Jonson's imagination, the figure of the poet Horace adumbrating Jonson's idea of himself. And it is in *Poetaster* that we find the earliest English instance of the form of opening scene—in the young man's town lodging—that we earlier traced back to *Epicoene*. But in *Poetaster*, of course, the city is Rome, not London. The time of day is not mentioned, though it feels early. But it is a striking fact that Ovid, the young man revealed in his lodging, is a law-student, who spends all his time writing poetry; and his first visitor is his father, who has come to upbraid him for neglecting his legal studies. The scene, though set in Rome, could just as well be in one of London's Inns of Court. It seems plausible to suppose that the kind of levee scene I described earlier is Roman in provenance and satirical in its original form.[1]

Both the formal satires of Augustan Rome and the amorous elegies, which are themselves often satirical, are full of a sense of indoor urban life, of rooms and doors, and of windows opening onto streets thronged with passing crowds. This is precisely the impression we have in the earliest, and one of the best, of Elizabethan non-dramatic satires: the first satire of Donne's.[2] The poem opens in the poet's tiny book-filled study. He is called on by a restless friend and, halfway through the poem, they leave the chamber for a stroll through the crowded street. The poem is

[1] The Roman *salutatio*, the ceremonious early-morning visit of clients to their patron, presumably contributed something to the conception.

[2] For a full account of this poem, see Barbara Everett's Chatterton Lecture, 'Donne: A London Poet', in *Proceedings of the British Academy*, 1972.

usually dated 1593; for the first time in an original English poem
we hear the urban and social note that is soon to become dominant
in drama. We find here too the contrast between the private
chamber, almost cell (Donne calls it 'this standing wooden chest',
where is he 'coffin'd'), and the most public and social of settings,
the open street. Donne possesses a highly developed sense of
interiority, which finds expression not only in this satire but in
several poems ('The Good-Morrow', 'The Sun Rising' among
them) in *Songs and Sonnets*. It seems likely that in this matter Jonson
was responding to Donne's lead.

Of the three Roman satirists, the one who is, it seems to me,
closest in spirit to the Elizabethan satirists is neither Horace nor
Juvenal but Persius. Indeed the importance of Persius for this
period of English satire seems much under-estimated. Persius, the
most austerely religious-minded of the three, had a high reputation throughout the Middle Ages and the Renaissance, culminating at the beginning of the seventeenth century in the edition of
his poems by Casaubon, who gave him the first place among the
satirists.[1] Donne is closer in style and sometimes in mood to Persius
than to either of the other two, and it is not altogether surprising
that he should actually have been addressed as 'Persius' in a
contemporary English poem.[2]

Persius's Third Satire opens with the poet still in bed, though
the morning is nearly over. A friend calls, and reproaches him for
his laziness: he should be up and about. I shall quote it in Dryden's
somewhat free version:

> Is this thy daily course? the glaring Sun
> Breaks in at ev'ry Chink: The Cattle run
> To Shades, and Noon-tide Rays of Summer shun.
> Yet plung'd in Sloth we lye; and snore supine,
> As fill'd with Fumes of undigested Wine.
>   This grave Advice some sober Student bears,
> And loudly rings it in his Fellows Ears.
> The yawning Youth, scarce half awake, essays
> His lazy Limbs and dozy Head to raise:
> Then rubs his gummy Eyes, and scrubs his Pate;
> And cries I thought it had not been so late:

[1] R. G. M. Nisbet, 'Persius', in *Critical Essays on Roman Literature: Satire*
(1963), ed. J. P. Sullivan, p. 40. Persius receives an inverted form of praise in
Epicoene, when Sir John Daw remarks: 'And Persius, a crabbed coxcomb, not to
be endured.' (II. iii. 71).

[2] R. M. Alden, *The Rise of Formal Satire in England* (Philadelphia, 1899),
p. 76. The reference is to Epigram 84 in the second book of Thomas Freeman's
Rub and a Great Cast (1614).

My Cloaths, make haste: why when! if none be near,
He mutters first, and then begins to swear:
And brays aloud, with a more clam'rous note,
Than an *Arcadian* Ass can stretch his throat.

As Professor Nisbet says, this is 'one of the most vivid pictures in Persius'; and it must be, if not the earliest levee scene in European literature, at least a very early instance, offering a precedent therefore to all those other levee scenes we can trace in English comedy. In fact, as Housman was apparently the first to point out, this dialogue of Persius' is spoken not by two persons, the man in bed and his reproachful visitor, but by two parts of the poet's own mind: 'the satirist's higher and lower selves'.[1] So this bedroom vignette is no more, for Persius, than a way of embarking on his philosophical discourse. But in Elizabethan times it was taken literally (as it was later by Dryden) as a dialogue between two men, and it is unlikely that so lively a passage would have been overlooked by interested readers.

It was probably, then, both the development of metropolitan forms of life in London in the late sixteenth century and the influence of Roman satirical poetry that contributed to the interiorizing of space in English drama. Jonson was the first to show a sustained interest in it, not only in *Every Man In His Humour* and *Poetaster* (whose 'Apologetical Dialogue', printed after the text of the play, is set in 'The Author's Lodgings') but preeminently in *Volpone* (1605), whose claustrophobic bedroom scenes are especially close to the world of Roman satire. In *Epicoene* itself, the theme is announced in different ways: first in the opening scene in Clerimont's lodging, and later in the entire conception of Morose, with his obsessive craving for enclosure— his 'huge turban of nightcaps on his head', his 'room with double walls and treble ceilings', and his repeated cry 'Bar my doors, bar my doors!' And after *Epicoene*, his two single-house plays, *The Alchemist* (1610) and *The New Inn* (1629), though very unequal in quality, continue to explore the imaginative possibilities of interior space.

In these same years other writers, attempting an early form of comedy of manners, showed a similar interest in putting private rooms or lodgings on the stage and even in the scenic possibilities,

---

[1] Nisbet, p. 53. Independently, Barbara Everett suggests (*Donne: A London Poet*, p. 250) that Donne's first Satire proceeds through a method of internalized debate, the stay-at-home scholar and the restless friend both representing aspects of the poet himself. As she notes, Donne's practice here owes something to Persius.

following *Volpone*, of the levee situation itself.[1] So Chapman opens
his comedy *The Widow's Tears* (printed 1612, but perhaps written
as early as 1606) with a morning scene: 'Tharsalio *solus, with a glass
in his hand, making ready*'; but Chapman makes little of it, and the
scene is set in a vague Cyprus. More interestingly, Marston has a
scene in *What You Will* (printed 1607) which much more vividly
evokes the appurtenances of an actual bedroom: '*Laverdure's
lodging*'. '*One knocks. Laverdure draws the curtains, sitting on his bed,
apparelling himself; his trunk of apparel standing by him.*' Laverdure
calls his servant: '*Enter Bidet, with water and a towel.*' The dialogue
that follows between master and servant might almost be out of a
Restoration comedy: Laverdure, a French fop, looks forward to
the heroic extravagances of Lord Foppington in Vanbrugh's
Relapse. Marston's scene, however, does not open the play and
therefore lacks structural emphasis, and is set in Venice, so
forfeiting topographical immediacy. But *What You Will* appeared
just two years or so before *Epicoene* and was written for the same
company of boy actors; and undeniably the other ingredients for
the levee formula—morning in the gallant's lodging, dialogue between master and servant, and visits from social acquaintances—
are all here.

VII

By opening *Epicoene* with Clerimont in his London lodging, and by
constructing for him a long unhurried conversation with his
friends, Jonson at one stroke brought Jacobean comedy into a
mode that made it instantly available to the Restoration.[2] In
doing so he was obeying the inner logic of the development of
comedy during the previous ten years; for now, by boldly locating
his action in London, and not only in London but in the fashionable quarter which his audience knew best, he was giving it the
immediacy and realism for which those earlier comedies had, less
effectively, all along been striving. Jonson's solution to the problem
of setting must have come with the force of revelation.[3]

[1] Jonson's own *Staple of News* (1626) opens with a levee scene based, as
Herford and Simpson note, on Horace, *Satires* (II. iii. 226–37).

[2] Whether consciously or not, Etherege seems to have modelled the opening
scene of *The Man of Mode* on Jonson's scene. Etherege's scene in turn furnished
a model for Congreve's in *Love for Love*.

[3] R. V. Holdsworth's edition of *Epicoene* has a useful guide to criticism of the
play. The following seem to me the most noteworthy: Jonas A. Barish, *Ben
Jonson and the Language of Prose Comedy* (Cambridge, Mass., 1960); Ian Donaldson, *The World Upside-Down* (Oxford, 1970); Terence Hawkes, *Shakespeare's
Talking Animals* (1973); Edward B. Partridge, *The Broken Compass* (1958);

The levee or getting-up-late scene, placed with the utmost emphasis at the opening of the play, amounts to an icon of status and property-based social power. It demonstrates the gentleman's ability to do nothing; while others get up early to work, he sleeps. The gentleman, idle in his lodging, strikes an attitude as richly symbolic in its way as that of the king seated on his throne; and just as the monarch and courtier have been central figures on the Renaissance cultural scene, so the propertied gentleman, with an estate in the country and lodgings in town, will dominate the coming gentrified bourgeois age. It is, moreover, from out of the fashionable, socially poised privacy of Clerimont's upstairs town apartment that the attack is to be sprung on the unfashionable, anti-social privacy of Morose's house. And crucial to Clerimont's lodging is the sense, wholly implicit, of its being a stoutly defended social citadel from which forays can be made of a superior, patronizingly dismissive nature. Only those who belong to the inner circle are freely admitted. His two friends come and go unannounced and unbidden, whereas others must wait downstairs until they are given permission to come up. So Sir Dauphine asks Clerimont for La Foole's full name.

> *Clerimont.* Sir Amorous La Foole.
> *Boy.* The gentleman is here below that owns that name.
> *Clerimont.* 'Heart, he's come to invite me to dinner, I hold my life.
> *Dauphine.* Like enough. Pray thee, let's ha' him up.
> *Clerimont.* Boy, marshal him.

And the Boy's reply—'With a truncheon, sir?'—pertly suggests that La Foole is to be admitted only under guard. In all this, the sense of inner and outer that results, of superior and inferior, of élite and multitude, is one that looks back to the satires of Donne and Persius as well as forward to Jonson's successors such as Congreve. But whereas in Persius the discourse would have been governed by the search for some kind of wisdom, what we find here in Clerimont and his friends is that their undoubtedly superior judgement and wit have been reinforced by an elusive social superiority, an exercise of social power, elegant in expression but aggressive in temper, which gives them, as a group, unquestioned authority to amuse themselves at the expense of others. They are instances of those 'fashionable People' who, as

L. G. Salingar, 'Farce and Fashion in *The Silent Woman*', *Essays and Studies*, NS xx (1967). My approach has most in common with L. G. Salingar's, which anticipates me on a number of points. His admirable essay was the first to investigate the immediate social milieu of *Epicoene*.

Steele put it in his remarks on the Town, are 'distinguished from the rest by some Eminence'.

I have already glanced at Clerimont's opening exchange with his boy servant. When Truewit arrives, he at once draws attention to Clerimont's pleasurably idle way of life, so continuing the topic which the play has already broached; and despite the desultory informality of his talk it should not be overlooked that what Jonson is doing is building up a description of the style of living of Clerimont and his class almost as formal as the allegorical tableau of Volpone worshipping his gold. Truewit's theme is waste of time. Clerimont lives frivolously, lying late in bed, listening to his own songs, doing nothing positive: 'Why, here's the man that can melt away his time, and never feels it! What between his mistress abroad and his ingle at home, high fare, soft lodging, fine clothes, and his fiddle, he thinks the hours ha' no wings or the day no post-horse. Well, sir gallant,' he goes on, firmly identifying him with the class of town gentlemen for which usually Jonson had little affection, 'were you struck with the plague this minute or condemned to any capital punishment tomorrow, you would begin then to think and value every article o' your time, esteem it at the true rate, and give all for't.' Truewit speaks almost in the voice of the Old Testament preacher[1] or the not wholly dissimilar voice of the Stoic Persius. And when Clerimont replies 'Why, what should a man do?', the resonance of his question for a moment condemns him out of his own mouth. In any case, he goes on to say, he can postpone being serious till when he is old: 'then we'll pray and fast.' This gives Truewit his cue, and he goes off into his 'act'—as a moralizing preacher: 'Oh, Clerimont, this time, because it is an incorporeal thing and not subject to sense, we mock ourselves the fineliest out of it, with vanity and misery indeed . . .'—until, still not making any headway with his imperturbable friend, he abruptly abandons the whole topic and switches to social matters of more immediate interest.

Through Truewit's burlesque performance, with its apparently genuine streak of seriousness, Jonson is stating the terms within which his comedy is to be taken. The moral considerations which, for Jonson, were of permanent and constant validity, are here going to be as if suspended, postponed to some unspecified future occasion. That *Epicoene* is not to be a moral comedy Truewit's ineffectual appeal to serious matters, quickly abandoned, makes

---

[1] As in Proverbs 6:9: 'How long wilt thou sleep, O sluggard? when wilt thou arise out of thy sleep?' Cf. the passage from Archenholz, quoted at p. 226, n. 2 above, for West End 'idleness' as seen by an eighteenth-century visitor.

clear. We have to do with a play whose bearings are instead predominantly social (Partridge rightly calls it 'this play about society').[1] Indeed one chief effect of the interiorization of the drama, its withdrawal into enclosed rooms, is to focus attention on behaviour rather than action. Comedy, switching allegiance from romance to satire, will be less concerned with telling a story of human action than with appraising and scrutinizing manners.

Some critics think Jonson is outright hostile to the gallants in this play. He is against them, they think, precisely because they belong to the ranks of the idle rich. It seems to me more complicated than that. He certainly fixes them with his envious, resentful gaze: he knows everything that can be said against them. Yet he refrains from condemnation. They are not exposed to satire or unfavourable comment. Nor are they ever ridiculous. Even when Truewit misjudges the situation and officiously tries to scare Morose out of marriage, he does not altogether lose his dignity. What saves the three friends is their language and their intelligence. They speak with a quick-glancing allusiveness and a nervous yet graceful volubility. They have an exquisitely exclusive style. It exquisitely shuts them in and shuts other people out. In effect Jonson's presentation is to say to each of them: 'Anyone who can talk like you is my friend'. So despite, and perhaps because of, the fact that their presence surrounds the action with an air of aristocratic idleness, Jonson is not, on the face of it, making them his targets. In any case neither Clerimont nor Truewit gets anything out of the day's business, except amusement; only Sir Dauphine gets his unnatural uncle where he wants him. So they are above mercenariness, mere gain. They are also above making any bid for our sympathies. We are not required to like them in order for the play to succeed; hence the lack of warmth, the heartlessness even, which at times may dismay the reader or spectator. But the lack of warmth goes with the society-orientated amorality: the play is without a heart for the same reason that it lacks a love interest. It is scrupulously external in its treatment of the workings of society.

The idea of society governs the whole play, dictating the dialogue's choice of topics and the incidents that make up the action. 'Society' so understood involves not so much the primary familial ties or the basic passions of the individual as the unavoidable exigencies of living with others in the same small social system, the relationships people form merely in virtue of the fact that they make part of an aggregate of persons such as

[1] Yale edition of *Epicoene* (New Haven and London, 1971), p. 12.

themselves: neighbours, acquaintances, colleagues, friends chosen
through the accidents of propinquity; persons whose typical
doings are those exhibited by the play: exchanging greetings,
hearing news, retailing gossip, discovering secrets or withholding
them, forming clubs, cliques and cabals, engaging in idle talk, and
inventing both occasions for getting together and excuses for
holding aloof. Since social living inevitably entails competitive-
ness, the recurring motives are those of enhancing one's own
reputation or damaging that of others, self-advertisement, keeping
up appearances, and hence sexual flirtatiousness and sexual boast-
ing, as well as snobbishness, social climbing, and all forms of
showing off. All these topics and others are aired in *Epicoene*, most
obviously in the follies of the knights, the Collegiate Ladies, and
the Otters, but also in the behaviour of the three gallants, whose
fluidly changing interrelationships enact some of the moment-to-
moment volatilities of ordinary social interchange. At times
Epicoene sounds almost like Swift's *Polite Conversation* in the attention it gives to the banal niceties of small-talk, the games, the
gambits, the minuscule stratagems, the clichés. And it listens hard
for the sillinesses of vogue-words and the exaggerations ritually
required of their members by social gatherings: 'Has Sir John Daw
used me so inhumanly?' cries Sir Amorous La Foole. His effetely
socialized 'inhumanly' was to be picked up by Congreve's Tattle
in the similar town-world of *Love for Love*: 'How inhuman! . . .
Gentlemen, this is the most inhuman proceeding—. . . Oh inhuman!'

   Society in this understanding of the term is the arena of a
power-struggle that never stops—where the power is by definition
not political or military or erotic but social power. The play's preoccupation with social power is equally manifest when it is
approached from a quite different direction. It has long been
established that the chief dramatic model for *Epicoene* is Aretino's
comedy *Il Marescalco* (*The Stable-Master*, printed in 1533).[1] This
play both is set at and was actually performed at the ducal court of
Mantua. Its action is in some ways not unlike that of Beaumont's
Woman Hater. An elderly bachelor, suspected of pederasty, is
tormented for the entire length of the play by being forced into
marriage, as he thinks, by the Duke. Much of the action consists of
his desperate attempts to wriggle out of what to him is an utterly
intolerable fate. The force that compels the victim–hero towards
his dreaded marriage is nothing less than the political power of

   [1] Translated by George Bull, in *Five Italian Renaissance Comedies* (Harmondsworth, 1978), ed. Bruce Penman.

the Duke. But when Jonson wrote his own play he introduced a decisive change in setting it not in a ducal court but in the fashionable part of London. The political courtly element is simply removed, leaving the play's power-system one involving more or less equal private citizens, gentlemen (some of them knights) and ladies, who struggle for different forms of precedence. The effect is to focus attention on to purely social pressures.

If the persecution of Morose owes something to a courtly entertainment, the same can be said for the subsidiary action in the fourth act of the play. This is the intrigue which brings together in a duel the two timorous and terrified combatants Sir Amorous La Foole and Sir John Daw. It is usual for editors of *Epicoene* to take it as established that Jonson's source here was Shakespeare. As Herford and Simpson say: 'The "duel" of Daw and La Foole (IV. v) is palpably built on that of Aguecheek and Viola.' The resemblance between the two scenes is not in doubt; but I question whether *Twelfth Night* should really be thought Jonson's source. It seems to me much more likely that Jonson's true source here is to be found in Sidney's *Arcadia* (3. 13)—the extended farcical episode which shows the craven braggarts Damoetas and Clinias brought by a series of ruses into a full-scale hand-to-hand fight in front of the two armies: the 'combat of cowards' as Sidney calls it. This is one of the most ambitious comic set-pieces in the whole of the *Arcadia*; and given the fame of this work throughout the early Stuart period, it seems more likely that, in this of all his plays, Jonson would have wished to align himself with Sidney rather than with a fellow-practitioner in the theatre. A comparison between the 'combat of cowards' in Sidney, Shakespeare, and Jonson would in any case show, I believe, that Jonson is much closer to Sidney than to Shakespeare.[1]

[1] Like Jonson, Shakespeare is probably himself indebted to Sidney here; but he introduces the complicating factor of Viola-Cesario's mistaken identity, and whereas he eliminates Sidney's contemptuous tone, Jonson retains it. There is in addition one verbal link which strengthens the case for Jonson's debt to Sidney. Near the beginning of the relevant chapter, Sidney uses the unusual word 'dotes', meaning 'natural gifts': '. . . not a little extolling the goodly dotes of Mopsa'—Mopsa, the foolish daughter of the cowardly Damoetas. Jonson seems to have noticed this promising word and incorporated it into *Epicoene*, where Clerimont says to Daw: 'I muse a mistress can be so silent to the dotes of such a servant' (II. iii. 91). Here, as Holdsworth notes, the word not only means 'natural gifts' but carries the latent satirical sense 'stupidities'—as it probably does also in Sidney. Sidney himself may have taken the idea for his 'combat of cowards' from the famous romance *Amadis de Gaule*. See John J. O'Connor, *'Amadis de Gaule' and its Influence on Elizabethan Literature* (Rutgers, 1970), p. 191.

My reason for mentioning the possibly Sidneian derivation of this episode is that it helps to bring out the aristocratic nature not only of the play's sources but of its own social assumptions. Essential to both Aretino's and Sidney's comedy is a posture of pride of rank on the part of the perpetrators of the jest (complemented by an unquestioning deferentiality among the lower orders) and a dismissive contempt for the eccentric or degenerate victims of it. In Sidney's aristocratic romance, Damoetas and Clinias are despicable buffoons, not much better than apes dressed in ermine. Sidney's writing is often genuinely funny, but always with a sharp edge and with a total lack of sympathy for his cowardly pair which stops us forgetting the social distinctions involved. Something of this steely Sidneian hauteur permeates Jonson's duel scene. Jonson is after all writing a comedy for and about the upper classes; and although he never writes about them with the insider's ease which Beaumont and Fletcher brought to the drama, his play is designed to leave its gentry-audience with a strong sense of class-solidarity and class-satisfaction. In order to minister to this final sense of social well-being, unworthy members of the order must be seen to be degraded and expelled from it.

Sir Amorous La Foole and Sir John Daw are both low-quality knights, and the unsparing treatment meted out to them is clearly related to their unmerited honours. Indeed in the last two acts, where La Foole and Daw are made, by repeated interrogation, to confess to having enjoyed sexual favours from Epicoene, it is hard not to feel that Jonson is disagreeably forcing the issue. Neither La Foole nor Daw has previously boasted of his conquests; La Foole especially has been earlier established as ninny rather than knave, and to see him baited at length by Clerimont and his friends makes Jonson's strategy not so much amusing as unpleasant. It is possible, on the other hand, that Jonson intends the malice and even cruelty of his tormentors to be exposed to the audience's disapproval; they behave in a way which recalls the bored irresponsibility of the town gentry as described by the young Count in Beaumont's *Woman Hater*. And when at one point Daw offers to cut his arm off as reparation (IV. v. 119–20) and Sir Dauphine accepts the offer, Truewit's response—'How! Maim a man forever for a jest! What a conscience hast thou?'—makes it clear that, for Truewit as for Jonson, there are limits to be observed in even the most sadistic practical joking. Sir Dauphine, the most coolly reserved of the three gallants, and the only one with a title, is also the most coolly ferocious.

In its social attitudes, as we have seen, the play looks back to the court-world of Sidney and Aretino as well as forward to the town-world of Congreve and his contemporaries. A few of its scenes anticipate Congreve in another way. Congreve was criticised by some critics of his time for writing not true comedy but a 'Bundle of Dialogues'; his plays were, they thought, defective in plot and action.[1] Despite Jonson's care in *Epicoene* to control his plot in all its elaborate complexity, quite a lot of the second half especially can give an effect of dialogue rather than drama, of polite conversation meticulously mimicked by marionettes. It is perhaps this slightly desiccated subhuman level of characterization and dialogue (at least in the fourth and fifth acts) that helps explain the absence of *Epicoene* from the modern stage. But not only that: its comedy of torment and teasing is too relentless, too nakedly exposed in its sheer unpleasantness, simply too prolonged, to make much appeal to a modern audience. Despite the genuinely funny passages and single lines, the play's mirth is finally less than infectious.[2]

The central episode of *Epicoene*, however, breaks free of the attenuated verbalism that may, for modern producers, throw doubt on the play's potential in the theatre. Here the form taken by the action is a favourite one of Jonson's. People from one urban area *invade* another. They force their way within the precincts of a private house, with an effect of gross violation. The idea of invasion, of the violation of territorial rights, was present as early as *Every Man in His Humour*, where the jealous Thorello/Kitely's house was invaded by impertinent and noisy strangers (in the revised version Jonson introduces the term 'invade' near the play's opening, where Knowell Senior says to Stephen: 'I would not have you to invade each place, / Nor thrust yourself on all societies . . .'; the earlier text had 'intrude'). *Volpone* too suffers an invasion—in his case, a one-woman invasion in the form of Lady Would-be: 'All my house, / But now, steam'd like a bath, with her thick breath'. And invasion on a far bigger scale is what Morose's house suffers when La Foole's quarter-day party is maliciously diverted into it. Indeed social invasion—people pushing their way into places where they are not wanted—forms the dominant stage image of *Epicoene*, a picture embodying the vexation, almost the horror, of close social living, and more especially the exhausting pressure

---

[1] See Maximillian E. Novak, *William Congreve* (New York, 1971), p. 78.

[2] *Epicoene* seems to have had only one professional production in recent times, that at the Oxford Playhouse in 1967. On that occasion, it seemed to me, the play at several points came across as so ill-natured as to lose the sympathy of the audience.

of other people's personalities. Of course Morose is a selfish, unlikeable misanthrope, whom all discourses but his own afflict; and as such he is subjected to a traditional ritual of punishment. But in so far as he is also the representative, as he is to some extent, of human sensibility shrinking from the noise and congestion of Jacobean London, he draws to himself some—however little—of our sympathy, whether Jonson saw it that way or not.

In a longer perspective, the fetidly gregarious nature of Morose's persecution assumes a social meaning in accord with wider developments in Jonson's London. His play shows people forced into social intimacy with an effect of horrible abrasiveness. And in doing so, it dramatizes that pressure for greater living space, that growing social desire for segregation and exclusion and leisured privacy, which was already finding public expression. Without in any way advocating it, or even adverting to it, Jonson shows town and city moving apart.

To think of Shakespeare in the midst of these forward-looking London matters is to be struck by how very far away he is from them. The only mention of the Strand in his plays is in *Henry VIII*, in a scene that may in any case be by Fletcher. At the time when Jonson was writing *Epicoene*, Shakespeare was embarking upon his final romances: *The Winter's Tale* and *The Tempest* were only one or two years ahead. The thought may serve to remind us how various and capacious, how resistant to simplifying formula, is the drama of the early Jacobean period.

APPENDIX

THE LATER WEST END TRADITION

In this Appendix I add a few notes and quotations to indicate the development of West End comedy from the mid nineteenth century onwards, and I take a little further some of the themes already touched upon: the town gentleman; the levee scene; and the West End of London.

It is in the early nineteenth century that this tradition of comedy comes closest to disappearing altogether. At this time even the best Restoration comedies began to lose the hold on the stage which they had maintained throughout the eighteenth century. In the 1840s, however, attempts were made to adapt the older comedy of manners to new social conditions and tastes. These mid-Victorian plays are undoubtedly slight and thin and even 'puerile' (to use the word which Henry James applied to Robertson's comedies); but they have a certain historical importance in that they helped to attract a fashionable audience back into the theatre, and so prepared the way for the nineties drama of Pinero, Wilde, and Shaw.

Dion Boucicault's comedy *London Assurance* (1841) sets most of its action in a country house, but it opens in London at the Belgrave Square home of Sir Harcourt Courtly. Sir Harcourt is still in bed, and his son Charles, having just come home after a night on the town, has to solicit the butler's help in keeping up his pretence of being a paragon of virtue. He narrowly misses walking into his father who, still in a dressing-gown, has descended from his bedroom. The scene is a variant on the levee formula, showing at the same time both Sir Harcourt's comfortable way of life and his son's profligacy. The bulk of the play does not concern us; but it ends with a resounding reaffirmation of the gentlemanly ideal. Sir Harcourt is addressing his son and his son's friend:

And these are the deeds which attest your title to the name of gentleman? I perceive that you have caught the infection of the present age. Charles, permit me, as your father, and you, sir, as his friend to correct you on one point. Barefaced assurance is the vulgar substitute for gentlemanly ease; and there are many who by aping the *vices* of the great, imagine that they elevate themselves to the rank of those whose faults alone they copy. No, sir. The title of a gentleman is the only one *out* of any monarch's gift, yet within the reach of every peasant. It should be engrossed by *Truth*—stamped with *Honour*—sealed with *good-feeling*—signed *Man*—and enrolled in every true young English heart. CURTAIN.

London Assurance demonstrates, over two hundred years after *Epicoene*, that West End comedy is still closely associated with the social outlook of the gentry. And the title of gentleman is still prized, as it was in the seventeenth century, as being beyond the gift of a monarch.

Boucicault's later comedy *Old Heads and Young Hearts* (1844) opens with a highly traditional morning scene: '*The Temple. The Interior of Littelton Coke's Chambers, meagrely furnished.* COKE *is discovered at breakfast, reading the paper.* BOB, *cleaning a Meerschaum,* R.' Between reading out items of news, Coke expresses his sense of poverty and laments his lack of success in his profession. Bob remarks: 'But your father, at his death, sir, left you 700*l* a year.' To which Coke replies: 'To support 7000 appetites he bequeathed me at my birth . . .' Boucicault seems to be recalling here, in a general way, Valentine's poverty in Congreve's *Love for Love*, but more particularly the striking exchange between Valentine and his father Sir Sampson in Act II. Here, Sir Sampson brutally disclaims responsibility for his son: '. . . Come, Uncase, Strip, and go naked out of the World, as you came into 't.' To which Valentine replies: 'My Cloaths are soon put off:—But you must also deprive me of Reason, Thought, Passions, Inclinations, Affections, Appetites, Senses, and the huge Train of Attendants that you begot along with me.' Faint though it

is, Coke's echo of Valentine shows the presence of Congreve in early
Victorian comedy and hence the continuity of the tradition. At the same
time Boucicault's play illustrates the persistence of the link between
the gentleman and the legal profession, here symbolized in the Inns of
Court setting.

Among Edward Bulwer-Lytton's plays is *Not So Bad As We Seem, or,
Many Sides to a Character*, a historical extravaganza in neo-Restoration
form, with an action set in London during the reign of George I. (It
was first performed in 1851, at Devonshire House, Piccadilly, before
Queen Victoria and the Prince Consort.) The opening scene shows
'Lord Wilmot's *Apartment* in St. James's.' The valet Smart appears:

Smart (showing in a Masked Lady). My Lord is dressing. As you say,
madam, it is late. But though he never wants sleep more than once a
week, yet when he does sleep, I am proud to say he sleeps better than any
man in the three kingdoms.
Lady. I have heard much of Lord Wilmot's eccentricities—but also of
his generosity and honor.
Smart. Yes, madam, nobody like him for speaking ill of himself and
doing good to another.
Enter WILMOT.
Wilmot. 'And sleepless lovers just at twelve awake.' Any duels to-day,
Smart? No—I see something more dangerous—a woman. (*To Smart*).
Vanish.

The cast-list for this royal performance included some well-known
names: Lord Wilmot was played by 'Mr. Charles Dickens', Smart by
'Mr. Wilkie Collins'. The connection of the play with Restoration
comedy is, though indirect, quite clear, not only in the nature and form
of the scene but in the hero's name (alluding, like the name of the hero of
Jane Eyre, four years before, to John Wilmot, Earl of Rochester). As
usual, the lateness of the hour receives comment.

T. W. Robertson's comedy *Society*, usually said to have opened a new
chapter in Victorian drama, was first acted in 1865. The play was put on
by Marie Wilton and her husband Squire Bancroft, who were pioneers
in the process of bringing back fashionable audiences into the theatre; as
much as anyone, they helped to establish the present West End theatrical
system. *Society* opens in the hero's rooms, which are once again in the
Inns of Court: 'Sidney Daryl's *Chambers in Lincoln's Inn*.' His servant
Doddles is on stage. A visitor is the first to speak.

Tom (without): Mr Daryl in?
Doddles: Not up yet. (*Enter* Tom Stylus, Chodd Jun., *and* Chodd Se.)
Chodd Jun. (looking at watch): Ten minutes to twelve, eh, guv?
Tom: Late into bed; up after he oughter; out for brandy and sobering
water.
Sidney (within): Doddles.

Doddles: Yes, sir!
Sidney: Brandy and soda.

We soon learn that Sidney is 'in his bath'—a new addition to the levee formula. For all the piquancy of its class comedy and the novelty of its realistic décor, Robertson's comedy is traditional in more ways than is usually allowed. The Chodds are intruding City types, tasteless but moneyed; Sidney is feckless but genteel. The next scene is set in '*The interior of a Square at the West End*': it brings on Sidney's fiancée, who is to be boorishly pursued by Chodd Junior. However remote in style from Jonson, Etherege, and Congreve, *Society* operates within the well-trodden precincts of town-and-city comedy.

Wilde's *Importance of Being Earnest* (1895), the best known comedy of manners from the end of the century, is in some ways a deliberate throw-back to the aestheticism of Congreve, though Gilbert's *Engaged* is a more immediate influence. Its opening scene is thoroughly traditional in orientation, but Wilde removes any suggestion of mere literariness by inventing a convincing variation on the levee formula. It is set not at morning but in the afternoon, so that the expected visitors are coming for afternoon tea. The opening dialogue between master and servant (compare *Epicoene* and *Love for Love*) is a fine instance of this traditional form, with Lane the butler effortlessly upstaging his employer.

During this same period of the revival of West End comedy, London also saw the rise of music-hall, the indigenous art-form of the East End. Many of its songs focus on the West End, and once again—for the first time in any notable way since the early seventeenth century—the Strand is singled out as the most illustrious street in London. (Not that earlier writers had ignored it: Dr Johnson and Lamb had paid it tribute; and Disraeli, in *Tancred*, remarked airily that 'the Strand is, perhaps, the finest street in Europe'). To judge from these music-hall songs, many East Enders regarded walking down the Strand as the height of social ambition. But the Strand is now much more a centre of West End entertainment than of fashionable life—by this time, of course, the true centre of fashion had long moved further west.[1] Still, in this period the mere mention of the Strand conferred glamour on the speaker, often ironically disclaimed—like the remark used by Marie Lloyd as a favourite opening gambit: 'Sorry I'm late—I got blocked in the Strand.' One of the songs written for the male impersonator Ella Shields, 'Burlington Bertie from Bow', was a sequel to an earlier number of Vesta Tilley's, a plain 'Burlington Bertie'. In

[1] 'The Strand is remarkable as containing more theatres than any other street in London': see H. B. Wheatley's *London Past and Present* (1891), iii. 323. Since Wheatley wrote, the Gaiety and the Tivoli, among others, have been demolished; Irving's Lyceum is no longer in use as a theatre, and (as it seems at the time of writing) the Adelphi may undergo a similar fate.

the sequel, Bertie has come down in the world and lives in Bow (in East
London); and his words trace a new variant on the West End levee
formula:

> I'm Bert, p'raps you've heard of me,
> Bert. . . . you've had word of me . . .
> I dress up in fashion, and when I'm feeling depressed,
> I shave from my cuff all the whiskers and fluff,
> Stick my hat on and toddle up West.
>
> I'm Burlington Bertie,
> I rise at ten-thirty, and saunter along like a toff,
> I walk down the Strand, with my gloves on my hand,
> Then I walk down again with them off . . .[1]

In a small way the song is a fantasy of fashionable leisure: it exploits the
Cockney angle on the West End and, as so often, picks out what was
most enviable to the working-class man—the gentleman's supposed
freedom from the imposition of early morning rising. (The upper-class
lady's freedom too: the high point of the comic tradition we are
considering could be said to be the scene in *The Way of the World* in which
Millamant declares: 'Positively Mirabell, I'll lie a-bed in a morning as
long as I please'.)

A real-life 'toff' of the same period was Somerset Maugham, although
he began his career working hard as a doctor in one of London's
hospitals. He worked even harder as a writer. In a few years he was to
have three plays running concurrently in the West End. One of them,
Lady Frederick (written in 1904, first acted in 1907), is a fair instance of
the turn-of-the-century transmutation of West End comedy, with its
strong infusion of 'Gallic' worldly wisdom and with the well-tried
formulas of the *pièce bien faite* given a new, but not too novel, twist. It even
has an excellent specimen of the levee scene, but with the usual
arrangement reversed by having it open the last (third) act instead of
the first, and by making the protagonist a woman. This is the scene—
it enjoyed a mild notoriety for a time—in which the 'mature' Lady
Frederick (i.e. between thirty and thirty-five) admits her innocent
young suitor to her dressing-room and, in order to disillusion him, lets
him see her make herself up: '*She comes through the curtains. She wears a
kimono, her hair is all dishevelled, hanging about her head in a tangled mop. She is
not made up and looks haggard and yellow and lined. When* MERESTON *sees her he
gives a slight start of surprise.*' The play is set, however, not in London but
in Monte Carlo, though it might as well be London since the characters
are entirely West End people. When she has despatched the young man,
she finally agrees to marry her faithful admirer, 'a very well-dressed man
of forty-odd', who—in reply to her remark 'I've got half a mind to retire
from the world and bury myself in a hermitage'—says 'So have I, and

[1] Daniel Farson, *Marie Lloyd and Music Hall* (1972), p. 137.

I've bought the lease of a little house in Norfolk Street, Park Lane.' She replies: 'Just the place for a hermitage—fashionable without being vulgar.'

Maugham brings us back nearly to the age of Noel Coward, whose entry into the West End theatre can be symbolized by a moment in his autobiography as he glides in a taxi through the Strand. The time is August 1918; Coward is eighteen, and has just been unexpectedly released from the army 'in a state of indescribable happiness. At Liverpool Street I took a taxi and drove through the City streets. It was twelve noon, in the full tide of traffic, and the hot August sun beat down upon taxis and trucks and drays and red friendly buses. It also beat down with kindly impartiality upon the Gaiety, the Vaudeville, the Savoy, and the Adelphi theatres and I pictured the cool pre-matinée gloom of their interiors . . .'[1]

I suggested earlier that the West End comic tradition, begun by Ben Jonson and his contemporaries, came to an end with Noel Coward and *his* contemporaries. But if we wish finally to settle upon a name with which to associate the close of this tradition (if it has in fact come to a close), I think we can do better than Noel Coward. We should look outside the theatre to prose fiction: the novels and stories of P. G. Wodehouse. Wodehouse's narrative technique is of course thoroughly theatrical; he himself was an expert writer of scripts and lyrics. But more perhaps than anyone since the early Thackeray, he has given a fresh mythopoeic currency to the idea of the West End. His earliest stories were appropriately published in the *Strand* magazine, to which he remained faithful until it closed down; and such titles as *A Gentleman of Leisure* (his first novel) and *Piccadilly Jim* (which is actually set in America) point to one of his persistent stamping-grounds. Bertie Wooster is the stylized, yet wholly convincing, apotheosis of the idle West End gentleman: perpetually young, unmarried, unworried about money, a life-member of the Drones Club, he habitually stays in bed of a morning as long as he pleases. Levee scenes are not infrequent in Wodehouse. *The Code of the Woosters* (1938) opens with one:

> I reached out a hand from under the blankets, and rang the bell for Jeeves.
> 'Good evening, Jeeves.'
> 'Good morning, sir.'. . .

Wodehouse, himself an extraordinarily hard worker by any standards, is likely to have had mixed views on the affluent idlers of his fiction. Indeed one of his critics, Owen Dudley Edwards, goes further, finding in his early fiction particularly a critical attitude to his upper-class characters: '. . . Wodehouse time and again returns to the theme of resolute and hard-working young men and women as a foil to aristocratic drones. . . . it is the bourgeois attack on the privilege and non-productivity of

---

[1] *Present Indicative* (1937), p. 101.

Emrys Jones

the aristocracy.'[1] A divided response to the town gentleman is something we meet throughout this comic tradition, from Jonson and Beaumont onwards: a vicarious delight in his uninhibited style of life together with a never quite fully suppressed reserve or irritation at his freedom from the necessity to work: 'what is a gentleman but his pleasure?'

[1] *P. G. Wodehouse* (1977), pp. 69–70.

SHAKESPEARE'S LIARS

By INGA-STINA EWBANK

Read 21 April 1983

My theme is words and men (and women)—the raw material of Shakespeare's drama. If language is one of the glories of Shakespearian man, as he uses it for feats of self-discovery and revelation, and for intercourse with others, it is also one of his chief perils, as he not only uses but also abuses it. Language gives him the power to create and to destroy. Like Time in *The Winter's Tale* it both 'makes and unfolds error'; it can reveal truth, but it can just as easily be the instrument of deception. It all depends on the man or woman who speaks it, and on the listener. Or, in the words of Montaigne, writing his essay 'Of Liars': 'Nothing makes us men, and no other meanes keeps us bound one to another, but our word.'[1] My subject is Shakespeare's liars, as men and women who most keenly demonstrate both the glory and the peril of trading in words.

I do not think that Shakespeare was a proto-modernist who believed that words as such lie, and whose plays are about the deceptiveness and inadequacy of language.[2] When Feste announces that 'words are grown so false I am loath to prove reason with them', or when, as in *King Lear*, the frailties of speech are at the very heart of the experience of the play, then the limitations and the falseness are in the speakers and their worlds, not in the medium as such. If words are double, this makes them all the more useful as dramatic tools. Nowhere, perhaps, do we see this more clearly than in the fondness— which Shakespeare shares with other dramatists of the period— for puns on the word 'lie' itself. In sonnet 138 the play on the

[1] 'Of Lyers', in *The Essays of Montaigne Done into English by John Florio Anno 1615*, ed. George Saintsbury, i (1892), 44. The original essay, 'Des menteurs', is dated 1572-4.

[2] In this respect I agree with Margreta de Grazia, whose article 'Shakespeare's View of Language: An Historical Perspective', *Shakespeare Quarterly*, 29 (1978), 374-88, has a useful summary of writings (mainly from the 1970s) on Shakespeare's mistrust of language.

two senses forms a kind of action, from the worldly wise paradox
of the opening lines,

> When my love swears that she is made of truth,
> I do believe her, though I know she lies,

to the achieved *modus vivendi* of the concluding couplet:

> Therefore I lie with her, and she with me,
> And in our faults by lies we flattered be.[1]

The Clown who delivers the fatal 'worm' to Cleopatra makes
particularly effective use of the same pun by compounding it with
a play on 'die'; and, with rather less sexual innuendo but no less
irony, Hamlet and the First Gravedigger try to outwit each other
with a pun on lying—in what is in fact going to be Ophelia's
grave. And there is that extraordinary scene in *Othello* (III.iv.
1-19), between Desdemona and the Clown who makes comic
capital out of not knowing where Cassio 'lies'—a scene which has
nothing to do with plot and everything to do with the multiple
horrors of lying in that play. If it provides relief, this is dubiously
comic, at a point in the structure where Iago's lies have already
begun to work and where, only a few minutes later, Othello is
going to find the word 'lie' gruesomely expressive: 'Lie with her—
lie on her? We say lie on her when they belie her.' The force of the
pun is, by this time, less in Othello's mind than in the audience's;
there it reverberates as the 'belying' of Desdemona slides out of
control and she dies with a lie, however white, on her lips, while
ironically the first and only occurrence of the word 'liar' in the
play is in Othello's still unenlightened (though by fundamentalist
standards true) statement: 'She's like a liar gone to burning hell.'
In each of these examples words prove their slipperiness, but
Shakespeare proves the power of words—even in their very
slipperiness—to interpret human relationships, extend the mean-
ings of situations, and establish formal connections between
apparently unrelated parts of a dramatic action. To look at
Shakespeare's liars is to affirm his interest in what people do to
themselves and to each other through words. What I want to talk
about, then, is lying—quite unambiguously in its dictionary
definition of speaking falsely, telling untruths—as one feature of
that landscape of people which makes up Shakespeare's theatre.

One assumes that Shakespeare the man thought telling the
truth was better than lying. Shakespeare the poet knew that his

---

[1] All Shakespeare quotations in this lecture are from Peter Alexander's
edition of *The Complete Works* (1951).

art was always open to accusations of mendaciousness from the Apemantuses (and strict Platonists) of his world:

Apemantus. Art not a poet?
Poet. Yes.
Apemantus. Then thou liest.
  (*Timon of Athens*, i. i. 221–3)[1]

But Shakespeare the dramatist, though I doubt if he would have agreed with those who believe that the origin of language is in man's need to lie, must have been grateful for the human inability, or unwillingness, to stick to truth—for the dramatic potential in man's sheer capacity for lying. For truth, as Montaigne says, has 'no more faces than one . . . But the opposite of truth has many-many shapes, and an undefinite field'.[2] In the 'undefinite field' of Shakespearian drama there is an almost infinite variety of lies. At one extreme is the lie as a social convenience, seen, for example, in the Jamesian ambiguities which Polonius instructs Reynaldo to utter in spying on Laertes, taking care not to call these 'indirections' anything so crude as lies ('. . . put on him / What forgeries you please . . .'; '. . . slight sullies . . .'; '. . . breathe his faults so quaintly . . .') and also to point out that the end justifies the means:

See you now
Your bait of falsehood take this carp of truth.
    (*Hamlet*, ii. i. 19 ff.)

At the other extreme are the lies of such moral magnitude and effect that they are able to kill body and soul, disrupt society, and overturn universal order, as imaged in Pisanio's lines when watching Imogen read Posthumus' letter—lines which remind us that, while Shakespeare may anticipate Henry James, he was a contemporary of Spenser and familiar with an iconography in which Calumny is the arch enemy of Truth:

What shall I need to draw my sword? The paper
Hath cut her throat already. No, 'tis slander,
Whose edge is sharper than the sword, whose tongue
Outvenoms all the worms of Nile, whose breath

---

[1] Kenneth Muir, writing on 'Shakespeare's Poets', in *Shakespeare the Professional* (1973), discusses the irony with which Shakespeare treats poets in his works—possibly 'to protect a heart he would not wear upon his sleeve' (p. 40).

[2] *The Essays of Montaigne*, i. 44.

> Rides on the posting winds and doth belie
> All corners of the world. Kings, queens, and states,
> Maids, matrons, nay, the secrets of the grave,
> This viperous slander enters.
>
> > (*Cymbeline*, III. iv. 30–7)[1]

If there are many kinds of lies, there are many sorts of liars, too. Lying can be as literally part of a life-style as it is with Falstaff, fathering lies like himself, 'gross as a mountain, open, palpable', and articulating his philosophy on the battlefield of Shrewsbury:

> Counterfeit? I lie, I am no counterfeit: to die is to be a counterfeit; . . . to counterfeit dying, when a man thereby liveth, is to be no counterfeit, but the true and perfect image of life indeed;   (*1 Henry IV*, v. iv. 113 ff.)

or with that 'infinite and endless liar' Parolles, who can think of no better way of lying about someone than to say that he, too, is a liar: 'He will lie, sir, with such volubility that you would think truth were a fool' (*All's Well*, III. vi. 9 and IV. iii. 235–6). But it can also be an act as unnatural as it seems to Coriolanus in the market-place ('Must I / With my base tongue give to my noble heart / A lie that it must bear?' *Coriolanus*, III. ii. 99–101), or as foreign as it is to Isabella in the final scene of *Measure for Measure*. 'To speak so indirectly I am loath', she tells Mariana, as she rehearses the instructions given her by the Duke,

> I would say the truth; but to accuse him so,
> That is your part. Yet I am advis'd to do it;
> He says, to veil full purpose.
>
> > (*Measure for Measure*, IV. vi. 1–4)

This range, of course, is a reminder of the range of moral perspectives on lies and liars in the plays. Shakespeare is no fierce fundamentalist. We must not assume that he himself accepts, or wishes us to accept, Falstaff's lie with quite the ease of Hal:

> For my part, if a lie may do thee grace,
> I'll gild it with the happiest terms I have;
>
> > (*1 Henry IV*, v. iv. 156–7)

---

[1] In Hadrianus Junius's *Emblemata* (Antwerp, 1565) the theme of *Veritas Filia Temporis* is treated in an emblem (LIII) where, under the motto 'Veritas tempore reuelatur, dissidio obruitur', Time (or Saturn) is represented as rescuing his daughter, Truth, from a cave where she has been oppressed by Discord (*Lis*), Envy (*Inuidia*), and Calumny (*Calumnia*). D. J. Gordon draws attention to the pessimism of this, as against the optimism of the poem which Geoffrey Whitney attaches to the same picture when he uses it in *A Choice of Emblems* (1586). See *Journal of the Warburg and Courtauld Institutes*, 3 (1940), 228–40.

but nor can we doubt that he glories in the sheer creativeness of Falstaff's lying wit. More often than not, lying is part of a complex exploration of moral values; often, too, it is part of a dramatic inquiry into what *is* true. 'If I should tell my history', Marina insists, 'it would seem / Like lies, disdain'd in the reporting' (*Pericles*, v. i. 117–18). With Montaigne, Shakespeare no doubt disdains lying as 'an ill and detestible vice', but he also shows the difficulty of knowing and judging a liar—much as Montaigne does in his several essays dealing with lies, not least in the one entitled: 'It is folly to measure the true and false by our own capacity.'[1]

Measure for Measure is perhaps the play which most peremptorily challenges that 'capacity' as we respond to the liars in the play. The world of Vienna is open to great perversions of truth, as Angelo's case shows, and as the disguised Duke tells Escalus: 'There is scarce truth enough alive to make societies secure' (III. ii. 213–14). The Duke tries to revive truth by the big lie of his disguise. Though he is voluble about Lucio's form of lying, his 'slanderous tongue' and 'back-wounding calumny', his own device is, throughout the play, surrounded by a notable unwillingness to call a lie a lie. The only two characters who explicitly call others liars[2] are, comically, Elbow fulminating against Pompey

---

[1] Florio's translation of this title is: 'It is folly to referre Truth or Falshood to our sufficiencie' (*The Essays of Montaigne*, i. 191–6). The version quoted is from *The Complete Works of Montaigne*, translated by Donald M. Frame (no date). In 'Of Lyers', lying is 'an ill and detestible vice' (*The Essays of Montaigne*, i. 44); in 'Of giving the lie' (dating from 1578–80) it is 'a horrible-filthy vice' (ii. 402). It is interesting that one editor of the essays finds himself prompted to write a three-and-a-half page note to the last mentioned passage in which he defends Montaigne against the accusation of being, himself, a liar. See *Œuvres Complètes de Michel de Montaigne*, Les Essais, IV, ed. A. Armaingaud (Paris, 1926), pp. 271–4.

[2] To be called a liar, Montaigne points out, 'is the extremest injury, may be done us in words' (*The Essays of Montaigne*, ii. 402), and he goes on to note the irony that we tend to defend ourselves most ardently 'from such defects as we are tainted with'. Thus Iago to Emilia: 'Filth, thou liest' (*Othello*, v. ii. 234). As Touchstone knows, giving someone the Lie Direct is the point of no return in duelling; we see this in deadly earnest in *Richard II*, I. i and in *King Lear*, v. iii. 140; and humorously in Sir Andrew Aguecheek's challenge to Caesario/Viola (*Twelfth Night*, III. iv. 149). In extremis, Coriolanus and Young Siward give the lie to, respectively, Aufidius and Macbeth (*Coriolanus*, v. vi. 103 ff. and *Macbeth*, v. vii. 10). Hamlet creates an imaginary duel situation and, characteristically, makes a vivid image of a clichéd intensifier: 'Who…gives me the lie i'th' throat / As deep as to the lungs?' (*Hamlet*, II. ii. 568–9). The response to being given the lie acts as a test of nobility in *Pericles*, II. v. 54 ff. and, humorously, in *The Winter's Tale*, v. ii. 129. Otherwise, high-born characters call others liars only in states of extreme emotion (Lear, Leontes, Cleopatra), whereas others, of a lower social

for describing his wife as a 'respected' woman, and, drastically, Lucio in words which freeze on his lips in that moment when he tears off the Friar's hood to find that he has revealed the Duke:

Why, you bald-pated lying rascal, you must be hooded, must you?

(v. i. 350)

It is tempting to say that Lucio here provides a kind of safety valve for our ambivalent feelings about the Duke. His own plot is articulated in a language of euphemisms. Isabella is instructed to go and lie to Angelo about lying with him (for that is what she is having to do, though the lying, like the bed-trick, is enacted off-stage) in a language of 'indirections' which would do credit to Polonius, let alone more recent politicians: 'answer his requiring with a plausible obedience; agree with his demands to the point; only refer yourself to this advantage . . . If for this night he entreat you to his bed, give him promise of satisfaction' (and she a nun, about to make quite a different kind of promise). In the scene where Mariana—again out of hearing—is initiated into the plan, Isabella comes straight from this interview with Angelo, to report with no sign of embarrassment that 'I have made my promise / Upon the heavy middle of the night / To call upon him' (iv. i. 32–4). The ends of the lie, it is obvious, will justify the means— though even this point is made by careful circumlocution:

If you think well to carry this as you may, the doubleness of the benefit defends the deceit from reproof.   (iii. i. 248–9)

In the end the Duke decides to lie to Isabella, too, to 'keep her ignorant of her good, / To make her heavenly comforts of despair / When it is least expected' (iv. iii. 105–7). Meanwhile she trusts his therapeutic purpose: 'for 'tis a physic / That's bitter to sweet end' (iv. vi. 7–8). This refrain—'sweet end'; 'full purpose'; 'least expected'—suggests that the 'euphemisms' in the play are there not so much to obscure deceit and draw attention from the lie perpetrated as to thrust our imaginations forward, to the promised end. They point the structure for us and help us to select from possible responses. Isabella's immediate response to the Duke's account of his plot provides a model in which the truth of actuality gives way to a fiction with a purpose: 'The image of it gives me content already; and I trust it will grow to a most prosperous perfection' (iii. i. 250–1). In other words, we are

status, utter the accusation more readily and thoughtlessly (Falstaff and his companions; Kate and Petruchio in *The Taming of the Shrew*; Abraham to Sampson in *Romeo and Juliet*).

dealing less with the Duke and Isabella as liars and more with Shakespeare as a liar—the playwright, finding in the lie a useful dramatic structure.

In the Comedies we are obviously not asked for moral outrage at the feigning which is part of the game of *homo ludens*. Transvestite heroines embody and enact the structural and thematic movement of their respective plays, through deceit to truth. When they tell outright lies, as in the developed fictions which both Julia and Viola use to convey their 'real' feelings, then the emotional result is truth, not falsehood.[1] In the world of the romantic comedies, just as young women will practise deceit to gain the right, true end, so young men will be swaggerers and—as in the high-spirited passage where Portia plans her disguise—'tell quaint lies' (*Merchant of Venice*, III. iv. 69). Yet, the perspective may shift suddenly, to lay bare the potential perniciousness of lying. There is more than comic wit in Beatrice's diatribe against men who 'are only turned into tongue, and trim ones, too. He is now as valiant as Hercules that only tells a lie and swears it', especially as it is spoken just after she has asked Benedick to 'Kill Claudio'—a Claudio deceived by a malignant lie (*Much Ado*, IV. i. 287 ff.). Later in the same play the belied Hero's uncle attacks Claudio and Don Pedro in a scene where justified moral outrage threatens to unbalance the comedy, and in a language which anticipates that of Jonson's and Middleton's 'roarers':

> Boys, apes, braggarts . . .
> Scrambling, out-facing, fashion-monging boys,
> That lie and cog and flout, deprave and slander.
>
> (v. i. 94–5)

And the conceit with which Leonato articulates the denouement of *Much Ado about Nothing*—'She died, my lord, but whiles her slander liv'd' (v. iv. 66)—looks forward to *The Winter's Tale*, even as it speaks more poignantly than Leonato intended, of lying as a deadly sin.

The Tragedies are more directly concerned with such lies. Lying (if often dressed up as omission of truth) dominates the political world of *Hamlet*, the plot of *Othello*, and so much of the first Act of *King Lear* that the Fool, pointedly, asks to 'learn to lie'. The moral chaos of *Macbeth* is epitomized by 'th' equivocation of the fiend / That lies like truth' (v. v. 43–4). I do not want to sound as if I were suggesting that all Shakespeare's dramatic art can be reduced to a study of lying: there are plays, such as *A Midsummer*

[1] Cf. *The Two Gentlemen of Verona*, IV. iv. 139 ff. and *Twelfth Night*, II. iv. 106 ff.

Night's Dream, where hardly anyone lies, except the fiction itself:
'Else the Puck a liar call.' But there are also plays, like *Othello*,
which pivot on a lie. They are plays, of course, where human
intrigue controls the design.

Unless we are habitual liars, we lie for a purpose: a lie tends to
be teleological. Furthermore, it is in the nature of lies that they are
rarely momentary phenomena or isolated acts. They tend to grow
into actions: a lie, once spoken, tends to have to be elaborated,
supported by further lies, until its ramifications spread beyond the
liar's control, and sooner or later a revelation (brought about by
Time the Revealer or more directly by human ingenuity) will
take place. Our little everyday, 'white', lies may not be quite
so Aristotelian in their course; but any more elaborate lie—
pernicious or salutary—is ideal as a design for a plot structure.
Shakespeare seems particularly conscious of this in *Much Ado about
Nothing*: Don John's slanderous lie is first rehearsed in Act II, scene
ii, where Borachio rapidly draws up the scenario for 'the death of
this marriage'; it is then practised on Claudio and Don Pedro in
Act III, scene ii, and the scene of supporting evidence is enacted off-
stage and reported by Borachio to Conrade in Act III, scene iii. The
lie and the 'proof' of its truth are then again reported and reviewed
in the church scene (IV. i), none of those present realizing that
Borachio has been overheard and 'comprehended' by the Watch.
The lie draws attention to itself as plot logic; hence the effectiveness in the design of the unexpected: Hero's swoon and the Friar's
counter-lie which keeps her 'dead' until Dogberry has finally got
around to revealing that Don John and his companions are 'lying
knaves'. In contrast to this neat pattern, Iago's plan emerges
piecemeal, from a general notion of 'abusing' Othello's ear, as
circumstances and Othello's nature play into his hand: ''Tis here,
but yet confus'd. / Knavery's plain face is never seen till us'd'
(*Othello*, II. i. 305-6).

To look at *Othello* is also to be reminded that what comes to be
really characteristic of Shakespeare's art is not lying as plot
dynamics but lying and being lied to, or about, as character
experience—the exploration of what the lie does, of how it
transforms both the liar and the belied. I say 'comes to be', for we
need only compare Don John to Iago, Claudio to Othello or
Leontes, and Hero to Imogen, to see how much more fully the
experiences of agents and victims of lies are articulated in the later
plays. But I am not suggesting a simple evolutionary process from
early to late, or from comedy to tragedy and tragicomedy. One of
the very earliest Shakespearian liars is the aptly named Proteus

in *The Two Gentlemen of Verona*.[1] When it comes to the point, he is
a bad liar, unimaginatively producing two identical lies:

> I grant, sweet love, that I did love a lady;
> But she is dead . . .
> I likewise hear that Valentine is dead.
>
> (IV. ii. 101–9)

But in the monologue where he deliberately sets about perverting
the truth—resolving to break his oath of love and faith to his
mistress Julia and his friend Valentine, so as to be free to woo
Silvia—he demonstrates a kind of perverse imagination which is
nothing less than a model of how the liar uses words to reconstruct
his world:

> I will forget that Julia is alive,
> Rememb'ring that my love to her is dead;
> And Valentine I'll hold an enemy,
> Aiming at Silvia as a sweeter friend.
> I cannot now prove constant to myself
> Without some treachery us'd to Valentine.
>
> (II. vi. 27–32)

As far as human relationships go, this—spelled out with the
antithetical stiffness which is the idiom of the play—is a mere
diagram; but translate the diagram into action, and we have
a world where 'nothing is but what is not', and where characters
would have to define themselves in Iago's language: 'I am not
what I am.' Indeed, the disguised Julia finds just this when she has
to woo Silvia on Proteus' behalf:

> I am my master's true confirmed love,
> But cannot be true servant to my master,
> Unless I prove false traitor to myself.
>
> (IV. iv. 99–101)

Proteus does not reach his new self without a struggle with the old—

> I cannot leave to love, and yet I do—
>
> (II. vi. 17)

[1] A. B. Giamatti, 'Proteus Unbound: Some Versions of the Sea-God in the
Renaissance', in *The Disciplines of Criticism*, ed. P. Demetz *et al.* (New Haven,
Conn., and London, 1968), discusses the two Renaissance traditions of Proteus:
'as *vates* and poet' and 'as *magus* and sinister manipulator of words'. His point,
that these traditions 'support one another, providing reciprocal tension and
balance, for each depends on the other for the reservoir of ambiguity that gives
Proteus, and language, the potency to adapt and to signify' (p. 455), is relevant
to Shakespeare's Proteus, and to my argument in this lecture.

and, though this sounds more like the paradoxes of Richard III ('I am a villain; yet I lie, I am not') than the agonized breaking-down of a Leontes or an Othello ('I think my wife be honest, and think she is not'), *The Two Gentlemen of Verona* still contains a blueprint of the creative power of the liar: making new selves and new relationships and a world in which the old values—constancy, honour, friendship, love—have been inverted.

At this point I must conclude this brief survey of the 'many shapes' of lying, in the hope that there has run one thread through it: the uselessness of speaking of something like 'the concept of the liar in Shakespeare'. His interest in lying is, not surprisingly, not an abstract one, but an interest in human predicaments: those of a liar, of one who is lied to, and (especially in the slander plots to which he almost obsessively returns) of one who is lied about.

Needless to say, this does not mean that Shakespeare does not explore the wider—we may call them 'philosophical'—aspects of dealing with that which is not true. Even Proteus gives us glimpses of that condition of chaos which Montaigne analyses in the essay 'Of giving the lie':

> Our intelligence being onely conducted by the way of the Word: Who so falsifieth the same, betraieth publik society. It is the onely instrument, by means wherof our wils and thoughts are communicated: it is the interpretour of our soules: If that faile us we hold our selves no more, we enter-know one another no longer.[1]

Jacobean tragedy generally was much concerned with that falsifying of the word which, in Montaigne's phrase, 'betraieth publik society'. Though Shakespeare chose not to set his tragedies in the tyrannical and hypocritical courts of Jacobean drama, they all show, in one way or another, his appraisal of the rhetoric of the world of *realpolitik*. Repeatedly in his Histories and Roman plays the dialogue demonstrates that gap between rhetoric and truth which Montaigne laments, earlier in the same essay: 'Now-adaies, that is not the truth which is true, but that which is perswaded to others.' But what he uniquely dramatizes is the horror—both more personal and more universal—of a lie so transforming the sense of self and others that 'enter-knowledge' becomes impossible and dialogue as such meaningless. The victims of slander experience this most poignantly, as when Desdemona, treated like the whore Othello thinks she is, cries out to him:

---

[1] *The Essays of Montaigne*, ii. 402–3.

> Upon my knees, what doth your speech import?
> I understand a fury in your words,
> But not your words.
>
> (*Othello*, IV. ii. 31–3)

Hermione, who is more articulate, sees only too clearly the Catch 22 position of such a victim:

> Since what I am to say must be but that
> Which contradicts my accusation, and
> The testimony on my part no other
> But what comes from myself, it shall scarce boot me
> To say 'Not guilty'. Mine integrity
> Being counted falsehood shall, as I express it,
> Be so receiv'd.
>
> (*The Winter's Tale*, III. ii. 20–6)

In the mockery of a trial to which she is subjected, even the verdict of the oracle is deemed a lie. Yet her defence rings with a lucid sense of self and an understanding of the impasse she is in which echo the voice of Shakespeare's sonnet 121. This poem—''Tis better to be vile than vile esteemed'—is perhaps his most direct account of the activity of lying as seen from the point of view of the belied. The first two quatrains challenge slanderers who 'in their wills count bad what I think good'; the third quatrain makes the kind of self-assertion which is possible when, as a sonneteer, you have the whole stage to yourself:

> No; I am that I am; and they that level
> At my abuses reckon up their own.
> I may be straight though they themselves be bevel;
> By their rank thoughts my deeds must not be shown.

But when you are confronted with an accuser convinced that your 'integrity' is 'falsehood', then the logic of 'I am that I am' dissolves into nonsense. Both Hero and Desdemona try, each in her own words, to make such a statement. Each responds to a 'catechizing' (*Much Ado*, IV. i. 77) in what seems to her the only natural and logical way. To Claudio's demand that she 'answer truly to your name' Hero replies:

> Is it not Hero? Who can blot that name
> With any just reproach?
>
> (*Much Ado*, IV. i. 79–80)

And to Othello's question 'Why, what art thou?' Desdemona answers:

> Your wife, my lord; your true and loyal wife.
>
> > (*Othello*, IV. ii. 35)

But each has her answer invalidated and flung back: Hero with a flat reply to what was intended as a rhetorical question ('Marry, that can Hero') and Desdemona with a bitterly ironical invitation to 'Come, swear it, damn thyself'. To be belied is to find oneself living in a fiction, without a self and a language, as Hermione sees:

> You speak a language that I understand not.
> My life stands in the level of your dreams.
>
> > (*Winter's Tale*, III. ii. 77-8)

Shakespeare's liars, on the other hand, often seem to be very good at forging an identity and a language for themselves. Iago has built a solid fiction of an 'honest' self; Iachimo is given a whole scene to take notes from which he later constructs his account of having slept with Imogen. Yet neither seems to have a particularly lively imagination. Nor (whatever some *Othello* critics say) are they at the imaginative centre of their respective plays. There we find heroes who, if they are liars, are so in a far more complex fashion, and part of our response to their prismatic, volatile selves is precisely to question when they are lying and when telling the truth. When, almost in one breath, Hamlet tells Ophelia 'I did love you once' and 'You should not have believ'd me; ... I loved you not' (*Hamlet*, III. i. 115-19), then who is deceiving whom, and where is Hamlet most true to himself? And how true was he in that somewhat embarrassing attempt at telling his love in 'numbers' which Polonius reads out:

> Doubt truth to be a liar;
> But never doubt I love.
>
> > (II. ii. 117-18)

As for Othello, where doth truth stop and fiction begin in that tendency to self-dramatization which most critics agree is one of his central characteristics? And where does fiction shade into a lie? 'The notablest liar', writes Anthony Munday, 'is become the best Poet'. And he continues to expound this point in what sounds like a de-glamourized version of Othello's tales of 'antres vast and deserts idle', or of those travellers' tales which even the sceptical Antonio and Sebastian are brought to credit in the banquet scene of *The Tempest*:

Our nature is led awaie with vanitie, which the auctor perceauing frames himself with novelties and strange trifles to content the vain humors of his rude auditors; faining countries never heard of; monsters and prodigious creatures that are not; as of the Arimaspie, of the Grips, the Pigmeies, the Cranes, & other such notorious lies.[1]

As Othello tells of 'the Cannibals that each other eat, / The Anthropophagi, and men whose heads / Do grow beneath their shoulders' (*Othello*, I. iii. 143-5), he holds his sophisticated auditors spellbound. But, though he is a good poet, the defensive situation which he is in makes Munday's stricture more relevant than the Sidneian apology that 'he nothing affirms, and therefore never lieth'.[2] What Othello affirms, of course, is above all the effect on Desdemona of his 'poetry'—his surely at least semi-fictional narration. He is telling a tale about telling a tale, and, if there is a fictional element, he is as truly moved by it as Hamlet perceived the First Player to be by his own delivery of Aeneas' tale 'But in a fiction, in a dream of passion' (*Hamlet*, II. ii. 545). His report of Desdemona's responses is authenticated by a colloquial simplicity of style which makes *oratio obliqua* sound like direct quotation:

> She swore, in faith, 'twas strange, 'twas passing strange;
> 'Twas pitiful, 'twas wondrous pitiful.
> She wish'd she had not heard it; yet she wish'd
> That heaven had made her such a man . . .
>
> (I. iii. 160-3)

He would have been the envy of Astrophil who, seeing his mistress more moved by fiction than by fact, cries out: 'I am not I. / Pity the tale of me' (*Astrophil and Stella*, sonnet 45). To suggest that Othello deliberately falsifies the true story of his life and his wooing of Desdemona would be to sink to the level of Iago's version: that 'she first lov'd the Moor, but for bragging and telling her fantastical lies. To love him still for prating?' (II. i. 220 ff.). But it seems peculiarly ironical, in a play so full of ironies, that Othello and Desdemona are brought together by one persuasive fiction, to be

[1] Anthony Munday, *A second and third blast* . . . (1580), reprinted in E. K. Chambers, *The Elizabethan Stage*, iv (Oxford, 1923), 211. This might also have been a description of Autolycus with those marvellous ballads which his 'rude auditors' are so anxious to be told are 'true' (*The Winter's Tale*, IV. iv. 253 ff.).

[2] Sir Philip Sidney, *An Apology for Poetry*, ed. Geoffrey Shepherd (1965), p. 123.

sundered by another. It also seems that Shakespeare finds peculiarly fruitful dramatic material in that border area between imagination and lying. When is a lie not a lie? When does a child stop having a lively imagination and turn into a liar? These questions are presumably as old as man himself, or at least as language itself; and they have certainly teased playwrights other than Shakespeare. We need only think of Ibsen's *Peer Gynt*, which opens with a mother accusing her son of lying—'Peer, you're a liar!'—and proceeds to follow and criticize Peer's 'round-about' dealings with truth, but which also contains the moving scene where the poet/liar Peer literally talks his mother through her death agonies in a fiction of a sleigh-ride to Soria-Moria Castle and to a meeting with St Peter and with the Lord Himself. In that border area lies hover ambivalently, with potentials for good or ill; and out of it Shakespeare fetches some of his most striking dramatic situations.

Perhaps the most striking of these is the scene in *King Lear* where Gloucester falls over an imaginary cliff, created entirely by Edgar's words. I make no apology for turning, here, to the exceedingly well known, for the emotional impact of this scene and its sheer dimensions—physical, familial, and spiritual—are such as to make it easy to forget that it is built on the biggest lie in all Shakespeare. (No doubt such forgetting is precisely one of the points of the scene.) Gloucester's two sons both lie to him: Edmund consistently and in pursuit of a well-prepared scheme for acquiring Edgar's land; Edgar spontaneously, selflessly, and to save his father. In Act iv, scene vi, Edgar has to lie very hard— the more active verbs, like 'feign' and 'forge',[1] which crop up as Elizabethan synonyms for 'lying', would be more appropriate here—to deceive Gloucester. In his new and painful state of vision, Gloucester is a resistant object, as he was not when Edmund set to work on him. His nagging questions and Edgar's answers, as the scene opens, have that solidity of specification, that adherence to the practical evidence of the senses, which is characteristic of the play (as in the newly awakened Lear's 'Be your tears wet?'):

[1] As when Exeter, in *1 Henry VI*, iii. i. 190, speaks of how the dissension between the peers 'Burns under feigned ashes of forg'd love.' In the Prologue to Act v of *Henry V* the Chorus asks the audience to 'behold / In the quick forge and working-house of thought, / How London doth pour out her citizens', thus providing a link between literal and metaphorical uses of the word 'forge'. 'The quick forge . . .' is obviously the imagination—the faculty which the Chorus is forever appealing to—and one is reminded how easily a word signifying the making of something out of nothing can slide over to become a synonym for lying.

Gloucester. When shall I come to th'top of that same hill?
Edgar. You do climb up it now; look how we labour.
Gloucester. Methinks the ground is even.
Edgar.   Horrible steep.
          Hark, do you hear the sea?
Gloucester.   No truly.

(*King Lear*, IV. vi. 1–4)

The text provides stage directions for what Jan Kott has called the 'pantomime' of the scene,[1] but it also draws attention to Edgar's efforts at lying as such. Though Gloucester admits Edgar's reasoning that 'your other senses grow imperfect / By your eyes' anguish', he continues to insist that Edgar's voice is altered and that he is 'better spoken'. At this point Edgar abandons his attempts to counter Gloucester's incredulity by argument and resorts to a simple imperative—'Come on, sir; here's the place. Stand still'—and to the *tour de force* of the imagination which, on the bare stage, creates out of nothing 'the place', the steepness, and the receding depth:

> . . .yond tall anchoring bark
> Diminish'd to her cock; her cock, a buoy
> Almost too small for sight.

(ll. 18–20)

Details of evocative poetry also function very precisely to keep the lie 'solid':

> The murmuring surge
> That on th'unnumb'red idle pebble chafes
> *Cannot be heard so high.*

(ll. 20–2; my italics)

However resistant, Gloucester is in one respect an ideal object of a lie: a blind man having visual reality created for him. He is convinced, but the dialogue does not dwell on his imaginary sightseeing. The depth means only one thing to him, and his self-obsessed participation in the scene is defined by the simplest of responses to Edgar's great speech: 'Set me where you stand.' As Gloucester dismisses him—again, taking nothing for granted: 'Go thou further off; / . . . and let me hear thee going'—and kneels to take his farewell of life, Edgar justifies his lie:

> Why I do trifle thus with his despair
> Is done to cure it.

(ll. 33–4)

---

[1] Jan Kott, *Shakespeare Our Contemporary* (1965; paperbook edn. 1967), p. 113.

Whether the need for a justification is Edgar's or Shakespeare's, or (as I think likely) both, the argument is familiar and traditional. The end justifies the means, but in this case both the end and the means are extreme, and Edgar defends his deceit much as St Augustine defended Christ against the accusation of lying.[1] Little attention was given to justifying his initial disguise as Poor Tom: 'Whiles I may scape / I will preserve myself' (II. iii. 5–6). But by this stage in the play his counterfeiting is no longer in the service of pure survival; it has gathered a missionary purpose, and the extremity of the lie and its aim turns Edgar into a maker of parables.

In the postlapsarian part of the scene the intended 'cure' is achieved, with Edgar acting in a new persona—but only after the 'true' features of the fictive situation have been further substantiated. First there is the height, which is now above them:

> Look up a-height; the shrill-gorg'd lark so far
> Cannot be seen or heard. Do but look up.
>
> (ll. 58–9)

This makes the point both that the new Edgar figure is not supposed to know that Gloucester is blind, and that the fictive lark is too high up to be audible. Then there is a palpable testing of Gloucester's soundness of limb, the accompanying lines thick with implicit stage directions. The two kinds of evidence—the height and the wholeness—give an extraordinary concreteness to Edgar's words, 'Thy life's a miracle.' It needs only one more lie, the story of the fiend-like 'thing' into which Edgar now turns his previous incarnation, to make the moral inescapable:

> Think that the clearest gods, who make them honours
> Of men's impossibilities, have preserved thee.
>
> (ll. 73–4)

This assertion of miracles and their purpose could, of course, be said to be the crowning lie of the scene (and it would be, if this were

---

[1] In Book II of *Quæstiones Evangeliorum*. See J.-P. Migne, *Patrologiæ cursus, Ser. Lat.*, xxxv, col. 1362. Edgar *could* have justified his disguise as Poor Tom much as Sir Walter Ralegh, in his scaffold speech, justified having feigned sickness: by appealing to the precedent of King David. 'The Prophet David did make himself a Fool, and did suffer Spittle to fall upon his Beard to escape the hands of his Enemies, and it was not imputed to him a sin': 1 Samuel 21: 13. See Stephen J. Greenblatt, *Sir Walter Ralegh: The Renaissance Man and His Roles* (New Haven, Conn., and London, 1973), chapters 1 and 2.

Shakespeare's end-game). But the moral proof of the pudding is in the eating, and this particular lie completes the 'cure' of Gloucester:

> I do remember now. Henceforth I'll bear
> Affliction till it do cry out itself
> 'Enough, enough' and die.

> (ll. 75–7)

The scene, then, is in a tradition, both secular and religious, of salutary deception. In a secular sense, Edgar—though far from court—has lied to Gloucester in the educative fashion recommended by Castiglione when he advises the courtier to feign 'in order to win the mind of the prince so that he may speak the truth effectively':

beguiling him with salutary deception; like shrewd actors who often spread the edge of the cup with some sweet cordial when they wish to give a bitter-tasting medicine to sick and over-delicate children.[1]

But another and much stronger sense reaches beyond the sugared pill, to the metaphysical marvel of 'men's impossibilities' being found to be divine possibilities. Editors gloss these lines with a reference to Luke 18: 27: 'The things which are impossible with men are possible with God.'[2] In Shakespearian terms Gloucester's experience is seen as something akin to Pericles' when, with a dawning sense of the miracle which is about to happen, he wills himself to credit the history of Marina's life 'to points that seem impossible' (Pericles, v. i. 123). Not that Gloucester himself articulates the wonder of the impossible proving possible, as heroes and heroines of the Last Plays do. His own lines merely enunciate a moral recovery—from which he is to lapse and be pulled back again by Edgar in Act v, scene ii. But for the audience in the theatre who have had the benefit of watching and listening

---

[1] *The Book of the Courtier*, translated by Charles Singleton (New York, 1959; Anchor Books edn.), p. 294.

[2] Kenneth Muir, in the Arden edition of *King Lear* (1952), quotes Furness. While not doubting the similarity to the passage in *Luke*, I think Edgar's lines also reminiscent of, if not necessarily echoing, Montaigne's essay: 'It is follie to referre Truth or Falshood to our sufficiencie.' Experience, says Montaigne, has taught him 'that so resolutely to condemne a thing for false, and impossible, is to assume unto himselfe the advantage, to have the bounds and limits of Gods will, and of the power of our common mother Nature tied to his sleeve. . . . For to deeme [unlikely events] impossible, is by rash presumption to presume and know how farre possibilitie reacheth. If a man did well understand, what difference there is betweene impossibilitie, and that which is unwonted . . .' (*The Essays of Montaigne*, i. 192–3).

to the whole scene—all the lies and all the truths, and all the lies which transform themselves into truths—it must surely grow into something of greater constancy: an apology for lying and even a model of the truth of fiction—the kind of truth which leaves behind, as irrelevant, questions of mendaciousness. Edgar's lie effects Gloucester's rebirth, and both together affect the audience's sense of man's possibilities.

As far as the possibilities of the liar go, this scene also makes the obvious point that, while lies may create something (and in this case a whole landscape, geographical and spiritual) out of nothing, they cannot exist in a vacuum: they need, or rather assume, an audience. The 'prosperity' of a lie, as of the 'jest' which Rosalind speaks of to Berowne,

> lies in the ear
> Of him that hears it, never in the tongue
> Of him that makes it;
>
> (*Love's Labour's Lost*, v. ii. 849–51)

and, though Shakespeare is, throughout his plays, much concerned with the image of the tongue—'double', or 'candied', or 'poisoned'—he is equally, if not more, concerned with the infected or abused ear. The Ghost in *Hamlet* sees 'the whole ear of Denmark / ... by a forged process of my death / Rankly abus'd'; Regan (of all people) tells Gloucester that Lear is 'apt / To have his ear abus'd'; and Antigonus can only think that Leontes' ear has been 'abus'd, and by some putter-on'. The ear, in these cases, is the image of the mind. (Leontes is, of course, his own audience.) For, if the creation of a lie is a matter of the imagination, its action involves the imagination not only of the speaker but also of the listener—who, like the implied reader in certain modern theories of fiction, collaborates with the liar. Iago's skill lies in knowing how to turn Othello into such a collaborator. Other liars find their objects only too ready to collaborate. Lear goes more than half-way to meet Goneril and Regan in their professions of love; and both Beatrice and Benedick, in their respective scenes of staged overhearing, rush to embrace the idea that they are beloved. Credulity like Malvolio's stems from an only too obliging imagination—

> *Fabian.* What dish o'poison has she dress'd him!
> *Sir Toby.* And with what wing the staniel checks at it!—
>
> (*Twelfth Night*, ii. v. 104–5)

which we have seen exercised, before any deceit is practised on him, in conjuring up a scene of married, *arriviste*, bliss. He believes

Maria's delightfully lying letter because he wants to: 'I do not now fool myself to let imagination jade me; for every reason excites to this, that my lady loves me' (II. v. 145). The shattering of a vision of self based on a lie ends, in this case, in pretty dark comedy, with 'Sir Thopas' trying to convince the allegedly mad Malvolio that 'That that is is'; but Sir Toby's words to Maria which anticipate this, at the end of the gulling scene, could as well have been spoken to Goneril or Regan at the end of the first scene of *King Lear*: 'Why, thou hast put him in such a dream that when the image of it leaves him he must run mad' (II. v. 172–3).

Shakespeare's interest in how human beings affect one another—how, in T. S. Eliot's phrase, they 'modify' one another—means that he takes a particular interest in the interaction of the liar and the one lied to. The liar has the power of transforming another being: of replacing 'that that is' with a 'dream' or an 'image'. The instrument of lying is rhetoric. At the end of such rhetoric, at its extreme, there can be a soul-making, as in the case of Gloucester; but there can also be what Strindberg calls 'soul-murder':[1] the action where (as in *Miss Julie*, and even more in *Creditors*) one person takes another to pieces, eating out his will and vision of himself, and either puts him together into a different being or destroys him altogether. Strindberg thought the play of *Othello* an instance of such soul-murder, and Othello's questions of Iago in the last scene—

> Will you, I pray, demand that demi-devil
> Why he hath thus ensnar'd my soul and body?—
>
> (*Othello*, v. ii. 304–5)

suggest that he would have agreed. In the process of 'ensnaring' Othello there is surprisingly little lying as such. Technically, the only real lie Iago tells in the scene which takes Othello from an unquestioning lover to a jealous revenger is the account of how he 'lay with Cassio lately' and witnessed that gentleman's amorous dream. In itself, this is a lively fiction, circumstantially documented, and supported by fabricated quotations. But it comes late in the scene, when Othello is already well in the grip of a passion which prevents him from questioning Iago's story. Less than sixty lines earlier—though ages ago, in psychological

---

[1] In the essay 'Själamord' ('Soul-Murder'), in *Vivisektioner* (*Vivisections*): *Samlade Skrifter av August Strindberg*, ed. John Landqvist, xxii (Stockholm, 1914), 188–201.

time—he had still been able to reach out, through an 'if', to the
possibility of Iago's lying:

> If thou dost slander her and torture me,
> Never pray more . . .
> For nothing canst thou to damnation add
> Greater than that.
>
> (III. iii. 371–7)

Now he can only groan in response 'O monstrous! monstrous!', the
text suggesting that his imagination has translated Iago's lying
words into a true scene, and one which requires action: 'I'll tear
her all to pieces.' Before this, Iago's strength lies, of course,
in insinuations, perfectly timed and structured into an act of
persuasion far more potent than any formal rhetorical structure.
He tells Emilia no more than the truth when in the last scene he
explains:

> I told him what I thought, and told no more
> Than what he found himself was apt and true.
>
> (v. ii. 179–80)

Over the scene, Iago's discourse eases into fiction almost im-
perceptibly, rather as Renaissance prose narrative tends to do,
behind a screen of prefatory apparatus and authenticating
analogues ('I know our country disposition well . . .'; 'She
did deceive her father, marrying you . . .'). Consummately
he establishes his credibility and affirms his reputation as a
fellow 'of exceeding honesty', achieving his false ends by telling
the truth:

> I do beseech you,
> Though I perchance am vicious in my guess,
> As, I confess, it is my nature's plague
> To spy into abuses, and oft my jealousy
> Shapes faults that are not—that your wisdom
> From one that so imperfectly conjects,
> Would take no notice.
>
> (III. iii. 148–55)

So Othello takes notice, and Iago achieves ends more sudden and
violent even than the 'monstrous birth' he envisaged at the end of
Act I. From the very beginning of this dialogue we see and hear
how Othello's imagination translates Iago's negative rhetoric into
positive images:

> By heaven, he echoes me,
> As if there were some monster in his thought
> Too hideous to be shown . . .
> And didst contract and purse thy brow together,
> As if thou then hadst shut up in thy brain
> Some horrible conceit.

(ll. 110 ff.)

Normally there is much virtue in 'as if': a bridge which enables us to move from that which is to that which is not, and back again. But Iago makes sure that Othello's traffic is one-way, stopping any attempt of his to return to his original image of himself and of Desdemona, and forever beckoning him on towards the chaos which at the beginning of the scene had simply been the sign of impossibility ('I do love thee; and when I love thee not / Chaos is come again', ll. 92-3). When Iago disappears briefly from the scene, Othello's soliloquy shows just how far he has travelled:

> I had rather be a toad,
> And live upon the vapour of a dungeon,
> Than keep a corner in the thing I love
> For others' uses.

(ll. 274-7)

The brief appearance of Desdemona means a flicker of a chance to return to base: 'If she be false, O, then heaven mocks itself!' But by the time Iago and Othello are both together on stage again, 'Othello's occupation's gone' and Desdemona's identity is gone, too:

> Her name, that was as fresh
> As Dian's visage, is now begrim'd and black
> As mine own face.

(ll. 391-2)

The effect of a lie, Montaigne stated in the essay 'Of giving the lie' which I quoted earlier, is that 'we hold our selves no more, we enter-know one another no longer'. The scene in *Othello*, to the subtlety of which I have been able to do scant justice here, not only confirms these statements but also shows why and how they are true. To explain away the scene in terms of the Elizabethan stage convention of the calumniator always being believed[1] is to cut out the heart of the scene: the fascination with the power which words can wield over man's imagination, making him accept as real that

[1] Cf. E. E. Stoll, *Othello: An Historical and Comparative Study* (Minneapolis, Minn., 1915).

which they signify. Obviously it is convenient, indeed necessary, in the concentrated time-span of a play to foreshorten acts of persuasion. *Richard III* is full of examples of this, and so are all the plays, notably the Comedies, which operate more by patternings of language, structure, and theme than by explorations of the troubled workings of the human mind. *Much Ado About Nothing* might well seem to belong in that category: Claudio leaps at Don John's lie in a few, mainly monosyllabic, lines which suggest a kind of conventional shorthand. But even then the shorthand hints at the negative, teasing technique of activating the victim's own imagination which Iago is to use on Othello:

> *Claudio*. Disloyal?
> *Don John*. The word is too good to paint out her wickedness; I could
>   say she were worse; think you of a worse title, and I will fit
>   her to it.
>
> (*Much Ado*, iii. ii. 96 ff.)

Similarly, the sense of shattered identity, and of a world transformed, in Claudio's speeches in the near-tragic church scene looks forward to *Othello*. Hero seemed to him 'as Dian in her orb, / As chaste as is the bud ere it be blown'; but now she is 'more intemperate in [her] blood / Than Venus, or those pamp'red animals / That rage in savage sensuality' (iv. i. 56–60). And so his vision of reality is forever changed:

> . . . fare thee well, most foul, most fair! Farewell,
> Thou pure impiety and impious purity!
> For thee I'll lock up all the gates of love,
> And on my eyelids shall conjecture hang,
> To turn all beauty into thoughts of harm,
> And never shall it more be gracious.
>
> (iv. i. 102–7)

As we have seen earlier, the lie acting on Claudio has transformed his Hero into another Hero. As we see (or rather hear) here, his shock—of lost 'enter-knowledge'—is conveyed in a language of paradoxes and oxymorons. Through the neat patterning of his idiom there beats a kind of hysteria: the logic of a chaos where contradictory statements are equally true. It is soon to reappear in Troilus' reaction to a situation which, as facts go, is almost exactly the reverse of Claudio's. He witnesses Cressida's faithlessness, but tries *not* to believe 'th'attest of eyes and ears'. He stays on stage after the meeting between Cressida and Diomed in order to 'make a recordation to my soul / Of every syllable that here was spoke',

> But if I tell how these two did coact,
> Shall I not lie in publishing a truth?
>
> (*Troilus and Cressida*, v. ii. 116-17)

The intensity of Troilus' wish to transform the truth into a lie takes him into that agonized state of apprehension where, to paraphrase Sir Thopas, 'that that is is not'. Claudio never really doubts that 'foul' has merely *seemed* 'fair'; but Troilus' line 'this is, and is not, Cressid' challenges both the imagination to create and language to signify. Yet Troilus is not a Macbeth; he does not linger in a state where 'nothing is but what is not'. 'This is, and is not, Cressid' is also the pivot-line of a speech with a large and completed action—a soul-making. It begins with the series of *if* clauses in which all that he has so far believed and valued most dearly is brought in to prove the truth a lie:

> If beauty have a soul, this is not she;
> If souls guide vows, if vows be sanctimonies,
> If sanctimony be the gods' delight,
> If there be rule in unity itself,
> This was not she.
>
> (ll. 136-40)

This way, it would seem, madness lies; but not in a play as analytical as *Troilus and Cressida*. Troilus recognizes the 'madness of discourse' in which he is engaged, and the speech moves to a plateau where he takes a conspectus of his own predicament:

> Within my soul there doth conduce a fight
> Of this strange nature, that a thing inseparate
> Divides more wider than the sky and earth;
>
> (ll. 145-7)

and from where he slides to the inevitable recognition of a loss of faith: 'The bonds of heaven are slipp'd, dissolv'd, and loos'd.' The speech ends as his imagination grapples in disgust with the new Cressida:

> The fragments, scraps, the bits, and greasy relics
> Of her o'er-eaten faith, are bound to Diomed.
>
> (ll. 156-7)

In the brief remainder of the play Troilus is driven only by the fury of disillusionment and a kind of exhaustion of the imagination. He tears up a letter from Cressida as 'words, words, mere words' (v. iii. 108); and when Hector is dead, 'there is no more to say' (v. x. 22).

Macbeth, on the contrary, lives for the better part of his play in that state of mind, and language, where 'horrible imaginings' are more real than reality. At the beginning of his first appearance on stage he meets the witches: at the end of that same scene he pulls aside to contemplate the words of these 'imperfect speakers'. Like Troilus he analyses the shock of a confrontation which has shaken his very being; but his analysis, unlike Troilus' coherent and progressive argument, moves through questions which have no answers, or only unspeakable ones, to a self-analysis which stops at description:

> My thought, whose murder yet is but fantastical,
> Shakes so my single state of man
> That function is smother'd in surmise,
> And nothing is but what is not.
>
> (*Macbeth*, i. iii. 138–41)

By the act which makes the 'fantastical' murder a reality, Macbeth creates around him a world of unimagined horror, where scenes of bloodshed alternate with scenes in which he discusses the reality of what he has seen—or imagines that he has seen. From his own point of view, of course, he ends up as the victim of a lie. When Birnam wood does come to Dunsinane, he begins to 'doubt th'equivocation of the fiend / That lies like truth' (v. v. 43–4); but it is only in his penultimate speech in the play, when his sense of bearing 'a charmed life' has been shattered by the truth about Macduff's mode of birth, that he finally abandons belief in the witches' prophecies:

> And be these juggling fiends no more believ'd
> That palter with us in a double sense,
> That keep the word of promise to our ear,
> And break it to our hope!
>
> (v. viii. 19–22)

He has been a willing victim. Act i, scene iii makes it clear that 'the imperial theme' has been as much in his mind as ideas of social advancement were in Malvolio's, and that his imagination is all too ready to supply what the 'imperfect speakers' have left unsaid. He is even his own Iago in adducing corroborative evidence:

> This supernatural soliciting
> Cannot be ill; cannot be good. If ill,
> Why hath it given me earnest of success,
> Commencing in a truth?
>
> (i. iii. 130–3)

Later, in Act IV, he is desperately anxious to interpret the visual and verbal signs of the Apparitions as truths to live by. Meanwhile he has himself turned liar: though it is Lady Macbeth who teaches him to lie, in Act I, scene vii where he learns that 'False face must hide what the false heart doth show', when it comes to the public scene after Duncan's murder, he lies far more elaborately than she. Separating words from truth, Macbeth 'betraieth publik society'; but in their progressive alienation from each other—beginning with his bizarre mixture of ruthlessness and solicitude in wishing her to 'Be innocent of the knowledge, dearest chuck, / Till thou applaud the deed' (III. ii. 45-6)—he and Lady Macbeth also illustrate Montaigne's point about lost 'enter-knowledge'. By the time she dies, unlamented, life itself has become to him an absurd fiction: 'a tale / Told by an idiot, full of sound and fury, / Signifying nothing' (v. v. 26-8).

But, of course, we do not see the play from Macbeth's point of view only (though the fullness with which we see his viewpoint is a major reason for the fascination of this villain-hero); nor do we see him only—or even primarily—as a dupe and a liar. If the witches' words wield a terrible power over Macbeth's imagination, it is because he is presented to us, above all, as a man with a terrible power to apprehend that which is non-existent. Holinshed's Macbeth, as Henry N. Paul pointed out in his book, *The Royal Play of 'Macbeth'*, had no imagination.[1] Paul suggests that, in endowing Macbeth with an excess of it, Shakespeare was under the influence of Montaigne's essay 'Of the force of Imagination'. Certainly the subject was in the air, and it interested King James, who at the end of August 1605 attended an Oxford debate on the question 'an imaginatio possit producere reales effectus?' Though I doubt Paul's conclusion—that Shakespeare wanted the witches to be purely figments of Macbeth's imagination—I think it very plausible that Shakespeare knew the Montaigne essay. As will be obvious by now, I feel that Montaigne's thinking on liars, and Shakespeare's, often cross-illuminate each other; and also that both vitally connect lying with the imagination. The real point, however, is not whether Montaigne was a source for *Macbeth* but that both the essay and the play are concerned with the *transforming* power of the imagination. The essay is typically discursive and personal. It begins on the 'very great conflict and power of imagination' suffered by the writer himself, and on the sympathetic identification with others which this leads to; and it ends on a kind of

[1] (New York, 1948; reprinted 1971), p. 61.

apology for his own writing. But the bulk of the essay consists of
specific and striking examples of the interaction of mind and body,
particularly in sexual relations; and of cases where anticipation
has turned into actuality, somewhat drastically cutting across the
natural course of events: the man found to be already dead when
reprieved on the scaffold, or the person transformed on his/her
wedding day from a woman to a man! As stories go, there is little
connection with *Macbeth*. What does connect the two works is
the exploration of the leap from idea to actuality, from one form
of being to another, from nothing to something—or, in terms of
Macbeth, from a 'fantastical' to an actual murder, from 'a dagger
of the mind' to the dagger which kills Duncan, from a mention
of Banquo to his real (or is it?) appearance at the banquet.

Macbeth is not one of Shakespeare's obvious liars; yet his
experiences of the 'reales effectus' of the force of the imagination
in the play are strangely akin to those of the act of lying and
being lied to in other Shakespeare plays. The best illumination
of that kinship which I know of is in that speech of Leontes'
which has been called 'the obscurest passage in Shakespeare':[1]
the lines in which he passes from unfounded suspicion to certainty
of Hermione's adultery. I would not presume to remove the
obscurity as such, but merely to suggest that these lines both
discuss and enact processes which are central both to lying and to
the imagination. I have to quote the passage in full:

> Affection! thy intention stabs the centre.
> Thou dost make possible things not so held,
> Communicat'st with dreams—how can this be?—
> With what's unreal thou coactive art,
> And fellow'st nothing. Then 'tis very credent
> Thou mayst co-join with something; and thou dost—
> And that beyond commission; and I find it,
> And that to the infection of my brains
> And hard'ning of my brows.
>
> (*Winter's Tale*, i. ii. 138–46)

The strained vocabulary and tortured syntax of the speech as
a whole are clearly in character, as those of a man whom
Hermione describes as 'something . . . unsettled'. Polixenes is
simply nonplussed by this address to 'Affection': 'What means
Sicilia?' The answer, presumably, is that Sicilia does not so much
'mean' as discover, in the course of an interior monologue, that
which is not. The first four-and-a-half lines of the quoted passage

[1] M. van Doren, *Shakespeare* (1939), p. 316.

are, I take it,[1] an analysis of his own state of mind by way of an answer to his own questions in the preceding half-line: 'Can thy dam?—may't be?' Like Troilus he watches his mind mastered by an overwhelming passion ('affection'). What he perceives is something very like the action of the creative imagination: making the impossible possible, dreams and 'what's unreal' real—all this out of 'nothing'. The trouble is that in Leontes a more than usual state of emotion is not balanced by a more than usual order. Logic would suggest that, if the image of an adulterous Hermione can be created out of nothing, then it should be seen for what it is: a 'dream', 'unreal', etc. But Leontes gives the lie to logic, and even as he speaks he begins to enact the perilous imaginative leap from 'nothing' to 'something'. Within a few lines the idea of adultery has been transformed into reality; and his brows are almost as hard as those of the fellow in Montaigne's essay who, having dreamt of being cuckolded, woke up in the morning with horns in his forehead, or as sore as Othello's when he rejects the handkerchief. The speech pivots on the illogical 'then'; and in the second four-and-a-half lines a series of cumulative, and cumulatively perverse, and-clauses form something very like the rhetorical figure of climax, or *gradatio*. Again, it is in character: this is the rhythm of mind of a man who, as if he were Iago and Othello rolled into one, has begun to fabricate and accept his own evidence ('Thou mayst . . .; and thou dost . . .; and I find it') and will increasingly do so, finding it in the most innocent word and gesture. At the same time the lines are also a model of the imagination as the breeding-ground of lies. Leontes, as he speaks, creates the thing he imagines.

The point, clearly, can be glossed by Theseus' famous speech about 'the lunatic, the lover, and the poet', being 'of imagination all compact' (*A Midsummer Night's Dream*, v. i. 7–8). When, as in the case of Leontes or Othello, lovers turn in a manner into lunatics, *their* 'shaping fantasies' are a destructive version of the poet's; they too turn to shapes 'the forms of things unknown' and give 'to airy nothing / A local habitation and a name'. Obviously I am not suggesting that Theseus' sneer at the imagination is Shakespeare's. Even locally Theseus' attitude to 'these fairy toys' is subverted by his own mythical identity, and Hippolita's retort

[1] In the appendix on this passage in his Arden edition of *The Winter's Tale* (1963), J. H. P. Pafford leans towards the opinion that Leontes is analysing Hermione's behaviour (pp. 165–6); but he also quotes H. G. Goddard (*The Meaning of Shakespeare*, 1951, p. 651), who considers that Leontes is diagnosing his own case.

confirms the status of 'fancy's images' by simply producing the proof of the pudding. Around Theseus there is the whole *Dream*, and around that play the whole Shakespeare corpus, to provide, implicitly, the same proof. Even so, the pursuit of Shakespeare's liars must finally lead us to listen with a measure of respect to Theseus. For, one thing the corpus of plays also shows is how perilously close, in their creation of something out of nothing, are lunatics, lovers, and poets—and liars.

But it would be wrong to end on the perils of this closeness: on the imagination and its operation through language as potentially lethal toys. If Leontes is a liar, so is Paulina. If Macbeth transforms reality, so does Prospero. The salutary lying which we have looked at—in the comedies, in *Measure for Measure*, in Edgar—is most clearly seen as redemptive and re-creative in the Last Plays. And yet a case could also be made for these plays—in themselves so explicit about their own fictive nature as 'old tales'—as most keenly presenting the tension between the destructive and the creative potentials of lying. There are Iachimo's lies, and Leontes' self-created perversion of the truth, and Prospero's account of how Antonio came to usurp the Dukedom of Milan,

> like one
> Who having into truth, by telling of it,
> Made such a sinner of his memory,
> To credit his own lie—he did believe
> He was indeed the Duke.
>
> (*The Tempest*, I. ii. 99–103)

Prospero, whose magic deceptions aim to redeem 'three men of sin', is vehement in accusing first Ariel and then Caliban of lying (I. ii. 257 and 344); and Ariel engineers one whole comic and rancorous scene in the subplot by strategic interjections of 'Thou liest' (III. ii. 40 ff.). I do not wish here to involve the whole question of theatrical art as lying (as embodied when Costard's claim, 'I Pompey am' meets with Berowne's retort, 'You lie, you are not he'; *Love's Labour's Lost*, v. ii. 543–4).[1] But when, in the Epilogue to *The Tempest*, Prospero throws the whole lie of his art into the lap of the audience, then we are left with a sense of the huge ambivalence of what is truth—a sense provoked by all Shakespeare's great liars.

Among those, finally, we should note the Friar in *Much Ado About Nothing*. In a play where characters' behaviour and

[1] The subject has recently been explored in Jonas Barish's monumental study, *The Antitheatrical Prejudice* (Berkeley, Los Angeles, and London, 1981).

language are, for ill and good, altogether rather devious, his plan
for giving out that Hero is dead makes him perhaps the biggest liar
of them all. He expounds his scheme with a fullness—right down
to the contingency plan[1]—which suggests a zest for fiction-
making. At the same time he declares his aim as morally
therapeutic: to 'change slander to remorse' (IV. i. 211), but even as
he utters this justification, he sees its limitations: 'But not for that
dream I of this strange course' (l. 212). The words 'dream' and
'strange', which Shakespeare so often connects with the workings
of the imagination, signal the way which the Friar is moving to
identify the end which really justifies the means: the effect on
people's minds when they think Hero is dead. That effect will be,
as it were, the creation of the 'real' Hero. In describing how
this transformation will apply to Claudio, the Friar speaks what
I think is a somewhat neglected Shakespearian passage on the
power—quite literally creative—of the imagination:

> When he shall hear she died upon his words,
> Th'idea of her life shall sweetly creep
> Into his study of imagination,
> And every lovely organ of her life
> Shall come apparell'd in more precious habit,
> More moving, delicate, and full of life,
> Into the eye and prospect of his soul,
> Than when she liv'd indeed.
>
> (IV. i. 223-30)

Claudio does indeed, in Act V, hear a great deal about how Hero
'died upon his words', but his mourning rites give little sense
that he lives up to the Friar's expectations. The ritual of the
denouement—the revelation of 'Another Hero' who 'died . . .
but whiles her slander liv'd' (v. iv. 60 ff.)—substitutes for any
dramatic realization of a morally transformed and reborn
Claudio. The Friar's vision remains, however, as a statement
of what the imagination may achieve, a statement to be set at
the side of Sidney's assurance that the poet makes 'things . . .
better than Nature bringeth forth'.[2] The Friar's lie will stimulate
the imagination; and the imagination, imitating the creative
processes of nature, will deliver a 'golden' Hero as against the

---

[1] i.e. 'And if it sort not well, you may conceal her, / As best befits her
wounded reputation, / In some reclusive and religious life, / Out of all eyes,
tongues, minds, and injuries' (ll. 240-3).

[2] *An Apology for Poetry*, ed. Shepherd, p. 100: 'Nature never set forth the earth
in so rich tapestry as divers poets have done, . . . Her world is brazen, the poets
only deliver a golden.'

Hero who 'liv'd indeed'. The metaphor which contains the essential justification of the lie also suggests the magnitude of the issues involved: 'But on this travail look for greater birth' (l. 213).

In the end, then, perhaps the clue to Shakespeare's liars lies in metaphor—the verbal device which transposes fact into fiction and vice versa, and which so does 'make possible things not so held'. The Elizabethans were proud of the copiousness of the English language and the ease with which it lent itself to figures of speech; but there was also an undertow of suspicion of metaphors, as articulated by Puttenham:

> As figures be the instruments of ornament in euery language, so be they also in a sorte abuses or rather trespasses in speach, because they passe the ordinary limits of common vtterance, and be occupied of purpose to deceiue the eare and also the minde, drawing it from plainnesse and simplicitie to a certaine doublenesse, whereby our talke is the more guilefull & abusing.[1]

'For', he concludes, 'what els is your *Metaphor* but an inuersion of sence by transport'. Shakespearian drama contains a number of characters who share Puttenham's opinion. Phebe, for one, very forcefully subjects Silvius' lovesick 'transport' to the acid test of 'sence' (*As You Like It*, III. v. 10 ff.). Timon tackles the 'guilefull & abusing' aspects of metaphorical language in his dialogue with the hypocritical Poet who is reaching for a cliché to describe the unspeakable way in which Timon has been treated by the Athenians. 'I am rapt', says the Poet, 'and cannot cover / The monstrous bulk of this ingratitude / With any size of words'; and Timon ruthlessly refers him back to plain truth: 'Let it go naked: men may see't the better' (*Timon of Athens*, v. i. 62–5). Obviously this is not to say that Shakespeare equates the truth of poetry with nakedness: in *As You Like It* we are also told by Touchstone, that specialist on lies, that 'the truest poetry is the most feigning'. Obviously metaphor is one of his own chief vehicles for communicating with his audience and guiding our responses. Even as he does so, though, he also sometimes tells us about the perils of metaphors which acquire the potency of life-lies. George Eliot, writing of poor Mr Casaubon who 'had imagined that his long studious bachelorhood had stored up for him a compound interest of enjoyment, and that large drafts on his affection would not

[1] George Puttenham, *The Arte of English Poesie* (1589), Book III, chapter vii ('Of Figures and figuratiue speaches'); Scholar Press reprint (Menston, 1968), p. 128.

fail to be honoured', moves naturally from the specific case to a generalization:

> ... we all of us ... get our thoughts entangled in metaphors, and act fatally on the strength of them.[1]

The King of Navarre and his followers in *Love's Labour's Lost* are *almost* fatally entangled in the metaphors which they apply to their studious bachelorhood. But it is perhaps Brutus who most clearly demonstrates George Eliot's dictum, when he prepares the killing of Caesar as a ritual—

> Let's be sacrificers, but not butchers, Caius.
>
> .   .   .   .
>
> Let's carve him as a dish fit for the gods,
> Not hew him as a carcase fit for hounds—
>
> > (*Julius Caesar*, II. i. 166–74)

only to find, when it comes to it, that sacrifice becomes butchery.

If the ability to create one's own imaginative reality is a peril, and if thinking and speaking in metaphor epitomizes this peril, then metaphor ought to be fatal to Cleopatra, to whom hyperbolical imagery is a way of life—and death. Her vision of truth does not go naked; it not only dresses itself in, but lives in, the images she creates of herself in her death-scene, or of Antony after his death. When she has recounted to Dolabella her 'dream' of Antony ('His face was as the heav'ns . . .'), she turns to him for confirmation:

> Think you there was or might be such a man
> As this I dreamt of?

Instead, he gives her the lie: 'Gentle madam, no.' This 'no' provokes one of the most emphatic accusations of lying in all of Shakespeare's plays, as Cleopatra throws the lie back at Dolabella:

> You lie, up to the hearing of the gods.
> > (*Antony and Cleopatra*, v. ii. 93–5)

Who is the greater liar, Cleopatra or Dolabella? Clearly, plainness and singleness is not the only touchstone of perception (unless we think that the true vision of Antony is simply as 'a strumpet's fool'). Cleopatra would seem to be reaching through to that theory of understanding which holds that all cognition is the

---

[1] *Middlemarch*, Book I, chapter ix (Penguin edn.), p. 111.

apperception of one thing through another,[1] leaving behind the Dolabellas of this world to ponder (as this Dolabella seems to be beginning to do: 'Your loss is, as yourself, great'; l. 101) Montaigne's insight that 'It is folly to measure the true and false by our own capacity.'

Shakespeare's contemporary, the poet and playwright George Chapman, writes in the Preface to his translation of Homer that there is no 'such reality of wisdomes truth in all humane excellence as in Poets fictions'.[2] Shakespeare gave such truth to his greatest liars: the gift of saying that which *is not* and of making us see and know that it *is*. Such lying is a godsend, even 419 years after his birth and in an age which sets its faith in computers rather than in dramatic poets. To the student of Shakespeare, computer-consciousness lies partly in becoming conscious that a computerized Concordance cannot distinguish between the two senses of 'lie' but jumbles them all together into 341 indiscriminate 'frequencies'.[3] The one thing, it seems, that a computer cannot do is to lie, in the senses I have tried to explore in this lecture. Perhaps the time has come when we shall have to learn to say 'I lie, therefore I am.'

[1] Cf. Hans Vaihinger, *The Philosophy of 'As if'*, translated by C. K. Ogden (1924), p. 29.

[2] In J. E. Spingarn, ed., *Critical Essays of the Seventeenth Century* i (Oxford, 1908), 67–8.

[3] This is merely to state a fact, not to bite the hand which has fed me: Marvin Spevack's invaluable *Harvard Concordance to Shakespeare* (Cambridge, Mass., 1973).

THE DRAMATIC STRUCTURE OF SHAKESPEARE'S *KING HENRY THE EIGHTH*: AN ESSAY IN REHABILITATION

By GLYNNE WICKHAM

Read 3 May 1984

AT least two questions have to be asked about Shakespeare's *King Henry VIII* before any profitable attempt at critical analysis of its particular form and content can begin. The first is why Shakespeare let twelve years pass between providing his actors with *Henry V* for performance at the Curtain and the composition of *Henry VIII* during 1612, a performance of which on 29 June 1613 resulted in the destruction of the Globe playhouse by fire. The second is why he chose not to write a play about Henry VII to link his *Richard III* with *Henry VIII*.

Any answer to either question must finally remain speculative since Shakespeare failed to supply answers himself. However, we do possess the evidence of the troubles encountered by the authors of the play of *Sir Thomas More* when attempting to get it licensed for performance by the Master of the Revels in the early 1590s, to warn us that the dangers surrounding any discussion of a Tudor monarch on the stage were sufficient to deter a professional play-maker from devoting much time or energy to writing a play with Henry VII or Henry VIII as title-role, while Elizabeth I was still alive. Even after James I's accession in 1603, time enough would have to pass for it to be known whether he was likely to adopt a more relaxed attitude towards public discussion of the conduct of Tudor monarchs. In this lecture it will be my purpose to argue that he did—at least with certain provisos—and that Shakespeare knew this by the time that *Cymbeline* and *The Winter's Tale* were safely in the repertoire of the King's Men.

The question then remains of why he opted to write *Henry VIII* rather than a play about Henry VII or both. Here the simplest and most probable answer lies in the facts of history itself. When the authors of *1066 and All That* described a British sovereign as 'a good King' they usually meant that chronicles of that reign failed to record sufficient subject-matter of a scandalous and notorious character to be worth writing about at any length. In this sense Henry VII was an exceptionally 'good King'. Under his rule peace succeeded civil war; dynastic marriages replaced war abroad; the national economy recovered; learning and letters flourished. Yet none of these admirable achievements supply material that invites attention from a dramatist. The single exception is the pathetic insurrections led by Lambert Simnel and Perkin Warbeck, the one from Ireland and the other from Holland, both of which were swiftly and easily suppressed. In one of them John Ford was later to find the seeds of drama; but even his interest is focused on the personality of the unfortunate Warbeck and the psychology of self-deception, *not* on Henry VII. Shakespeare, moreover, may well have felt that he had already said all he wished to say about Henry VII in the closing Acts of *Richard III*. So much then for the 'missing' play of *Henry VII*.

Two further questions, however, require an answer. The first of these is why it should have appeared 'safe' to write a play about Henry VIII around 1611/12. An answer is that the playwright Samuel Rowley had already taken the temperature at the Revels Office in obtaining a license in 1605 for his rumbustious defence of the King and the Protestant Reformation, *When You See Me You Know Me. Or the famous Chronicle Historie of Henry the eight.*

The second question is why should Shakespeare have decided to construct his play in a manner so strikingly different both from his own earlier 'Histories' and from Rowley's play. I wish to argue now that the answer to both these questions rests in Shakespeare having wanted to say something about Henry VIII, and more particularly about Queen Katherine of Aragon, which his patron, James I, actually wanted to be said and widely heard at that particular time.

John Munro when editing the play for *The London Shakespeare* (1957) wrote disparagingly of its structure in his Introduction:

Although primarily dramatic and spectacular, the play attempts to reconcile the tragic and unmerited falls of Buckingham and Katherine, the self-provoked fall of Wolsey and the foretoken of the fall of Cranmer, with the rise of Anne Bullen and the felicitous birth of Elizabeth, and, finally, the exaltation of James as the King appointed to carry on the divine mission of the Tudors.

As a plot synopsis this could scarcely be bettered. However, he then continues,

The dramatic result is a series of ill-fitting episodes, smothered in pageantry, and redeemed by some magnificent speeches and situations.

It is no wonder that, apart from questions of style, it has been so frequently stated that Shakespeare cannot have been responsible for the general structure of the play.   (iv. 1149)[1]

Is that really the best that can be said of it? Or has Munro left out of his account any factor or factors in his appraisal of the play that might lead to a more favourable verdict? One such factor, altogether ignored by all critics known to me, is the measure of topicality that the play possessed for its original audiences which is now lost on us.[2] This lies at the very heart of the drama, the advent of the Reformation and the burden of responsibility for an event which still eclipsed all others in its political implications and reverberances. The Scottish James VI had succeeded to the English throne in 1603 because he was a Protestant lineally descended from Henry VII. The Gunpowder Plot had been hatched in 1605 because he was a Protestant, and had been designed to assassinate both him and his heirs in favour of a Roman Catholic alternative. Yet James's mother, Mary Queen of Scots, had been a Catholic and had been executed by Elizabeth I accused of conspiring to assassinate her. Behind that lay memories of Mary I, her consort Philip II of Spain, and the fires of Smithfield; and behind Mary I lay the figure of her mother, Katherine of Aragon, whom Henry VIII had divorced in order to marry Anne Bullen, the mother of Elizabeth I, aided and abetted by Cardinal Wolsey and the papal legate Cardinal Campeius. A hotter political potato than this could scarcely have been plucked from the embers of remembered history in 1611. In other words, it stands to reason that a play which places Queen Katherine's trial and Henry's subsequent wedding at the centre

[1] As it forms no part of my purpose within this lecture to discuss attribution, it suffices here to state that I accept the normal critical view that Shakespeare collaborated with John Fletcher in writing it, being responsible for the ordering of the action, or 'invention', himself as well as for most of the major set-piece scenes, and leaving the linking passages to Fletcher in the manner of contemporary portrait painters, who, having taken full responsibility for the likeness and posture of the sitter, left it to apprentices to complete the costume and background.

[2] R. A. Foakes in his edition of the play for the 'Arden Shakespeare' does at least relate it to the courtship and wedding of the Princess Elizabeth to the Elector Palatine, Prince Frederick (see Introduction, pp. xxx-xxxv); but he omits to mention that among the many suitors for the Princess between 1609 and the wedding itself were several Roman Catholics, not the least being Philip III of Spain (then a widower) whose candidature was strongly favoured by Queen Anne.

PLATE III

Katherine was the youngest child of King Ferdinand and Queen Isabella of Spain. She arrived in England in October 1501, when she was still only fifteen, and married Arthur, Prince of Wales in St Paul's Cathedral on 14 November, only to become a widow five months later. In 1509 she was married again to her brother-in-law, Henry VIII, and crowned Queen of England on 24 June in Westminster Abbey. Divorce proceedings commenced in the Legatine Court specially set up in the Great Hall of Blackfriars in May 1529. The king finally abandoned her in July 1531. She died, a virtual prisoner at Kimbolton Castle, in January 1536.

Reproduced with the kind permission of the National Portrait Gallery.

of the action could only hope to meet with the censor's approval if it was structured in such a way as to be ideologically acceptable: in short, it was passed by the Revels Office for performance because it said something about these highly charged historical events that the King in Council wanted said.

I wish now to suggest, therefore, that what James and his Ministers wanted said was that Katherine of Aragon, although both a Spaniard and a Roman Catholic, was a woman more sinned against than sinning: and from the way her scenes are written it is difficult to believe that Shakespeare did not share that view of her himself. Indeed, the play is so structured as to ensure that the audience's sympathies are carefully and consistently directed towards her and then retained by her, notwithstanding the more flamboyant scenes which follow in Act V, and the repeated pattern of Fortune's turning wheel.[1] The short Epilogue confirms this view. From the Privy Council's standpoint, however, it was no less important that Henry VIII, Anne Bullen, and Elizabeth I should be detached and exculpated from any personal responsibility for Katherine's fate. This Shakespeare achieves by laying all blame squarely at the door of Anti-Christ, Pope Clement VII, and his diabolic agents Cardinal Wolsey (who likens his own fall to Lucifer's) and the egregious papal legate, Campeius (a latter-day Iscariot). With both these objectives accomplished, Shakespeare can move safely towards the final apotheosis of James VI and I, revealing this to be the culmination of a messianic vision of an imperial future for the British, predestined by Divine Providence and brought to fruition through the Reformation.

Before turning to the text itself to explore the way in which Shakespeare manipulates his materials to this threefold end, I must beg leave to substantiate my claim that all three of these objectives had special relevance at the time he was writing the play. Reduced to essentials they can be expressed as follows: the harmony that is bred from union begets peace and prosperity.[2] God, as King James repeatedly told his subjects in his speeches,

[1] This pattern and its recurrence in the other Romances is fully discussed by Frank V. Cespedes in '"We are one in fortunes": The Sense of History in *Henry VIII*', *English Literary Review*, vol. x, no. 3 (Autumn, 1980), pp. 413–38.

[2] For fuller discussion see G. Wickham, 'Romance and Emblem: A Study of the Dramatic Structure of *The Winter's Tale*', *Elizabethan Theatre III*, ed. David Galloway, 1973, pp. 82–9; 'Masque and Anti-Masque in *The Tempest*', *Essays and Studies 1975*, ed. R. Ellrodt, pp. 1–14; and 'Riddle and Emblem: A Study in the Dramatic Structure of *Cymbeline*', *English Renaissance Studies*, 1980, ed. John Carey, pp. 94–113; also Roy Strong, *Britannia Triumphans*, 1980.

had brought an end to all the speculation and anxiety that had bedevilled the last two decades of Elizabeth's reign by reuniting the Kingdoms of Scotland and England within his person, just as God had terminated the Wars of the Roses a century earlier in the marriage of Henry VII and Elizabeth of York: and if England had prospered under the Tudors, how much more so would the re-united Kingdom of Britannia, Great Britain, flourish under the Stuarts. A start had been made in the Peace Treaty signed with Spain in 1604; Guy Fawkes's devilish gunpowder treason had mis-carried; the future looked brighter still. When James's son Henry, created Prince of Wales in 1610, inherited the throne, he would truly reunite Wales, Ireland, Scotland, and England within an imperial diadem embracing colonies in the New World. And in his sons Henry and Charles, and his daughter Elizabeth, James rested his hopes of a still more resplendent achievement in the ultimate reunion of a sadly divided Christendom through judicious dynas-tic marriages. Not for nothing did he welcome as his motto on arriving in England, *Beati Pacifici*: Blessed are the Peacemakers; for the reward he foresaw for his subjects in God's good time was to be nothing less than a *Pax Britannica* as stable, widespread and durable as the former *Pax Romana*; in short, a Protestant Empire grounded on London, and led by the predestinately elect nation of Great Britain.

Poets, pageanteers, and playmakers had swiftly battened on these romantic ideals, adorning them in the mythological meta-phors of Trojan Brutus, the prophet Merlin, and the sleeping King Arthur formerly bestowed on the house of Tudor, and exploiting such legendary early British kings as Lear and Cymbeline, to advance them further. James had encouraged them himself by matching words with deeds. The burial arrangements made for his predecessor and his murdered mother in the King Henry VII Chapel at Westminster provided his subjects with both an explicit example and an emblem of practical peacemaking: bury the past: forgive and forget. The wedding of Lord Hay, leader of the Scottish peers, and the Lady Honora Denny, heiress to an English peerage, celebrated at Court and crowned with a Masque commissioned from Thomas Campion in 1606, again served to translate an abstract idea into recognizable, concrete terms of reference. And, if Scots, instead of fighting the English, could marry them, why should Protestants not marry Catholics and thus spread peace and prosperity through union further still?

It was within this climate of opinion that negotiations started in earnest in 1609 to find an appropriate bride and groom for

Prince Henry and the Princess Elizabeth: and it was against this background that one awkward ghost had still to be laid to rest, the tarnished image of a Spanish Princess married to a King of England for more than twenty years, mother of his first child, yet ultimately disgraced, rejected and left alone to die as a virtual exile in a foreign land. This could hardly be regarded as a good advertisement for a repeat performance. No wonder the King and his Ministers thought it high time to set the record straight: yet in setting it straight, the over-riding image of a divinely chosen, elect nation being led by a latter-day Moses and a second Joshua into a promised land of imperial dimensions must in no way be sullied or despoiled.

Shakespeare, I suggest, set out in 1612 to lay this ghost, fully aware of the urgency and importance attaching to this task. It was one worthy of the King's Men. Who better placed to tackle it? Title and Prologue combine as signposts to an understanding of the company's intent. Audiences were told that they were to see and hear a play called 'The Famous History of the Life of King Henry the Eighth', probably sub-titled 'All is True' when it first appeared. No word of Henry himself in the Prologue, and none of the other characters are named; but there is an unusual insistence upon the realism with which both the story and the persons in it are to be treated in this play. *Truth* will reward those who pay for admission; this *truth* has been 'chosen'; clowning and ribaldry can only serve to undermine the recipients' sense of the *truth* of the actions represented, and have accordingly been deliberately avoided. The events to be discussed are 'serious', 'weighty', 'full of state and woe'.

> Those that can pity here
> May, if they think it well, let fall a tear.

Hitherto, it has generally been assumed that *Henry VIII*, because it is known to have been performed at the Globe on 29 June 1613, must therefore have been written for, and first performed at, the Globe. Admittedly R. A. Foakes, in editing the play for 'The Arden Shakespeare' in 1968, encouraged the idea of earlier performances;[1] but what no one has recognized, as far as I am aware, is that this play could just as easily have been written for first performance in the King's Men's Private Playhouse in the Blackfriars, which they had recovered for their own use in August 1608.[2] Once this is remarked, then the probability that the play

[1] Op. cit., pp. xxx–xxxi.
[2] On James I's decision to disband the Company of Boys known as the

was conceived for presentation at the Blackfriars through the winter season of 1612/13 and then transferred to the Globe in the summer of 1613 has to be taken very seriously, since that Playhouse had been fashioned out of the great open room, or hall, formerly known as the Parliament Chamber—*itself the actual site of Queen Katherine's trial in 1528.*

If, temporarily, we accept this hypothesis, an explanation is at once forthcoming for the extraordinary insistence upon 'truth', already remarked upon, and for the no less extraordinary insistence upon verisimilitude in many of the play's exceptionally long and detailed stage-directions. In other words, if Shakespeare intended, as I am now arguing that he did, to re-enact the Queen's trial some eighty years on within the walls of the Court-room where it had originally been held, but before a new jury of Jacobean playgoers, then accuracy and verisimilitude (or at least the semblance of both) must have assumed a special importance for author, actors, and audience alike.

With that said, let us now apply this hypothesis to the existing Folio text, and examine such consequences as this may have on an understanding of the play's dramatic structure.

The play itself begins some eleven years after Henry VIII's accession with a vivid if retrospective account of the Field of the Cloth of Gold of 1520. Within fifty lines, however, this descriptive setting is angled to discredit its prime begetter, Cardinal Wolsey. 'Ambitious finger' ... 'fierce vanities' ... 'spider-like out of his self-drawing web' . . . thus the Dukes of Norfolk and Buckingham describe his contribution. Lord Abergavenny probes deeper:

> . . . I can see his pride
> Peep through each part of him. Whence has he that?
> If not from hell, the devil is a niggard,
> Or has given all before, and he begins
> A new hell in himself.

The allusion is transparent: if Wolsey is the Pope's principal representative in England, so Lucifer was the brightest of God's angels. They proceed to attribute the unprecedented extravagance of the Field of the Cloth of Gold to deliberate scheming on Wolsey's part to ruin the nobility, only to be interrupted by the entrance of Wolsey himself in great pomp and circumstance. Battle is swiftly joined between him and Buckingham who now

Children of the King's Revels whose manager, Henry Evans, had leased the playhouse from the Burbages between 1600 and 1608, see G. Wickham, *Early English Stages*, vol. ii, pt. 2 (1972), pp. 129–36.

views Wolsey as 'This holy fox, or wolf, or both', an ironic comment in the event since further discourse is cut short by the arrest of Buckingham on Wolsey's orders.

Scene 2 introduces the audience to the King and Queen. Katherine's role is highly significant. It is analogous both to Esther's when pleading for the Jews before Ahasuerus and to that of the Virgin Mary as intercessor for sinful man before God. Here she takes cause with London's merchants and artisans reduced to penury by Wolsey's taxes with little thought for herself or any danger in which such action might place her.

> I am much too venturous
> In tempting of your patience, but am boldened
> Under your promised pardon. The subjects' grief
> Comes through commissions, which compels from each
> The sixth part of his substance, to be levied
> Without delay; and the pretence for this
> Is named your wars in France.

Nothing could be better calculated to win her the immediate sympathy of the public.

Wolsey side-steps her accusations by passing the buck to the Judges. Nevertheless, the King acts on the Queen's advice and orders a free pardon to be given to everyone who has failed to pay the tax. Wolsey passes this instruction on to his secretary, but tells him to attribute the sudden pardon to his own 'intercession'. This action, combined with the Cardinal's scarlet hat behind which it is given, could only serve to confirm the audience in the impression of devilish viciousness gleaned earlier of Wolsey from Buckingham's comments. This viciousness—fox and wolf at once—is then displayed in action as Wolsey cajoles a bribed and perjured servant of the Duke into accusing him of treason. Again the Queen intervenes to plead for charity, but in vain. Buckingham must stand trial: Wolsey's voice still rings more loudly in the King's ear than Katherine's.

The action then shifts to Wolsey's Palace, where the Cardinal is depicted as host at a banquet worthy of the Borgias. Henry himself is to be the principal guest, leading a troupe of mummers disguised as shepherds. The Queen has not been invited, but Sir Thomas Bullen's young daughter, Anne, has. Once Henry, now unmasked, has met her, Wolsey adopts the role of Pandarus and escorts the flirtatious couple to refreshments in his private apartments. The pastoral setting supplied by the shepherd-masquers can scarcely be coincidental: the care already taken to

equate Wolsey with Lucifer serves deftly to translate the close of
this Act into a sixteenth-century Garden of Eden shortly before
the Fall. Neither Henry nor Katherine can now stop what must
follow, but the blame for it has been firmly planted on a Cardinal
in an adder's coat.

Act II opens with Buckingham's finale. Shakespeare denies us
the trial scene deliberately: that he must hold in reserve. Instead
he employs an eye-witness to describe to an absentee what has
happened. If words are to be believed, then not only did the trial
itself represent a miscarriage of justice, but responsibility for
that rested with the perjured clergy guided and suborned by the
envious Cardinal. As the eye-witness observes, this has become
a routine.

> And generally, whoever the King favours
> The Cardinal instantly will find employment,
> And far enough from Court too.

Nor are these sentiments confined to courtiers playing the power-
game. As the absentee responds:

> All the commons
> Hate him perniciously, and, o' my conscience,
> Wish him ten fathom deep.

Buckingham then appears on his way to the scaffold. He is urged
to speak his mind. What is notable, when he does so, is that he
never directs one word of blame towards the King. The dramatic
purpose of his harrowing and pitiful farewell is not, however, an
end in itself: rather is it designed to prepare the audience to fear for
the Queen's safety. The execution procession has no sooner left the
stage than the second of the two Gentlemen who began the scene
by discussing Buckingham's trial informs his companion of,

> . . . an ensuing evil, if it fall,
> Greater than this.

Pressed to explain himself, he confides a rumour that has recently
reached him.

> Either the Cardinal,
> Or some about him near, have, out of malice
> To the good Queen, possessed him (i.e. the King) with a scruple
> That will undo her . . .
> . . . The Cardinal
> Will have his will, and she must fall.

Thus we are brought back to the image of the Paradise Garden
that closed Act I. With Lucifer abroad in it, Eve must fall: but

this time Adam must be lured first. What is 'this scruple that will undo her'? We only have to wait some ten more lines for the answer. As the Lord Chamberlain observes to the Duke of Norfolk,

> It seems the marriage with his brother's wife
> Has crept too near his conscience.

'No' replies Suffolk, 'his conscience has crept too near another lady.' A rash ripost! Yet Norfolk immediately confirms it and adds a damning rider.

>   'Tis so.
> This is the Cardinal's doing, the King-Cardinal.
> That blind priest, like the eldest son of fortune,
> Turns what he list. The King will know him one day.

Still the King's fault lies only in ignorance of the devilish machinations being practised upon him. The Queen is wholly excused by Norfolk. Wolsey, he remarks, having first schemed to introduce the King to Anne Bullen, then plants the idea of incest in his mind, stirring up a turmoil of doubts, dangers, fears and despairs.

> And out of all these to restore the King,
> He counsels a divorce, a loss of her
> That, like a jewel, has hung twenty years
> About his neck, yet never lost her lustre;
> Of her that loves him with that excellence
> That angels love good men with, even of her
> That, when the greatest stroke of fortune falls
> Will bless the King:—and is not this course pious?

In reply to this ironic rhetorical question Suffolk declares open war on the Cardinal.

>   ... so, I leave him
> To him that made him proud, the Pope.

Most of the cards are now face-upwards on the table. Time can thus be foreshortened: the papal legate has arrived; he and Wolsey are free to work their fiend-like ends upon the innocent King and Queen of England; but by now Jacobean audiences have also been equipped by this skilful playmaker to serve as jurymen on the conduct of all four. To hammer home the point Shakespeare then provides the King with these four lines:

> The most convenient place that I can think of
> For such receipt of learning is Blackfriars:
> There ye shall meet about this weighty business:
> My Wolsey, see it furnished.

In those four lines the equating of the Parliament Chamber, the site of the original trial, with the existing Private Playhouse is made explicit for all present to hear and see.

Before the Queen's trial can begin, however, one more card has to be turned upwards—Anne Bullen's. Promptly we meet her expressing dismay at the turn events have taken, pitying Katherine's predicament, and vowing that she will never allow herself to take her place as Queen. In all this she is mocked by a companion resembling Juliet's nurse. When Anne swears that by her 'truth and maidenhead' she would not be a queen, this shrewd woman replies,

> Beshrew me, I would,
> And venture maidenhead for 't: and so would you,
> For all this spice of your hypocrisy.
> You that have so fair parts of woman on you
> Have too a woman's heart, which ever yet
> Affected eminence, wealth, sovereignty;
> Which, to say sooth, are blessings; and which gifts—
> Saving your mincing—the capacity
> Of your soft cheveril conscience would receive
> If you might please to stretch it.

This is a devastating exposure. With her card now face-upwards, Anne can be dismissed from the drama that is to follow in Blackfriars. At this point it would perhaps be as well to recapitulate, in the manner of one of those chess problems in newspapers showing the state of play and the number of moves white has in which to checkmate black, on how Shakespeare has manipulated audience sympathies to date, in preparation for the play's central event, the trial of the Queen.

In one sense the Buckingham scenes in Acts I and II are non-events, since the ambiguous story of his treason is not an end in itself, only a means to another end: his guilt or innocence, in other words, are left in some doubt; all that is certain is that he was rash in his choice of personal servants and in the trust he placed in them. What these scenes really exist to do is to show audiences that Henry VIII is no less rash, in human terms of reference, in the trust he places in his ministers; that the leader of them, Wolsey, is as devious as could be expected of any ecclesiastic owing his allegiance and authority to the Pope, and as ambitious as Lucifer who had succeeded in deceiving God himself. This exonerates the King, but it bodes ill for the Queen if she is courageous enough to step between the Cardinal and his own ends. This she does, first by pleading for the citizens against unjust and ruinous taxation, and then as an intercessor for Buckingham. Wolsey promptly counters these dangerous moves, first by arranging to place Anne Bullen within Henry's acquaintanceship and then by expressing doubts to Henry about the legitimacy of his marriage. Thus Satan comes to tempt the old Adam in Henry's mortal nature with a nubile apple, and to employ the niceties of legal small-print, with the Pope's help, to ensure that he will yield. Lastly, Anne's role within this diabolic plot is also glossed to protect her against any charge of having been a prime mover in the events to follow; she is no more than the unfortunate but essential instrument chosen by Wolsey, as it seems, to effect his revenge on Katherine. Young, beautiful, and unschooled in politics, but wholly feminine in her nature, she is fully aware of what could result from the situation in which she finds herself to have been placed. Like Henry, therefore, from the audience's standpoint, she is still an innocent within the Machiavellian game orchestrated by Anti-Christ.

It is against this moral backcloth that Katherine's trial begins: discerning spectators may well have noticed parallels with Hermione's situation in Act III of *The Winter's Tale*. No actress worth that name could ask for a better start.

The re-enactment of the historical event in Blackfriars Hall begins with a blaze of pageantry: the stage-direction covering the order of proceedings is itself fourteen lines long. Significantly the trial starts with these words from Wolsey:

> Whilst our commission from Rome is read,
> Let silence be commanded.

This supplies Katherine with her cue to launch into one of the best known audition pieces in the canon:

> Sir, I desire you do me right and justice,
> And to bestow your pity on me . . .

This plea, and the forty-five lines that follow it are addressed directly to the King, but it is the two Cardinals who intervene with answers to prevent him replying to her request for Spanish lawyers. She, in turn, accuses Wolsey to his face of pride, cunning, and all uncharitableness. Her courage is only matched by her simplicity, for in her refusal to be judged by Wolsey it is 'unto the Pope' that she appeals—

> To bring my whole cause 'fore his Holiness,
> And to be judged by him.

—whereupon she sweeps out of the hall, a woman patently more sinned against than sinning, and every inch a Queen. It is a *tour de force* and one that succeeds in moving the King at last to speak: what is more, her conduct has recovered his admiration for her: she is 'the queen of earthly queens'.

Wolsey is at once on the defensive: nor can anything be quite the same again. Henry excuses him and, at his suggestion, offers the audience a seventy-line account of how the lack of a male heir, conjoined with the possible illegitimacy of his only daughter, so disturbed him as to make it imperative, in the nation's interest, to settle the matter once and for all. Campeius, in supporting his resolve, sinisterly suggests that the Queen's proposed appeal should be blocked. This proves to be the last straw for Henry, who abruptly closes the scene with an unexpected aside to the audience:

> I may perceive
> These Cardinals trifle with me. I abhor
> This dilatory sloth and tricks of Rome.

He summons Cranmer: Fortune's wheel has started to turn.

Act III opens like the last act of *Othello*. The Queen, still loyal to her husband, but now wracked with anxiety and foreboding, like Desdemona, takes comfort in music.

> In sweet music is such art,
> Killing care and grief of heart
> Fall asleep, or hearing die.

This touching scene is interrupted by a visitation from Wolsey and Campeius. In the interview which follows Shakespeare wrings the changes on his audiences' emotions, as the dialogue alternates between the obsequious counselling of the two Cardinals and the Queen's dignified, doubting and contemptuous responses. Campeius rashly rebukes her rising anger and provokes a devastatingly frank ripost.

> The more shame for ye. Holy men I thought ye,
> Upon my soul, two reverend cardinal virtues;
> But cardinal sins and hollow hearts I fear ye.
> Mend 'em, for shame, my lords. Is this your comfort?
> The cordial that ye bring a wretched lady,
> A woman lost among ye, laughed at, scorned?
> I will not wish ye half my miseries:
> I have more charity. But say, I warned ye:
> Take heed, for heaven's sake, take heed, lest at once
> The burthen of my sorrow fall upon ye.

The scene continues for another hundred lines, but it is all over

bar the shouting, the tears, the wringing of hands. As Katherine
herself observes,

> Like the lily,
> That once was mistress of the field and flourished,
> I'll hang my head and perish.

Maybe, if that is heaven's high purpose; but her prophecy, like
Cassandra's, will swiftly come to pass through the agency of the
Reformation. Cranmer is at work; Campeius has fled to Rome;
Wolsey, much to his alarm, has discovered Anne Bullen to be a
secret Lutheran; rumour has it that the pragmatic King will
resolve his own and the nation's dilemma by marrying her forth-
with. All that is still controllable. What is not is the letter he has
sent to the Pope which, in error, gets delivered to the King. When
Henry hands him this damning evidence of his own avarice and
double-dealing, he knows the game is up.

> Nay then, farewell!
> I have touched the highest point of all my greatness;
> And, from that full meridian of my glory,
> I haste now to my setting. I shall fall
> Like a bright exhalation in the evening,
> And no man see me more.

Charged by others with extortion, duplicity, and viciousness,
Wolsey ironically answers his accusers in the language Katherine
had used to him—'officious lords', 'curious courses', 'men of
malice',—but with the vital difference that the audience, who had
believed Katherine, now disbelieve him, more especially on
hearing Surrey address him as 'thou scarlet sin'! The longer this
goes on, and as the list of Wolsey's deceptions is catalogued by his
accusers, so the need for a thorough Reformation of a totally
corrupt 2nd Estate becomes self-evident. At least it brings Wolsey
to self-knowledge at last. Left to meditate, he soliloquizes
memorably and philosophically on the personal catastrophe
prophesied by the Queen; and, in conclusion, recognizes that,

> . . . when he falls, he falls like Lucifer,
> Never to hope again.

And so the way is clear to move on to Anne's marriage and
coronation. Both are conveyed to us as matters of fact without any
further discussion of the rights and wrongs of either. As Wolsey
admits,

> The King has gone beyond me. All my glories
> In that one woman I have lost for ever.

In other words Anne was God's chosen instrument who, with the
King's assistance, would occasion Wolsey's fall and, with it, bring
about the Reformation. Cranmer and Cromwell are left to effect
it. And so we move to her coronation, but we will be denied any
closer acquaintance with her. Her name will recur, briefly, in the
dialogue when she gives birth to a daughter, the Princess Elizabeth, but that is all: in that role she will neither speak nor be seen.
Her role is over. Yet Katherine is destined to return, and in one of
the play's most moving scenes. Old, isolated, ill, and ignored
during the coronation celebrations, we meet her next with her few
loyal retainers at Kimbolton Castle. It is an astonishing scene, its
ritualistic simplicity contrasting sharply with the garish pomp and
circumstance of the preceding scene. With all passion spent and
music at the close, it offers us a theatrical representation of the
supreme Christian virtue of Fortitude. Starting with a recital of
the circumstances of Wolsey's death it moves on to an exchange of
obituaries; the first, supplied by Katherine, of his vices; the second
supplied by Griffith, her usher, of his virtues. Katherine sums up.

> After my death I wish no other herald,
> No other speaker of my living actions,
> To keep mine honour from corruption,
> But such an honest chronicler as Griffith.
> Whom I most hated living, thou hast made me,
> With thy religious truth and modesty,
> Now in his ashes honour. Peace be with him!

Shakespeare has shown us a woman who has loved her neighbours
as herself and honoured both God and the King, his appointed
deputy on earth. She has endured suffering with patience, dignity
and humility; and now, with true Christian charity, she forgives
her arch enemy. Shakespeare rewards her with a dream which
bears a close resemblance to pictures of the Assumption of
the Virgin Mary as depicted by such Mannerist painters as
Correggio, Guido Reni, and Murillo.

Choreographed in all probability by the King's dancing
master, Monsieur Hieronimus Herne,[1] six seraphic children

enter, solemnly tripping one after another . . . clad in white Robes,
wearing on their heads Garlands of Bay, and golden Vizards on their
faces, Branches of Bays or Palm in their hands.

As they dance they pair off and each pair in turn holds a spare

[1] It was he who, according to Ben Jonson, choreographed the grotesque
dance for the King's Men to provide in the anti-masque to *The Masque of Queens*,
presented at court by the Queen and her ladies in 1609.

garland over Katherine's head while the others curtsy to her. The stage-direction in Folio ends as follows:

And so, in their Dancing vanish, carrying the Garland with them. The Music continues.

As Katherine wakes, she fancies she still sees these angelic beings and addresses them as 'Spirits of peace'.

This powerful icon of a martyr's crown awaiting a soul that has lived and died for her faith provides a fitting prelude to a gesture of reconcilement from her husband and a final reckoning. When told by Capucius that he brings commendations and comfort from the King, Katherine responds,

> O my good lord, that comfort comes too late:
> 'Tis like a pardon after execution.
> That gentle physic, given in time, had cured me;
> But now I am past all comforts here but prayers.
> How does his Highness?
> *Capucius.*   Madam, in good health.
> *Katherine.* So may he ever do! and ever flourish
> When I shall dwell with worms, and my poor name
> Banished the kingdom!

Yet even as she speaks these words, Shakespeare is repealing in Blackfriars that very banishment which an English Court had imposed upon her in Blackfriars.

With failing strength she dictates her last will and testament, and bequeaths to her faithful attendants instructions for her funeral.

> Let me be used with honour. Strew me over
> With maiden flowers, that all the world may know
> I was a chaste wife to my grave. Embalm me,
> Then lay me forth; although unqueened, yet like
> A queen, and daughter to a king, inter me.
> I can no more.

And there ends the finest death scene Shakespeare ever wrote: and with it ends Act IV. Why then add Act V? It's there, in my submission, to wrench the play back into time-present. This is effected by the birth and christening of the Princess Elizabeth. The latter is entrusted to Thomas Cranmer who, as Archbishop of Canterbury, is a fit mouthpiece for prophetic utterance. Following a panegyric on Elizabeth's future achievements, he proceeds,

> Nor shall this peace sleep with her; but, as when
> The bird of wonder dies, the maiden phoenix,

> Her ashes new create another heir
> As great in admiration as herself,
> So shall she leave her blessedness to one—
> When heaven shall call her from this cloud of darkness—
> Who from the sacred ashes of her honour
> Shall starlike rise, as great in fame as she was,
> And so stand fixed. Peace, plenty, love, truth, terror,
> That were the servants to this chosen infant,
> Shall then be his, and like a vine grow to him.
> Wherever the bright sun of heaven shall shine,
> His honour and the greatness of his name
> Shall be, and make new nations. He shall flourish,
> And, like a mountain cedar, reach his branches
> To all the plains about him. Our children's children
> Shall see this, and bless heaven.

And so Fortune's wheel has come full-circle. The children's children cited here by Cranmer are now the very same spectators who are watching him deliver this prophecy. Peace, plenty, love— the familiar Jamesian aspirations—and with them the first-fruits of an imperial future for God's chosen Protestant people have become realities.

My claim, therefore, is that Shakespeare set out to offer more in *King Henry VIII* than just a rag-bag of 'ill-fitting episodes, smothered in pageantry, redeemed by some magnificent speeches and situations' to humour jolly, jingoistic theatre-goers at the Globe. Rather is this play as carefully and artistically designed as all its immediate predecessors. Its structure is governed by a single unifying purpose, underpinned by the fortuitous conjunction of the former Parliament Chamber and contemporary Private Play-house within the dissolved Priory of Blackfriars. That purpose, at its simplest, is to redeem *in the national interest* the slanders cast in 1531 upon the name of Katherine of Aragon on British soil. As dramatic narrative, it is a chunk of national history: as art it is a Requiem Mass and an entombment.

The dying Hamlet, as you will recall, calls on Horatio to render him a final favour.

> O good Horatio, what a wounded name,
> Things standing thus unknown, shall live behind me!
> If thou didst ever hold me in thy heart,
> Absent thee from felicity awhile,
> And in this harsh world draw thy breath in pain
> To tell my story.

I suggest that it was this voice, or one very like it, that rang in

Shakespeare's ears as he set about the rehabilitation of Katherine, Princess of Aragon and Queen of England, when composing *The Famous History of the Life of King Henry the Eighth or, All is True* for production by the King's Men in their playhouse at Blackfriars in 1612.[1]

[1] Shakespeare is quoted from J. J. Munro, *The London Shakespeare* (6 vols), 1957.

POSTSCRIPT
1993

A presumptive chronology for the composition, rehearsal and first perform-ances of Shakespeare's King Henry VIII *by the King's Men, 1612–1613.*

May, 1612.   A contract of marriage signed between the Princess Elizabeth (daughter of James I and Goddaughter of Elizabeth I) and Prince Frederick, Elector Palatine, a leader of the Protestant cause in Germany (see pp. 121–2 above).

August, 1612.   London theatre season ends. The Master of the Revels orders the King's Men to prepare a play relevant to the wedding for performance at Court, and informs them that the bridegroom will arrive in London in September to be invested as a Knight of the Garter prior to his wedding in November.

October, 1612.   Shakespeare and Fletcher complete *King Henry VIII*: wardrobe construction and rehearsals start as new theatre season opens in London.

November 7th, 1612.   Death of Henry Stuart, Prince of Wales: all theatres closed until Christmas. The wedding is postponed.

January, 1613.   *King Henry VIII* re-rehearsed to open at Black-friars in readiness for Court performance during the wedding festivities in February.

February 14th, 1613.   The wedding.

February 16th, 1613.   (*Shrove Tuesday*). The King's Men called to Court to perform *King Henry VIII*, but a Masque is preferred.[1]

February 17th, 1613.   (*Ash Wednesday*). All theatres closed through Lent.

[1] 'Much expectation was made of a stage play to be acted in the Great Hall at Westminster by the King's players where many hundred of people stood attending the same; but it lapsed contrarie, for greater pleasures were preparing'. See E. K. Chambers, *William Shakespeare*, ii. 343.

April/May, 1613.   Summer theatre season opens. *King Henry VIII*
re-rehearsed for presentation at the Globe.

May/June, 1613.   *King Henry VIII* enters the repertoire of the
King's Men at the Globe. The theatre burns down during a
performance on June 29th.

Three letters describing this event survive dated June 30th, July
2nd and July 4th. The first (from Thomas Lorkin to Sir Henry
Pickering) refers simply to 'the play of Henry VIII':[2] in the
second, Sir Henry Wotton tells Edmund Bacon, 'The King's
players had a new play called *All is True* which was set forth with
extraordinary pomp and majesty. . . .':[3] in the third, a London
merchant informs a friend in Somerset, Richard Weeks, that,
'On Tuesday last there was acted at the Globe a new play called
All is Triewe which had been acted not passing 2 or 3 times
before . . .'.[4]

'New', the play unquestionably was for Globe audiences; but
with its exceptionally large cast, elaborate costumes and stage-
properties and the time required for rehearsal, I submit that it
cannot have opened at the Globe in May, 1613, without prior
exposure to audiences elsewhere. This could easily have been
achieved in the brief pre-London season at Blackfriars,—a
surmise supported by the whole structure of the text and its
detailed stage-directions (see p. 123 above and the arguments
advanced by R. A. Foakes, Arden ed. xxx-xxxv) in the context of
the wedding.

[2] Logan Pearsall Smith, *The Life and Letters of Sir Henry Wotton* (1907), ii.
32.
[3] C. K. Pooler, *King Henry VIII*, Arden ed. (1915, 1936), citing B. L. Harl.
MS. 7002 f.268.
[4] See *King Henry VIII* ed. John Margesson, New Cambridge Shakespeare,
1–3, citing M. J. Cole, *Shakespeare Quarterly* 32 (1981), 352.

THE REIGN OF KING EDWARD THE THIRD (1596) AND SHAKESPEARE

By RICHARD PROUDFOOT

Read 23 April 1985

THREE years ago, when this lecture was last delivered in Burlington House, Emrys Jones began by revealing that his title, 'The First West End Comedy', far from introducing a revolutionary reading of *The Merry Wives of Windsor*, had nothing to do with Shakespeare. As the directions to British Academy Shakespeare lecturers allow them the choice of any topic concerned with the history of English drama, his decision was to speak about Ben Jonson's *Epicene*. Last year, Glynne Wickham, lecturing on *King Henry VIII*, deliberately avoided reference to the question of the authorship of a play generally conceded to be the collaborative work of Shakespeare and his younger colleague, John Fletcher—for all its inclusion in the First Folio. Today I shall talk on a topic which may, or may not, be Shakespearian, and I intend to postpone the question of whether or not it is until very late in my lecture.

Neither of the lectures to which I refer was delivered on 23 April. When I was invited to give this year's lecture, it was suggested that 'the birthday' might be a suitable date for it. The date had some bearing on my choice of topic. The day wherein our author's birth is celebrated in his role of National Poet of England is the anniversary of the foundation of the chivalric order of St George, better known, from soon after its inception in 1348, as the Order of the Garter. Edward III founded it, and the pleasantly scandalous myth of its foundation, first recorded by Polydore Vergil in his *Anglicae Historiae*, is among the few scraps of information about his long reign still widely current.

Alas, we do not know beyond reasonable doubt that we are right in celebrating today William Shakespeare's 421st birthday—and I do not offer any solution to the perplexed question of his authorship of the historical play *The Reign of King Edward III*, which—to cap my catalogue of frustrations—fails to include the stageworthy episode at the victory ball for the battle of Crécy, held at Calais in 1347, when a court lady lost a garter, and the gallant king, retrieving it, also retrieved his own reputation by coining the Garter motto, '*Honi soit qui mal y pense*'.

William Shakespeare did die on 23 April. The tradition that it was also his birthday dates only from the eighteenth century. His baptism on the 26th tells against it: by normal usage, a baby born on the 23rd would have been baptized on the next holy day, the 25th, St Mark's Day. On the whole, the 21st, the 22nd—even perhaps the 25th—look likelier as his true date of birth, sadly depriving him both of an 'especially appropriate' birthday and of the strange chance of matching in life the fate of his Cassius, dead on his birthday, or his Cleopatra, dead soon after the gaudy night of a final birthday party.[1] Edward III did not die on 23 April, but he did make his last official public appearance on this day in 1377, when he created two new young knights of the Garter, his grandsons, Richard of Bordeaux and Henry Bolingbroke, the future kings Richard II and Henry IV.

Just as Shakespeare ought to have had the patriotic tact to be born on St George's Day, but may not have, he as surely ought to have written a play about the philoprogenitive monarch whose seven sons and factious descendants supplied the matter for eight of the ten plays printed as his 'Histories' in 1623, and to whose story he alludes in those plays some twenty times. That he may indeed have written such a play has been the claim of scholars, critics, enthusiasts, and even a few editors, since it was first mooted by Edward Capell in 1760. In the preface to his *Prolusions*, a trial volume of short edited texts preliminary to his complete edition of Shakespeare, Capell wrote as follows of one of them, listed in the table of contents as 'Edward the third, a Play, thought to be writ by SHAKESPEARE'.

But what shall be said of the poem that constitutes the second part? or how shall the curiosity be satisfy'd, which it is probable may have been rais'd by the great Name inserted in the title-page? That it was indeed written by SHAKESPEARE, it cannot be said with candour that there is any external evidence at all: something of proof arises from resemblance between the stile of his earlier performances and of the work in question; and a more conclusive one yet from the consideration of the time it appear'd in, in which there was no known writer equal to such a play: the fable of it too is taken from the same books which that author is

---

[1] S. Schoenbaum, *A Documentary Life of Shakespeare* (Oxford, 1975), p. 20.

known to have follow'd in some other plays; to wit, *Holinshed's* Chronicle, and a book of novels call'd the Palace of Pleasure: But, after all, it must be confess'd that it's being his work is conjecture only, and matter of opinion; and the reader must form one of his own, guided by what is now before him, and by what he shall meet with in perusal of the piece itself.[1]

If Capell's claim remains 'conjecture only, and matter of opinion' over two centuries later, it is mainly because candour still compels the acknowledgement that 'external evidence' remains conspicuously absent. True, in 1656 a catalogue of plays published with an edition of Thomas Goff's *The Careless Shepherdess* lists *Edward III* as Shakespeare's. As it also gives him *Edward II* (Marlowe's tragedy) and *Edward IV* (thought to be by Thomas Heywood), it is hard to see what evidential purpose this list can serve. I propose to attempt some discussion of the anonymous play of *Edward III*, printed in 1596, in which I shall refrain from conjecture about the identity of its author. Then, time and your patience thus allowing, I will speak a little on that question. The first part of my contention is that understanding has sometimes been hampered by a natural desire to further or challenge the association of it with Capell's 'great Name'.

The Reign of King Edward the Third, as published by Cuthbert Burby early in 1596, after entry on the Stationers' Register on 1 December 1595, makes a singularly unattractive little book. Most pages contain a tight column of verse speeches, their beginnings not even signalled by indentation, relieved only by the occasional spaced and centred entry direction. The tightness of the setting allowed the printer, Thomas Scarlet, to squeeze 2,600 lines of text into nine and a half quarto gatherings. Typesetting was by formes, from cast-off copy. This method of setting, which robbed compositors of the aid of an intelligible context, together with what must have been a difficult hand, resulted in a profusion of misprints arising from misreading. Thus three French towns sacked by the English, 'Harfleu, Lo, Crotay', appear as 'Harslen, Lie, Crotag' (vi [III. i].20).[2] More alarming misreadings include the ludicrous 'I will throng a hellie spout of bloud' for 'I will through a Hellespont of bloud' (iii. 152 [II. ii 156]). This line roused Swinburne to paroxysms of rage against the blameless author for

---

[1] *Prolusions* (London, 1760), pp. ix–x.

[2] Quotations from the play are taken from the text of my forthcoming edition for the Clarendon Press. References include, within square brackets, act and scene numbers from the edition in C. F. Tucker Brooke, *The Shakespeare Apocrypha* (Oxford, 1908).

inflicting on his auditors 'the shock of this unspeakable and incomparable verse'.[1]

Speech prefixes are frequently misprinted, misplaced, or omitted. Stage directions, though sparse, are serviceable. They are undetailed about matters of staging: the use of 'above' is never specified, though two scenes imply its use in their dialogue (ii [I. ii], viii [III. v]), and entries by separate doors are only once described by the technical terms *'at one doore'* and *'At an other doore'* (iii [II. ii] 0.1–2). Cues for sound effects, which the play uses freely, are amply provided, suggesting that the manuscript used as printer's copy, though evidently not a theatrical prompt-book, represented a play conceived in very practical theatrical terms. In three or four places obscurity appears to result from misplacing of verse lines or longer passages, conjuring up the vision of an authorial manuscript with marginal alterations or additions. Beneath its superficial flaws, the text of the quarto gives every sign of completeness and of derivation from copy of high authority. The only known early reprint was printed in 1599 by Simon Stafford, again for Burby. Four subsequent transfers of the copyright, between 1609 and 1639, leave room for conjecture that other editions may once have existed. The title-pages of both quartos state that the play *'hath bin sundrie times plaied about the Citie of London'*. No company is named and it is unclear whether 'about' should be construed as within or without the city.

Although no company or playhouse is named on its title-page, the play must have belonged to one of the four adult companies active in the early 1590s, the Queen's Men, Lord Strange's Men, the Earl of Pembroke's Men, and the Admiral's Men. Equally, the only playhouses outside the city of London at which it could have been acted were the Theatre, the Curtain, and the Rose. Performances inside the city could have been at any of the inns whose yards were used for plays. Something can be deduced from the printed text about the resources of the company and the playhouse. An action requiring a large cast of characters has been plotted with care and resourcefulness to be actable, with much doubling, by eleven men, three or four boys, and about ten non-speaking extras. Staging requires no more than two doors for entries, with an invitation to use 'above'. The countess's reference to 'the great Starre-chamber ore our heads' (iii [II. ii]. 161) invites a gesture to the stage canopy 'heavens' to accompany the appeal to a higher court than the king's. Sound effects are many and

---

[1] A. C. Swinburne, *A Study of Shakespeare* (London, 1929), p. 264.

ambitious. They include cannon shot for the naval battle of Sluys (iv [III. i]) and '*A clamor of rauens*' (xiii [IV. v]. 18). Performance in a properly equipped playhouse seems at least to be envisaged, while the casting requirements are those of a full company working in London rather than a touring group.

The doubling has one striking result. Although the Dauphin, Charles, duke of Normandy, is captured at Poitiers with his father and his young brother Philip, he does not appear with them in the final scene. In fact, Charles did escape from Poitiers, to begin an outstandingly effective career as regent and later king of France. But it is no scruple of historical accuracy that occasions his absence. The playwright has a higher card to play. King David II of Scotland is, quite unhistorically, brought over by his captor, John Copeland, to be delivered to King Edward in person at Calais—and the role of King David (seen before only in scene ii) is clearly designed to be doubled with the Dauphin. The point of my reference to these details is to dispel from the outset the thought that *Edward III* can be the work of any poet but one who was proficient and professionally experienced in theatrical composition, who knew the resources of his playhouse and his acting company, and who wrote his play to accommodate and exploit them.

The play apparently enjoyed a continuing reputation. Thomas Heywood, in his *Apology for Actors* (1612), chose it to exemplify the power of historical drama to 'new mold the harts of the spectators and fashion them to the shape of any noble and notable attempt'.

What English Prince should hee behold the true portraiture of that [f]amous King *Edward* the third, foraging France, taking so great a King captiue in his owne country, quartering the English Lyons with the French Flower-delyce, . . . would not bee suddenly Inflam'd with so royall a spectacle, being made apt and fit for the like atchieuement. So of *Henry* the fift: (fol. B4)

That Heywood is referring to our play and no other is confirmed by his inclusion of 'the Countesse of *Salisbury*' (fol. g1v) among examples for the imitation of chaste women, who are 'by vs [the actors] encouraged in their virtues'. Heywood was not the first defender of the stage to jump on the patriotic history play as a reassuring instance of the power of art to shape life. Thomas Nashe, in a well-known passage in *Pierce Penniless*, wrote:

What a glorious thing it is to haue *Henrie* the fifth represented on the stage, leading the French King prisoner, and forcing both him and the Dolphin to sweare fealty.[1]

This is our best evidence that the reign of Henry V had been dramatized by the summer of 1592. The play Nashe refers to does not survive, unless *The Famous Victories of Henry V*, published in 1598, stands in some debased relation to it. In *The Famous Victories*, King Henry does receive homage from the Dauphin in the final scene, but he is not a prisoner, neither is his father, who pays no homage, though the duke of Burgundy does. The reference to royal captives rather recalls the end of *Edward III*, with the triumphant return of Edward from Calais at the head of a party containing 'three kings, two princes, and a queene' (xviii [v]. 243). I do not mean to imply that Nashe was confusing the two plays, rather to point to the obvious resemblance between the careers of the victors of Crécy and Agincourt, and to associate patriotic plays about both with the spirit of the years following the failure of the Spanish Armada in 1588. It seems a pity that the chronicler Edward Hall allotted the tag 'Victorious Acts' to the reign of Henry V. Transferred to the stage, it would have suited *Edward III* much better than the sad fragment we know as *The Famous Victories of Henry V*.

The story of the reign of King Edward III (1312–77) offers a variety of interests. It was a period of rapid military and political development, a period, like the reign of Elizabeth I, in which English national identity was strongly asserted and the longevity of the sovereign helped to validate an image of royal excellence harder to associate with an Edward II, an Edward VI, or a James I. Edward's reign saw the outbreak of what would become the Hundred Years' War; it was savagely punctuated by two visitations of the plague. The king enjoyed unprecedented success in holding his nobility and his own large family in a union of loyalty and singleness of purpose without which his military exploits against the Scots and the French would have been unthinkable. He had a harder time persuading a succession of parliaments to go on raising the cash at least to service the debts incurred by those exploits. His reign began in his minority and its early years were overshadowed by the ascendancy of Roger Mortimer, earl of March, the lover of his mother, Isabelle, daughter of Philippe V of France, nicknamed 'le Beau'. The murders of his father, Edward II, and his uncle, Edmund, earl of Kent, probably implied a risk to young Edward's own life. His

[1] *The Works of Thomas Nashe* (ed. R. B. McKerrow, Oxford, 1958), i. 213.

resolution and the loyalty of his closest friends, among them William Montacute, later earl of Salisbury, achieved the arrest of Mortimer and the Queen at Nottingham Castle in 1330 and the summary execution of Mortimer. Edward's declining years were difficult too. After an active and brilliant military career in which he asserted his control over the Scots and came within striking distance of winning the French crown, he withdrew into an increasingly private retirement. The death, in 1369, of his queen, Philippa of Hainault, mother of his twelve children, diminished his concern for his royal duties. Too heavy a reliance on the comfort and advice of the mistress of his old age, Alice Perrers, was enough to tarnish even his heroic image. When he died, most of what he had won in France had been lost again, though Calais remained under English control until the French recovered it in 1558, at the end of the reign of Mary Tudor. A further sad blow was the eclipse of his eldest son, 'Edward, Black Prince of Wales' (*Henry V*, II. iv. 56). The victor of Poitiers returned to Bordeaux from his Spanish expedition of 1367 a sick man. Ill health forced him to resign his rule over English Aquitaine to his brother John of Gaunt and to return to England, where he predeceased his father, leaving his own surviving second son to succeed in 1377 as King Richard II.

The reign, as retailed by the sixteenth-century English chroniclers, offered two clear opportunities to a dramatist. Christopher Marlowe saw one of them, though naturally his treatment of the accession of Edward III takes second place to the tragedy of his father, and it is Edward II and Mortimer who dominate the closing scenes of his play. Ben Jonson too began a play on 'Mortimer his Fall', but he wrote no more than a synopsis, an opening soliloquy for Mortimer, and a scrap of spirited dialogue between Mortimer and the queen. He conceived the play in Greek form, with heavy reliance on choric narratives, one of which was to tell of the murder of Edward II. The conclusion was to be a wholesome '*Celebration of the Kings Justice*', to follow young Edward's arrest and execution of Mortimer.[1] Jonson abandoned his play—or rather he found a more congenial and less wholesome vehicle for a study of Machiavellian ambition pitted against Machiavellian statecraft when, in 1603, he wrote *Sejanus his Fall* instead.

Our author avoided Edward's early years, perhaps because Marlowe had handled them already, more certainly because

[1] *Ben Jonson*, vii (ed. C. H. Herford and P. and E. Simpson, Oxford, 1941), p. 59.

Isabel's liaison with Mortimer was an undesirable element in a play in which her role was to afford her son an unimpeachable title to the throne of France. Instead, he went for the other, the heroic theme, this time quite certainly with Marlowe in mind. As many critics have remarked, *Edward III* was written by a poet heavily under the influence of *Tamburlaine*.

Edward III is an exercise in variation on a very few themes. Three nations, four theatres of war, twenty years of history, and a wide array of major and minor figures from the chronicles have been reduced with skill and economy to a stage action which, if undeniably repetitious, avoids monotony of treatment and achieves its own high degree of shapeliness and coherence. A range of military actions on different fronts is shaped into a single sequence of interlocking episodes. (Here I must digress to point out that the division of the play's eighteen scenes into five acts, introduced by Capell, is misleading. The true structure is tripartite, though as it happens phase 1 corresponds to Capell's acts I and II, phase 2 to act III and phase 3 to acts IV and V.) Edward's offensive against France in pursuit of the crown (1345–7) is launched in scene i. There follows the main action of phase 1, based on a romantic myth loosely connected with his counter-offensive against the Scots in 1341—his violent infatuation with the countess of Salisbury. This occupies scenes ii and iii. In the second phase, before the authentic events of the expedition of 1345 are staged or reported, we hear an extended report on the naval battle of Sluys fought in 1340 (scene iv). Then we proceed to the crossing of the Somme and the battle of Crécy (scenes vi–viii). Phase 3 treats chronology with similar freedom. The siege and fall of Calais (1346–7) are presented in scenes x and xviii, which frame an extended presentation of the battle of Poitiers (1356), occupying scenes xii–xvii. These two chronologically and topographically distinct events are linked by conflation of yet more quite unconnected matters. The English support, in 1344, for John de Montfort's attempt to seize the dukedom of Brittany, together with an exploit of one of Edward's most glamorous leaders, Sir Walter Manny, related by Froissart[1] as happening in 1346, provide the action of scenes ix and xi. In them, the earl of Salisbury (the play's equivalent to Manny) is implausibly captured on the field of Poitiers while travelling from Brittany to rejoin King Edward at Calais.

The radical reshaping of the material serves several ends. It lets

---

[1] *The Chronicles of Froissart* (ed. W. P. Ker, London, 1901), i. 306–8.

the playwright include seven English victories, staged, related, or merely alluded to. Bringing Poitiers forward by ten years means that Prince Edward, historically a man of twenty-six, can be presented as still the brilliant adolescent, freshman in the school of honour, whom we have just seen winning his spurs at Crécy. Each phase of action culminates in a climax of danger for its central figure, which is then resolved by his escape. The first phase ends when the king, faced with the virtuous countess's resolve rather to kill herself than yield to him, is restored to a true sense of his honour as king and as husband. The relation of the love action to the surrounding war is underlined by insistent military imagery, as the Scottish siege of Roxburgh Castle, raised without a fight, gives way to a more insidious danger to the countess from Edward's 'lingring English seege of peeuish loue' (ii. 189 [II. i. 23]). The second and third phases reach more predictable climaxes with Prince Edward's jeopardy in his two great battles. At Crécy, in a heightened version of Froissart's account, the king refuses not one but three requests to send aid to his cornered son, on the grounds that 'we gaue him armes to day, /And he is laboring for a knighthood' (viii [III. v]. 17–18). The prince wins his spurs, returning to his father '*in tryumph, bearing in his hande his shiuered Launce, and the King of Boheme, borne before, wrapt in the Coullours*' (viii [III. v]. 60. 1–3). This is a hard act to follow. Phase 3 accordingly varies the pattern, allowing the spectators the double satisfaction, first of seeing the prince's miraculous victory against overwhelming odds at Poitiers, then of watching with superior knowledge as the king and Queen Philippa first learn from Salisbury of the inevitability of their son's defeat and death and then welcome his arrival at newly-won Calais, this time with a bag consisting of King John of France and his son Philip.

The playwright's freedom with chronology has consequences for his handling of his characters. King Edward and the Black Prince, indeed, appear chiefly in actions for which there is warrant in the chronicle sources. The king's role is confined to command, leaving active participation in the fighting to the prince. English solidarity is reinforced by the continued presence of three lords, Derby, Audley, and Robert of Artois. Artois, a French exile, strengthens our sense of the justice of Edward's claim to the French crown. It is he who first presents it, in the opening scene. Restatements of his right are also put into the mouths of French characters. Artois later appears beside the prince at both big battles. Audley's only moment of glory in the chronicles is at Poitiers. The play introduces him in the first scene, expanding his role into that of Aged Experience, the proper foil and companion for the prince's Youthful Valour.

The earl of Salisbury is harder to place. He enters the play only in scene ix. After he does so, no reference is ever made to the countess, whose husband we must presume him to be. As his actions are mainly borrowed from Sir Walter Manny, this need not much surprise us. Only the threat of summary execution when he is captured relates him to the historical Salisbury, who was similarly treated in 1339.[1] His name matters, though. It is our cue for recognizing that the episode of his search for a passport to travel to Calais, in the third phase of action, stands in thematic relation to the countess episode in the first. Salisbury's survival depends on awakening the Dauphin's sense of princely honour, and on the Dauphin's resistance to his father's will. Similarly, the countess escapes suicide—or a fate worse than death—by reawakening the lustful King Edward to a true sense of *his* honour. Few details in the play argue so strongly for care in plotting and for unity of conception as the balance struck between the quite separate actions that centre respectively on the countess and the earl of Salisbury.

On the French side, the main alteration of history is to name the king of France 'Iohn of Valoys' (i [I. i]. 37) in its opening scene. As John only succeeded his father, Philippe VI, in 1350, all his actions in the play except his capture at Poitiers are in fact his father's. Clearly the playwright decided that two French kings were one too many: besides, he wanted to introduce John's two sons with their father in the Crécy sequence by way of preparation for their more prominent share in the action at Poitiers.

Though I have so far referred to the chronicle sources of *Edward III* without much particularity, it should be apparent that I assume consultation of more than one. Beyond possibility of doubt, the playwright made careful use of Lord Berners's English version of the chronicles of Froissart, which depend in their turn, for this early period of Froissart's work, on the writings of an older French writer, Jean le Bel. Froissart sticks very close to le Bel, as became clear when le Bel's long-lost work resurfaced after five hundred years in the nineteenth century. Our author also used Holinshed—who taught him, among other things, to spell the names of French towns misprinted in the 1596 quarto. He appears to have consulted one of Stow's chronicles too, on the evidence of a small detail: Stow alone speaks, as does the play, of the emperor's appointment of Edward as lieutenant-general of the Empire,

---

[1] *Froissart*, i. 132–3.

where the others call him vicar-general. Altogether, the play is as remarkable for the quantity of authentic detail it packs in as for its cavalier way with chronology.

The tone of the play's portrayal of King Edward and the Black Prince is closer to the sanctimonious English jingoism of Holinshed and Stow than to the chivalrous generosity of Froissart, a writer of broad and international sympathies. Prince Edward's rhetoric smacks strongly of what A. P. Rossiter, in another connection, called the 'Hotspurious'. He comes close to a later description of him by John Webster:

> Hee that like lightning did his force aduance,
> And shook toth' Center the whole Realm of *France*,
> That of warme bloud open'd so many sluces,
> To gather and bring thence sixe *Flower de Luces*.[1]

After Poitiers, he greets King John, who has fought heroically in the face of foreseen defeat, with the derisive lines:

> Now Iohn in France, and lately Iohn of France,
> Thy bloudie Ensignes are my captiue colours:

> (xvii [IV. ix]. 1-2)

This is a far cry indeed from Froissart's prince who won the praise of friend and foe by the humanity and humility with which he treated his royal captive.

Sir, methynke ye ought to rejoyse, though the journey be nat as ye wolde have had it, for this day ye have wonne the hygh renome of prowes and have past this day in valyantnesse all other of your partie: sir, I say natte this to mocke you, for all that be on our partie that sawe every mannes dedes, ar playnly acorded by true sentence to gyve you the price and chapellette.[2]

The play's King Edward is the king of the woodcut portrait that heads his reign in the chronicles of Holinshed and Stow. It shows an armed man, with a crown on his helmet, looking suspiciously over his right shoulder, an orb clutched in his left hand and in his right a sword on which two more crowns are broached. To the crowns of England, France, and Scotland, the play adds a coronet, sent in homage by Mountford, duke of Brittany.

Another familiar image of Edward derived from coins first struck in 1344. They bear the device of the king as King of England and Lord of France. Crowned and armed with his sword and with a shield quartered with the arms of England and France,

---

[1] *A Monumental Column* (London, 1613), B1.
[2] *Froissart*, i. 384.

he stands on a ship, its sails filled with a following wind. The device commemorated his naval victory off Sluys in 1340. In 1894, J. K. Laughton, editor of state papers relating to the Spanish Armada, wrote of it:

> ·It was no mere coincidence which led to the adoption of such a device in 1344, four years after the most bloody and decisive victory of western war . . . which by giving England the command of the sea, determined the course of the great war which followed.[1]

The device, he added, was 'still in use under Elizabeth, telling to those who could understand it that the might and majesty of England rested on her navy'. These facts may help us to understand the play's treatment of two of its battles, Sluys and Poitiers. The connection between the naval engagements of 1340 and 1588, which saved England from two of the most acute risks it has ever faced of invasion across the Narrow Seas, was not lost on our playwright. His account of Sluys differs radically from the chronicle narrative. The divergent details, as K. P. Wentersdorf pointed out, include several drawn from accounts of the Armada.[2] Among them are a description of Edward's fleet as a 'proud Armado' (iv [III. i]. 64); heavy and anachronistic emphasis on naval gunnery; the use of the name '*Nom per illa*' for a French warship (one of Drake's squadron was the *Nonpareil*); and, most strikingly, this image for the English formation:

> Maiesticall the order of their course,
> Figuring the horned Circle of the Moone,
>
> (iv [III. i]. 71–2)

We may compare Petruccio Ubaldino's description of the Spanish formation:

> their fleete was placed in battell araie, after the maner of a Moone cressant, being readie with her horns & hir inward circumference to receiue either all, or so manie of the English nauie, as should giue her the assault, her hornes being extended in widenes about the distance of 8. miles.[3]

Historically, the Black Prince's victory at Poitiers depended on leading the dismounted French men-at-arms into a trap, a lane where four but went abreast, between hedges manned by the

[1] J. K. Laughton (ed.), *State Papers Relating to the Defeat of the Spanish Armada*, i (London, 1894), ix–x.

[2] 'The Date of *Edward III*', *Shakespeare Quarterly*, xvi (1965), 227–31.

[3] P. Ubaldino, *A Discourse Concerning the Spanish Fleet Invading England in the Year 1588* (London, 1590), p. 7.

redoubted English longbowmen. The play will have none of this, substituting a French trap, in which the English are not only outnumbered but surrounded. Audley's description of the French positions once more alludes to the Armada formation:[1]

> Behinde vs too the hill doth beare his height,
> For like a halfe Moone opening but one way,
> It rounds vs in:
>
> (xii [iv. iv]. 30-2)

Both battles, Sluys and Poitiers, are thus assimilated with memories of the Armada narrative which the playwright could presumably rely on his audience to supply.

During the probable period for the play's composition, say 1590-5, English soldiers were continually in action in France and Brittany, fighting on behalf of Henry of Navarre against his Catholic opponents and their Spanish allies. In addition to the Armada references, its presentation of the siege of Calais, while following its chronicle sources with some fidelity, shows remarkable resemblances to accounts of the siege of Paris published in England in the early 1590s.[2]

One other work, Marlowe's *Tamburlaine*, has left a pervasive mark on *Edward III*. Both plays dramatize an almost unbroken succession of battles. Edward's campaign in France shows many similarities to Marlowe's version of the campaigns of his younger Scythian contemporary. Among these are his adversary's scornful view of him as 'A theeuish pyrate, and a needie mate', and his offer of 'Exceeding store of treasure, perle, and coyne' as an incentive to the English army to fight 'manfully' (vi [iii. iii]. 53, 67, 71). Edward's threats against Calais echo those of Tamburlaine against Damascus and he is ready, when he thinks his son dead, to promise savage revenge:

> ... in the stead of tapers on his tombe,
> An hundred fiftie towers shall burning blaze,
> While we bewaile our valiant sonnes decease.
>
> (xviii [v]. 173-5)

We may also think of Tamburlaine in an earlier scene, when Edward seeks for poetic expression of the perfections of the countess of Salisbury. The important episode of the king's love for the countess comes, as Capell said, from William Painter's

---

[1] The point is made by F. Lapides in his edition of *Edward III* (London and New York, 1980), p. 33.

[2] See, e.g. *A Letter . . . from . . . Saint Denis* (London, 1590), B3ᵛ-4.

Palace of Pleasure (1566–7). Capell did not add that Painter's story itself comes from Matteo Bandello's *novella* of 1554, which was a fictional expansion of the episode as described by Froissart. The play uses much that is in Painter, but it follows Froissart in making both characters married, so that the catastrophe of the king's wooing cannot be a nuptial. The playwright enlarges on stray references to Edward's courtiers in Froissart and Painter to integrate characters from the military plot with the romantic episode. Derby, Audley, and the Black Prince all come to Roxburgh Castle, ready and eager to embark for France. Their presence heightens the tension of the king's temporary alienation from his proper royal role. When Audley arrives, he is curtly dismissed by Edward:

> *Audley.* I haue my liege, leuied those horse and foote,
> According to your charge, and brought them hither.
> *King.* Then let those foote trudge hence vpon those horse,
> According too our discharge and be gonne.

> (iii [ii. ii]. 30–3)

Painter supplies two extra characters: Warwick, as father of the countess, and Edward's secretary, though a third, the countess's mother, is relegated to a single passing mention (at ii. 536 [ii. i. 727]), doubtless to keep down the demand for boy players. From Painter's discreet and obedient secretary, the playwright has developed Lodwick, the first opponent to the king's pursuit of the lady, a subtle upholder of right values who, when called on to compose a love-poem, uses his awareness of its intended recipient to present the king instead with the opening lines of a verse sermon against adultery. His is the only comic part in the play: it persuades us, from the very inception of the king's passion, that the outcome will be a happy one. Not for nothing did John Barton include his first dialogue with King Edward in his popular dramatic anthology, *The Hollow Crown*.

Much conjecture and controversy surrounds the question whether this romantic episode bears any relation to historical events, indeed, whether the countess of Salisbury in it is more than a conventional figure of fiction. The topic deserves a separate lecture, so a brief summary must suffice. Both versions of the story known to the playwright are clearly fictitious. Chapters 76, 77, and 89 of Froissart's first book charmingly elaborate a romantic moral tale, a cliff-hanger of virtue in danger, of wifely continence and constancy preserved by royal recovery from unbridled passion to the right reassertion of self-government. The themes were dear to

English playwrights of the 1590s and earlier. They abound in plays like John Lyly's *Campaspe*, Robert Greene's *James IV* and *Friar Bacon and Friar Bungay* or the anonymous *A Knack to Know a Knave*. The moral is proverbial: 'He is not fit to rule others that cannot rule himself.' No one in the sixteenth century could possibly have known that Froissart, usually slavish in his following of Jean le Bel, here rewrote him. Recovery of le Bel's chronicle uncovered a very different story, the tragic tale of the violent rape of Alice, countess of Salisbury, by King Edward, of the reactions of his friend, her husband, and of her miserable death.

Michael Packe, in a recent biography of Edward III which has not, in this particular, won universal assent, presents documentary evidence held to substantiate the central fact of le Bel's story, despite much divergence of detail.[1] What concerns us as readers of the play is that the fictional countess in it may owe something to three historical originals. They are:

1. Catherine, countess of Salisbury, wife of Edward's closest friend and for some time governess of the royal children.

2. Joan, 'the Fair Maid of Kent'. She was countess of Kent in the right of her father Edmund, half-brother to Edward II, and countess of Salisbury only in expectation and only during the years of her second (and bigamous) marriage to Catherine's son, William Montacute junior. After the dissolution of her marriage to him and the death of her first husband, Sir Thomas Holland, she was to remarry, with the Black Prince, and give birth to Richard II.

3. Alice, never countess of Salisbury, but wife of Edward Montacute, the earl's youngest brother. In 1341, it was probably she and her husband who held Wark Castle (not Roxburgh) against the Scots. She, if anyone, was the victim of King Edward's lust. She died in 1351, after being violently beaten by her husband, whose prosecution was quashed by the king.

The countess in the play combines the title of Catherine with her daughter-in-law's fabled attractions. Alice, lost to memory with le Bel's chronicle, strangely survived in the fictional tradition—or at least her name did. Bandello called his countess of Salisbury 'Ælips', and variants of that name, Alice among them, recur in derivative versions of his story, more than a dozen of which were already known by the end of the sixteenth century.[2] Bandello

---

[1] M. Packe, *King Edward III* (ed. L. C. B. Seaman, London and Boston, 1983), pp. 105–23, 175–8.

[2] See G. Liebau, *König Eduard III. von England und die Gräfin von Salisbury* (Berlin, 1900).

may have invented the name, or he may have heard of Edward's mistress, Alice Perrers, but the remote possibility remains of a tradition of an 'Alice, countess of Salisbury', with whom Edward's name was associated, whether romantically or shamefully—a tradition fresh enough to prompt, and to survive, the whitewash job performed by Queen Philippa's good servant Froissart when he turned le Bel's tale of rape and remorse into one of wholesome morality and romantic sentiment.

What is critically useful here is chiefly a sense that in its treatment of the countess story, as much as in its treatment of Edward's campaigns, the play is pulling its punches. Serious issues are broached, but the serious potential of pain in both actions is evaded or sublimated, either into rhetoric or into a poetry that is more often lyrical or epic than engagedly dramatic. The tone of the countess scenes is well captured by Cyrus Hoy, who writes of the 'utter simplicity' of moral bearings in our playwright's handling of an episode 'fully stocked with a store of romantic, not to say erotic, potential which the Jacobean dramatists and their successors would prove themselves adept in the art of exploiting'.[1]

Criticism of *Edward III* has habitually taken as its focus the question of the Shakespearian or un-Shakespearian quality of the writing. Risking the charge of perversity or evasiveness, I propose to comment briefly on some other aspects of the play. As I do so, I cannot help reflecting how hampering it is to have had no opportunity of seeing it performed. William Poel, indeed, adapted the countess scenes into a one-acter, *The King and the Countess*, which was acted, evidently with some success, on rare occasions in 1890 and 1897. It was revived at the Old Vic for his centenary in 1954.[2] In 1977, a BBC radio series of twenty-six episodes drawn from Elizabethan history plays and called *Vivat Rex* included in its third and fourth parts heavily cut selections, mainly from the countess scenes and the Crécy and Poitiers sequences. Recent rumours of an intended production at the Nottingham Playhouse have proved over-optimistic (though new hopes have since arisen of a production at the Greenwich Theatre in the early summer of 1986). The play is clearly conceived in terms of performance and of the physical resources of its theatre.

The challenge of the heroic subject is to avoid monotony and bathos. *Edward III* achieves a modest success on both counts. It

---

[1] 'Renaissance and Restoration Dramatic Plotting', *Renaissance Drama*, ix (1966), 261–2.

[2] R. Speaight, *William Poel and the Elizabethan Revival* (London, 1954), pp. 73, 122–3, 190.

never stages any fighting. The nearest we get to it is the spectacle of the Black Prince chasing the French just before his moment of gravest peril at Crécy. Military trappings, though, are much in evidence. Many scenes demand weapons, armour, or flags, while the sound effects most in demand are trumpets and drums. Though the imagery of storm, smoke, and darkness pervades the battle scenes, thunder is not called for. Battles are narrated in formal and sometimes long messengers' speeches. Among the most impressive is this characterization of the advance of Edward's forces through northern France. It is spoken by a nameless French refugee:

> Flie cuntry men and cytizens of France.
> Sweete flowring peace the roote of happie life,
> Is quite a bandoned and expulst the lande,
> In sted of whome ransackt constraining warre
> Syts like to Rauens vppon your houses topps.
> Slaughter and mischiefe walke within your streets,
> And vnrestrained make hauock as they passe:
> The forme whereof euen now my selfe beheld,
> Vpon this faire mountaine whence I came,
> For so far of as I directed mine eies,
> I might perceaue fiue Cities all on fire,
> Corne fieldes and vineyards burning like an ouen,
> And as the leaking vapour in the wind
> Tourned but a side, I like wise might disserne
> The poore inhabitants escapt the flame,
> Fall numberles vpon the souldiers pikes.
> Three waies these dredfull ministers of wrath
> Do tread the measures of their tragicke march:
> Vpon the right hand comes the conquering King,
> Vpon the lefte his hot vnbridled sonne,
> And in the midst our nations glittering hoast,
> All which though distant yet conspire in one
> To leaue a desolation where they come.

> (v [III. ii]. 46–68)

The imagined mountain top from which this panoramic view is taken recurs. The French at Poitiers are in hilltop positions, and King John sends Salisbury to witness their expected victory from

> . . . a loftie hill,
> Whose top seemes toplesse, for the imbracing skie
> Doth hide his high head in her azure bosome,
> Vpon whose tall top when thy foot attaines,
> Looke backe vpon the humble vale beneath,

Humble of late, but now made proud with armes,
And thence behold the wretched prince of Wales,
Hoopt with a bond of yron round about,

(xiii [IV. v]. 113–20)

Chivalry is theatrical. To the pictorial theatricality of these panoramas, the play adds the spectacle of the formal investiture of the Black Prince in his arms before Crécy and of his battered but triumphant return.

The alternation of love and war in scenes ii and iii cannot continue in the later scenes in France, but tone and pace are still carefully varied. The strongest emotions are evoked in scenes of quiet tension which precede or follow those of belligerent rhetoric, the clearest instance being the scene before Poitiers when the aged Audley counsels and comforts the Black Prince as he contemplates the imminence of death.

Without experience of the play in performance, it is harder to speak confidently of visual effects, but a few may be suggested. Actions are sometimes linked in pairs or larger patterns. In scene ii [I. ii], in an action memorably described by Froissart, the countess descends from her battlements to open the castle gates to the king. The play elaborates his reluctance to enter, forcing her to plead for the royal visit which will imperil her honour. After Crécy, it is Edward's turn to descend from the 'little hill' (viii [III. v]. 2) to which he has withdrawn and reward his victorious son with knighthood. As at Roxburgh Castle, so at the siege of Calais, the opening of the gates is a significant action. The gates open twice and each time six men emerge: in scene x [IV. ii], they are poor men, driven out by the captain to save provisions; in scene xviii, the six burghers whose surrender Edward has imposed as a condition of clemency come out, '*in their Shirts, bare foote, with halters about their necks*' (xviii [v]. 0. 1–2). The two sieges are thus linked and a contrast is suggested between the earlier treachery of the king's assault on a loyal subject and his final magnanimity towards defenceless enemies. Only two identified women appear in the play. The early prominence of the countess has its counterpart in Queen Philippa's arrival in the last scene, 'big with child' (x [IV. ii]. 45), as so often. Any vestige of blame attaching to Edward for the adulterous frenzy in which he was ready to contemplate killing his wife is removed by that wife's entry, visibly in enjoyment of his conjugal attentions, to repeat the countess's role of moderator of his passions as she kneels to plead for the lives of the six burghers.

Thematic links as well as visual relate different areas of the episodic action to each other. Sometimes they correspond with patterns of character. The two kings, Edward and John, are contrasted in terms of right to and possession of the French crown. They exchange mutual accusations of tyranny, clearly justified by John's readiness to turn the field of Crécy to a 'poole of bloode' and a 'slaughter house' (vi [III. iii]. 116-17) and as clearly refuted by Edward's acts of generosity and mercy. Admittedly this balance is only maintained by the expedient of transferring to the Black Prince an English bloodthirstiness which contrasts him with the varieties of arrogant timidity displayed by the French princes.

The historical subject is much concerned with oaths of allegiance, whether to one's monarch, or in the form of homage to a feudal lord. In the play, Edward refuses homage to John for a French dukedom, claiming the right of sovereignty over him. Mountford sends a coronet to Edward in token of his homage for the dukedom of Brittany. Both the countess and her father, Warwick, are tricked by Edward into swearing to help to relieve his distress before they learn that its cause is his guilty passion for the lady. Both escape with honour. The countess does so by opposing her marriage vows to her duty to the king:

> He that doth clip or counterfeit your stamp
> Shall die my Lord, and will your sacred selfe
> Comit high treason against the King of heauen,
> To stamp his Image in forbidden mettel,
> For getting your alleageance, and your othe?
> In violating mariage sacred law,
> You breake a greater honor then your selfe.
> To be a King is of a yonger house
> Then to be maried: your progenitour,
> Sole raigning Adam on the vniuerse,
> By God was honored for a married man,
> But not by him annointed for a king.

> (ii. 420-31 [II. i. 255-66])

Warwick keeps the letter of his oath to the king, first wooing his daughter for him, then applauding her opposition. 'It is the purpose that makes strong the vow; / But vows to every purpose must not hold', as William Shakespeare would one day write in his *Troilus and Cressida* (v. iii. 23-4). Oaths regain prominence in the Salisbury/Villiers scenes. Unexpectedly, the outcome of this action is to vindicate French honour. Villiers, a French prisoner, is released, on his parole to return, to obtain a passport for Salisbury from his childhood friend, Charles, the Dauphin. 'Thus once I meane to trie a French mans faith' is Salisbury's comment (ix [IV. i]. 43). Charles urges Villiers to break his parole, insisting on the superior force of his oath of allegiance. Villiers resists, impressing Charles to the point of granting the passport. When Salisbury is captured at Poitiers, the action is repeated, Charles in turn resisting his father, King John, thus saving Salisbury from hanging on the next tree and his own honour from impeachment. This vindication of the honour of a soldier and of a prince stands in direct relation to the vindication of the countess's honour as a faithful wife. The theme recurs in a lighter vein in the final scene, when King Edward applauds the refusal of Copeland to surrender King David of Scotland to Queen Philippa, on the grounds that he loves the king's person more than his name (xvii [v]. 83-7).

As with themes, so with images. Critics who believe in collaborative authorship, particularly those who want to assign to Shakespeare the countess scenes and little more, have seriously understated the extent to which those scenes owe their metaphoric richness to material derived from the military action. To cite one clear instance: the king's line, 'Ah but alas she winnes the sunne of me' (iii [II. ii]. 66), uses a military image that would have been strongly impressed on the mind of any poet who had just read Froissart. Both at Sluys and at Crécy, the English tactics included 'winning the sun' of the French. Conversely, the military action contains images drawn from love and marriage, notably Prince Edward's plea to Audley:

> Thou art a married man in this distresse,
> But danger wooes me as a blushing maide:
> Teach me an answere to this perillous time.

> (xi [IV. iv]. 130-2)

Although time must have a stop, history has no ending. A playwright's first decision must be where to start and where to conclude his action. To conflate the victory of Poitiers, the taking of Calais, the winning of Brittany and the capture of David II at Neville's Cross into a single final scene is as strong a statement of commitment to English patriotic values as can easily be imagined. Philip Edwards writes of the ending of Shakespeare's *Henry V* that, 'while it is quite legitimate for an historical dramatist to conclude his play at a moment of actual triumph and peace, the feeling which he may give of the achievement being final and the peace permanent belongs to the experience of art'.[1] Shakespeare added an epilogue to *Henry V*, reminding his audience of the disasters to

[1] *Threshold of a Nation* (Cambridge, 1979), p. 112.

follow, 'Which oft our stage hath shown'. In *Edward III*, before
Poitiers, King John of France hears a riddling prophecy of French
defeat. It ends:

> Yet in the end thy foot thou shalt aduance,
> As farre in England, as thy foe in Fraunce.

> (xi [IV. iii]. 72-3)

He sees that this could foretell his future success in invading
England, only to recognize his error at the end, as a prisoner
awaiting shipment to England:

> Accursed man, of this I was fortolde,
> But did misconster what the prophet told.

> (xviii [V]. 214-15)

Was the author of *Edward III* aware that, by the 1590s, the
prophecy had an ironic ring? That, though Englishmen were
fighting in France, it was in support of Henry of Navarre and
not of any English territorial claim? That now England's foot
extended no further in France that France's in England? If so, he
excluded the awareness from his play.

In *Shakespeare and the Rhetoricians*, a challenging enquiry into the
ways in which understanding of sixteenth-century rhetoricians'
ideas of the topic of invention may help us to a truer picture of
what an Elizabethan poet might have supposed he was doing,
Marion Trousdale observes that 'a play in which attitude is
predetermined is not by virtue of that fact bad. A point of view,
even if doctrinaire, ought not to occasion suspicion of the art.'[1]
Edward III appears to reflect the working of an artistic intelligence
of the highest order on material which, though far from merely
uncongenial, is in many ways constricting. Intelligence and
theatrical professionalism warm into full imaginative engagement
only sporadically, and not always for long at a time. It is most
apparent where we might expect it, in the fictional episode of the
countess of Salisbury, where rhetorical energy takes off into flights
of poetic and emotional power and where a comic spirit, starved
elsewhere by the heroic theme, enjoys brief nourishment. Here,
and in the dialogue of Prince Edward and Audley before Poitiers,
the playwright was free of the burden, self-imposed though it
probably was, of a quantity of historical material whose mere
exposition must have taxed his constructive powers. Slackness of
imaginative engagement with the patriotic matter is reflected in
the play's repetitiveness. Some of the repetitions, among them the

[1] (London, 1982), p. 124.

much-studied 'recurrent images' and those patterns of action and theme to which I have referred, may be felt to develop cumulative meaning. Others, I submit, more likely reflect an orderly mind writing at speed and under some pressure to meet a deadline.

One lapse of imaginative concentration curiously damages the play's handling of Edward's claim to the French crown. Arguing that the disparity of numbers between his own small force and the surrounding French multitudes at Poitiers can be minimized by speaking of each as merely one army, Prince Edward hits on a positively Freudian analogy:

> There is but one Fraunce, one king of Fraunce,
> That Fraunce hath no more kings, and that same king
> Hath but the puissant legion of one king?

> (xii [IV. iv]. 61–3)

The prince may refer to the office rather than the man, but it is natural to identify that 'one king' with John of Valois—and the prince is fighting for his father's claim that he, rather than John, is truly the one king of France. Inevitably, our minds move forward to another King John—Shakespeare's—and to a more extended debate as to just who may be the true King of France.

And Shakespeare?

Can *Edward III* be accommodated within any panoramic view of his works? Without arguing the case, may I draw your attention to some of the points of contact. Like *Romeo and Juliet*, *Othello*, and *Troilus and Cressida*, *Edward III* combines stories of love and fighting, integrating them with each other by cross-reference of theme and image. Like *3 Henry VI*, *Richard III*, and *Measure for Measure*, it shows man in authority using his position to attempt to coerce the love of a subject. Like *Lucrece*, it employs the image of siege warfare for a sexual assault. Like *Romeo and Juliet*, *Love's Labour's Lost*, and *Richard II*, it uses recurring metaphors, of which the siege is one of the most prominent, as a structural technique. As in *The Two Gentlemen of Verona*, rather more than half of the action consists of duologues. Like *The Two Gentlemen*, *Love's Labour's Lost*, and *As You Like It*, it introduces cynical comment on the use of poetry in courtship. Like *3 Henry VI*, *Richard II*, and *King John*, it is written in verse throughout. Like *1 Henry VI*, *King John*, and *Henry V*, it dramatizes English wars in France. It shares with *King John* a central concern with the rival claims of strong possession and right for the crown of France (though not that of England). Its treatment of King Edward and the Black Prince includes an element of the educative theme central to *Henry IV*.

Unlike *Henry V*, it has not discovered the expedients of choric commentary and comic subplot to alleviate the pressures of an heroic military action. Like *Richard III*, *Macbeth*, and *The Winter's Tale*, it uses prophecies to control audience expectations. Like *1 Henry IV* and *Henry V*, it celebrates military honour. Unlike *The Merry Wives of Windsor*, it makes no reference to the Order of the Garter. Like *The Two Gentlemen*, *Love's Labour's Lost*, *All's Well that Ends Well*, and *Measure for Measure*, it dramatizes conflicts of loyalty and explores the proposition that there may be circumstances in which one must break an oath to find, or preserve, one's self. Like *Hamlet* and *Measure for Measure*, it treats of the art of dying well.

Some of these analogies are closer than others—but the list is only illustrative. Of verbal parallels, especially with the earliest plays and the poems, I need say nothing. They are legion, and they have been thoroughly explored.[1] The line 'Lillies that fester, smel far worse then weeds' (ii. 617 [II. i. 451]), shared by the play and Sonnet 94, is only the most famous, and was one of the earliest clues on the trail that has led to the convergence of the play and the name of Shakespeare.

It is more than time to ask some simple questions. They are not independent of each other. When was *Edward III* written? For whom was it written? Who wrote it? The casting pattern corresponds exactly with the findings of Scott McMillin's investigation of five plays that make up the known repertoire of Pembroke's Men.[2] Three of them, adaptations of Shakespeare's *Taming of the Shrew*, and *2* and *3 Henry VI*, were printed, in reported texts, in 1594 and 1595. Pembroke's Men were among the three companies that had acted *Titus Andronicus* before it was printed in 1594. Their fifth play is Marlowe's *Edward II*. MacDonald Jackson has demonstrated that the reporter of the *Henry VI* plays distorted several passages under the influence of his knowledge of *Edward III*.[3]

Pembroke's Men remains an obscure company. We know that it broke up before September 1593. We are less sure when it was formed, probably, though, in 1591 or 1592. In June 1592 plague deaths rose to the point at which London playhouses were closed.

---

[1] See especially V. Østerberg, 'The "Countess Scenes" of "Edward III"', *Shakespeare Jahrbuch*, lxv (1929), 49–91; K. P. Wentersdorf, 'The Authorship of "Edward III"' (Ph.D. thesis for the University of Cincinnati, 1960).

[2] 'Casting for Pembroke's Men', *Shakespeare Quarterly*, xxiii (1972), 141–59.

[3] '*Edward III*, Shakespeare, and Pembroke's Men', *Notes and Queries*, ccx (1965), 329–31.

They stayed shut for some eighteen months. If *Edward III* was written for Pembroke's Men, then late 1591 or early 1592 seem the likeliest dates of composition. The players who made up the company came from two others, Lord Strange's Men and the Queen's Men. From Strange's Men they acquired their four Shakespeare plays, from the Queen's Men they probably added to their repertoire *The Famous Victories of Henry V*, *The Troublesome Reign of King John*, *The True Tragedy of Richard III*, and the old play of *King Leir*. G. M. Pinciss has pointed out that the plays which Shakespeare knew well enough to quote from or parody in later years include several from this repertoire.[1] Shakespeare also knew *Edward III*—so well that there are few of his plays from 1594 onwards that have not been shown, more or less convincingly, to reflect that knowledge. It is most apparent in the two plays whose actions most resemble the elements of *Edward III*, namely *Henry V* and *Measure for Measure*. The degree of similarity has been fully demonstrated, most impressively by Kenneth Muir.[2]

Cuthbert Burby entered the manuscript, possibly an authorial one, on the Stationers' Register on 1 December 1595. On 28 November the Admiral's Men at the Rose had presented a new, or refurbished, play of 'harey the v', playing it thirteen times between that date and 15 July 1596.[3] The coincidence seems hardly casual. Someone evidently decided, late in November 1595, that the stage career of *Edward III* was sufficiently in decline to warrant selling it for publication.

These facts will afford the circumstantial basis at least for a romantic hypothesis that could connect Shakespeare and *Edward III*. It goes like this. Shakespeare wrote the play, in 1591 or 1592, for Pembroke's Men. He may for a time have belonged to the company, long enough to acquire an actor's familiarity with their repertoire. He wrote it after *2* and *3 Henry VI*, at a time when he already had in mind a long poem about the rape of Lucretia (alluded to in the play as 'her whose ransackt treasurie hath taskt / The vaine indeuor of so many pens' (iii [ii. ii]. 192–3]). Either he took his manuscript with him when he joined the Lord Chamberlain's Men in 1594, or it remained in the hands of some other member of Pembroke's Men. In either case, the Admiral's Men's 'harey the v' put paid to its hopes of revival, or—to retain

---

[1] 'Shakespeare, her Majesty's Players and Pembroke's Men', *Shakespeare Survey*, xxvii (1974), 129–36.

[2] *Shakespeare as Collaborator* (London, 1960), chapters ii, iii.

[3] *Henslowe's Diary* (ed. R. A. Foakes and R. T. Rickert, Cambridge, 1961), p. 33.

our sense of the speculative—provided a natural occasion for the publication of a play on so closely related a subject. The latter hypothesis may explain the reprinting of *Edward III* in 1599, the year of Shakespeare's *Henry V*.

The subsequent history of the text is easier to account for. The 1599 reprint came at an awkward moment. Complaints had been heard from Scotland in the previous year that 'the comedians of London should scorn the king and the people of this land in their play'.[1] We do not know what play is meant, but once James VI of Scotland had grown (or shrunk?) into James I of Great Britain, only a hardy stationer would have risked his ears by venturing into print with this exchange between King David and Douglas.

> *King David.* Dislodge, dislodge, it is the king of England.
> *Douglas.* Iemmy my man, saddle my bonny blacke.
> *King David.* Meanst thou to fight, Duglas we are to weake.
> *Douglas.* I know it well my liege, and therefore flie.

> (ii [i. ii]. 56–9)

We may recall that when *Henry V* was printed, in 1600, no Captain Jamy appeared. This is the case of supporters of Shakespeare's authorship of *Edward III* who wish to account for its absence from the First Folio. It is a strong one. As for its omission from Francis Meres's list of titles in *Palladis Tamia* (1598), it may suffice to remember that *Henry VI* is not there either.

Any reader of *Edward III* who is reasonably well-versed in Shakespeare will feel the attraction of Capell's invitation to the exercise of personal connoisseurship. As I have quoted from it, many of you have probably been accepting that invitation— though I missed out the best bits, deliberately, because Professor Muir has scooped them all in his account of the play! But connoisseurship cannot solve the historical problem or answer the question 'Did Shakespeare write it?'.

Investigators have, in recent years, increasingly sought grounds more—or do I mean less?—relative than personal sensibility. No doubt aesthetic estimates must affect our thinking. But if we feel drawn to ask 'Is it good enough for Shakespeare?', we must reflect that the Shakespeare we are to consider is the author of *Henry VI*, *Richard III*, and *The Taming of the Shrew* rather than *Twelfth Night*, *King Lear*, and *The Tempest*. The author, too, of the Ovidian narrative poems, and of the sonnets. To follow Swinburne's line in urging his authorship of *Henry V* as 'one single and simple piece of evidence that Shakespeare had not a finger in

[1] E. K. Chambers, *William Shakespeare*, i (Oxford, 1930), 65.

the concoction of *King Edward III* will no longer do—if it *ever* did.[1] Investigation of the play's language, particularly its exceptionally large vocabulary, and of its imagery, particularly those associative links described as 'image clusters', is far on the way to demonstrating a kind and degree of connection between the whole play and the early works of Shakespeare that amounts to a strong positive case for his authorship—or that of some person unknown.[2] The same evidence by now implies the improbability of the play's being the work of any other known playwright of the early 1590s. Here, however, much work of validation and verification remains to be done, mainly by way of systematic study of those other writers.

The incipient bardolatry that led Capell to offer *Edward III* as a new and minor jewel in Shakespeare's crown has yielded, as Shakespeare studies have grown from cottage craft to heavy industry, to an uneasy sense that we may instead be busy unearthing a skeleton from his cupboard. What is unequivocal is that *Edward III* now stands squarely on the frontier of the Shakespeare canon. Five plays omitted by the editors of the First Folio have been strongly backed as wholly or in part his work. Three of them now generally find a place in collected editions. *Pericles* was in print as his by 1609; *The Two Noble Kinsmen*, as the product of his collaboration with Fletcher, in 1634. Both have now moved from the 'Apocrypha' to the 'Works'. The lines in *The Book of Sir Thomas More* attributed to him on the evidence of handwriting, style, and language, have also won an enigmatic niche, often as an appendix. The 'lost play' of *Cardenio* can hardly follow suit. Even if Lewis Theobald's *Double Falsehood*, printed in 1728, derives from an authentic Jacobean manuscript of a play by Fletcher and Shakespeare, the text he printed is avowedly a thorough adaptation for eighteenth-century stage conditions. *Double Falsehood* may even be a double palimpsest—to wit, Theobald's reworking of Thomas Betterton's adaptation of the Jacobean original.[3]

Edward III was more in evidence in the nineteenth century than it is today. But its tentative appearances, as a 'doubtful play', in

[1] *A Study of Shakespeare*, p. 274.

[2] M. Bell, 'Concordance to the Shakespeare Apocrypha' (MA thesis for the University of Liverpool, 1959); K. P. Wentersdorf, 'The Authorship of "Edward III"'; E. T. O. Slater, 'The Problem of "The Reign of King Edward III" (1596): A Statistical Approach' (Ph.D. thesis for the University of London, 1982).

[3] See J. Freehafer, '*Cardenio*, by Shakespeare and Fletcher', *PMLA*, lxxxiv (1969), 501-13.

complete editions of Shakespeare ceased when the new broom of reintegrationist scholarship reasserted the authority of the Folio canon against the extravagances of such as J. M. Robertson. Its inclusion was, in any case, easier in an age when it was still respectable to regard *Henry VI* as Shakespeare's revision of other men's work and to reject *Titus Andronicus* outright.

Publishers of multi-volume editions, whose stake in Shakespeare might suffer little if *Titus* and *Henry VI* were to vanish from their lists, may view with concern any move to promote yet another early history to canonic rank. Even outside the canon, the play has been separately published only four times in our century. It is harder to see why single-volume complete works should continue to exclude what has become, by the process of elimination I have just outlined, the sole remaining 'doubtful play' which continues, on substantial grounds, to win the support of serious investigators as arguably the work of Shakespeare. Such inclusion would at least shift the burden of proof onto the sceptics, while ensuring renewed access to a play obtainable only in an expensive reprint of an American dissertation[1] or from the fast-disappearing shelves of second-hand English drama.[2]

[1] F. Lapides (ed.), *The Raigne of King Edward the Third: A Critical, Old-Spelling Edition* (London and New York, 1980).

[2] Since this lecture was delivered, an edition in modernized spelling by George Parfitt has been published in the Nottingham Drama Series. Though commendably inexpensive, and though level-headed in its brief but informative introduction and commentary, it presents a grossly inaccurate text.

THE CORRIDORS OF HISTORY: SHAKESPEARE THE RE-MAKER

By GIORGIO MELCHIORI

Read 23 April 1986

THE title of this lecture is not meant as a pun. Though, as you know, in Italian *re* means king, I do not intend to suggest that in writing his histories Shakespeare was assuming the role of king-maker—what I want to stress instead is that the histories, like all his other plays, are better approached by keeping firmly in mind the fact that Shakespeare was first and foremost not a political thinker but a man of the theatre, a supreme expert in a trade or a business—show business—that in many of its essentials has not changed much through the centuries. The most notable change perhaps is in nomenclature: now we speak of the media and of mass response, and compile charts on viewers' or listeners' attendance, but in the first Elizabeth's time the only mass media available were the theatre and the preacher. A frequent mistake we make in trying to draw parallels between then and now is that of using as a term of reference the present-day stage, while we should rather focus on film and television.

To be more specific: leaving aside the private or academic shows, the Theatre and the other London playhouses were built in the 1570s and 1580s to provide entertainment as a money-making proposition. What mattered was the effectiveness of the enter-tainment provided, the story, the action and the acting—not the message or the literary qualities of the show. Of course, some men of letters joined in, but without claiming authorship: they simply contributed their particular skills in exchange for a fee. It took quite a while before popular audiences began to value the names of some theatre poets as a guarantee of a good afternoon's enter-tainment: the title-pages of plays that got into print counted on the names of the companies that acted them rather than on those of the authors. Shakespeare is a case in point: *Titus, Romeo, Richard III* and even the first part of *Henry IV* appeared anonymously, and we have to wait till 1598 to see his name on the title-page of a play.

The parallel is once again with the cinema, where the text of the show is a script in which a number of people have a hand (or at least a main finger, as Thomas Heywood was to say about his contribution to the stage),[1] and which is further modified during the 'shooting'. Henslowe's diary from 1597 to 1603 hardly ever records a payment to a single author for a play: this collaborative practice must date back a number of years, though apparently it petered out at the turn of the century, and possibly somewhat earlier in the case of the Chamberlain's men. In one respect the parallel with the cinema does not hold; while the film, once made, is permanently recorded and remains unchanged (except for possible censorial intervention, manipulation by distributors, or damage to the copy), the play changes with each individual performance so that the printed text of a Shakespeare play, as Stanley Wells so beautifully put it, is merely 'the snapshot that got taken'[2] among the numberless ones that remain unrecorded.

My purpose, though, is to call attention to two common practices in the film industry which were foreshadowed in Elizabethan show business. The best known is that of the sequel or follow-up: when a film has been particularly successful, the same firm and team of actors and script-writers devise new and frequently preposterous adventures for the popular hero, from Tarzan to Frankenstein, from Rocky to Rambo. Incidentally, this has nothing to do with radio or television serials, from the Archers to Coronation Street, to Dallas, to the innumerable and literally endless tele-novellas: these develop from the serial novels of the last century. The sequels instead were certainly practised by the Elizabethans: there would have been no *Death of Robert Earl of Huntington* if his *Downfall* had been a flop.

The second and less noted practice is that of the re-make: when a film has been successful, after a few years a rival company produces a new version of the same subject—especially if drawn from a novel or from history—with a completely different cast and director, possibly a new slant to the story, and hopefully improved technical devices. This is exactly what happened in the Elizabethan or Jacobean theatre, where the rivalry between companies was as fierce as that in the modern film world—and I put it to you that Shakespeare was the greatest expert in re-makes for the Chamberlain's/King's men. We know for certain that at least

---

[1] In the 'Address to the Reader' in his *The English Traveller* (1633) Thomas Heywood claimed that he 'had either an entire hand, or at least a maine finger' in no less than 220 plays.

[2] Letter in *Times Literary Supplement*, 18 January 1985.

three major plays of Shakespeare were new treatments of subjects which had been successful on the stage before, when they had been acted by the Admiral's or the Queen's men. The 'ur-*Hamlet*' is unfortunately lost, of the Admiral's *Troilus* there remains only a leaf of the plot, and probably the much earlier *True Chronicle History of King Leir* would never have got into print if Shakespeare had not produced his masterly re-make of it. Unlike the common run of current film re-makes, Shakespeare's are not just forms of revamping past successes: he went back to the sources of the earlier versions and recast the stories his own way, leaving the treatments presented by the rival companies far behind.

It is my contention that Shakespeare acquired his skill as a re-maker at an early stage and more precisely that he was led to it by the popularity of the history or chronicle play on the public stage in the late eighties and throughout the nineties of the sixteenth century. I shall not enter into the question of the much debated relationship between the *Henry VI* plays and *The Whole Contention*, or even between *Richard III* and the anonymous *True Tragedy*: as David Bevington remarks in *Tudor Drama and Politics*,[1] theatrical censorship became much more sensitive to topical references of what we would now call a political nature from 1593 onwards. The feeling of unrest in the country induced the Master of the Revels to put an end to the tolerance which in previous years had permitted the emergence of what I would call 'alternative histories'—plays for the public theatre criticizing the abuses of authority and underlining the rights of the common people. I suggest that Shakespeare's first re-makes are to be seen within this context, which is better defined in theatrical rather than in strictly political terms. I must refer at this point to my experience in editing with Vittorio Gabrieli *The Book of Sir Thomas More*.[2] There is no time to enter into all the problems set by this play, and I must be content with offering some of the conclusions we have reached. In the first place, far from being an accumulation of stylistically discontinuous fragments, *Sir Thomas More*, once all the additions are put in their proper places, is one of the best

---

[1] D. Bevington, *Tudor Drama and Politics* (Cambridge, Mass., 1968), pp. 230 ff.

[2] Our edition was published by Adriatica Editrice (Bari) in 1981, but we are preparing a completely new and augmented one for the Revels Plays series (Manchester U.P.). The references in the present paper are to Greg's edition (Oxford, Malone Society Reprints, 1911). Act, scene, and line numbering in the quotations from Shakespeare's plays (but not necessarily spelling and punctuation) are from the Riverside Shakespeare (ed. G. Blakemore Evans, Boston, 1974).

constructed plays of the age. It is a coherent whole, dramatically effective: the authors of the additions show a fine sensitivity to the needs of the stage, the smooth sequence of the different scenes within a solid framework represented by the traditional pattern of the *De casibus virorum illustrium*. None of the additions is a gratuitous interpolation: most of them act instead as dramatic links tightening up the overall theatrical structure. But there is one inconsistency, not on the theatrical, but on what I would call the ideological level. Throughout the original version of the play in the hand of Anthony Munday the London citizens are shown as justified in their resentment against the aliens. The behaviour of John Lincoln, the leader of the popular rebellion against the insolent strangers, is nothing short of noble, or even heroic:

> Then to you all that come to viewe mine end,
> I must confesse, I had no ill intent,
> but against such as wronged vs ouer much.
> And now I can perceiue, it was not fit,
> that priuate men should carue out their redresse,
> which way they list, no, learne it now by me
> obedience is the best in eche degree.
> And asking mercie meekely of my King,
> I paciently submit me to the lawe.
> But God forgiue them that were cause of it.
>
> (*619–28)

Lincoln's death parallels very closely that of More at the end of the play:

> I confesse his maiestie hath bin euer good to me, and my offence to his highnesse, makes me of a state pleader, a stage player, (though I am olde, and haue a bad voyce) to act this last Sceane of my tragedie (†1931–4).

In a much earlier scene Surrey and the other noblemen had justified the citizens' resentment against what is described in Holinshed as 'the insolent sawcinesse' and 'the diuelish malice' of the aliens, offending 'against all honestie, equitie, and conscience' (Holinshed, iii. 840).[1]

The arguments against the strangers put forward by Lincoln in the famous addition in hand D are of a completely different nature and tone:

> . . . he that will not see a red hearing at a harry grote, butter at a levenpence a pounde meale at nyne shillinge a Bushell and Beeff at fower nobles a stone lyst to me   (Add. II. 123–5).

[1] References are to the enlarged 1587 edition of Holinshed's *Chronicles*.

... our Countrie is a great eating Country, argo they eate more in our
Countrey then they do in their owne   (II. 127-8).
... they bring in straing rootes, which is meerly to the vndoing of poor
prentizes for whate a sorry psnyp to a good hart   (II. 130-1).

This is the language of Jack Cade and his followers: the rightly
indignant citizens of the earlier scenes, who later, when sentenced
to death, are ready to face it with dignity and even a touch of
humour, become in the hand D addition an irresponsible rabble
in the hands of a clownish demagogue.

Now, from the moment it was suggested that hand D was
Shakespeare's—and I share this opinion—attention and praise
concentrated on these three additional pages, and the rest of the
play was at best disregarded because it did not fit in with the
Shakespearean fragment. In other words the paradoxical view
was taken that the whole should suit the part, instead of the other
way round. My concern here is to enquire into the reasons for this
unfitness. I take the *More* fragment to be an early instance of
Shakespeare rewriting—not re-making, but the one process is a
first step in the direction of the other—a scene written originally
by somebody else. It is not a question of the poorer literary or
dramatic quality of Shakespeare's addition, or of its interrupting
the flow of the action; on the contrary, the passage in hand D is
probably from this point of view superior to the lost scene that it
replaces: it handles beautifully the rhetoric of persuasion and it is a
masterly treatment of a crowd scene. But it does not belong to the
context created by the original author of *More*: this is a different
crowd from the one presented in the previous scenes. I have
attempted elsewhere a conjectural reconstruction of the lost
original version;[1] I wish to focus now on More's admirable speech
in this addition, which is perfectly structured by dovetailing two
main arguments. The transformation of forensic oratory into
poetry is achieved by placing a forceful restatement of the Tudor
doctrine of the sacrality of kingship within the context of Christian
compassion for the oppressed. The pathos of More's plea in favour
of the strangers is enhanced if we take into account a further
topical context: in 1592-3 there was in London a strong re-
emergence of anti-alien feeling, culminating in the seditious
rhyme posted on the wall of the Dutch churchyard on 5 May 1593,
of which unfortunately we know only the first four lines:

> You, strangers, that inhabit in this land,
> Note this same writing, do it understand,

[1] 'Hand D in *Sir Thomas More*: An Essay in Misinterpretation', *Shakespeare
Survey*, xxxviii (1985), 101-14.

>   Conceive it well, for safeguard of your lives,
>   Your goods, your children and your dearest wives.[1]

—a threat that was taken so seriously by the Privy Council as to
cause the arrest of a number of suspects, among whom was the
playwright Thomas Kyd. (A further consequence was the interrogation and indirectly the death of Christopher Marlowe.) The
rhyme in the Dutch churchyard ended with an ultimatum to the
strangers to leave the country. More's plea, in Shakespeare's
fragment,

>   ymagin that yo^u see the wretched straingers
>   their babyes at their backs, w^t their poor lugage
>   plodding tooth ports and costs for transportacion . . .

>   (Add. II. 197–9)

recalls More's own description of the condition of the evicted
tenants in *Utopia*[2] in order to provide a point by point reply to the
rhyme. The reaction of the crowd to the speech, 'letts do as we
may be doon by' (a Christian proverb from the sermon on the
mount), is exactly the same as had been the decisive argument
with which on 23 March 1593 Henry Finch obtained the rejection
in the House of Commons of a bill against the aliens in London.[3]
It reflects exactly the view of the authorities on the question of
the strangers in 1593, which I believe is when Shakespeare wrote
his addition. I suggest therefore that the rewriting of the scene,
replacing what must have been in the original version a more
sympathetic presentation of the case for the May Day rebels, was
motivated by the events of the time. This is not tantamount to
accusing Shakespeare of being a time server: we should take into
account that the theatre in the Elizabethan age was the nearest
equivalent to the modern mass media, entailing a certain caution
in those who work for them, as well as a very different conception
of political issues.

My point is that some of the same reasons obtaining in the rewriting of one scene of *Sir Thomas More* were at work also in the
early Shakespearean re-makes of popular history plays. But the
significant thing is that at least in two instances even the re-made
plays got into some sort of trouble of the same nature.

Such considerations seem predominant in the case of *Richard II*,
which was undoubtedly intended to counteract the utterly

---

[1] John Strype, *Annals of the Reformation* (London, 1725–31), iv. 168.

[2] *Utopia* (Robinson's translation, 1551), sig. C7v.

[3] See P. Maas, 'Henry Finch and Shakespeare', *Review of English Studies*, NS iv
(1953), 142.

negative presentation of the figure of the king in the titleless anonymous manuscript play, variously known as *Woodstock* or *The First Part of Richard II*. To call Shakespeare's play a re-make is perhaps stretching a point: what I feel is that it was originally conceived as such—as a rival stage presentation of Richard's reign—but the determination to stress the other aspect of the king's figure, his role as victim extenuating his abuses as a morally weak ruler, forced the playwright to focus on later developments in Richard's reign. Paradoxically the intention of presenting the king in a more favourable though necessarily still ambiguous light, though resulting in an extraordinary artistic and dramatic achievement, involved further problems of a political nature, as is shown by the omission of the deposition scene in the first three editions of the play and by much more serious trouble at the time of the Essex rebellion.

Commercial reasons are instead predominant in the decision to re-make a long-standing success of the rival company of the Queen's men, a company that by the mid nineties was in a phase of rapid decline. *The Famous Victories of Henry V* had held the stage triumphantly in the eighties as, among other things, a vehicle for the popular clown Tarlton.[1] Unfortunately the *Famous Victories* that went into print in 1598—probably because of the success of a Shakespearean play on the subject—is a much reduced and wretchedly reported text of a play that originally must have been in two parts. The Chamberlain's men's idea was surely to re-make the original *Victories*, known to them at least through performances, into two plays: one, *Henry IV*, mainly concerned with the youthful private misdemeanours and thorough reformation of Prince Hal, the other, *Henry V*, dealing with the famous victories proper, without forgetting to make the audience merry with Katherine of France. I shall concentrate on the first of these two plays, planned as the company's history for the year 1596 in the same way as *Richard II* had been the history for 1595. The obvious approach was to preserve the general outline of the previous play, describing the pranks of the prince and his companions which were surely responsible for the earlier popularity of the *Famous Victories*, but to turn it into a proper history by injecting into the

[1] John Dover Wilson's argument ('The Origins and Development of Shakespeare's "Henry IV"', *Library*, 4th series, xxiv (1945), 9–11) that *Famous Victories* is an awkward conflation of two separate Queen's men's plays of different dates, which are the real sources of Shakespeare's re-makes, does not prevent us from considering *Victories* as Shakespeare's model, since the two plays are lost.

new version large sections derived from Holinshed's and Stowe's chronicles that should provide the supporting framework. The delicate point was the behaviour of the prince at the beginning of the *Victories*, presented as the personal promoter of such abuses as that of robbing his father's receivers and intimidating them into silence. Three ways were found to attenuate this negative impression: the first and most far-reaching was the creation out of history and legend of a counterpart to the prince among the rebels—the impulsive and heroic Hotspur, over whom the prince was to triumph in the end showing that he was the better man; no historical or other source attributes to the prince the actual killing of Hotspur. A second more direct way was not to let the prince be a robber in his own person: he pretends to organize the robberies but in fact he merely robs the robbers and returns the booty to the rightful owners. Thirdly, the main responsibility for the prince's (attenuated) misbehaviour was attributed to the influence of a more mature 'Councellor of youthfull sinne'.[1] *Famous Victories* had called the most authoritative of the knights who seconded the prince in his enterprises Sir John Oldcastle, familiarly Jockey, though he was also the most moderate among them. Oldcastle therefore became the misleader of youth in Shakespeare's re-make of the play. Shakespeare would be the readier to accept the name for this new creation of his if he had been influenced at some time by the attitude of the English Roman Catholics toward the historical Oldcastle Lord Cobham, in contrast with his celebration by Foxe as a Protestant proto-martyr. This opens up a very controversial field of speculation, which I shall touch upon only very briefly. Ernst Honigmann has recently pointed out the youthful Shakespeare's connection with eminent Lancashire Catholic families,[2] and I find that the typical interjections of the Hostess in *2 Henry IV* are reminiscent of, and to be found only in, the language attributed to Lady More by Sir Thomas More's great biographer Nicholas Harpsfield, in a forbidden book widely circulated in manuscript (eight copies are still extant) in recusant households.[3] It is worth noticing that Harpsfield had published in Antwerp in 1566 those Latin *Dialogues* (another book treasured

[1] The description is from the Prologue of *The First Part of Sir John Oldcastle*, by Munday, Drayton, Wilson, and Hathway (1599); see P. Simpson's edition (Oxford, Malone Society Reprints, 1908).

[2] See E. A. J. Honigmann, *Shakespeare: the Lost Years* (Manchester, 1985), *passim*.

[3] *The life and death of Sir Thomas More, knight, sometymes Lord high Chancellor of England, written in the tyme of Queene Marie by Nicholas Harpsfield, L.D.* (ed. Elsie Vaughan Hitchcock (Early English Text Society, os clxxxvi), 1932), 92–9.

by recusants) containing a virulent attack against Oldcastle as a pseudo-martyr, which Foxe furiously refuted in page after folio page of his *Acts and Monuments*.[1] I am not suggesting—as has recently been done—that Shakespeare created the character of Oldcastle as a bitter satire of the Lollards and Puritans in general—and I shall not follow Alice-Lyle Scoufos[2] in her belief that the prince's words in *1 Henry IV*, II. ii, 'Oldcastle sweats to Death, And lards the lean earth as he walks along' is an example of grisly wit alluding to the terrible martyrdom of Oldcastle, hanged in chains over a burning pyre. I think that Shakespeare's first and foremost preoccupation in re-making the first part of *Famous Victories* was that of producing as entertaining a play for the London audience as possible, while providing a much stronger historical background to the events, and at the same time extenuating the prince's misbehaviour by shifting responsibility for it on to a new, much amplified, comic character. In *Victories* the task of providing rough and ready clowning was entrusted to Derrick the Carrier, while Shakespeare transferred it to one of the knights: I am convinced that Will Kemp took originally the role of scarlet-nosed Rossil—the nickname of Sir John Russell, playing on the Italian for 'red'/'rosso', who was later to become Bardolph[3]—while Oldcastle, developed into a major comic and not clownish part, was taken by an actor with a much wider range than that of the professional clown.

My conclusion is that the history acted in 1596 by the Chamberlain's men was Shakespeare's re-make as *Henry IV* of the first part of the *Famous Victories*, centring on the figures of the prince, of his outsize evil angel, Oldcastle, and of his mirror image, Hotspur, acting as his involuntary good angel. The idea that *Henry IV* was originally not only conceived, but actually performed on the stage as a single play was advocated most forcibly some forty years ago by John Dover Wilson.[4] Since then, though, it has lost some of its credit. This is surely due in some measure to the habit of looking at Shakespeare's histories as grouped into tetralogies, a sound and helpful notion in the terms Tillyard presented it,[5] but

---

[1] See 'A Defence of the Lord Cobham, Against Nicholas Harpsfield' in J. Foxe, *Acts and Monuments* (ed. J. Pratt, 1874), iii. 348–402.

[2] Alice-Lyle Scoufos, *Shakespeare's Typological Satire: A Study of the Falstaff-Oldcastle Problem* (Athens, Ohio, 1979), pp. 76 f.

[3] See G. Melchiori, 'Reconstructing the ur-*Henry IV*' in *Essays in Honour of Kristian Smidt* (ed. P. Bilton, L. Hartveit, S. Johansson, A. O. Sandved, and B. Tysdahl, Oslo, 1986), 59–77.

[4] In the paper mentioned on p. 171, n. 1.

[5] E. M. W. Tillyard, *Shakespeare's History Plays* (London, 1944), *passim*.

seriously misleading if understood as implying that Shakespeare
actually planned in advance to produce sequences of four plays as
organic units. If, in order to underline the consistency of the
historical sequence, we must speak in terms of tetralogies, let me
suggest that the second of them is formed by *Edward III*, a play
written not long before 1595, which Richard Proudfoot in his
Shakespeare Lecture last year[1] so convincingly claimed as part of
the Shakespeare canon—*Richard II, Henry IV*, and *Henry V*.

Nobody doubts that there must have existed an earlier version
of the *Henry IV* play or plays with Oldcastle instead of Falstaff, but
the latest proposal is simply to replace, in Part I of the Shakespeare
text as we have it now, the name of Falstaff with that of Oldcastle.
Editors who do not follow this injunction, we are told, 'join
defenders of the corrupt and derivative Vulgate, against the
reforms of Erasmus'.[2] I am afraid I must be classed with the
defenders of the Vulgate, not because I do not believe that in
many instances it would be enough to substitute one name for
the other in order to get to what Shakespeare originally wrote—
I did so myself a moment ago when, in quoting a well-known line
from Act II scene ii, I restored Oldcastle's name for the
present unmetrical 'Away, good Ned! Falstaff sweats to death'—;
in my opinion what Kristian Smidt has recently called the
'unconformities'[3] that are scattered in large numbers through
both parts of *Henry IV* bear witness to a process of adaptation,
rewriting, and especially amplification of materials originally
organized in a much tighter and more economic dramatic
structure. I have attempted elsewhere a reconstruction of this
original structure, what I call the ur-*Henry IV*,[4] that is to say
Shakespeare's one-play version of the history, featuring Oldcastle,
Harvey, and Rossill instead of Falstaff, Peto, and Bardolph
respectively, as well as the episode of the box on the ear of the Lord
Chief Justice, but ignoring altogether the second rebellion and the
Gaultree episode and many sections of the comic scenes in the first
and practically all those in the second Part of the plays as we have
them now.

I have no time to go into details: what matters is that such a play
could not have been presented on the stage at a more unfortunate

[1] *Proc. British Academy*, lxxi (1985), 159–85.
[2] Gary Taylor, 'The Fortunes of Oldcastle', *Shakespeare Survey*, xxxviii (1985), 85–100.
[3] K. Smidt, *Unconformities in Shakespeare's History Plays* (Atlantic Highlands, New Jersey, 1982).
[4] See p. 173, n. 3.

time. Henry Carey, first Lord Hunsdon, the Lord Chamberlain and patron of Shakespeare's company, had died on 22 July 1596, and though the company remained under the patronage of his son, George Carey, second Lord Hunsdon, the office of Lord Chamberlain was transferred to William Brooke, Lord Cobham. It was a short-lived transfer because the Lord Cobham died in March 1597 and the office was then returned to the younger Carey, so that the company was able to resume the name of Chamberlain's men; but these few months were enough for the Lord Cobham, as supervisor of all public entertainments, to be shocked by the success of a play featuring his martyred ancestor Sir John Oldcastle as its main comic attraction (though surely his part was by no means as extended as that of Falstaff in the later versions). The company, now known as Lord Hunsdon's men, was forced to withdraw the play just after discovering the formidable appeal of the newly created character of the fat misleader of youth. To throw away altogether such a promising script would have been a sorry waste. The obvious solution was to produce, as the history for the next season 1597, a re-elaboration of the same play on Henry IV, removing from it the offending presentation of the Protestant martyr, but not the character himself; on the contrary, Falstaff, now no longer identified with Oldcastle, the historical Lord Cobham, should be given ampler scope to delight the London audience: the tavern scenes (now *1 Henry IV*, II. iv, and III. iii) were much extended, and his portrait was rounded off with the introduction, at the crucial point of the battle that was to mark the prince's utter reformation and transformation, of Falstaff's catechism on honour (v. i).

The expansion of Falstaff's role entailed the problem of his relationship with the prince. In re-making the first part of *Famous Victories* Shakespeare had attenuated the direct responsibility of the prince, in line with the picture provided towards the end of *Richard II* (v. iii) by Bolingbroke, enquiring about his 'unthrifty son' 'with unrestrained loose companions . . . Which he, young wanton and effeminate boy, Takes on the point of honour to support So dissolute a crew' (ll. 1, 7, 10–11). The ur-*Henry IV* was the story told in unambiguous terms of this wanton boy who, out of a misguided sense of loyalty to loose companions, had gone so far as to box the Lord Chief Justice on the ear; exactly that episode—his acceptance of being sent to prison—marked the young man's awakening to a sense of personal responsibility, the beginning of his reformation, of that crescendo that gave him heroic stature at Shrewsbury, leading to his coronation and the rejection of his 'dissolute crew'. In the rewriting of the re-make the greater space allowed to Falstaff as an obvious box-office draw entailed the risk of enrolling the prince too firmly on his side in the early scenes, diminishing the credibility of an unprepared revulsion from wanton ways. The solution was to show from the beginning the prince's awareness of his difference from Falstaff and his crew, by underlining that his living as Falstaff's shadow, sharing his language and attitudes, was mere pretence. Hence the introduction of the well-known soliloquy at the end of the very first scene in which the prince appears (now *1 Henry IV*, I. ii. 204–26):

> I know you all, and will awhile uphold
> The unyoked humour of your idleness, . . .
> I'll so offend, to make offence a skill,
> Redeeming time when men least think I will.

After this self-revelation the scene with the Lord Chief Justice would be out of character, as being appropriate to a misguided boy, not to one intent on redeeming time; so it must go, and be replaced with an action more in keeping with such premisses.

I agree with Harold Jenkins's brilliant surmise[1] that at some point in the writing—or rather rewriting—of the new Act IV Shakespeare must have realized that all the additional material concerning Falstaff and the prince could not be fitted into a single play. There would be no room for the last scenes of the ur-*Henry IV*, such as the death of the king and the rejection of Oldcastle/Falstaff. These scenes, I think, were set aside for possible future use, and the play was planned as culminating in the battle of Shrewsbury, leaving no doubts as to the transformation of the prince into the victorious Henry V—and leaving no doubts either as to the retribution of the 'irregular humorists'. The latter objective was achieved by a masterly device that only a professional man of the theatre could have thought of. Taking a hint from *Famous Victories*, where the episode of the box on the ear of the Lord Chief Justice is immediately followed by its comic re-enactment by Derrick the Clown and his partner John Cobbler, in the new *Henry IV* the suppressed scene with the Justice was now replaced with what is known as the play-acting scene (II. iv. 378–481), where the prince, impersonating his father, condemns 'that villainous abominable misleader of youth, Falstaff', and, when Falstaff, impersonating the prince, pleads 'Banish not him thy Harry's company—banish plump Jack and banish all the world', replies in his own person as well as the king's 'I do, I will'.

---

[1] In *The Structural Problem in Shakespeare's Henry IV* (1956).

I am suggesting that *1 Henry IV* was written, or rewritten, in 1597, as a self-sufficient play with an open ending. So, if it did not meet with success on the stage, some of the scenes left over from the ur-*Henry IV* could be conflated into the opening scene of *Henry V*, the re-make of the second part of *Famous Victories*— after all in the *Victories* the rejection of the prince's companions, the archbishop's arguments for the English rights to the French crown, the episode of the tennis balls with the declaration of war, and the confirmation in office of the Lord Chief Justice were all rolled into one single scene.[1] If the rewritten play was instead successful, all the material left over and much more could be incorporated in a straight sequel to it. In other words, when *Part One* of *Henry IV* was completed and first performed in 1597, *Part Two* had not yet been planned—it was at most thought of as an open option.

The exceptional number of Quarto editions of *Henry IV, Part One*, shows how well the first Falstaff play was received: the option must be taken, the history for the 1598 season must be a sequel to *Henry IV*. The task was not easy: what was left over from the ur-*Henry IV* could fill at most one act with historical material and a couple of scenes with comedy. The only chance of reinforcing the historical side was to turn once again to Holinshed and include the second rebellion and the unsavoury Gaultree episode—an awkward decision, because, in the hurried replacement of offending names in the ur-*Henry IV*, Shakespeare had picked on that of Bardolph for Russell, but now he could not avoid introducing a duplication, since the historical Lord Bardolph had played a major role in the second rebellion. On the other hand the best way of strengthening the comic scenes was the creation of a host of new characters as well as extending the parts of those who had already appeared: here are Pistol, Doll Tearsheet, Justice Shallow and Justice Silence—allusive names that could figure well in a moral interlude. It is significant that *Part Two* should be introduced by Rumour 'painted full of tongues', the only case (apart from Time in *Winter's Tale*) in which Shakespeare presents on the stage an allegorical personification.[2] *Part Two* acquires, for better or worse, a new dimension: not history but a revisitation of known events in the key of moral allegory, so that when Falstaff enters it is easy to recognize him as the morality Vice. And, as Lionel Knights

[1] Scene ix in the Praetorius facsimile edition of *Famous Victories* (introd. P. A. Daniel, London, 1887).

[2] See G. Melchiori, 'The Role of Jealousy: Restoring the Q Reading of *2 Henry IV*, Induction, 16', *Shakespeare Quarterly*, xxxiv (1983), 327–30.

pointed out,[1] the play in its final form is run through by the theme of time, of man's subjection to time and physical decay, so macroscopically presented in the figure of Falstaff—a different Falstaff from that of *Part One*, as the Lord Chief Justice remarks (*2 Henry IV*, I. ii. 178–86):

> Do you set down your name in the scroll of youth, that are written down old with all the characters of age? Have you not a moist eye, a dry hand, a yellow cheek, a white beard, a decreasing leg, an increasing belly? Is not your voice broken, your wind short, your chin double, your wit single, and every part about you blasted with antiquity? and will you yet call yourself young? Fie, fie, fie, Sir John!

Knights recognizes that 'the tone of *Henry IV Part II* is entirely different from the tone of detached observation of the earlier plays', it is 'markedly a transitional play. It looks back to the Sonnets, and the earlier history plays, and it looks forward to the great tragedies.'[2]

This is true, though the obvious morality element in the earlier group of histories lacked the new complexities of the later one. They offered themselves in fact as mere chronicles, culminating in the monstrous apparition of Richard Crookback, duly defeated by that mirror of knighthood, Richmond, the founder of the Tudor dynasty bringing about—as the historian Edward Hall put it— the union of the two noble and illustrious families of Lancaster and York. History was approached single-mindedly as the record of events full of sound and fury, leading towards one great goal, not—as that misleading historian and schoolmaster, Mr Deasy in Joyce's *Ulysses*,[3] was to put it—the manifestation of God, but at least, in Edward Hall's words, the triumph of peace, profit, comfort, and joy in the realm of England.[4]

I think that Shakespeare's occasional collaboration in a play like *Sir Thomas More*, presenting a problematic view of recent history, with so many topical references to current events, must have awakened, or reinforced, his awareness that such a simple conception of the historical process would not hold. Then there came the re-makes, partly motivated—like his contribution to

---

[1] L. C. Knights, 'Time's Subjects: The Sonnets and *King Henry IV, Part II*' in his *Some Shakespearean Themes* (London, 1959), pp. 45–64.

[2] Ibid., p. 63.

[3] J. Joyce, *Ulysses* (critical edition ed. H. W. Gabler, New York, 1984), 69.

[4] E. Hall, *The Union of the Two, Noble and Illustre Famelies of Lancastre and Yorke* (1548), as quoted in G. Bullough, *Narrative and Dramatic Sources of Shakespeare*, iii (London, 1960), 17.

More—by the wish, or the necessity, of taking into due consideration the sensitivity of the censor regarding the presentation of the
negative side of authority, particularly royalty. *Richard II* is a case
in point: in reacting to the negative view of Richard in *Woodstock*,
Shakespeare had to alter the focus of history itself, no longer the
conflict between the powers of good and those of evil represented
in two opposing factions, but a conflict inborn in human nature
itself. Richard is a contradictory personality to be explored *per se*.

No less contradictory is his successor, *Henry IV*, at one and the
same time a wise and rightful ruler with a noble mission, and a
guilt-ridden usurper. *Famous Victories* shirked the problem by
leaving the king in the shadow, but in the re-make, where he had
the title role, it was solved by feats of eloquence, like the soliloquy,
now in *Part II*, iii. i, 'How many thousand of my poorest subjects
. . .'—paralleling the magnificent oratory of More in Shakespeare's contribution to the earlier play. The most remarkable
development, though, is one I have already mentioned: the
introduction, in the rewriting of the ur-*Henry IV* as *Part One*, of the
prince's self-revealing soliloquy right at the beginning of the play
(i. ii. 206–12):

> Yet herein will I imitate the sun
> Who doth permit the base contagious clouds
> To smother up his beauty from the world,
> That when he please again to be himself
> Being wanted, he may be more wondered at
> By breaking through the foul and ugly mists
> Of vapours that did seem to strangle him.

The historical prince, in contrast with the tavern-hunting
wanton and effeminate boy (*and* with the impulsive and out-
spoken Hotspur), follows a deliberate policy. His character is
ambivalent, but deliberately so, while the inner conflicts of
Richard II and Henry IV were presented as part of their natures.
Hal is from the beginning the political man—not necessarily the
Machiavellian, the deceiver for deception's sake, but rather the
statesman who calculates the impact of his behaviour in respect of
the interests of the institutions. What emerges here is the relationship between history and politics, a problem that had not been
faced at all in the early histories, where the motives of the action
were represented by naked thirst for power and conquest, the
generous pursuit of national ideals, or the most villainous forms
of plotting and counter-plotting. Like T. S. Eliot's Gerontion,
Shakespeare has now realized that

> History has many cunning passages, contrived corridors
> And issues, deceives with whispering' ambitions,
> Guides us by vanities . . .[1]

The realization that policy—a word regularly used in Shakespeare's time with negative or at most ironical connotations—could be an instrument in the pursuit of noble ends, conditions both parts of *Henry IV* on the stylistic level as well. From the unified language of *Richard II*, based on the principles of the highest rhetoric, we move to a constant alternance of high and low, a see-saw that in *Part Two* tends to become unbalanced. In fact there the relationship between the prince and Falstaff is completely changed, or rather it hardly exists. The only time—apart from the final scene—they are together in the tavern at Eastcheap (II. iv), the prince appears in another traditionally political role: that of the disguised ruler spying on the actions of his subjects. After which Falstaff becomes a recruiting officer in the provinces (III. ii)—surely a role transferred from the earlier part of the history, where it really belongs[2]—and this time he recruits soldiers for a war that does not take place because of the 'policy' of prince John of Lancaster, who entraps the rebels at Gaultree with false promises. *Part Two* is the triumph of policy: the last meeting of the prince, now King Henry V, with Falstaff—the rejection scene—is in fact no meeting at all: Henry has become a personification of kingship. In a recent haunting re-make of the two parts of *Henry IV* into one by the Italian avant-garde company Collettivo di Parma, instead of saying 'I know thee not old man', the king stood motionless under a spotlight at the back of the stage throughout the scene, a monument to himself, singing a little Brechtian song underlining his utter alienation.[3]

The king comes fully into his own of course in *Henry V*, which we all know was the history performed by the Chamberlain's men in the 1599 season. There is no mistaking the dominant figure in this history: apart from those of Hamlet, Richard III, and Iago, that of King Henry is the longest part that Shakespeare ever wrote for one of his characters, 8,338 words according to Marvin Spevack's *Concordance*,[4] nearly one third of all the words spoken in this long

---

[1] T. S. Eliot, *Collected Poems, 1909–1935* (London, 1936), 37–9.

[2] This opinion is widely shared by recent editors of the play, and repeated in Kristian Smidt's book referred to on p. 174, n. 3.

[3] The performance is amply documented in L. Allegri, *Tre Shakespeare della Compagnia del Collettivo / Teatro Due* (Firenze, 1983).

[4] M. Spevack, *A Complete and Systematic Concordance to the Works of Shakespeare*, 6 vols. (Hildesheim, 1968–80).

play. History, in it, is physically present in the frequent intervention of the Chorus—the positive side of Rumour in *Henry IV,
Part Two*. Without Falstaff, without the English background of
tavern, inn, or village life, the comic unhistorical scenes in the play
create a new dramatic *genre* which I would call 'comedy of
language', or rather 'languages', with the four captains, Fluellen,
Gower, Macmorris, and Jamy and their marked national accents
and features, and with the French, from the boastful Dolphin to
Princess Katherine, already singled out as a source of merriment
in the Epilogue to the previous history. The part of King Henry
himself is constantly played on two distinct linguistic registers:
the noble oratory of the great verse speeches, based on ample
rhetorical patterns of immediate appeal (the proper use of rhetoric
is to produce consensus), and on the other hand the subtle dia-
lectical prose speeches, ironical and unashamed of sophistry—a
sophistry apparent not only in the wooing of Katherine, but even
more in the night scene before Agincourt (IV. i), in which once
again Henry takes over the role of disguised ruler.

The dispute over Shakespeare's positive or negative view of
Henry's character is basically idle, though it has stimulated a
variety of lively stage productions. What in fact emerges from
the stylistic duality of Henry's part is not his humanity but the
portrait of a statesman, of the *homo politicus*. It is perhaps wiser
at this point to let the figures in Spevack's *Concordance* speak for
themselves. The relation between the two registers used in Henry's
speeches, which I mentioned before, is roughly 69 per cent verse
to 31 per cent prose. It is interesting to ascertain in which other
leading characters in Shakespeare's plays a similar ratio between
verse and prose is maintained, since I believe that the proportion
of prose to verse is a revealing, because unconscious, criterion in
the construction of character. Other English histories cannot be
taken as terms of reference: after *Henry V* Shakespeare wrote none
(apart from the collaborative and much later *Henry VIII*). Perhaps the fact itself (Shakespeare forsaking the writing of histories)
is intrinsically significant: we should ask ourselves whether it was
due to the decline of the *genre* in contemporary theatre, or rather to
Shakespeare's new consciousness of the primacy of the exploration
of the individual character and of the motives of human behaviour
over the chronicling of events. His last history play, *Henry V*, had
yielded him the character of the politician, ambiguous even when
pursuing noble ends. The moralized lives of the great Romans
presented by Plutarch were better suited to the pursuit of the
exploration of individual character in history. The nearest thing

to an English history play after *Henry V* is *Macbeth*, and it is to be
wondered if Macbeth's statement that life 'is a tale told by an
idiot, full of sound and fury, signifying nothing' does not represent
the author's ultimate view of history.

Let us go back now to the statistical data, for what they are
worth, that can be extrapolated from Spevack's exhaustive *Concordance*. After Hamlet, and apart from Macbeth (who speaks only
in verse) and Timon (whose linguistic register is constant to the
point of monotony), there are only two other characters who
speak over 30 per cent of the words of the plays in which they
appear. The first is the duke in *Measure for Measure*—the *deus ex
machina* in a sinister story, a ruler in disguise with a vengeance.
The fundamental ambiguity of his role is borne out by that of his
language, alternating the high sententiousness of his moralizing
speeches in verse with plotting and planning—apparently all for
good—in prose: and the proportion between the two registers is
very close to that which we find in Henry: 69.4 per cent verse,
30.6 per cent prose. Stepping out of history into fiction, the
politician follows more devious ways: the disguised ruler pursues
justice through the deceits of the bed-trick and the pretended
capital execution—through many cunning passages and con-
trived corridors.

At this point it is perhaps no surprise to find that nearly the
same proportion between verse and prose (71 to 29) obtains in
another character who, like Henry, speaks over 32 per cent of the
words in the play where he appears, though not in the title role:
Iago in *Othello*. There is some variation within the registers of
his language, the subject of masterly studies such as those of
Madeleine Doran or Alessandro Serpieri:[1] sophistry, the rhetoric
of negation, reticence and suspension, affect his verse—and
especially his extended soliloquies—as much as his prose, and the
latter is at times degraded to the coarseness of barrack language.
But the outer balance is the same: the variation is in degree, not
in kind. Freed from the fetters of history, the politician reveals
a deeper layer of ambiguity: 'I am not what I am.'

The parable is complete: from the wanton Prince Hal turned
into the victorious Henry V, through the duke of dark corners
in Vienna, to the 'ancient' in the Venetian army. Is this the
inevitable progress of the politician? I prefer to think that this is
the lesson of History. Three hundred years later, Mr Deasy's

---

[1] M. Doran, 'Iago's *If*—Conditional and Subjunctive in *Othello*' (1970) in
her *Shakespeare's Dramatic Language* (Madison, 1976), pp. 63-91; A. Serpieri,
'*Otello': L'Eros Negato* (Milano, 1978).

statement in *Ulysses* that 'History moves to one great goal, the manifestation of God' was countered by young Stephen Dedalus with: 'History is a nightmare from which I am trying to awake.' This was written in 1916, and Eliot's 'Gerontion' at about the same time: it had taken Eliot and Joyce the experience of the First World War to discover the deception of History. Shakespeare learnt the lesson as a man of the theatre should: by *re-making* History—turning its deception into dramatic ambiguity, which is the true life of a play.

PLATE IV

Petruccio and Katherine: one of Frances Brundage's drawings for *The Children's Shake-speare* by E. Nesbit (1897). (*Birmingham Library Services*)

TALES FROM SHAKESPEARE

By STANLEY WELLS

Read 30 April 1987

SOME coincidences seem more coincidental than others. It is surely rather a manifestation of the spirit of the age than pure chance that 1807 saw the publication of two adaptations, each of twenty Shakespeare plays, designed to make those plays both more accessible to young readers and more suited to what their elders thought the young should be reading; chance may, however, be held responsible for the fact that both adaptations were undertaken by the less distinguished sisters of more distinguished brothers, and that over the years the brothers have received more than their fair share of credit for their sisters' work. One of the adaptations, published anonymously, was *The Family Shakspeare*, offering (literally) bowdlerized texts.[1] In its second edition, of 1818, this work was ascribed to Thomas Bowdler, MD; he is still frequently held responsible, though in 1966 it was shown that his sister, Henrietta Maria, undertook the initial task of expurgation, and that Thomas was responsible only for the plays added in the second edition.[2] This adaptation, now relegated to library basements and mentioned only to be derided, enjoyed many years of success; Jaggard records some thirty-five editions between 1807 and 1900.[3]

The other adaptation, *Tales from Shakespear. Designed for the use of young persons*, was ascribed on its first publication to Charles Lamb; not until the seventh edition, of 1838, was his sister's name added to the title-page, though Charles had made it quite clear in letters to his friends that Mary wrote fourteen of the tales and that he had contributed only six—the tragedies—along with 'occasionally a tail piece or correction of grammar ... and *all* of the spelling'.[4]

[1] *The Family Shakspeare*, 4 vols. (London, 1807).
[2] Noel Perrin, 'The Real Bowdler', *Notes and Queries*, NS xiii (1966), 141–2.
[3] William Jaggard, *Shakespeare Bibliography* (Stratford-upon-Avon, 1911).
[4] Edwin W. Marrs, Jr (ed.), *The Letters of Charles and Mary Lamb*, 3 vols. (Ithaca and London, 1975–8); ii. 256 (Charles Lamb to William Wordsworth, 29 Jan. 1807).

The Lambs' letters give a charming picture of the process of composition, the brother and his mentally unstable sister (she had already stabbed her mother to death) writing, as Mary says, 'on one table (but not on one cushion sitting) like Hermia & Helena in the Midsummer's Nights Dream, or rather like an old literary Darby and Joan. I taking snuff & he groaning all the while & saying he can make nothing of it, which he always says till he has finished and then he finds out he has made something of it ...'.[5] Mary, too, groaned, complaining, according to Charles, 'of having to set forth so many female characters in boy's clothes'.[6] She gets stuck (understandably) in *All's Well*; Charles writes to Wordsworth that he encourages her with flattery, and we know that the flattery succeeded because a few days later Mary writes to Sarah Stoddart that she is 'in good spirits' because Charles has told her that *All's Well* is 'one of the very best' of her stories.[7]

The *Tales* were composed for The Juvenile Library, published by William Godwin and his second wife, Mary Jane, known to the Lamb circle as 'the bad baby', and execrated by Lamb for her inept choice of topics for illustration, which included a picture of Hamlet with the grave-diggers, even though the scene 'is not hinted at in the story, & you might as well have put King Canute the Great reproving his courtiers'.[8] Payment was at the rate of three guineas per tale, and initial publication was in two volumes, though eight individual tales were also issued separately in chapbook versions which are now, according to David Foxon, 'probably the greatest rarities of more recent English literature'.[9]

The Lambs' Preface contains a modest statement of their aims and methods. The *Tales* are intended to introduce young readers to the study of Shakespeare, whose own words are used whenever possible; in narrative passages, 'words introduced into our language since his time have been as far as possible avoided'. The *Tales* are 'faint and imperfect stamps of Shakespear's matchless image ... because the beauty of his language is too frequently destroyed' by the need to change verse into prose; even where, 'in

[5] *Letters*, ii. 228–9 (Mary Lamb to Sarah Stoddart, 30 May–2 June 1806).
[6] *Letters*, ii. 233 (Charles Lamb to William Wordsworth, 26 June 1806).
[7] *Letters*, ii. 233, 237 (Charles Lamb to William Wordsworth, 26 June 1806; Mary Lamb to Sarah Stoddart, 2 July 1806).
[8] *Letters*, ii. 256 (Charles Lamb to William Wordsworth, 29 Jan. 1807).
[9] 'The Chapbook Editions of the Lambs' *Tales from Shakespear*', *The Book Collector*, vi (1957), 41–53, quotation on p. 41.

some few places', 'his blank verse is given unaltered, as hoping from its simple plainness to cheat the young readers into the belief that they are reading prose', it still suffers by being taken out of context. The *Tales* are written mainly for 'young ladies . . . because boys are generally permitted the use of their fathers' libraries at a much earlier age than girls are'; and boys are encouraged to explain the hard bits to their sisters, and even to read pleasing passages from the original plays to them, 'carefully selecting what is proper for a young sister's ear'. When the young readers are old enough to turn to the plays for themselves, they will discover many surprises not hinted at in the *Tales*. And the last paragraph of the Preface—written by Charles—expresses the wish that in the future 'the true Plays of Shakespear' will prove 'enrichers of the fancy, strengtheners of virtue, a withdrawing from all selfish and mercenary thoughts, a lesson of all sweet and honourable thoughts and actions, to teach you courtesy, benignity, generosity, humanity: for of examples, teaching these virtues, his pages are full'.

Though the principal aim is clarification and simplification, there are hints also of a certain moral protectiveness; fraternal selection of 'what is proper for a young sister's ear' is precisely akin to Miss Bowdler's expunging of 'any thing that can raise a blush on the cheek of modesty'.[10] There is, too, an implied assurance that reading Shakespeare is good for you; an assurance that may have been particularly welcome to parents at a time when the child attending the theatre might be, as Wordsworth had recently put it,

> environ'd with a Ring
> Of chance Spectators, chiefly dissolute men
> And shameless women . . .
> While oaths, indecent speech, and ribaldry
> Were rife about him . . .
> (*The Prelude* (1805), vii. 385–90)

Both Mary and Charles reduce the plays' complexity, concentrating where possible on a single story-line. The Gloucester plot disappears almost entirely from *King Lear*; *The Merchant of Venice* loses the caskets and, almost, Lorenzo and Jessica. Theseus makes only a fleeting appearance at the opening of *A Midsummer Night's Dream*, and all that remains of the mechanicals is a nameless clown 'who had lost his way in the wood' and who stands in for

[10] *The Family Shakspeare*, i. p. vii.

Bottom in the episode with Titania. Low comedy episodes and characters—Christopher Sly, Juliet's Nurse, Paroles, Cloten, Touchstone and Jaques, even Sir Toby, Sir Andrew, and Malvolio—all disappear entirely or are reduced to the merest ciphers. Humour suffers greatly, as Lamb admits in his Preface; many of the comedies are brought closer to the romance tales on which they are founded.

Shakespeare's own tendency to idealize his sources is heightened: the bed trick in *All's Well* becomes a 'secret meeting', and Helena is not pregnant at the end; in *Measure for Measure*, Claudio had simply 'seduced a young lady from her parents' (though Isabella does speak to Claudio of Angelo's demand that she 'yield' her 'virgin honour'). There are no bawds or brothels in either *Measure for Measure* or *Pericles*, and bawdy language is almost totally expunged. In those pre-Partridge days, however, Mary Lamb—like Miss Bowdler—could retain Graziano's closing couplet about 'keeping safe Nerissa's ring'.

Along with omission and reduction there is also a little elaboration. The narrative mode encourages additional exposition, comment, and even interpretation. Some additions are purely explanatory: 'In those times wrestling, which is only practised now by country clowns, was a favourite sport even in the courts of princes' (*As You Like It*); 'though it is not the custom now for young women of high birth to understand cookery, it was then' (*Cymbeline*). There are some gently humorous comments—'fathers do not often desire the death of their own daughters, even though they do happen to prove a little refractory' (*A Midsummer Night's Dream*)—, some moralistic ones—Antigonus' ursine death was 'a just punishment on him for obeying the wicked order of Leontes' (*The Winter's Tale*), —and some aphoristically generalizing ones that have won the praise of commentators.[11] Some additions reveal preconceptions about the characters and their actions, sometimes with important interpretative consequences: Prospero is 'an old man', and it is as a result of 'his magic art' that Miranda fell in love so suddenly; and Antonio's silence at the end of *The Tempest*, always interpreted by modern critics as a sign that he is unrepentant, suggests to the more generous-minded Mary Lamb that he was 'so filled . . . with shame and remorse, that he wept and was unable to speak'.

[11] E.g. Alfred Ainger, Introduction to his edition (1879): Mary Lamb 'constantly evinces a rare shrewdness and tact in her incidental criticisms'. See also Edmund Blunden, *Charles Lamb and his Contemporaries* (London, 1937), p. 74.

Interpretative elaboration is particularly prevalent at the ends of stories: Mary Lamb is in no doubt that, after the events shown in *Measure for Measure*, 'the mercy-loving duke long reigned with his beloved Isabel, the happiest of husbands and of princes'; nor is there anything tentative about her conclusion to *All's Well that Ends Well*: Helena 'at last found that her father's legacy was indeed sanctified by the luckiest stars in heaven.' But Charles is even more apt than Mary to offer explicit interpretation; indeed, his elaboration of the role of Kent in *King Lear* has caused Jonathan Bate—who finds that Charles's *Tales* 'form a kind of creative commentary' on Shakespeare—to suggest that perhaps Lamb 'saw himself as a Kent-figure, characterized by loyalty and honesty, a willingness to remain in the shadow of the great souls around him, a preference for plain language, prose to the verse of Wordsworth and Coleridge'.[12]

The reception of the *Tales* on publication was in general lukewarm, with one notable exception. There are seven reviews, all anonymous, mostly very brief.[13] Criticism centres on moral purpose. In spite of the Lambs' efforts to avoid causing offence, the *Literary Panorama* regretted that 'morals ...' had not 'been deduced from such incidents as afford them'. Though *The Anti-Jacobin Review* thought that the *Tales* were told 'as decently as possible', it did not consider them 'very proper studies for female children'; and the Lambs had properly put their foot in it by telling girls that there are parts of Shakespeare that they should not read till they are older: 'This only serves as a *stimulus* to juvenile curiosity, which requires a *bridle* rather than a *spur*.' The only really enthusiastic praise of the *Tales* is in a notice in the *Critical Review* which places the volume firmly in the context of the current debate about children's literature, a debate with which Lamb was himself concerned. In a letter to Coleridge of 1802 he had complained that didacticism was supplanting imagination in children's books: 'Science has succeeded to Poetry no less in the little walks of Children than with Men. ... **Damn them**. I mean the cursed Barbauld Crew, those **Blights** &

---

[12] 'Lamb on Shakespeare', *The Charles Lamb Bulletin*, NS li (1985), 76–85, quotations on pp. 76 and 84. On Lamb's implicit criticism of Shakespeare see also Joan Coldwell (ed.), *Charles Lamb on Shakespeare* (London, 1978), esp. pp. 12–15.

[13] *The Anti-Jacobin Review* (26 March 1807), p. 298; *Critical Review*, ii, no. 1 (May 1807), 97–9; *The Monthly Mirror*, NS ii (July 1807), 39; *The Literary Panorama* (3 Nov. 1807), pp. 294–5; *Gentleman's Magazine*, lxxviii, no. 2 (Nov. 1808), 1001; *The British Critic*, xxxiii (May 1809), 525; *The Satirist* (1 July 1809), p. 93.

Blasts of all that is ***Human*** in man & child.'[14] The writer in the
Critical Review is entirely of Lamb's mind: 'We have compared it
[the *Tales*] with many of the numerous systems which have been
devised for rivetting attention at an early age, and insinuating
knowledge subtilly and pleasurably into minds, by nature averse
from it. The result of the comparison is not so much that it rises
high in the list, as that it claims the very first place, and stands
unique, and without rival or competitor, unless perhaps we
except Robinson Crusoe.' The *Tales* 'will effect more than all the
cant that ever was canted by Mrs Trimmer and Co. in all their
most canting and lethargic moments.'

For the rest, the highest praise comes from *The Gentleman's
Review*, saying that the 'very pretty Tales ... may interest the
mind at an age when the plays themselves cannot be properly
appreciated'. 'Very pretty Tales' has seemed apt enough to later
ages as a description of what the Lambs produced. These *Tales*
are generally undemanding; their literary quality is modest.
They have been praised for narrative clarity, for ease of style, for
an understanding of the needs of a child's imagination. They
have been seen as a manifestation of the Romantic interest in
childhood, and as a blow on behalf of the arts in the education of
the young.[15] But, as even so sympathetic a critic as Lord David
Cecil wrote, their success 'is a little surprising; for the tales are
told in a gentle undramatic manner, unlikely, one would have
thought, to excite children in Lamb's day, let alone many years
later'.[16] Nevertheless, A. Hamilton Thompson, writing (in 1915)
in *The Cambridge History of English Literature*, claimed that 'the
collection forms one of the most conspicuous landmarks in the
history of the romantic movement'.[17]

This initially surprising claim may be supported by consideration of the volume's publishing history. During the Lambs'
lifetime, it enjoyed a modest success. It was reprinted in 1809 and
1810, and appeared in three more editions by the time Charles
Lamb died, in 1834. By the time Mary died, in 1847, there had

[14] *Letters*, ii. 82.

[15] See e.g. F. J. Harvey Darnton, *Children's Books in England* (London, 1932),
3rd edn., rev. by Brian Alderson (Cambridge, 1983), p. 192: 'They provide a
defence of poesy by a kind of nursery introduction to it in prose.'

[16] *A Portrait of Charles Lamb* (London, 1983), p. 127. An extreme reaction is
that of Robertson Davies: 'Shakespeare was a poet and, if you rob him of his
poetry, you reduce him to tedious stuff like Lamb's Tales From Shakespear
(1807), which I was given as a child and which turned me off Shakespeare for
many years' (Toronto *Globe and Mail*, 1 August 1987).

[17] Vol. xii, *The Nineteenth Century* (Cambridge, 1915), p. 189.

been five more editions, making eleven in all. After this, edition
succeeded edition with increasing, and increasingly astonishing,
rapidity. To chart their progress fully would require a biblio-
graphical study which so far as I know has not been undertaken,
and which would be difficult to prepare accurately, because even
the copyright libraries seem to have wearied of giving shelf-room
to the full spate of editions and reissues. The British Library has
many that are not in the Bodleian; the Bodleian has some that are
not in the British Library; the picture is complicated by the
existence of selections, simplified versions, reprints of individual
tales, foreign reprints in English, and translations. With that
proviso, let me say that I have evidence of close on 200 editions in
English, and of at least forty translations extending beyond the
major European languages to Burmese, Swahili, Japanese,
Macedonian, Chinese (in 1905, the first Chinese translation of
Shakespeare in any form), Hungarian, and the African dialects
Ga and Ewe. I won't bore you with the detailed statistics
(painfully though these have been acquired), but some indication of the periods of greatest popularity may be of interest.
Reprints of English versions continue steadily after Mary Lamb's
death until 1873 (by which date there had been fifteen, in sixty-
four years). Then—doubtless under the influence of Forster's
Education Act of 1870—they accelerate rapidly. 1879 was a
bumper year, with seven editions, three of them in Calcutta.
There are sixteen editions in the 1880s, ten in the 1890s, and
thirty-six in the first decade of the twentieth century. From 1910
to 1920 there are twenty-six, and then numbers dwindle a bit:
eleven in the 1920s, twelve in the 1930s, eleven in the 1940s,
thirteen in the 1950s, fourteen in the 1960s. I have no reliable
figures for more recent years, but *Books in Print* reveals ten
editions currently on the market.

I adduced these figures initially to support Thompson's assertion of the volume's importance 'in the history of the romantic
movement'. They show that the *Tales* became a classic with a
popularity matching that of *Alice in Wonderland*. I say 'a classic'
rather than 'a children's classic' because it is clear that the *Tales*
(like *Alice*) is both read by adults and chosen by adults as a book
suitable for children, not necessarily by children as a book that
they are anxious to read for themselves. Indeed, its very title—
unlike, say, *Charlie and the Chocolate Factory* or *Five on a Treasure
Island*— requires knowledge, or information, along with cultural
aspirations. Thompson's own support for his assertion is that the
Tales 'is the first book which, appealing to a general audience and

to a rising generation, made Shakespeare a familiar and popular author and, in so doing, asserted the claims of the older literature which, to English people at large, was little more than a name'.[18] But this gives too much weight to the volume's declared function of serving as an 'introduction to the study of Shakespeare'. In fact there is a sense in which the *Tales* supplanted Shakespeare, becoming an object of study in its own right, a book that itself required to be introduced and explained to young readers, and on which they could expect to be examined, sometimes in conjunction with a few extracts from the plays on which it is based, sometimes as an independent text. This can be seen by looking at some of the more important editions, which fall into two main streams: those intended for a general readership, and those specifically presented for use in schools.

In the early period particularly, it is not always easy to distinguish between the two. As early as 1843, a reprint is furnished with a Chronological Table (beginning with *Pericles*, 1590, and ending with *Twelfth Night*, 1613); and Charles Knight's edition of 1844, whose Advertisement states that the *Tales* 'have become as attractive to adults as to those for whose use they were originally intended', seems aimed at the more earnest kind of general reader; he adds 'a few *Scenes*'—such as the dagger soliloquy and murder scene from *Macbeth*—'which may be advantageously read after the perusal of the Tale, to furnish some notion of the original excellence of the wonderful dramas upon which the Tales are founded'. These extracts are lightly annotated with explanatory glosses. An edition of 1879 in Macmillan's Golden Treasury series includes an admirable Introduction by Canon Alfred Ainger (author of the volume on Lamb in the English Men of Letters series), setting the background of the *Tales* and offering an appreciation of the Lambs' methods, especially Mary's 'casual and diffused method of enforcing the many moral lessons that lie in Shakespeare's plays'. This, says Ainger, is why 'these trifles, designed for the nursery and the schoolroom, have taken their place as an English classic. They have never been superseded, nor are they ever likely to be.' Thus the volume was canonized. An edition of 1893, attractively presented in four slim, elegant volumes, provides 'a continuation by Harrison S. Morris', unmoralistic retellings of the sixteen remaining plays carefully done and including characters that the Lambs would certainly have dropped, such as Costard and

[18] Thompson, *loc. cit.*

Jaquenetta (in *Love's Labour's Lost*) and the Clown in *Antony and Cleopatra*.

Alfred Ainger had stressed the value of the *Tales* as an introduction to Shakespeare. Andrew Lang, in an Introductory Preface to an edition of 1894, disputes this, arguing that children 'are best introduced to Shakespeare by Shakespeare himself', that they 'do best to begin with the plays themselves, afterwards Lamb's Tales may bring them back to the originals'. (Does he mean, I wonder, that because they don't understand the plays they will read Lamb, and will then be able to understand the plays?—If so, why not start with Lamb?) Although Ainger's was not specifically a school edition, he had stressed that 'a knowledge of Shakespeare' was more and more 'coming to be regarded as a necessary part of an Englishman's education'. Not so, says the disputatious Lang: 'Alas, it is not Shakespeare, but the notes of Editors that are now a necessary part, not of an Englishman's education, but of an English boy's "cram", for the purpose of examiners.' We should read for pleasure: 'It is a misery to turn classics into schoolbooks.' Lang's essay, clearly not intended for young readers, is consciously anti-academic; he doubts whether 'the exquisite English of Lamb and his sister will attract the infants of today', and regrets the omission of the comic bits. One is left with the impression that Lang wishes he had not agreed to write this Introduction.

The most physically impressive of all editions of the *Tales* is that prepared by F. J. Furnivall and published by Raphael Tuck in 1901. The two handsome volumes, bound in gilded white cloth, are adorned with a portrait of Shakespeare and a full-page photograph of the bushy-bearded, sage-like Furnivall (who at least had the decency to reserve himself for the second volume). This, one feels, is an edition for the rich man's library, one that might stand beside the New Variorum Shakespeare. It is, boasts Furnivall in the full flush of late-Victorian materialism, 'the grandest and most costly ... ever issued'. (It sold for 31s. 6d., with a cheaper issue at 22s. 6d., in a year when other editions were published for between 2s. 6d. and 7s. 6d.) Beyond being grand and costing a lot, its aims are uncertain. Furnivall writes characteristically quirky introductions on various topics, supplies a chronology (omitting *Titus Andronicus*, because 'Its story is too repulsive to be told in a book for boys and girls'), and sketches the stories of six plays omitted by the Lambs while declaring that 'for the Histories ... readers must turn to Shakspere's works', and opining that *Measure for Measure* is 'the gloomiest and most unpleasant of Shakespeare's comedies'. Furnivall is at his most sympathetic in his comments on the Lambs' reduction of Shakespeare's comedy: 'The odd thing is, that two such humourful folk as Mary and Charles Lamb were, two who so enjoyed Shakspere's fun, made up their minds to keep all that fun (or almost all) out of his plays when they told the stories of them to boys and girls who so like fun too ... I can't help thinking that most boys would like the fun put into the Tales, and the stories cut shorter; but they can easily get it all in the plays themselves, so there's no harm done' (i. p. xi).

Furnivall's edition is expensively illustrated with indifferent pictures by H. Copping; and a number of less elaborately presented editions have been newly illustrated. Indeed, some seem primarily intended as vehicles for the work of particular artists. Routledge's Sixpenny Series in 1882 had forty quite striking engravings by Sir John Gilbert. In 1899 Dent's Temple Classics for Young People had twelve illustrations by Arthur Rackham; transferred to Everyman's Library in 1906, this edition is still in print; the Rackham illustrations are not as fine as those he did for *A Midsummer Night's Dream*, but it's a pity that the most interesting of them—a coloured one of Ariel and Caliban—is omitted at least from the paperback reprint, and that the delicacy of line which gives some of them a Beardsleyish quality has become much coarsened in successive reprints. Heath Robinson illustrated an edition of 1902, and the Oxford edition of 1905 has sixteen illustrations unadventurously chosen from the Boydell Gallery; the same year saw a reprint in the Hampstead Library with a sensible introduction by George Sampson praising the Lambs for sounding 'no jarring modern note, nothing that causes the mind to forget the master-author upon whose plays the work is based'. In 1909 Mrs Andrew Lang came upon the scene, introducing a handsome, gift-book style edition which sold for five shillings. Her 'Life of Shakespeare' condescends to the young reader in a manner that makes us appreciate the Lambs' refusal to do so: 'Many a posy William picked for his mother, of "daffodils that come before the swallow dares" ...' An edition of 1911 adds additional tales by one Winston Stokes whose composition seems to have weighed heavily upon him: 'The writing' he says 'has presented untold difficulties; and to portray in foreign form the shifting battle-scenes of "Henry the Sixth", and guide the thread of an unbroken narrative among the horrors of "Titus Andronicus", must forbid an equal literary merit with Lamb's Tales, even if this had been attempted.' At any rate it was enterprising of him to include *Titus*, even though he glosses over what happens to Lavinia—she was 'subjected ... to cruel tortures'—and no pie is served at the feast. Many of the more recent editions have no special features, as if publishers had regarded them as self-propelling, non-copyright volumes assured of a steady sale with very little effort on their part. The Bantam edition of 1962 has an introduction by Elizabeth Story Donno which treats the *Tales* with a kind of cynical expectation that they will be used mainly as a crib to Shakespeare: she writes an historical introduction to Shakespeare's life, times, and stage without even mentioning the Lambs, provides an index of characters, and tells the stories of plays not treated by the Lambs in compressed synopses of about two pages each. J. C. Trewin balked the challenge of *Titus* (and of *Henry VIII*) in the twelve gracefully told tales that he added to the beautifully printed Nonesuch edition of 1964. His method resembles that of the Lambs except that he includes undisguised passages of verse at certain points. In 1979 O. B. Hardison briefly introduced a handsome paperback version illustrated with nearly a hundred pictures—some rare and fine, others rare and boring—selected from the Folger art collection.

The first edition of the *Tales* that seems explicitly intended for schools appeared in 1862, when Gordon's School and Home Series published sixteen of the *Tales* in four parts costing threepence each. A popular but unambitious Pitt Press edition of 1875 adds an 'appendix of speeches from three of the plays ... for the use of teachers who may wish to play the part of the elder brother of the Lambs' Preface, and to introduce their pupils at once to Shakespeare himself'. As might be expected, moral considerations are stressed in Victorian school editions; *Measure for Measure* is dropped from one of 1883 because 'teachers find objection to it'. The 1888 version in John Heywood's Literary Readers, edited by Alfonzo Gardiner, Headmaster of the Little Holbeck Board School (Leeds School Board), states as one of its aims 'to give such needful explanations as shall make the language and the allusions intelligible to young readers', and as another 'to show the many moral lessons that Shakespeare's plays enforce'. The glossarial notes include '*Immortal Providence*—The goodness of God to us, which never ceases'; there are Lists of Spellings, and vile illustrations. William P. Coyne's forbidding edition of 1895 numbers the lines of the tales in fives, offering them as fodder for a method of instruction that has little to do with the imagination and that illustrates the danger of confusing

Lamb with Shakespeare: the volume 'may be of practical service in offering themes for the always valuable class-exercise of paraphrase and analysis, and may supply the teacher with apt and admirable materials for, say, a contrast of the dramatic and narrative styles of writing, for an occasional discourse on the merits of Lamb's methods of criticism, or for an historical reference to the qualities of idiom and diction, which make the language of Shakespeare a model of strength, pith, and brevity.' This kind of didacticism is exactly the attitude of mind that Lamb thought he was combatting by retelling the *Tales* in the first place. Like other editors of this period, Coyne stresses the moral value not merely of the *Tales* and of Shakespeare but of the lessons to be learned from Charles Lamb's 'self-annihilating devotion . . . to the care and tutelage of his sister', which 'affords . . . one of the most touching and noble incidents in the range of literary annals'.

A number of editions around the turn of the century illustrate the growth of character criticism: one of 1899 provides 'Sketches of the Principal Characters', as does the Oxford and Cambridge edition of 1904. Such preoccupations are apparent too in the questions with which pupils are presented: 'Name three men whose characters you admire, and give your reasons . . .' (1899); 'What do you admire most in the characters of . . .' (1899); 'Can you justify Desdemona's choice of a husband?' (1904). The 1904 edition is particularly suggestive as to the educative methods applied to the *Tales*: 'short character sketches . . . will be found to contain . . . all the leading features of each character'; passages from the plays 'will afford useful practice in paraphrasing, in parsing, and in analysis; many of them are also suitable for committing to memory'; there is a section on 'Lessons to be derived from the Tale', and a statement that the editors 'have expunged without ceremony whatever seemed unsuitable for juvenile readers'. The detailed annotations are a curious mixture of the naïve and the over-sophisticated; the young reader who needed to be told that a dragon was 'a fabulous monster' might have been daunted when faced with the gloss '*peculiar*, special, particular: from Old Fr. *peculier*: Lat. *peculiaris*, one's own'.

Later school editions are less ambitious. A much used one is in Dent's King's Treasuries of Literature series (1920); it has eight tales with extracts from the plays and simple 'Literary Exercises', such as 'Which of the plays would you call tragedies?', 'Who is the jolliest person in the stories?', and—continuing the moral emphasis on Charles Lamb's treatment of his sister—'What was there heroic about Charles Lamb's life?' In 1934 A. C. Ward wrote: 'Only in the present generation has the repute of [the *Tales*] suffered a serious decline, under the influence of a new scholastic conviction that paraphrased and pemmicanised classics are a hindrance more than an aid to literary appreciation.'[19]

I hope I've said enough—and I fear I may have said too much—to indicate something of the function that the Lambs' *Tales* have fulfilled since their publication. Their work has undoubtedly become a classic, and if it is less used as a Shakespeare substitute in schools than it used to be, it still serves as a crib even to distinguished performers of Shakespeare: the actress Gemma Jones writes in *Players of Shakespeare* (1985) that, invited to play Hermione in *The Winter's Tale* at Stratford, she tried to read the play but, finding difficulty in understanding it, resorted to Charles and Mary Lamb, who, she says, 'tell me a tale'.[20] This pinpoints one of the attractions of the *Tales*: even an actress, accustomed to working with playscripts, acknowledges the easier comprehensibility of a third-person narrative.

Although the title 'Tales from Shakespeare' instantly evokes the Lambs, the classic status of their volume has not gone unchallenged; and I should like now to turn to some of the alternative versions that have been offered. Most are long-forgotten. Some may well have fallen virtually dead from the presses; others had a life that is now expired; some of the more recent ones have a vitality that may carry them alive and kicking into the next century—though by then, of course, they may have more competitors.

Although the Lambs may not have known it, fourteen of Shakespeare's plays had already been turned into short stories, in French. In 1783, J. B. Perrin, a London-based teacher of French to the English nobility and gentry, had published *Contes Moraux & Instructifs, à l'usage de la Jeunesse, tirés des Tragédies de Shakespeare*. Subscribers to the volume included David Garrick's widow, who took six copies, and the tales—which include histories and *Cymbeline* as well as tragedies—are based on theatrical versions, including Garrick's adaptation of *Romeo and Juliet*. Presumably Perrin worked from Bell's recently published theatre edition. His Preface is predictably preoccupied with the unities, and *Titus Andronicus* is declared fit to be performed only before cannibals.

---

[19] *The Frolic and the Gentle* (London, 1934), 1970 edn., p. 131.
[20] 'Hermione in *The Winter's Tale*' in Philip Brockbank (ed.), *Players of Shakespeare* (Cambridge, 1985), pp. 153–65, quotation on p. 153.

The principal function of this volume was later to be fulfilled by the many foreign-language translations of Lamb.[21]

Two rival volumes appeared during Charles Lamb's lifetime. One, *Tales of the Drama* by Elizabeth Wright Macauley, published in 1822, is interesting partly because its author was (in her way) both a poet and an actress. Her collection, drawing on the current theatre repertoire, includes tales based on plays by Massinger, Shirley, Rowe, Steele, Goldsmith, and Mrs Cowley, as well as six by Shakespeare. A publisher's Preface declares that she has attempted 'to preserve all the colloquial wit and scenic effect' and, above all, 'to render the whole strictly obedient to the most refined ideas of delicacy, subservient to the best purposes of morality, and conducive to the highest sense of religious awe, and love for a beneficent Providence'. Again one notes the purificatory function; and Miss Macauley's theatrical affiliations make it even clearer than in the case of the Lambs that she is trying, as her publishers say, to extend knowledge of the stage even 'to family circles where the drama itself is forbidden'. This curious volume is decorated with many pleasing little engravings, and the plots are both treated with some freedom—*The Winter's Tale*, for instance, begins with the episode of Antigonus and the bear and tells the preceding part of the story in retrospect—and also elaborated with verse passages written by Miss Macauley herself: thus, *The Merchant of Venice* includes an original verse invocation by Portia to 'the spirit of her venerated father', and ends with Miss Macauley's poetical thoughts on friendship. Lest there should be any danger of confusion, verse quotations from 'our immortal Avonian Bard' are marked with asterisks. The tone throughout is highly moralistic. This volume, never reprinted, might repay investigation by students of the theatre.

The principal interest of *The Juvenile Shakespeare, adapted to the Capacities of Youth* published in 1828 by Caroline Maxwell, a minor novelist, is that, including only plays with a historical basis, such as *Cymbeline*, *Titus*, and *Lear*, she nevertheless omits the major English historical plays while including the apocryphal *Thomas Lord Cromwell* and *Sir John Oldcastle*. This is an introductory volume, designed to tell the stories of the plays 'in the most simple and easy style ... and to introduce in the course of the narratives, some of the most beautiful passages which each contain, for study or recitation ...'. Again, moral purpose is

---

[21] Bertram Dobell writes briefly on Perrin in *Sidelights on Charles Lamb* (London, 1903).

rammed home: 'on no occasion has the fair purity of the infant mind been for one moment forgot ...' (Presumably Caroline Maxwell, like Macbeth, had no children.)

Around mid-century, Duncombe's Miniature Library published a series of Dramatic Tales, brief narrative versions of dramas, melodramas, extravaganzas, and pantomimes performed in London's minor theatres. These tiny volumes, each illustrated with a crude, often coloured engraving, sold for twopence each. Presumably they were on sale at the theatres, just as editions of the text as acted in grander performances could be bought at the Theatres Royal. The Library includes over twenty tales from Shakespeare, retold by a minor—indeed, minimal—playwright, Joseph Graves, which could be had either individually or in bound volumes accompanied by a Life of Shakespeare. Like Perrin's *Contes Moraux*, these tales are based on theatrical adaptations. At the end of *Richard II*, the Queen dies 'upon the corse of her unfortunate husband', as in Richard Wroughton's version acted by Kean in 1814 (and published in 1815). *King Lear* has its tragic ending, but, as in Tate, there is no Fool, and Edgar is in love with Cordelia; though he becomes King, he 'never afterwards formed any attachment; but devoted the remainder of his days in [*sic*] sorrow and mourning'. Most curiously, at the end of *A Midsummer Night's Dream* Theseus delivers an encomiastic defence of the drama as a beneficent moral and ethical influence, and instructs Philostrate to 'further its interests whenever opportunity offers'. This appears to be a flight of Graves's own fancy rather than a reflection of a theatre version.

After this, the Lambs' supremacy was unchallenged until 1880, when Mary Seymour published *Shakespeare's Stories Simply Told*, in two volumes. These are simple, sometimes simplistic versions, perhaps influenced by the Lambs—at any rate, making some of the same omissions—though including all the plays. Although the author is not over-moralistic for her time, she exercises some ingenuity in avoiding moral awkwardnesses: 'Claudio ... had for some time been leading a very bad life, which was quite forbidden by the laws of the city'; no mention is made of Juliet's pregnancy, Angelo is actually married to Mariana, but has 'cast her from him', and the bed trick becomes 'another interview'. All ends well, 'for Claudio became reformed in character, and when Isabella was made Duchess of Vienna her influence over the people was sufficient to exterminate the vices to which they had for so long been prone, and the state became once more prosperous and glorious'.

A sweetly pretty fancifulness characterizes Adelaide C. Gordon Sim's *Phoebe's Shakespeare*, of 1894, very clearly intended for
little girls—or presumably for one particular little girl, since the
Preface is addressed to 'My Dear Little Phoebe' and signed
'Auntie Addie'. 'Once upon a time ... there lived a most
wonderful man called Mr William Shakespeare. No one before
he lived ever made up such beautiful stories ... Mr Shakespeare
wrote some stories that even children can read and understand;
and I have written these down for you, and made them into this
book, because I want you to learn to know them, and to love
them, while you are still a little girl.' It's all very sweet and
charming; the plots have passed through an imagination and
come out far more heavily romanticized than by the Lambs,
though not totally lacking in moral fibre—Romeo 'should have
been a little more patient and less selfish, and [have] remembered
that he had no right to kill himself just because he was unhappy'.
Like other, later writers, Adelaide Sim brings Shakespeare
himself into the picture: 'Mr William Shakespeare was a poet,
and a poet is a person who *can* see fairies, and one lovely summer
night, when he was lying under the trees on the soft moss in the
woods, he heard and saw some wonderful things, and wrote them
down and made this story ...' Though the plots are simplified in
structure they are sometimes elaborated in detail, as in the way
The Tempest is rounded off: 'sailors tried to discover' Prospero's
island, 'but they have never found it to this day, and I don't
think they ever will, for, after Prospero and Miranda left, I
believe the fairies gave it to the mermaids, who took it down to
the bottom of the sea and used it for a palace, and Caliban went
down with it. He'll never be able to do any more mischief.' A
similar level of readership is envisaged by E[dith] Nesbit in *The
Children's Shakespeare* of 1897, which is prettily if kinkily illustrated with paintings and drawings in which children are portrayed in grown-up roles: we see a four-year old Romeo embracing a little dimpled Juliet, a tiny Hamlet histrionically banishing
a diminutive Ophelia to a nunnery (Pl. IV), and an innocently
merry little Malvolio with a suitably haughty young Olivia.[22]

By contrast to this kind of little-girlishness, there is a hearty,
self-conscious young-manliness about A. T. Quiller-Couch's *Historical Tales from Shakespeare*. The volume appeared in 1899,
during the last years of Queen Victoria, when English soldiers

[22] Edith Nesbit's retellings of Shakespeare went through several stages: see
the bibliography in Julia Briggs, *A Woman of Passion: The Life of E. Nesbit,
1858–1924* (London, 1987).

were fighting in South Africa. Patriotic fervour ran high, and
Quiller-Couch regarded patriotism as the 'great lesson' of
Shakespeare's history plays: indeed, they 'might almost serve as a
handbook to patriotism, did that sacred passion need one'.
Unfortunately there was one serious lapse: the portrayal of Joan
of Arc (in 1 *Henry VI*). Again the issue was exacerbated by
topicality: this was the period during which Joan was being
groomed as a candidate for canonization. Quiller-Couch would
like to believe that Shakespeare 'was always fair and just', that he
'had no hand in the slanderous portrait of Joan of Arc sent down
to us under his name'. In any case, 'no writer with a conscience
could repeat that portrait for the children in whom are bound up
our hopes of a better England than we shall see . . . here they will
not be given the chance; since today, if ever, it is necessary to
insist that no patriotism can be true which gives to a boy no
knightliness or to a girl no gentleness of heart.' In the play, you
will remember, Joan, condemned to death as a sorceress, disowns
her poor old father, claims to be of royal birth, and at first
proclaims her virginity, but then, finding her captors unmoved,
confesses she is with child, and claims first that the father is
Alençon, then that it is René, King of Naples; she is led cursing to
execution. Quiller-Couch's version is much closer to that with
which we are familiar from Bernard Shaw: 'A pile of faggots was
raised in the market place of Rouen, where her statue stands
today. The brutal soldiers tore her from the hands of the clergy
and hurried her to the stake, but their tongues fell silent at her
beautiful composure. One even handed her a cross he had
patched together with two rough sticks. "Yes!" she cried, "my
voices *were* of God!" and with those triumphant words the head
of this incomparable martyr sank on her breast. "We are lost",
muttered an English soldier standing in the crowd, "we have
burned a saint"'. This is adaptation in the service of propa-
ganda; and Quiller-Couch is even more blatant in some of his
footnotes. Of the closing speech of *King John* ('This England
never did, nor never shall, Lie at the proud foot of a conqueror
. . .') he writes that 'the lesson of this "troublesome reigne" is
summed up for us in the wise, brave, and patriotic words of
Faulconbridge—lines which every English boy should get by
heart'; and John of Gaunt's speech on 'this royal throne of kings'
is an 'incomparable lament', which 'may only be rendered in
Shakespeare's own words, which no English boy, who is old
enough to love his country, is too young to get by heart,
forgetting the sorrow in it'.

In his Preface, Quiller-Couch disclaims the attempt 'to round off or tag a conclusion' to the Lambs' 'inimitable work', and indeed his method is very different from theirs. In keeping with a movement of thought that I noticed in school editions of Lamb at this time, he says that he stresses 'the *characters* in these plays'. He adds a considerable amount of historical detail and back-ground—Falstaff, for example, was 'a poor gentleman shaken loose from the lower degrees of feudalism when that edifice began to rock and totter'—and draws attention to important changes of history. He reproduces and paraphrases much dialogue, and tells the stories at considerable length with that narrative flair that made him, in his time, a highly successful novelist. The volume had two new editions, in 1905 and 1910.

Quiller-Couch pays tribute to the 'easy grace' of the Lambs' style, but Sidney Lee, in his somewhat heavy-handed Introduction to Mary Macleod's *Shakespeare Story-Book* of 1902, complains that Mary Lamb 'had little of her brother's literary power' and claims (reasonably enough) that her omissions, in particular, justify the 'endeavour to supply young readers with a fuller and more accurate account'. In conclusion he stresses the tales' exemplary value: 'of both stories and characters proffering the counsel to seek what is good and true and to shun what is bad Shakespeare's pages are full.' Mary Macleod herself was a successful children's writer; her books include adaptations of Malory, Froissart, and Spenser, and *A Book of Ballad Stories* introduced by Edward Dowden, along with *Hilda at School* and *Tiny True Tales of Animals. The Shakespeare Story-Book* had a fourth edition in 1911 and appeared in Spanish translation the following year. She writes vigorously, provides some historical placing (beginning *Macbeth* with information about witchcraft, for example), and is capable of incisive comment: 'when trouble arose, the nurse's shallow, selfish nature became apparent, and poor Juliet was soon to learn that she must rely solely on her own strength and judgement in the sorrows that overwhelmed her.' Like Beerbohm Tree in his then-current production, she ends *Hamlet* with the flights of angels that sing the hero to his rest; and at times in her narrative passages she makes a strong attempt to convey a conception of the play in performance: 'And what was left for Shylock to answer? Baffled of his revenge, stripped of his wealth, forced to disown his faith, his very life forfeited—a hated, despised, miserable old man—he stood alone amidst the hostile throng. Not one face looked at him kindly, not one voice was raised on his behalf. Twice he strove to speak, and twice he failed. Then, in a hoarse whisper through the parched lips, came the faltering words: "I—am—content"'. 'Shylock', said *The Spectator*, 'is Mr Irving's finest performance, and his final exit is its best point . . . the expression of defeat in every limb and feature, the deep, gasping sigh, as he passes slowly out, and the crowd rush from the Court to hoot and howl at him outside, make up an effect which must be seen to be comprehended.'[23] It is difficult not to feel that Mary Macleod was influenced by Irving's interpretation.

I pass quickly over the relatively undistinguished versions of Lois Grosvenor Hufford (an American) in 1902, R. Hudson, an elementary and highly selective version of ten plays in 1907, and of Alice Spencer Hoffman (1911), and alight briefly on those of Thomas Carter, a Doctor of Theology who made his contributions to Shakespeare scholarship with *Shakespeare, Puritan and Recusant* (1897) and *Shakespeare and Holy Scripture* (1905), and who also, under a pseudonym, wrote improving books for boys, such as *Jeffrey of the White Wolf Trail* (1912), *Sinclair of the Scouts* (1911), both published by the Religious Tract Society, *The Stolen Grand Lama: An English Boy's Adventures in Wild Tibet* (*Boy's Own Paper*, 1917), and *Yarns on Heroes of India: a book for workers among boys* (Church Missionary Society, 1915). Dr Carter did not seek to abandon his more scholarly persona when he came to publish *Stories from Shakespeare* in 1910, and *Shakespeare's Stories of the English Kings* in 1912. I wonder if you can guess, for example, which play is being introduced here: 'On the great plain of Attica, watered by the Kaphisos and the brook Ilissus, and circled by its hills, Parnassus, Hymettus, Pantelicon, and Lycabettus, there stands the famous city of Athens. Not many miles away, the sunlit waters of unconquered Salamis, the Bay of Eleusis, and the bold Saronic Gulf enclose the land in a belt of purple sea.' That is how Thomas Carter seeks to lead his young readers into the world of *A Midsummer Night's Dream*. The didact is evident in, for example, the distancing of the opening of *Macbeth*: 'The great story of Macbeth is an illustration of the powers of imagination of conscience, working in a sensitive and highly-strung mind. . . . To feel the power of the story you must know its setting.' Carter elaborates detail in a manner that seems at times to anticipate the worst excesses of psychological criticism: 'Death had early taken away his [Shylock's] wife Leah; and

[23] *Spectator* (8 Nov. 1879); cited by Arthur Colby Sprague, *Shakespearian Players and Performances* (Cambridge, Mass., 1953, British edn., London, 1954), p. 116.

his daughter Jessica, too careless and too selfish to strive to learn the secret of a proud man's heart, had allowed his home to grow into a place of suspicion and coldness and bickering, wherein the strife of the world outside was carried within its walls, and dishonesty and treachery allowed to make havoc of its peace.' And at times he seems to occupy the pulpit rather than the story-teller's chair: 'as he [Lear] passes from our sight in a passionate agony of yearning for the. peace and light and love which dwelt for him in the pure and holy heart of Cordelia, we feel that the great writer in the words "Look there, look there!" lifts up the dark curtain for an instant that the light of the Eternal may shine through and speak of hope Beyond.' Carter makes immensely worthy, earnest attempts to turn the plays into improving short stories; it seems no accident that the copy of *Stories from Shakespeare* that I picked up in a second-hand shop had been presented as a school prize. Nor is it entirely surprising that when four of the verbose Carter's stories were reissued in 1937, they were 'adapted and rewritten within the thousand-word vocabulary'.

The batch of tales of which I have just been speaking, published from 1893 to 1914, coincides, you may have noticed, with the period during which the Lambs' *Tales* were at the height of their popularity. The new versions, in other words, seem not so much to have been driving the Lambs off the market as to have been supplying an alternative demand—partly (though only partly) by providing versions of plays that the Lambs had omitted. As reprints of the Lambs' *Tales* dwindled, so, for a while, did alternative versions. Even so, there are more than I can spare time to mention. There is a *Shakespeare Tales for Boys and Girls* dating apparently from around 1930 whose attitude to the events of *Measure for Measure* suggests a major shift in moral values: Claudio had been condemned 'for an act of rash selfishness which nowadays would only be punished by severe reproof'. Even so, there is no bed in the bed trick. Friars, we are told, 'are as nearly like nuns as men can be', and Claudio had 'a queer friend called Lucio' who was finally 'condemned to marry a stout woman with a bitter tongue'. At the end 'She [Isabella] was his [the Duke's] with a smile, and the Duke forgave Angelo, and promoted the Provost.'

Much more interesting is a forgotten volume of 1934 which I confess to regarding as something of a find. Called *Six Stories from Shakespeare*, it boasts as authors John Buchan, Hugh Walpole, Clemence Dane, Francis Brett Young, Winston Churchill, and

Viscount Snowden.[24] Each tells a different tale. I wondered if Churchill might have chosen *Henry V*; in fact his play is *Julius Caesar*. He displays a politician's shrewdness in his analysis of Brutus's arguments in favour of the assassination: 'Caesar must not be allowed even the chance of going wrong, the seed of potential tyranny must be killed outright, like a serpent in the egg. One could hear the sigh of relief and release with which he finally persuaded himself to acquiesce in this sophistry.' And in the Forum scene Churchill stands apart from the tale with a comment on the oratory: 'It can scarcely be necessary to remind the reader of what [Antony] said, for no speech in the history of the world is more famous, none better known. "Friends, Romans, countrymen ..." ... the words are alive on every tongue, and custom cannot stale them.' There Churchill treats Shakespeare as history, and comments on it (in 'custom cannot stale them') with a half-submerged quotation from Shakespeare himself.

But the most aesthetically interesting of these tales are those told by the professional novelists. Hugh Walpole creates a great sense of awed wonder in the narrator of the Lear story. John Buchan's narrative of *Coriolanus* is told at a tangent from Shakespeare's play, with old Publicola as the central character; as he takes his ease in various parts of Rome, the events are narrated to him by characters including the tribunes, Menenius, and Flaccus, with the result that the story acquires a distanced, retrospective quality. It ends with Flaccus telling Publicola of the hero's death:

'He died like a Roman', said Menenius.
'He might have been the Volscian king, but he was too noble', said Flaccus.
But old Publicola flung a fold of his cloak over his head and looked on the ground.
'It is as I feared', he said. 'He had no part in Rome. He had gone barbarian.'

And in *Hamlet* Francis Brett Young takes his cue from Hamlet's request that Horatio 'draw [his] breath in pain | To tell my story'. Again, the tale is told in retrospect; as narrator, Horatio is also (validly) a commentator, who sounds as if he had read, as well as met, *Hamlet* at Wittenberg: 'if the mere act of vengeance

---

[24] The stories had originally appeared as a series, 'Shakespeare's Plays as Short Stories', in the *Strand Magazine* (1933–4).

appeased [Hamlet's] devotion to his father's memory, I believe
that the artist in him took pleasure in the complicated hazards
against which it must be wreaked; I believe he took pains to
contrive his vengeance as a work of art ...' Paradoxically
enough, here, as in Buchan's *Coriolanus*, the narration of the
drama's events by an involved participant rather than a
detached, omniscient story-teller restores something of the dramatic mode. The best of these *Six Stories* seem to me to float free
from their models and to acquire value as fully realized short
stories in their own right.

Very different is the unemphatic, even laconic tone of the
scholar G. B. Harrison in his two volumes of *New Tales* of 1938
and 1939. Not for Harrison the rhetoric of Thomas Carter at
Lear's death—though there is a reflection of Bradley: 'So they
gathered round, watching Lear as he feebly knelt beside Cordelia. The little life left in him began to flicker. Suddenly he
thought that her lips moved, and with a cry of joy he fell over her
body.' Harrison's generally phlegmatic tone may be not unfairly
represented by the ending of his composite story 'Sir John
Falstaff', of which the last words are 'So that was the end of
Falstaff'. 'Nothing is here for tears ...'

As the Shakespeare quatercentenary of 1964 approached, so,
as if in anticipation, the number of new tales from Shakespeare
increased. In 1960 appeared Marchette Chute's version, summary in style and making no real attempt at imaginative reconstruction. Irene Buckman's *Twenty Tales from Shakespeare* of 1963,
nicely produced with excellent photographs of recent productions, has a short foreword by Peggy Ashcroft saying that,
whereas the Lambs' *Tales* 'were for the nursery and the fireside',
these are for 'the young playgoer and the young playgoer's
parents'. But these too are relatively summary in manner.

There is more life in Roger Lancelyn Green's two volumes
(twenty tales) of 1964. Christopher Fry, in a brief foreword,
remarks that Green had acted many of the minor roles himself,
and certainly he has theatrical touches. There seems, for example, to be a direct echo of Clifford Williams's 1962 production
of *The Comedy of Errors* in Green's '"Are you pleading with me,
fair lady?" asked Antipholus, looking behind him to see if she
was talking to someone over his shoulder.' The action is occasionally up-dated in the manner of modern-dress productions—Dr
Pinch is a psychiatrist, though his methods of treatment sound a
little archaic: 'Both your husband and your servant are suffering
from schizophrenia: I know the symptoms only too well. They

must be bound and laid in a dark room.' There are other fanciful additions—Leontes gave the old shepherd 'lands in Sicily where he settled down as a gentleman-farmer, and was able to employ Autolycus as a bailiff'; and Lady Macbeth helpfully tells Macbeth 'I know what it is to be a mother, for I had a child by my first husband.' But Green's tales are ultimately reductive because of a failure to match up to the emotional demands of the story, nowhere more evident than at the end of Shylock's trial: after the Duke has said that Shylock must sign a deed, we are told simply 'So Shylock went off home'!

More successful is Ian Serraillier's *The Enchanted Island: Stories from Shakespeare*, of 1964. Serraillier creates alternative titles: 'A Wild-Cat for a Wife', 'Bottom the Actor', 'Murder at Dunsinane', and so on. He does not aim to be comprehensive—there is, for example, no Viola plot in 'The Love-Letter' (based on *Twelfth Night*); Cesario *is* Orsino's page. There is no casket story in 'The Pound of Flesh'—Bassanio simply woos Portia—nor are there any young lovers in 'Bottom the Actor'. The tone is straightforward and clear, but uncondescending. Action is successfully visualized, though not necessarily in stage terms. We might once again take the ending of *King Lear* as a sample:

The field between the two camps was crowded with soldiers, Kent and Albany among them. Suddenly the ranks broke and in the silence a tragic figure stumbled forward. It was Lear, clasping Cordelia's limp body and crying out in a voice of anguish, 'She's gone for ever. She's dead as earth.'

Yet somehow he could not believe that she was really dead. He asked for a mirror to hold close to her mouth to see if there was any breath to mist the glass; then for a feather to see if it would stir on her lips. For a moment it seemed to stir—but only in mockery. .... All he could grasp was that Cordelia was in his arms, that she was dead and would never come to him again.

A moment later he too had gone, his living martyrdom ended at last. Death had come as a blessing, for he could endure no more.

The tone is unsentimental, unmoralistic, and there is no condescension.

One has the sense in Serraillier's volume, as in some of the others I have mentioned, that these stories are not primarily introductions to the study of Shakespeare, or even introductions to Shakespeare in performance, but the result, in however minor a way, of an interaction between the author's imagination and

Shakespeare's; the stories have their own independent interest, deeply indebted though they are to Shakespeare.

There may come a point in such a process at which tales cease being versions, or reinterpretations, of Shakespeare and assume a virtually independent life of their own. Such a point, approached in Serraillier's work, is reached and passed in Bernard Miles's popular *Favourite Tales from Shakespeare* of 1976 and *Well-Loved Tales from Shakespeare* of 1986. These are free, idiosyncratic fantasies on plays rather than retellings of them.

But it is pleasant to record that the most recent—or almost the most recent—of the retellings that I have traced is one that, in my opinion, brilliantly succeeds in translating both the substance and the effect of Shakespeare's plays into the narrative medium. In *Shakespeare Stories*, of 1985, Leon Garfield adopts a crisp, sharply metaphorical style, often employing bold images: Juliet stares down from her balcony 'with her willow hair weeping'; when Kate, the shrew, stormed through her father's house in a bad temper, 'doors kept going off like exploding chestnuts'; in Illyria, thatched cottages are 'neat as well-combed children'. Though Garfield's prose is not unmannered, it succeeds remarkably in providing an acceptable alternative to Shakespeare's poetry. Like the Lambs, Garfield omits some episodes—the Porter from *Macbeth*, the Nurse's introductory scene from *Romeo and Juliet*, the Pedant from *The Taming of the Shrew*—, but he displays a mastery of the plays' structural principles that enables him to transmute their essential features into the medium of the short story. This is apparent in, for instance, his use of analytical parallels to effect transitions: 'While one Harry was idly dreaming of the glory that would be his, the other Harry was much concerned with the glory that *was* his'; and 'Even as the casket that Jessica had thrown down from Shylock's window had contained her father's treasure, so one of the three closed caskets in Belmont contained another father's treasure.' Such comments put criticism to creative use.

The essential difference, it seems to me, between Garfield's method and the Lambs' is that where the Lambs provided a simplified reading experience as a preparation for a more complex and difficult experience of the same kind, Garfield seeks to convey in prose narrative the experience, not of reading the twelve plays that he includes, but of seeing them performed. Sometimes he visualizes action that could be used as stage business: Falstaff 'sat down and regarded his countenance in the diminishing bowl of a spoon' before saying 'why, my skin hangs about me like an old lady's loose-gown'; Polonius reads his list of entertainments offered by the actors who visit Elsinore 'from the company's extensive advertisement, which reached down, like a paper apron, almost to his knees'; and after the enraged Claudius has stopped the play and stormed out of the chamber, 'the bewildered Player King crept back to recover his tinsel crown. Then he went away, sadly shaking his head. The performance had not gone well.' It might almost be Hazlitt writing about Kean—and there is a Shakespearian touch in the sudden recognition of the Player's point of view. Garfield is best known as a writer for teenagers, and his volume is presented in a manner that seems intended primarily for young readers, but his transmuting power gives his stories a wider appeal; they are not pale reflections of Shakespeare, not introductory studies, but fully imagined re-creations with a life of their own.

I have, I know, given only a superficial survey of a literary subgenre which, though minor, has been too popular to be adequately considered within a single lecture. In recent years, theatrical adaptations of Shakespeare from the Restoration onwards have been much reprinted and studied. Prose adaptations have been almost entirely neglected, yet they have been immensely popular, and are often no less radical in their revisions and reinterpretations.[25] I don't suggest that I have identified an important new growth area in Shakespearian studies; but I hope I've said enough to suggest that the successive retellings of Shakespeare's stories offer a body of material that permits an interesting exploration of narrative techniques, that—like stage adaptations—they can reflect changing critical and moral perspectives on Shakespeare himself, that they are of sociological interest, especially in relation to the history of education, and that some of them are not negligible as prose fictions in their own right.[26]

[25] The most substantial study is by Maria Verch, 'Die Lambschen *Tales from Shakespeare* und ihre Nachfolger', *Shakespeare Jahrbuch 1980*, pp. 90–108. The Lambs' *Tales* are critically considered in J. Riehl, *Charles Lamb's Children's Literature* (Salzburg, 1980).

[26] The lecture as read concluded with a recording of a version of *Romeo and Juliet* from the audio cassette *One-Minute Classics*, conceived and written by Andy Mayer and Jim Becker and performed by John 'Mighty-Mouth' Moschitta (1986).

Editions cited

(a) Charles and Mary Lamb

Tales from Shakespear. Designed for the use of young persons ... By Charles Lamb. Embellished with copper-plates. 2 vols. (London, 1807)

Tales from Shakespear. 2 vols. (London, 1809)

Tales from Shakespear. 2nd edn. 2 vols. (London, 1810)
   (Duplicates the 1809 edition, except that this has a new title-page and the engravings of the first edition, and lacks the 'advertisement' of 1809.)

Tales from Shakespear, 6th edn. (London, 1838)

Tales from Shakspeare ... To which is added, the Life of Shakespeare (London, n.d.; *c*. 1843)

Tales from Shakspeare by Mr and Miss Lamb. A New Edition. To which are now added, Scenes Illustrating Each Tale. 2 vols. (London: Charles Knight and Co., 1844)

Tales from Shakespeare. 4 Parts (Edinburgh and London, 1862)
   (Gordon's School and Home Series; reprints sixteen tales)

A Selection of Tales from Shakspeare. Edited with an Introduction, Notes and an Appendix of Extracts from Shakspeare by J. H. Flather, M.A. (Cambridge, 1875)
   (Pitt Press; six tales)

Tales from Shakspeare. Edited, with an Introduction, by the Rev. Alfred Ainger, M.A. (London, 1879)

Lamb's Tales from Shakspeare: with 40 illustrations by Sir John Gilbert, R.A. (London, n.d. [1882])
   (Part of Routledge's Sixpenny Series)

Tales from Shakspere. With Illustrative Extracts from Shakspere's Plays (Annotated), and a Picture to each Tale (London, 1883)
   (Marcus Ward's Educational Literature; omits *Measure for Measure* 'to which teachers find objection'.)

Tales from Shakspeare. Ed. with explanatory notes, &c. for the use of schools, by A. Gardiner (Manchester, 1888)
   (John Heywood's Literary Readers; selected tales)

Tales from Shakespeare including those by Charles and Mary Lamb with a continuation by Harrison S. Morris. 4 vols. (London, 1893)

Tales from Shakspeare. Introductory Preface by Andrew Lang. Illustrations by R. A. Bell (London, 1894)

Tales from Shakspeare. Edited with introduction and notes and chronological tables by William P. Coyne M.A., 2nd edn. (Dublin and London, 1895)
   (Browne and Nolan's English Texts; selected tales. B.L. records only the 'second edition'.)

Tales from Shakespeare with twelve illustrations by A. Rackham (London, 1899)
   (Dent's Temple Classics for Young People; reprinted in Everyman's Library, 1906, etc.)

Tales from Shakespeare. With Introduction and Notes by C. D. Punchard B.A. (1899, etc.)
   (Eight tales)

Tales from Shakespeare. With Introductions and Additions by F. J. Furnivall ... Founder and Director of the New Shakspere and other Societies. 2 vols. (London, 1901)

Tales from Shakespeare. With 16 full-page illustrations by W. H[eath] Robinson (London, n.d. [1902])

The Oxford and Cambridge Edition of Tales from Shakespeare for Preliminary Students, with Introduction, Notes, Examination Papers, Extracts from the Plays, etc. Edited by Stanley Wood M.A., Editor of Dinglewood Shakespeare Manuals, etc., and A. T. Spilsbury, M.A., Senior Classical Master at the City of London School. 2 vols. (n.d. [1904, 1909]). (Selected tales)

Tales from Shakespeare ... With sixteen illustrations (London: OUP, 1905)

Tales from Shakespeare, edited, with an Introduction and Notes, by George Sampson. Illustrated by J. A. Walker (London, 1909) (Hampstead Library)

The Gateway to Shakespeare for Children. Containing A Life of Shakespeare, by Mrs Andrew Lang, A Selection from the Plays, and from Lamb's *Tales*. With Sixteen Coloured Plates and many other Illustrations (London, n.d. [1909])

All Shakespeare's Tales. Tales from Shakespeare by Charles and Mary Lamb and Tales from Shakespeare by Winston Stokes. Illustrated by M. L. Kirk (London, 1911)

Lamb and Shakespeare: Selected Tales with Extracts from the Plays (London, n.d. [1920]) (Dent's King's Treasuries of Literature; eight tales)

Tales from Shakespeare ... expanded ... to include the complete plays, with essays on the Elizabethan theater and Shakespeare's life and times. Edited and with an introduction by Elizabeth Donno (New York, 1962)

Tales from Shakespeare. All those told by Charles and Mary Lamb with 12 others newly told by J. C. Trewin (London, 1964)

Tales from Shakespeare. Foreword by O. B. Hardison (Washington, D.C.: Folger Books, 1979)

(b) Other authors

Six Stories from Shakespeare. Retold by John Buchan [*Coriolanus*], Hugh Walpole [*King Lear*], Clemence Dane [*The Taming of the Shrew*], Francis Brett Young [*Hamlet*], Rt Hon. Winston Churchill [*Julius Caesar*], Rt Hon. Viscount Snowden [*The Merchant of Venice*] (London, 1934) (Eight illustrations by Fortunino Matania)

Anon., *Shakespeare Tales for Boys and Girls* and 'When Shakespeare was a Boy' by Dr F. J. Furnivall, M.A. (London, n.d.; *c.* 1930?)

Buckman, Irene, *Twenty Tales from Shakespeare*, with a Foreword by Dame Peggy Ashcroft (London, 1963)

Carter, Thomas, *Stories from Shakespeare* ... With sixteen full-page illustrations by Gertrude Demain Hammond (London, 1910) (Eleven plays)

Carter, Thomas, *Shakespeare's Stories of the English Kings* ... With sixteen full-page illustrations by Gertrude Demain Hammond (London, 1912)

Chute, Marchette, *Stories from Shakespeare* (London, 1960) (All the plays)

Garfield, Leon, *Shakespeare Stories.* Illustrated by Michael Foreman (London, 1985)

Graves, Joseph, *Dramatic Tales founded on Shakespeare's Plays*, to which is added

the Life of this Eminent Poet, by Joseph Graves. Embellished with Superb Engravings (London, n.d. [1850?])
(Duncombe's Miniature Library; the tales appeared both individually and in various combinations.)

Green, Roger Lancelyn, *Tales from Shakespeare*, with a foreword by Christo-.pher Fry. 2 vols. (London, 1964)
(Twenty plays)

Harrison, G. B., *New Tales from Shakespeare* (London, 1938)
(Seven plays)

Harrison, G. B., *More New Tales from Shakespeare* (London, 1939)
(Five plays)

Hoffman, Alice Spencer, *The Children's Shakespeare*, Being Stories from the Plays with Illustrative Passages (London, 1911)
(Twenty plays; illustrated by Charles Folkard)

Hudson, R., *Tales from Shakespeare* (London, n.d. [1907])
(Ten plays, retitled (e.g. 'Rosalind and Celia', 'The Story of Perdita') and told in elementary fashion)

Hufford, Lois Grosvenor, *Shakespeare in Tale and Verse* (London, 1902)
(Fifteen plays)

Macauley, Elizabeth Wright, *Tales of the Drama* founded on the Tragedies of Shakespeare, Massinger, Shirley, Rowe, Murphy, Lillo, and Moore, and on the Comedies of Steele, Farquhar, Cumberland, Bickerstaff, Goldsmith, and Mrs Cowley by Miss Macauley (Chiswick, 1822)
(Includes *King John, The Winter's Tale, Richard II, The Merchant of Venice, Coriolanus,* and *Julius Caesar.*)

Macleod, Mary, *The Shakespeare Story Book* with Introduction by Sidney Lee. Illustrations by Gordon Browne (London, 1902)
(Sixteen plays; reprinted 1911)

Maxwell, Caroline, *The Juvenile Shakespeare, adapted to the Capacities of Youth* (London, 1828)
(Includes only plays with a historical basis (e.g. *Cymbeline, Timon of Athens, King Lear,* but omits e.g. *Henry IV, Henry V, Richard III* while including *Thomas, Lord Cromwell* and *Sir John Oldcastle.*)

Miles, Bernard, *Favourite Tales from Shakespeare* (London, 1976)
(*Macbeth, A Midsummer Night's Dream, Romeo and Juliet, Twelfth Night,* and *Hamlet*)

Miles, Bernard, *Well-loved Tales from Shakespeare* (London, 1986)
(*The Tempest, As You Like It, Othello, The Merry Wives of Windsor, Julius Caesar*)

Nesbit, E[dith], *The Children's Shakespeare* (London, n.d. [1897])

Perrin, J. B., *Contes Moraux Amusans & Instructifs, à l'usage de la Jeunesse, tirés des Tragédies de Shakespeare* (London, 1783)
(*Hamlet, Coriolanus, King Lear, Romeo and Juliet, Othello, Macbeth, Julius Caesar, Antony and Cleopatra, King John, Richard II, Henry IV, Henry V, Richard III, Cymbeline, Timon of Athens*)

Quiller-Couch, A. T., *Historical Tales from Shakespeare* (London, 1899)
(Reprinted 1905, 1910)

Serraillier, Ian, *The Enchanted Island: Stories from Shakespeare* (London, 1964)

Seymour, Mary, *Shakespeare's Stories Simply Told*, 2 vols. (London, n.d. [1880])
(Includes all the plays; reprinted 1883; German translation, 1890)

Sim, Adelaide C. Gordon, *Phoebe's Shakespeare*, arranged for children (London, 1894)

HAMLET: CONVERSATIONS WITH THE DEAD

By A. D. NUTTALL

Read 21 April 1988

'WHO's there?' says Barnardo, bravely, in the cold darkness on
the castle platform. These are the first words of the play, and it is
hard to see how they could be bettered.* They carry, as often in
Shakespeare, both an immediate meaning and a larger meaning,
which is not simultaneously present but can grow in the mind as
the play unfolds. Barnardo means only, 'Who goes there?', the
sentry's challenge. The larger meaning is, 'Who is there, in the
darkness, among the dead?' As I struggle to paraphrase, I find
myself in danger of opting too easily for the more usual phrases:
'Is there life beyond the grave?' 'Are there human existences on
the far side of what we call death?' But these fail to take account
of a certain grammatical peculiarity in Shakespeare's words; the
sentry's challenge, though formally in the third person singular,
is partly infiltrated by a sense of second person singular, arising
from the fact that the question posed is addressed to its presumed
subject. In which case we must modify our paraphrase, perhaps
to 'Who, of you who are dead, is there?' The very awkwardness
of the sentence is instructive. The English language naturally
resists such a combination of second and third persons. Yet some
such phrasing is needed, because *Hamlet* is not a cool treatise on
death but is instead about an *encounter* with a dead person.

If Barnardo's words are to work at all, beyond their immediate
sense, they must, so to speak, be set ticking, like a time bomb. All
that is needed for this purpose is that the words be set slightly
askew, so that the immediate meaning is felt to be in some degree
unsatisfactory or incomplete. This is done, wonderfully, by
Francisco's reply: 'Nay, answer me. Stand and unfold yourself!'
Francisco means, '*I* am the sentry on duty, so I should be the one

* All quotations from Shakespeare are, unless otherwise specified, from
William Shakespeare, *The Complete Works*, edited by Stanley Wells and Gary
Taylor (Oxford: Clarendon Press, 1986).

to issue the challenge. Now *you* tell me who *you* are'. This exchange, with its wrong-footing of Barnardo, is remotely linked to farce, as many things will prove to be as the play goes on (two comic sentries frighten each other). But here the sense of fear is of course much stronger than any intuition of the ridiculous. We may think that Barnardo should formally have taken over from Francisco before challenging strangers, but the whole point of the challenge is that friend and foe cannot be distinguished at first. Shakespeare for once holds back on the theatrical metaphor—he does not make Francisco say, as the Volscian says in *Coriolanus* (IV. iii. 48) 'You take my part from me, sir'—but some sort of self-reference seems nevertheless to be going on: the actor arriving pat upon his cue matches neatly with 'most carefully upon your hour' (I. i. 4) and 'Unfold yourself' is placed exactly to echo the other use of *unfold*: 'explain oneself to the audience; perform the exposition'. Thus we have fear, faintly absurd confusion and a question of identity, thrown out upon the dark. And all the while someone, or some thing—something other than Francisco—is there. At line 19 Horatio (if we follow the second Quarto) or else Marcellus, shrewdly responding to the extra warmth of Barnardo's welcome, asks, 'What, has this thing appeared again tonight?'

Forty-six years ago in his Annual Shakespeare Lecture to the British Academy, C. S. Lewis said that the thing to remember about *Hamlet* is that it is about a man 'who has been given a task by a ghost'.[1] There is no ghost in Saxo Grammaticus's version of the Hamlet story, though there is in Belleforest's. We do not possess the Elizabethan *Hamlet* which preceded Shakespeare's, but we know from Lodge's reference to it that it contained a ghost. Curiously, we *do* possess Kyd's inverse *Hamlet*—for *The Spanish Tragedy* is about a father avenging his son—and there the whole action is watched by a dead man. In the *Ambales Saga* there are angels, and in remote Greek analogues there are, as we shall see, dreams, oracles and visions of a dead father. Hamlet, in Shakespeare's play, is beckoned into the shadows by something which may be his father, may be the Devil, may even be, since our disorientation is so great, negation itself. He is then made party to the dark world, is changed utterly, cut off from marriage and friendship, made an agent of death. The Ghost tells him to wreak vengeance, but Hamlet notoriously finds himself strangely

---

[1] *Proceedings of the British Academy*, **28** (1942), 139–54, p. 147. Also in C. S. Lewis, *Selected Literary Essays*. (Cambridge University Press, Cambridge, 1969) 88–105, p. 97.

impeded. It is as if, having joined the shades, he finds himself drained of substance. He savages Ophelia, because she is life, ready for procreation, but for the rest he is lost, suddenly adrift in the paralysing liberty of a kind of solipsism; bounded by a nutshell he could count himself king of infinite space, but for his bad dreams (II. ii. 257). Such reality as persists figures, we notice, as mere nightmare to Hamlet.

'There is nothing either good or bad but thinking makes it so', he tells Rosencrantz and Guildenstern (II. ii. 250–1). Professor Harold Jenkins in the New Arden edition robustly rejects the notion that ethical absolutes are here discarded, pointing out that the phrase is commonplace and has reference not to morals but to happiness or taste.[2] Certainly the same thought can be found (though not perhaps with precisely the same force) in Spenser and also in Montaigne who knows it as a Stoic aphorism. But for all that, I suspect that Professor Jenkins is here *too* robust. There was always a seed of epistemological relativism within Stoicism itself; the rational man is exhorted to rise above seeming misfortunes, bereavement, say, or exile by exerting the power of reason, by reflecting that all must die, or that the good man is a citizen of the whole world and therefore cannot be exiled. One senses that reason is here being accorded, covertly, a fictive power to reconstruct reality according to the needs of the subject. Real reason, one feels, is an altogether more constrained affair. The Stoic philosopher in Johnson's *Rasselas*, when his daughter died, found the reality of loss simply insuperable: 'What comfort, said the mourner, can truth and reason afford me? of what effect are they now, but to tell me, that my daughter will not be restored?'[3] Of course it is true that in Stoicism the major constraint of a rationally ordered cosmos is always present. With this, reason must always accord, and so by implication keep relativism at bay. But what of *Hamlet*, a Post-Stoic text? Surely it is not only bad readers who sense that now this thought is in suspension, hanging between ancient and modern conceptions. The passage taken as a whole is so instinct with a vertiginous uncertainty as to what is real, what unreal, what is waking, what dream, that the relativism germinally present even in Senecan Stoicism grows suddenly stronger. Philip Edwards in the New Cambridge edition[4] accepts Professor Jenkins's note, but only after a concessive

[2] The New Arden edition of *Hamlet* (Methuen, London, 1982) pp. 467–8.
[3] *The History of Rasselas, Prince of Abyssinia*, Chap. 18, ed. Geoffrey Tillotson and Brian Jenkins (Oxford University Press, London, 1971), p. 51.
[4] *Hamlet, Prince of Denmark*, the New Cambridge Shakespeare, ed. Philip Edwards (Cambridge University Press, Cambridge, 1985), p. 129.

clause: 'While this phrase voices an uncertainty about absolutes which reverberates through the play, Jenkins, makes it clear . . .' and so on. The wilder meaning, which is as much epistemological as it is ethical, cannot be entirely excluded.

I have argued so far in terms of mere metaphysical affinity: Hamlet meeting the father who no longer is, becomes one with death and un-being. Meanwhile, however, other lines of interpretation are open to us. William Empson in the 1950s offered a brilliant explanation[5] in terms of Shakespeare's orchestration of styles, now naturalistic, now theatrical. It is likely, he suggests. that Shakespeare was approached to do a re-write of the immensely popular Ur-*Hamlet*. The audience which demanded this was not however quite like the audience which had been terrified in the 1580s by, as it might be, Kyd. The new audience was keen but it was also cool. Such audiences are, by a familiar paradox, notoriously 'tickle o' the sere', that is, a shade too ready to laugh. Meanwhile, the text of the old play, which Shakespeare had before him, was marred by a crippling improbability: the hero, simply in order that the dramatist might spin out the suspense, and for no other reason, continually delayed. Faced with this state of affairs Shakespeare had a choice. He could either render the delay ordinarily intelligible by interposing a series of practical obstacles, or else he could foreground the very oddity of the delay, make his hero comment musingly on his own inaction, and so transform an original error of construction into a psychological mystery. He chose the second course and in so doing solved his problem with the too-cheerful audience. They could now be given, to their great delight, serious pastiche of the old play, in those scenes in which Hamlet assumes his antic disposition, but at any moment the dramatist could wipe the smiles from their faces by showing that beneath the histrionics lay something which they just did not understand:

> I have that within which passeth show—
> These but the trappings and the suits of woe.
>
> (I. ii. 85–6)

The play thus runs on a stylistic oscillation, between a histrionic seeming and a reality which is at first light and naturalistic but is

[5] 'Hamlet when new', *Sewanee Review*, **61** (1953). 15–42; reprinted in a revised form as 'Hamlet' in William Empson, *Essays on Shakespeare* (Cambridge University Press, Cambridge, 1986), pp. 79–136.

ultimately beyond our understanding. The melodramatic style, entirely appropriate to revenge tragedy, is disparaged by Hamlet in his advice to the players, but used by him to perplex the Court.

Empson's account is vigorous and elegant, yet finally somehow dispiriting. He dispatches centuries of laboured speculation on the sources of Hamlet's inaction through a single, meta-critical move: 'You are all puzzled because you were meant to be puzzled; Hamlet is constructed as a mystery, and there's an end on't'. In certain psychological experiments doggedly conscientious academics are made to struggle with problems which they are led to believe have solutions but in fact have none. It is so with the audience and readers of *Hamlet*. There is a sense, Empson, implies, in which all that vivid adventurous thought was a waste of time.

Empson's thesis, in the simple form to which I have reduced it, resolves all difficulties by frankly placing sheer negation or absence in the centre. But this is too clear, too neat, and of course Empson knew that. Shakespeare may give us no ultimate answer but, equally, he refuses to make it unequivocally clear that no answer should be sought. The negative comfort is withheld as is the positive. Trails of suggestion are laid down, so that we can sense at once that certain interpretations, though they may indeed be irremediably speculative and insusceptible of a final determination, are manifestly more reasonable than others. With all his marvellous openness of mind, Empson brings to bear a spirit naturally and vigorously atheist, a robust confidence of absence. What is rather needed for *Hamlet* is, I would suggest, agnosticism.

Notice first how soon Hamlet's scheme of histrionic deception begins to go off the rails. At first indeed he out-Hamlets the Ur-*Hamlet* to bemuse the opposition. But, as he separates himself from all ordinary, truthful conversation with the living, his motivation decays. We sense, behind the feigned madness, a real disorder in his understanding. There is one moment, seldom picked up in the theatre, which shows this very exactly. In the play scene Hamlet says to Ophelia, 'What should a man do but be merry? For look you how cheerfully my mother looks, and my father died within's two hours'. Ophelia answers, 'Nay 'tis twice two months, my lord'. Hamlet answers, 'So long? Nay then, let the devil wear black, for I'll have a suit of sables. O heavens, die two months ago, and not forgotten yet!' (III. ii. 119–25) If we attend, as Empson taught us, to the shifting styles, we shall see that Hamlet speaks at first, not indeed in the ranting style, but in the 'wild and whirling' hyperbolical manner which is similarly, though less certainly, associated with the feigned madness. Ophelia is distressed by his flippant exaggeration and answers with what must be the truth, that 'twice two', that is *four* months have elapsed. Hamlet reacts at first with the same harsh jocularity: 'I'll have a suit of sables' but then seems to drop into an ordinary speaking voice: 'Oh heavens, die two months ago and not forgotten yet?' But when at last he drops the false mannerisms, *he still gets the time wrong*; Ophelia said four months; Hamlet, thinking that he is agreeing, says two. Does he not know any more? To be sure, we could be dealing with an authorial slip, or just careless writing. But the moment can be very powerful and is in fact in principle quite easy to convey to an audience. A pause, and a frown from Ophelia will do it.

An interesting possible example of this subtle orchestration going wrong in performance is provided by the bad Quarto stage direction at V. i. 254, directing Hamlet to leap into the grave after Laertes. The anonymous *Elegy* on the actor Richard Burbage[6] contains the line, 'Oft have I seen him leap into the grave'. This strongly suggests that the First Quarto stage direction is reflecting actor's practice rather than authorial intent (for the *writing* requires that Hamlet's demeanour be courteous at this point). It seems to me just possible that the *Elegy* is referring not to Shakespeare's play but to the old *Hamlet*, in which Burbage could conceivably have acted: the symmetrical structure of the line, 'No more young Hamlet, old Hieronymo' could be designed to mirror two inversely related plays by Kyd. If that were the case (since actors certainly leapt into the grave in later productions of Shakespeare's play[7]) it would mean that actors (themselves irremediably theatrical beings) could not resist carrying on in the manner of the old *Hamlet*, and ignored the subtler controls interposed by Shakespeare, all of which accords very well with Empson's perception of the psychology of the performance. But it remains more likely that Burbage behaved in this way in Shakespeare's play, in which case, while we can make no inferences back to the Ur-*Hamlet*, we may still note the histrionic mis-firing—the surviving sign of a now *ungovernable* theatricality in the principal actor.

[6] Printed in *The Shakespeare Allusion Book: A Collection of Allusions to Shakespeare*, compiled by C. M. Ingleby, L. Toulmin-Smith and F. J. Furnivall, re-edited by John Munro (1909), re-issued with a preface by E. K. Chambers, 2 vols. (Oxford University Press, London, 1932), Vol. 1, p. 272.

[7] See Arthur Colby Sprague, *Shakespeare and the Actors* (Harvard University Press, Cambridge, Mass., 1948), p. 178.

Even our inner selves are nourished by relations with others. The contrast between a supposedly primary, inviolable self and outward relational behaviour can be sustained only for brief periods. Hamlet sees a real tear in the eye of the actor *playing* Aeneas but can find no emotion in himself, despite the fact that his father has actually been murdered. This prompts in him the thought that role-playing can be *used*, not to deceive others but (with infinite pathos) to reconstruct some sort of motivational core, from the outside in. That is why we find at III. ii. 379 the 'Now could I drink hot blood' speech, in language which imperiously requires the 'Kyd style' of acting, but is delivered *in soliloquy*. Hamlet is now working, not upon others, but on his own, ill-nourished self.

We have passed from a logical to a psychological negative: instead of 'There is no answer' we have 'The terminal self proves to be a kind of nothingness', so that role-playing can shift from being a means of deception to being a means of constituting that which was at first seen as its antithesis. For those who relish anachronistic terms I would add, it smells of existentialism.

The critical formula, 'This is constructed as a mystery, therefore do not search for a solution', is really very odd. The feeling one gets is like the sense of sudden triviality in a philosophical argument, when someone replaces a synthetic with an analytic account; for example, A says that all voluntary action can be shown to be fundamentally egoistic if one investigates the unconscious forces involved, and B says, as if in warm agreement, that this is certainly true, since a man who acts voluntarily does what pleases him—because that is what 'voluntary' *means*.

In fact, as I have suggested, drama resists this sort of collapse into logically pure circles of non-explanation. If the audience and the good reader are to think, they must be given some food for thought. The critic who austerely abstains from the entire process on the ground that ultimate certainty is not to be had, will find himself or herself excluded from the vivid enjoyment of the rest, who are all thinking, imagining, guessing like mad.

It is curious how this sequence of critical moves recurs in history. If there is a modern Hamlet it is surely Dostoevsky's Raskolnikov. In a brilliant study Mikhail Bakhtin expressed disdain for those readers who are eager 'to philosophize with' the heroes of Dostoevsky.[8] L. C. Knights's rejection of motivational inference in 'How Many Children Had Lady Macbeth?' is in the

---

[8] *Problèmes de la Poétique de Dostoevski*, traduit par Guy Verret (Éditions l'âge d'homme, Lausanne, 1970), pp. 314–16.

same mode. The Empsonian example is, however, one stage further advanced: Empson does not argue that we should stop guessing because we are given images rather than people; instead he initially accepts the fact that audiences will make inferences, but declares those inferences contentless, on the (insufficient) ground that they fail to cohere in an unambiguous conclusion.

Let us, then, obey the play not the critics. If it helps us to wonder, let us do just that. It may seem that we have slid uncritically from the mystery of the Ghost to the mystery of Hamlet, but, if we have, the offence is venial. The embodied darkness without becomes a darkness within; in Act I the Ghost is visible to all who are present; in the closet scene he is visible to Hamlet alone. Together with the negatives of death, darkness, the unknown, we are offered possible positives. There seem to be shapes in this darkness and the good critic knows that such seeming must be respected. Hamlet's 'I know not "seems" ' (I: ii. 76) is in a manner savagely ironic; there is a sense in which he knows nothing else. To put the matter with an almost idiotic simplicity, it would be false to say, 'Hamlet went out on the platform one night, but there was nothing there.' Hamlet met with something, which may have been a devil, may have been nothingness somehow concentrated into an inverse, palpable intensity ... may have been his father. And it is this last thought that burns in his mind.

There is another poem in which the dispossessed leader of his people rejects the woman who loves him, visits his father in the world of the dead and returns, strangely dehumanised, with a mission. I mean the *Aeneid* of Virgil. Virgil took the ancient episode, familiar in Homeric epic as the *nekuia* or Questioning of the Dead, and morally transformed it by causing Aeneas to meet old Anchises in the Underworld. The ghosts in Homer cry, as old Hamlet cries, for blood. Behind the dominant Shakespearean meaning, 'vengeance', an older thirst for life and substance may still, obscurely, persist (think of the special poignancy of the Ghost's references to the Queen). In particular, we find in Virgil a peculiar interpenetration of horror with good, arising from the introduction of the father-motif. The grim House of Hades becomes gradually a green world with a larger sky than ours (*Aeneid* vi, 640) before the loved father meets his son again. In *Hamlet* the ghost comes from 'sulph'rous and tormenting flames' (I. v. 3). We learn later that the flames are purgatorial, but never quite lose the sense of a loved person, in the midst of damnation, obliging the hero to damnation. *Hamlet* is Shakespeare's *nekuia*.

But what if the loved father is also hated? This is the kind of remark to which Empson applies the epithet 'profound' as a term of abuse. It comes to us from the most famous post-Shakespearean theorist of father-figures, Freud. I ought to say now that I am unpersuaded, in general, by Freud's writings. I have never been convinced that adequate evidence exists for the theory that all male infants wish to murder their fathers and ravish their mothers. Nevertheless Shakespeare who thought of everything seems almost to have thought of this too. Hamlet, when he thinks of his father, seems unable to kill Claudius. But when he thinks of Gertrude's present relationship with Claudius, he can stab and kill. The first thing to reach us in III. iv is the setting. Traditionally, this is known as the bedroom scene, but it may be more correct to place it in the Queen's 'closet'. Either way the implication, more or less direct, is that the setting is intimate, not public; after all, closets normally open into bedrooms, are the place where one gets ready for bed. Moreover, before this scene is ended there will be talk of things that are done in bed. Indeed, to think of this as a kind of bedroom scene is not a peculiarly modern aberration. In the 1714 edition of Rowe's *Shakespeare* Du Guernier's drawing, illustrating III. iv. 97, 'Do you not come your tardy son to chide?' shows a sumptuous double bed in the background.[9] Of course such pictures do not always reflect theatrical practice. But they certainly do reflect what arose in the mind. Near the beginning of the scene Hamlet enters the curtained room, where Polonius is now hiding. He begins almost at once to bait his mother, and the baiting follows a swiftly rising sequence from 'You have my father much offended' (III. iv. 10) to 'You are the Queen, your husband's brother's wife. But— would you were not so—you are my mother' (III. iv. 15–16) (here I follow the Second Quarto reading). It is then that he adds, so menacingly that Gertrude thinks he is about to murder her, that he will set up a glass to show her her own inmost part. Gertrude's fear infects Polonius, who betrays his presence behind the arras. Hamlet—again, doubtless, because of the intimate setting—assumes that it is the King and strikes home without difficulty. The man who removed his father he cannot kill. The man who makes love to his mother he can kill.

In the dialogue which follows, the first rising sequence is re-enacted, more slowly. First we have the comparison of the two pictures in which Hamlet applies to his father the terms of

[9] The drawing is reproduced in the New Cambridge edition of *Hamlet*, p. 65.

classical mythology, Hyperion, Jove, Mars, Mercury, Super-ego language to the Freudians. This is followed by the reappearance, to Hamlet only, of the Ghost and that in turn is followed by the violence of '... the rank sweat of an enseamèd bed,/Stewed in corruption, honeying and making love/Over the nasty sty' (III. iv. 82–4), which, equally clearly, is 'Id language'. The licentious movement in the listener's imagination from 'enseamèd' meaning 'greasy' to 'semen' is assisted both by the context and by the echoic character of the word chosen. Of course such a presumption is not rigorously demonstrable. But it is part of my point that in practice theatre-goers, if not dead from the neck up, habitually indulge in such culpably loose inferences. Moreover Shakespeare knows and in some degree relies on this fact. Even Empson says, 'Some kind of sex nausea about his mother is what is really poisoning him'.[10] We still have not reached the full Freudian thesis: the son who is sexually jealous of the father and sexually drawn to the mother. But it is a tolerably economical explanation of what confronts us. Ockham—he of the famous razor—would be quite pleased with us.

We seem to be involved in an accelerating series of problems. If the Oedipal theory is itself baseless (as I suggested) how can such 'Oedipal' elements be present in *Hamlet* at all? Since Shakespeare cannot have derived these ideas from Freud must he not have derived them from life? But, if that is the case, can we continue to maintain that the Freudian theory is baseless? To this I offer two (less than adequate) answers. First, a theory which is implausibly asserted of all male infants is certainly much more credible if asserted of certain evidently disturbed adults. Secondly, Empson's abusive word, 'profound', may provide us with a useful clue. Freud was a verbal artist as well as a psychologist, and he specialised in *depth*—in going deeper, stripping away more coverings than any predecessor; and Shakespeare did the same. It is not so very surprising that a similarity of method should produce at times similar structures of psychological paradox. But, once more, to follow this through we must be prepared to obey the poem's imperative to guess, to assume—even, if necessary, to make temporary fools of ourselves.

The truth is, however, that Greek tragedy has a much closer analogue to Hamlet than Oedipus. I mean Orestes. For this we must go back to a yet earlier British Academy Shakespeare

[10] Op. cit., *Sewanee Review*, p. 202; *Essays on Shakespeare*, p. 112.

lecture, Gilbert Murray's 'Hamlet and Orestes',[11] given in 1914, some thirty-five years before Ernest Jones's psychoanalytic study, *Hamlet and Oedipus*.[12] Murray puts his case—at least until he mounts his hobby-horse, 'the Year Spirit' near the end—with disarming modesty. He uses, primarily, *Hamlet*, Saxo Grammaticus, the Ambales Saga, Aeschylus's *Choephoroe*, Sophocles' *Electra* and Euripides' *Electra*, *Orestes*, *Iphigeneia in Tauris* and *Andromache*. The case, at first unimpressive, becomes by gradual accumulation of detail overwhelming.

Murray begins with broad resemblances. The hero is the son of a King who has been murdered and succeeded by a younger kinsman; the dead King's wife marries this inferior successor; the hero, driven by supernatural commands, avenges his father. This gives us the vertebral column, as it were, of our analogy. Murray conceded that Hamlet, unlike Orestes, dies on achieving his revenge, but observes that in the earlier Scandinavian version he succeeds to the kingdom. In all the versions there is some shyness about the mother-murder: in Saxo the mother is not killed, in Shakespeare she is killed by accident, in the Greek version she is indeed deliberately killed but the horror of the killing drives the hero mad. It is important that in all the versions the hero is under the shadow of madness (Orestes, Murray says, has that in him which makes us feel that 'it is easy for him to go mad').[13] Like Hamlet in his mother's room, Orestes sees visions which others cannot see. Orestes is remarkable in Greek drama for soliloquy and for hesitation. This last point is put briefly by Murray but seems to me to be of immense importance for the history of drama. John Jones in his *On Aristotle and Greek Tragedy* brings out the difference between Euripides' Orestes in the play of that name and Aeschylus'. In the older play the hero is as it were crucified by conflicting external imperatives, but in Euripides the conflict is internalized and the tragic hero becomes the locus of hesitation, of an interior indeterminacy.[14] It is remarkable that the figure of Orestes should evoke from Euripides this feat of

[11] 'Hamlet and Orestes: a study in traditional types', *Proceedings of the British Academy*, **6** (1913–14), 389–412. A slightly modified version appears in Murray's Charles Eliot Norton Lectures under the title *The Classical Tradition in Poetry* (Oxford University Press, London, 1927), pp. 205–40.

[12] Jones had embarked on the Hamlet–Oedipus theme earlier, in his *Essays in Applied Psychoanalysis* (International Psychoanalytical Library, London and Vienna, 1923).

[13] *The Classical Tradition in Poetry*, p. 210.

[14] Chatto and Windus, London, 1962, pp. 272–3.

dramaturgy and that Hamlet should have so similar an effect upon Shakespeare. In Euripides' *Electra* (979) Orestes suspects that the god commanding him to take vengeance may be an evil spirit in disguise and in the *Orestes* (288–93) says that his father would not have wished him to kill his mother (think here of old Hamlet's 'Nor let thy soul contrive/Against thy mother aught' (I. v. 85–6)). Orestes, like Hamlet, dissembles his true feelings, is thought to be dead, but returns. Like Hamlet (and Ambales) Orestes is given to cynically violent language against women. Indeed at *Orestes* 1590 he is given what Murray describes as 'the horrible, mad line'[15] in which he says that he could never weary of killing evil women. Both, Murray observes, bully any woman they are left alone with.

Finally Murray turns to odd details, some of which are very striking indeed. In both traditions the hero has been away when the action begins (Phocis, Wittenberg); in both he goes on a ship, is captured by enemies who try to murder him and escapes (*Iphigeneia in Tauris*). In Saxo,[16] though not in *Hamlet*, the hero ties his dead soldiers to stakes to deceive the enemy, while in Euripides' *Electra* Orestes prays to his father to 'come, bringing every dead man as a fellow-fighter' (this, Murray concedes, may be just a weird coincidence). The father in both traditions dies without due religious observances. Hamlet has his friend Horatio as Orestes has Pylades. Hamlet in the Scandinavian versions is filthy, covered with ashes and rolls on the ground. At the beginning of *Orestes* the hero is found with his sister, ghastly pale, his hair matted with dirt and in *Iphigeneia in Tauris* he foams at the mouth and rolls on the ground (307). This is not prominent in Shakespeare's play, but Hamlet does appear before Ophelia with his doublet unbraced, his stockings fouled, 'pale as his shirt' (II. i. 79–82). Although there is no Ophelia in the Greek and no Electra in the northern story, there are signs that these two figures may themselves be analogically related. The pairing of this young woman with an old man who treats her as his daughter is present in Euripides' *Electra* (493, 563). Most telling of all, in all the Electra plays a peculiar effect is obtained by having Orestes first sight his sister in funeral garb or in a funeral procession (*Choephoroe*, 16; Sophocles, *Electra*, 80; Euripides, *Electra*, 107).

---

[15] *The Classical Tradition in Poetry*, p. 216.

[16] See Saxo Grammaticus *The History of the Danes*, 2 vols. (D. S. Brewer, Cambridge; Rowman and Littlefield, Totowa, New Jersey, 1979–80), Vol. 1, p. 100.

Compare with this Hamlet's 'What the fair Ophelia?' on seeing her carried to the burial.

But what can such an analogy, intricate as it is, mean? In these days of synchronic anthropology it is somehow bad form to worry about historical connexion, about who read what or the mechanics of transmission. Yet I must confess to an unregenerate discomfort in the face of a resemblance so detailed and yet, at the same time, so signally short on visible causal links.[17] It is hard, indeed, to avoid the sense that we have an oddly coherent body of stories, probably having at some early date an extensive oral provenance. I do not know whether at some crucial point a Norse story-teller told the tale to a Greek or vice versa, and I imagine no one does. But some such transmission is inherently probable— much more probable than the freakish array of coincidences which otherwise confronts us.

Nor do I know whether it is fair to find in such materials corroboration of one's own interpretation of Shakespeare's unique play. I have suggested, a little nervously, that there is something odd about Hamlet's relation to his mother. When we learn that in Saxo[18] Hamlet remained always in his mother's house and that in the Ambales Saga[19] he actually slept in his mother's room, we may begin to feel that we were not after all merely imagining things. Later, when he came to write *Coriolanus* Shakespeare read in Plutarch that his hero did not leave his mother's house even when he married,[20] and built wonderfully on the suggestion. Shakespeare certainly read Plutarch and probably did not read Saxo. But the author of the Ur-*Hamlet*, especially if it was indeed Kyd, is quite likely to have done so. Saxo is an important source, at one or two removes. It belongs quite clearly in the direct tradition of Shakespeare's story, as ancient Greek plays do not.

Yet the analogy expounded by Gilbert Murray nags at the mind. It can even, perhaps, be made to confirm our sense that behind the revenge story of *Hamlet*, blood for blood, lies a

[17] William F. Hansen describes the link between Hamlet and Orestes as 'possible' but adds that certainty in this matter seems to be unattainable. See his *Saxo Grammaticus and the Life of Hamlet* (University of Nebraska Press, Lincoln, Nebraska and London, 1983), p. 16.

[18] *History of the Danes*, Vol. 1, p. 84.

[19] Ambales Saga, *Capituli* XV, XVI and XVIII, printed with a translation in Israel Gollancz's *Hamlet in Iceland* (David Nutt, London, 1898), pp. 98–9, 101–3, 109.

[20] See the New Arden edition of *Coriolanus* by J. Philip Brockbank (Methuen, London, 1976), p. 317.

metaphysical drama of substance and unbeing. I saw the Ghost's persisting love for Gertrude as a kind of hunger for life in the midst of death, making him for a moment like the thirsting, bloodless shades in Homer's *Odyssey*. I suggested that Hamlet is paralysed partly because he has become one of them, a dead man walking among the living, opposite to life (which is Ophelia). Like the dead he cannot weep (tickle him and he might not laugh). All of this is grounded—but insecurely—in the text. Hamlet is dressed in black, in the garb of death; he talks to a ghost and later to skulls; his exchange with the gravedigger is a conversation of two persons expert in death. Thought to have been murdered, he returns, a lethal revenant, and kills others. Yet all these things could be turned, by an unsympathizing critic, in another, more commonsensical direction.

In the Greek tradition, however, the notion that Orestes is himself a kind of ghost is explicit (here, again, I am guided by Murray): in *Orestes* (385–6), Menelaus, meeting with Orestes, says

ὦ θεοί, τί λεύσσω; τίνα δέδορκα νερτέρων;
Gods! What do I see? Whom, of those that live in this Underworld, am I looking at?

And Orestes answers

εὖ γ᾽ εἶπας· οὐ γὰρ ζῶ κακοῖς, φάος δ᾽ ὁρῶ.
You say well. By reason of the evils I have suffered, I live not, but I see the light of day.

Later in the same play the messenger tells of the citizen who alerted him to this sudden appearance of Orestes: 'He said to me, "Can't you see Orestes walking near, to run the race of death?" and I saw the unlooked for phantom' (877–8). As Murray observed, Hamlet's sudden advancing to meet Laertes, in the funeral scene, 'This is I,/Hamlet the Dane' (V. i. 254–5) is like *Andromache*, 884, 'It is I, Agamemnon's and Clytemnestra's son, Orestes'. *Iphigeneia in Tauris*, 1361, has a similar ring: the self-announcing apparition. Moreover this is the play in which Orestes interrupts his own funeral rites (at line 67). When Hamlet says 'Horatio, I am dead,/Thou liv'st (V. ii. 290–91) the immediate meaning is, as at the opening, followed by a larger meaning which fills the play, this time retrospectively. Again a minor linguistic abnormality, the proleptic 'I am dead' for 'I am dying' (a little like the modern idiom, 'I am as good as dead') carries a potent charge. We are dealing, I surmise, with what must now be seen as an ancient European story, and that is public matter. Again—may we say?—the fear of a merely subjective reaction is less than it was. Presentiment looks more like intuition.

I have moved from a meta-critical insistence on the impossibility of explanation (Empson) to psychoanalysis and thence to ancient story patterns which, while they tend to confirm our sense of a certain strangeness in Hamlet's relation to his mother and Ophelia, push the range of reference further into the darkness, so to speak, forcing us to confront once more the embodied death and negation from which we began.

There has been much talk about this play because, I suggest, Shakespeare has given us much to talk about. There is meat for the psychologically minded and for the philosophically minded. The brilliant interplay of the substantial with the artificially (theatrically) constituted self is answered at another level by a disturbing displacement of sexual feeling. But the beginning and end of the play is death. That is why the powerful, complex analogy with Orestes is *critically* more fruitful than the looser analogy with Oedipus. Wittgenstein said that death is not an event in life (*Tractatus* 6. 4311). It is a philosophically imaginative remark, and full of the philosopher's contempt for the more usual uses of the imagination. It respects the logical uniqueness of death, which is, in the words of another philosopher, 'itself, and not another thing'. It reminds us of our confinement to life; when we think we talk about death, we really talk about dying or else, because of some natural intolerance of pure negation, we use our intelligence, as Richard II did, to people a vacuity—with ghosts, machinery of punishment—images, suitably darkened, drawn from our own order of things. Faced with this philosophic challenge, *Hamlet* fares better than most works of literature. Lewis was right to insist that it forces us to think not just about dying, but about 'being dead'.[21] For every more or less palpable image Shakespeare offers a correlative, undermining doubt. The ghost may not be a ghost. Startlingly, the Christian scheme of afterlife may be a delusion (the *play* raises this possibility, though only at moments). Death is not the metallically hard, systematic

---

[21] *Proceedings of the British Academy*, **28** (1942), p. 149; *Selected Literary Essays*, p. 99.

landscape of Dante nor is it plainly the simplified scheme of the
Reformers. It is an undiscovered country, or a dream-invaded
sleep. The days have passed when scholars could pretend that
agnostic thought was simply impossible in Elizabethan times.
Indeed, faced with the text of *Hamlet*, one wonders how they
could ever have done so.

The drama, however, hinges upon the initial encounter, and
an encounter must be with something. This element of the play,
one supposes, Wittgenstein would condemn as self-indulgence. I
have argued that inferences and associations which may appear
under the searchlight of a sceptical investigation to be less than
rigorous are not only permissible but in a way essential to a full
critical response. It does not follow that any comparison is as
apposite as any other. The story of Hamlet is nothing like the
story of Jairus's daughter (Mark 5). But it is a little like that most
haunting of Biblical narratives, which tells how Jacob met a man
and wrestled with him until the light came (Genesis 32). Traditionally the story is known as: 'Jacob and the Angel' but the Bible
itself seems to say what tradition dare not repeat: that Jacob
wrestled with God. Gunkel in his commentary on Genesis[22]
assembles copious analogues, showing the pattern of the ambiguous spirit who must depart when dawn breaks: 'It faded on
the crowing of the cock' (*Hamlet*, I. i. 138). I might have
struggled to frame from these materials some sort of bridge to the
Hamlet story. But my own licentious imagination, which is not
perhaps so very unusual, made the step long before I knew
anything of Gunkel's work. Hamlet never engages in physical
combat with the majestic being he meets in the night, but there is
a sense in which the rest of the play is taken up with his wrestling
with the Ghost. We may think also of 'Loving Mad Tom' in
which the world of darkness and death throws up an emissary
and a challenge:

With an host of furious fancies
Wherof I am commander,
With a burning spear and a horse of air
To the wilderness I wander.

[22] Hermann Gunkel, *Genesis: Übersetzt und Erklärt* (Vandenhoeck und
Ruprecht, Göttingen, 1964), pp. 359–65. Cf. Gerhard von Rad, *Genesis*, trans.
John Marks (SCM Press, London, 1972), p. 321.

By a Knight of ghosts and shadows
I summoned am to tourney
Ten leagues beyond the wide world's end.
Methinks it is no journey.[23]

Tom Stoppard's *Rosenkrantz and Guildenstern Are Dead* is more than a *jeu d'esprit*. His question, 'Where do they go when they leave the drama?' is in profound accord with Shakespeare's play, though he is readier than Shakespeare could ever be to defuse primitive anxieties with logical jokes. In *Timon of Athens* Shakespeare was to dramatize negation in a manner more acceptable, I suspect, to such as Wittgenstein. There, no images are in the end allowed. Timon's epitaph is worn away by the sea and he himself is no more. The emptiness, in all its intellectual purity, is almost fatal to the drama.

The implied argument I have attached to the name of Wittgenstein works in this way: the very force of *Hamlet*, which must be at bottom a force of imagery, presupposes an intellectual softness, an impulse self-indulgently to tame the unimaginable with conventional pictures. This argument would, I suppose, have seemed strong to many philosophers in the 1950s and '60s. But now philosophers seem less willing to dismiss as merely incoherent Hamlet's words 'There are more things in heaven and earth, Horatio,/Than are dreamt of in your philosophy' (I. v. 168–9). Perhaps it is the play rather than twentieth-century philosophy which perceives the full extent of our ignorance. If we do not know that death is any particular thing, equally we do not know that it excludes or is not any particular thing. If death is a sleep, there may be dreams in that sleep, and what kind of thing would that be ... ? Even today, in 1988, in clear daylight, do we know with confidence the answer to Barnardo's question: 'Who's there?'

---

[23] *The New Oxford Book of English Verse, 1250–1950*, ed. Helen Gardner (Clarendon Press, Oxford, 1972), p. 371.

JACOBEAN PLAYWRIGHTS AND 'JUDICIOUS' SPECTATORS

By LEO SALINGAR

Read 25 April 1989

WHEN Hamlet is lecturing the Players at Elsinore about practising truth to nature in their craft he admonishes them that 'this overdone, or come tardy off, though it makes the unskilful laugh, cannot but make the judicious grieve: the censure of which one' (he adds) 'must in your allowance o'erweigh a whole theatre of others'. Hamlet's ideas have a classical background. But hardly anyone in England had discussed plays or acting in quite those terms before, with the exception of Ben Jonson. About a year before *Hamlet*, in 1599, Shakespeares's company had given *Every Man out of his Humour*, that novel and deliberately programmatic work where Jonson appeals to 'judicious friends' and 'happy judgements' in his audience, as against the cavils of 'envious censors' and downright 'fools'.[1] The adjective *judicious* was still new to the language, and Hamlet underlines it by making it serve as a noun (the only place where Shakespeare uses it in this way). It gives the prince's pronouncement an extra touch of fastidiousness, even a hint of up-to-the-minute fashionable affectation, such as Jonson himself illustrates, very soon afterwards, in *Cynthia's Revels*, when Mercury praises Crites, the 'perfect' moralist and critic, as one who 'strives rather to be that which men call judicious, than to be thought so: and [who] is so truly learned, that he affects not to shew it'. Even so, Jonson in turn borrows straightforwardly from Hamlet in the self-justifying afterword to his next comedy, *Poetaster*, where he announces that he will now bring out a tragedy, for which the satisfaction of one 'judicious'

---

[1] *Every Man out of his Humour*, Induction, ll. 56–65, 131–3, 194–6, in C. H. Herford & Percy Simpson (eds), *Ben Jonson*, Vol. 3 (Oxford, 1927). (I have modernized spellings in all quotations in this paper).

person 'alone' will be sufficient, and equivalent to 'a Theatre'.[2] Between them, Jonson and Hamlet evidently launched the word; in the London theatres about 1600 it implied an important step in critical self-consciousness. Within the next few years, Middleton, Marston and other playwrights were hoping expressly for approval from 'judicious spirits'; by way of variant, Heywood appealed to 'judicial spirits' in his epilogue to *The Golden Age* in 1610. In the sequel, *The Silver Age*, Heywood appealed in his prologue to 'this judging Nation'.[3]

Judging and *judgement* were commoner words than *judicial* or *judicious*. In the Caroline theatre, as Michael Neill has pointed out, the buzzword of commendation was to be *wit* (covering dramatic construction as well as language).[4] *Wit* was already a prominent word in the dramatic vocabulary of Shakepeare's time. But during the last Elizabethan and early Jacobean years—from 1599, the moment of *Every Man out of his Humour*, to about 1613, the time of Shakespeare's retirement—the keyword in a dramatist's approach to his public was rather the word *judgement*. A few earlier plays anticipate this keyword. For instance, the Prologue to Lyly's *Midas*, acted by the boys of St Paul's in 1589, excuses the piece as a 'mingle-mangle' by alluding to the difficulty of conforming to changeable fashions and divergent tastes, but assures the 'Gentle-men' present that the actors are 'jealous of your judgements, because you are wise'; and Marlowe invites 'patient judgements' in his prologue to *Faustus*, as if tempering the notorious 'vaunt' he had delivered in *Tamburlaine*. But if we search back before 1599, to 1587—the probable year of *Tamburlaine* and of *The Spanish Tragedy* which, with Lyly's comedies, gave shape to the drama of Shakespeare's day,—we can only find a few such appeals to

[2] *Cynthia's Revels*, II.iii.132, and *Poetaster*, To the Reader, ll. 222–8, in Herford & Simpson, *Ben Jonson*, Vol. 4 (Oxford, 1932).
[3] Thomas Middleton, *The Family of Love*, Epistle to the Reader (1608), in A. H. Bullen (ed.), *Works*, Vol. 3 (1885); Marston, *Antonio's Revenge*, Prologue (1600), in H. Harvey Wood (ed.), *Plays*, Vol. 1 (Edinburgh, 1934); compare Barnabe Barnes, *The Devil's Charter*, Epilogue (1607); John Day, *Law Tricks*, To the Reader (1608); Fletcher, *The Coxcomb*, Epilogue (1609?); also Thomas Heywood, *The Golden Age* (1610) and *The Silver Age* (1611), in *Pearson Reprints* of *Heywood's Dramatic Works*, Vol. 3 (1874), pp. 79, 86.
[4] Michael Neill, '"Wit's most accomplished Senate": the audience of the Caroline private theaters', *Studies in English Literature*, **18** (1978). I have discussed topics related to the present paper in '"Wit" in Jacobean comedy' (1984), reprinted in *Dramatic Form in Shakespeare and the Jacobeans* (Cambridge, 1986).

'judgement': only five, perhaps,[5] out of some forty plays provided with prologues or epilogues or else published, within that dozen years, with epistles to a patron or to the reader. In contrast, the fifteen years from 1599 to 1613 yield at least thirty-five plays containing a similar appeal, out of eighty-four furnished with prologues or epilogues, or with prefatory addresses. Admittedly, more plays are extant altogether from the later period — perhaps 179 plays of all kinds, as compared with ninety-four. But it is noticeable that somewhat more plays from the later or Jacobean period contain extra-dramatic passages addressing the public directly, either from the stage or the printed text; and specific references to the idea of critical 'judgement' become much more frequent, arising in roughly one play out of every five, as contrasted with just over one in twenty.

'Judgement' required knowledge and understanding; in other words, classical learning. As in Lyly's prologue, it was the province of 'Gentlemen' — though members of the wider public that Marlowe, for example, was writing for might also be allowed to claim their share. Heywood's sequence of plays beginning with *The Golden Age* was intended as a course in popular education, dramatizing a cycle of Greek myths for 'this judging Nation', with a liberal dose of spectacle, from the stage of the Red Bull; but in the epilogue to the third play, *The Brazen Age*, Heywood observes that 'the learned ... only' can 'censure right' how well he has condensed his sources: 'The rest we crave, whom we unlettered call,/Rather to attend than judge'. This distinction between the

---

[5] Prologues to Lyly, *Midas* (1589); Marlowe, *Dr Faustus* (c. 1592); and Henry Porter, *Two Angry Women of Abingdon* (pub. 1599); Printer's preface (1591) to Lyly's *Endimion*; and cf. R. Wilmot's letter to 'the Gentlemen Students of the Inner Temple' and 'the Gentlemen of the Middle Temple' (1591), prefacing his *Tancred and Gismunda* (Hazlitt/Dodsley's *Old English Plays*, Vol. 7 [1874]). In addition, the prologue to *The Wars of Cyrus*, acted by the boys of the Chapel Royal, is addressed to 'gentle gentlemen,. ... worthy to judge of us' (ed. James Paul Brawner, *Illinois Studies in Language and Literature*, 28, Urbana, 1942). *The Wars of Cyrus* is a faintly classical anonymous blank verse piece, largely derived from Xenophon. Some scholars would date it c. 1588, i.e. after *Tamburlaine* (see E. K. Chambers, *The Elizabethan Stage*, Vol. 4 [Oxford, 1923], p. 58). It was printed in 1594. But Brawner would attribute it to Richard Farrant, Master of the Chapel Royal from 1576 to 1580, and he gives strong arguments for dating the play in or just after 1576 — possibly as the first play Farrant produced when he opened the (first) Blackfriars in that year as a private theatre (edn cit., pp. 12–20, 38–71). In any case, *The Wars of Cyrus* is probably the earliest extant play written for a private theatre and containing a prologue addressed to the 'judgement' of the 'gentlemen' gathered there. It strengthens the case for a special association between the idea of 'judgement' and private theatre audiences.

two grades of spectator is significant, though it is also significant that Heywood, an experienced actor-playwright, counts upon finding both at the same performance.

The emphasis on learning or judgement in prologues and the like after 1600 was in part the expression of what may be called a new wave of playwrights, Shakespeare's younger contemporaries, who began to write for the theatres after the disappearance of the first generation of University Wits. Chapman was an assertively self-taught scholar and so, in a sense, was Ben Jonson (who had the benefit of schooling at Westminster under the distinguished antiquarian, William Camden); John Marston, an Oxford graduate, was also a member of the Middle Temple, as likewise, it appears, was John Webster, who collaborated with him in his revised production of *The Malcontent* in 1604;[6] Heywood and Middleton had been students at Cambridge and Oxford; Thomas Dekker was an industrious pamphleteer as well as a playwright. For all of these men, a display of learning must have seemed natural and necessary, or at least advantageous. The so-called War of the Theatres, which excited attention in the wake of *Every Man out of his Humour*, was due, as Rosencrantz and Guildenstern explain to Hamlet, to the renewed opening of 'private' playhouses—Paul's in 1599 and the second Blackfriars in 1600—and the competition between the boy actors appearing there and the adult companies established in the public theatres. But the War was also a personal slanging-match between Jonson on one side and Marston with Dekker on the other. That meant that the stage was now a place where literary reputations could be built up or deflated. It was all the more important because there were insufficient openings for men with scholarly attainments; returns from publishing were meagre; and the benefits of patronage were elusive or disappointing.

But further, the writers' appeal for favourable 'judgement', which outlasted the two-or-three year War, signals a continuing change in the social composition of the London public. Evidently a bigger proportion of the public was coming from the ranks of the educated and the wealthy; courtiers, professional men and well-to-do Londoners like the circle of the letter-writer, John Chamberlain; students from the Inns of Court—a particularly prominent group; fashionable gallants, of uncertain status; and

[6] M. C. Bradbrook, *John Webster, Citizen and Dramatist* (1980), p. 28; on these writers as a group, see Alfred Harbage, *Shakespeare and the Rival Traditions* (New York, 1952), pp. 90–101.

an increasing number of country gentlemen visiting London for business or pleasure, especially during the terms when the law-courts were sitting, accompanied often by their wives. This increase in the numbers of wealthy playgoers does not mean that the poor and 'unlettered' were crowded out—in spite of the contention of Professor Ann Jennalie Cook that workmen, apprentices, servants and even shopkeepers had neither the time nor the money to go to plays.[7] On the contrary, in 1603, for example, a moralist, Henry Crosse, could lament that 'poor pinched, needy creatures', surviving on beggary, 'yet will make hard shift but that they will see a Play, let wife and children ... languish' as best they might. In 1609, in an often quoted passage of satire, Dekker cheerfully observed that 'The Theatre is your Poet's Royal Exchange', where 'your Gallant, your Courtier, and your Captain, had wont to be the soundest paymasters', but where 'the Farmer's son' is as free to come as 'your Templar', and

your Stinkard has the self-same liberty to be there in his Tobacco-Fumes, which your sweet Courtier hath: and ... your Car-man and Tinker claim as strong a voice in their suffrage, and sit to give judgement on the play's life and death, as well as the proudest *Momus* among the tribe of *Critic*;

and, rather less cheerfully, in a prologue of 1611, for the same Red Bull theatre where Heywood was delivering his digest of classical instruction, Dekker hit out at dramatists pandering to the masses:

A Play whose *Rudeness, Indians* would abhor,
If't fill a house with Fishwives, *Rare, They All Roar.*
It is not Praise is sought for (Now) but *Pence,*
Tho' dropp'd, from Greasy-apron *Audience.*

Whatever allowance we make for satiric exaggeration, statements like those surely confirm the presence in some number of lower-class playgoers. Indeed, about 1618, the Mayor of Exeter, resisting repeated visits from acting companies to his city, explained to

[7] Ann Jennalie Cook, *The Privileged Playgoers of Shakespeare's London, 1576–1642* (Princeton, 1981). Cook's conclusions have been accepted by Michael Hattaway in *Elizabethan Popular Theatre* (1982), pp. 44–50, but opposed by Martin Butler, in *Theatre and Crisis 1632–1642* (Cambridge, 1984), pp. 293–306, and by Andrew Gurr, *Playgoing in Shakespeare's London* (Cambridge, 1987), pp. xiii, 3–4.

the Privy Council that 'those who spend their money on plays are ordinarily very poor people'.[8]

Nevertheless, it seems likely that working men and the poor, however greedy for intervals of pleasure, must have cut down their attendance at plays after the years of dreadful hardship in the mid-1590s. We are told that after the years of dearth culminating in 1597 the buying-power of a London building worker's wages stood at the lowest point for 200 years; and over the next forty years, punctuated as they were by economic depressions, the recovery of wages in London and the provinces was both uneven and slight.[9] No doubt the effects of this economic hardship can be read in the records of acting throughout the provinces, where the number of players' companies and the number of their known visits had been rising steadily since the time of Shakespeare's childhood, only to fall away just as steadily soon after 1595.[10] If we could have statistical records about the middling and poorer classes' playgoing in London, I presume they would tell a very similar tale.

But meanwhile, playgoing by the well-to-do was evidently increasing. From the scattered records of London theatre attendances by known individuals, nearly all belonging to the gentry,

[8] Henry Crosse, *Vertues Common-wealth* (1603), in Alexander B. Grosart (ed.) *Occasional Issues*, **7** (1878), p. 118; Dekker, *The Gull's Hornbook* (1609), Chap. 6 (quoted, Gurr, *Playgoing* p. 222); *If This be not a Good Play, the Devil is in It*, Prologue (1611), in Fredson Bowers (ed.), *The Dramatic Works of Thomas Dekker*, Vol. 3 (Cambridge, 1958); letter from the Mayor of Exeter, in J. T. Murray, *English Dramatic Companies, 1558–1642*, Vol.2 (1910), p. 6.

[9] E. H. Phelps Brown & Sheila V. Hopkins, 'Seven Centuries of the Prices of Consumables, compared with Builders' Wage-Rates', App. B, *Economica*, **23**(n.s.) (1956). See Alan Everitt, 'Farm Labourers', and Peter Bowden, 'Agricultural Prices, Farm Profits, and Rents', in Joan Thirsk (ed.) *The Agrarian History of England and Wales IV, 1500–1640* (Cambridge, 1967), pp. 396–465, 593–695; John Walter & Keith Wrightson, 'Dearth and the Social Order in Early Modern England' (1976), in Paul Slack (ed.), *Rebellion, Popular Protest and the Social Order in Early Modern England* (Cambridge, 1984); C. G. A. Clay, *Economic expansion and social change: England 1500–1700* (Cambridge, 1984), Vol. 1, pp. 38–45, 49; Vol. 2, pp. 28–31.

[10] See my article, with Gerald Harrison & Bruce Cochrane, 'Les Comédiens et leur public en Angleterre de 1520 à 1640', in Jean Jacquot (ed.), *Dramaturgie et société ... aux XVIᵉ et XVIIᵉ siècles* (Paris, 1968), Vol. 2, pp. 531–2, 538–41. (The statistical tables I gave there are inadequate by now, in view of the data published subsequently in Malone Society *Collections* and in *Records of Early English Drama*; but I believe the new data still confirm my general account of a prevailing increase in plays by professional companies touring the provinces from about 1560 to about 1595, followed by a decline).

that have been assembled by Professor Andrew Gurr, it emerges that less than ten names can be assigned to the fifteen years before 1595, but a dozen names to the five years following.[11] And not only the number of well-educated playgoers but the kind of interest they expressed appears to have been changing after about 1595. As a student at Lincoln's Inn, John Donne was said to be 'a great frequenter of Plays'; he was lastingly impressed by *Tamburlaine* and *Dr Faustus* and later, as a friend of Jonson, penned a tribute to *Volpone*; but his interest in the theatre, as shown by his poems of the mid-1590s, such as his Satires, was chiefly an amused fascination with the actors' resplendent costumes.[12] About the same time, the verse epigrams of Sir John Davies of the Middle Temple show a lively interest in the foibles of playgoers, but not in the actors or the playwrights or their plays. But by 1598 a minor poet, Robert Tofte, was describing how his own amour had been affected by a visit to a theatre to see *Love's Labour's Lost*; in 1598 also, the literary gossip, Francis Meres, could parallel Shakespeare with Plautus and Seneca, revealing an extensive acquaintance with his work and extolling him as 'the most excellent' of English writers for the stage; and in 1599 another minor poet, the Cambridge man, John Weever, devoted admiring epigrams to Shakespeare and to Jonson, Marston and the actor, Edward Alleyn, on the same plane as eminent poets, Spenser and Daniel; while Marston, in his verse satires of the same year, portrayed a gallant, obsessed by plays and players, who could utter nothing else but 'pure *Juliet* and *Romeo*'.[13] We can see the emergence of connoisseurship in stage affairs, especially in the works of Shakespeare. Professor Gurr lists a gentleman who really kept a commonplace book like that of Marston's stage-struck gallant: a Mr Edward Pudsey, who, about 1600, noted down extracts, apparently from memory, after performances, from

[11] Gurr, *Playgoing*, App. I.
[12] R. C. Bald, *John Donne: A Life* (Oxford, 1970), pp. 72–4, 117, 195: see Donne, *Elegy* XV, lines 59–60; *Satires* I, l. 99, and IV, ll. 180–87; *To Sir Henry Wotton* ('Here's no more news ...'), ll. 19–21. Sir John Davies's *Epigrams*, Nos 1, 3, 7, 28, 39, 47 (1593?) contain satiric sketches of playgoers; see Gurr, op. cit.
[13] Robert Tofte, '*Love's Labour Lost*, I once did see a play ...', in *Alba* (1598) ed. A. Grosart (1880), p. 105; Francis Meres, *Palladis Tamia* (1598) in G. Gregory Smith (ed.), *Elizabethan Critical Essays* (1904), Vol. 2 pp. 317–18; John Weaver, *Epigrammes in the Oldest Cut & Newest Fashion* (1599), ed. R. B. McKerrow (1911), pp. 75, 76, 95, 96, 101; John Marston, *The Scourge of Villanie* (1599), Satire X 'Humours', ed. G. B. Harrison (1925), p. 107.

plays by Jonson, Marston, Chapman, Shakespeare and Dekker.[14] To give one more example of the evolution of educated or academic taste: back in 1580, and again in 1593, the Cambridge don, Gabriel Harvey, had ridiculed the professional stage in the spirit of Sir Philip Sidney; but about 1601 he made a note that Shakespeare's poems and his tragedy of *Hamlet* 'have it in them, to please the wiser sort'.[15] I presume that 'the judicious' were to be found, if anywhere, in the neighbourhood of the writers and gentlemen I have just mentioned.

Very likely it was this gathering interest in the stage shown by members of the gentry that made possible and encouraged the rise of the private theatres, where the boy actors flourished between 1599 and 1608, when Shakespeare's company, the King's men, in effect put a stop to their competition and then occupied Blackfriars in addition to the Globe. The private playhouses were relatively small and intimate, roofed in, artificially lit and expensive; Alfred Harbage describes them as coterie theatres in his impressive and influential study of *Shakespeare and the Rival Traditions*.[16] Although Harbage recognizes that audiences at Paul's, Blackfriars and Whitefriars must have overlapped to a large extent with those at the public theatres and that often the same poets wrote for both kinds of stage, he holds that the work of the private theatres was aimed at an exclusive clientele and expressed a self-conscious but rootless avant-garde, remote from the healthy national mainstream of the productions at the Globe, the Fortune and the Red Bull. Choristers by training, the boy actors excelled in music and elocution—and parody. Unlike the self-governing adult companies, they were controlled by their managers, who included literary men, such as Marston and Daniel. And no doubt these factors affected their styles and repertory. For instance, the private theatres ignored the type of national history play which had been popular in the 1590s and still sometimes appeared on the public stage under James I, now

---

[14] Gurr, *Playgoing*, pp. 200–1.

[15] Gabriel Harvey: see Smith (ed.), *Elizabethan Critical Essays*, Vol. 1, p. 125; Vol. 2, p. 261; G. Blakemore Evans (ed.), *The Riverside Shakespeare* (Boston, 1974), p. 1840.

[16] See above, n. 6. For comparison with Harbage, see the studies of the private playhouses in *Dramaturgie et Société* (n. 10, above), especially Jean Jacquot, 'La Répertoire des compagnies d'enfants à Londres (1600–1610): Essai d' interprétation socio-dramaturgique', pp. 729–82; and Reavley Gair, *The Children of Paul's: the story of a theatre company, 1553–1608* (Cambridge, 1982).

glorifying the Tudor past. Instead, the private theatres concentrated on satire and social comedy, in plays studded with parody and with topical allusions, genuine or suspected, that regularly brought their authors into trouble with the Privy Council. And the allusive, sophisticated manner and satiric bias of plays by Marston and others give some weight to Harbage's account of them as coterie drama. All the same, I think Harbage exaggerates the gap between the two kinds of theatre, because he underrates the prominence of the gentry at large among London playgoers and because he sets aside the more self-aware and self-critical tone of drama in general about the time of *Hamlet*.

One sign of this development, as I have partly indicated already, was a change in the style of prologues, which now much more commonly discuss the public's reaction to plays or voice the dramatist's hopes of success, in the manner of Terence, as well as, or instead of, introducing the plot. In particular, there was a new style for inductions—opening scenes where the delivery of a prologue is amplified, usually into dialogue between two or more speakers and sometimes with stage business. Earlier inductions had prepared for the mood of the main action, or recounted antecedent events, though they could also introduce the role of a spectator within the play, as in *The Spanish Tragedy* or *The Taming of the Shrew*. But with *Every Man out of his Humour* Ben Jonson brought in a new style of induction, where critical theory and the state of public taste are made the subjects of discussion, and the real spectators are provoked into critical engagement within the play. Before introducing two of the characters in the main play, Jonson provides a spokesman (who lectures the audience on the true meaning of 'humours' and on the difference between those who are and those who would like to appear 'judicious') together with two friends of the spokesman, one of whom sketches out the 'laws' and the classical history of comedy; and the two friends remain on stage to fill recurrent pauses in the main dialogue, one amiably questioning and the other obligingly explaining the methods the dramatist has used in his art. Jonson incorporates a theoretical disquisition that reminds a modern reader of the prefaces of Bernard Shaw. There were precedents in the theory-ridden comedies of Renaissance Italy, but Jonson goes further; if criticism can be defined as the deduction of general 'laws' or principles and their application to particular works of literature, then Jonson, after Philip Sidney, initiated dramatic criticism in England. But other inductions point in the same direction as *Every Man out of his Humour*. In the anonymous crime story, *A Warning for Fair Women*, also performed by Shakespeare's company in 1599, three speakers named Tragedy, History and Comedy debate what the public really want; and Heywood's early, undemanding romance, *The Four Prentices of London: with the Conquest of Jerusalem*, has three prologue speakers to forestall likely objections and to urge the 'clear-sighted Gentlemen' present 'with the eyes of their judgements' to look tolerantly on any unintentional 'errors'.[17] Marston competed with Jonson in his inductions. *Antonio and Mellida*, his first play for Paul's in 1599, was introduced by eight of the boys, with 'cloaks cast over their apparel', questioning the parts they were about to play and ridiculing theatrical stereotypes taken from *Tamburlaine*; two years later, *What You Will* opened with two friends of the author pouring scorn on habitual detractors (or 'Knights of the *Mew*') and—evidently against Jonson's dominance— rebutting the idea that what 'the world' thought of a play should be decided by 'three or four deem'd most judicious':

> *Music and Poetry* were first approv'd
> By common sense; and that which pleased most,
> Held most allowed pass: [your] rules of Art
> Were shap'd to pleasure, not pleasure to your rules.

Other inductions of the next few years bring spectators into the dialogue. Webster's, for the Globe production of Marston's *Malcontent*, has Burbage and other actors to justify the borrowing of the piece and its freedom in satire to two gallants who insist upon sitting on the stage, one of them a frequenter of Blackfriars, who has 'seen this play often' and complains 'it is a bitter play', although he '[has] most of the jests here in [his] table-book'. Again, in a Blackfriars play of 1606, *The Isle of Gulls* by John Day (a comedy that brought its producers into trouble), the Prologue begs 'gentlemen' to 'judge' the plight of the hard-working poet, after three representative playgoers have been heard on the stage, one gentleman demanding to hear 'vice anatomized', preferably with some 'great man's life charactered in't', the second wanting bawdry, and the third, 'a stately penned history'—which is scoffed at as 'fustian', with 'swelling comparisons, and bombast Epithets'. In the same year, in a Paul's prologue glancing at the same contradictions of taste, Francis Beaumont declared that 'inductions [were] out of date';[18] but he was then to provide a

---

[17] Richard Simpson (ed.), *A Warning for Fair Women*, in *The School of Shakespere*, Vol. 2 (1878); *The Four Prentices of London*, in *Heywood's Dramatic Works*, Vol. 2.

[18] Francis Beaumont, *The Woman Hater* (1606).

notable one himself, in *The Knight of the Burning Pestle*, where the naïve but vociferous demands of the grocer and his wife twist the actors' preparations entirely out of shape. And the liveliest of inductions about audience opinions was still to come, in Jonson's *Bartholomew Fair* of 1614, for the opening of a new public theatre, the Hope.

These inductions reveal a new climate of vocal theatrical criticism, even if it was not yet taking the form of essays or treatises. So do the dedications and prefatory letters which now become more common, as the playgoing public extends into a reading public as well. But it is striking, from these allusive references, that the dramatists are at least as much concerned with their audience and their audience's unpredictability as with their own guiding intentions. They have the precepts and examples of a common classical education to appeal to, but not the yardstick of a shared educated taste, such as writers were to assume by the age of Dryden. Critical 'judgement' was not so much a settled reality as an ideal, or perhaps a deferential supposition, even in what Harbage calls the theatres of the coteries.

Hamlet considers that the penny-paying groundlings 'for the most part are capable of nothing but inexplicable dumb-shows and noise'; but he has no more esteem for the elder statesman, Polonius, who had been 'accounted a good actor' in a university play in his youth: 'he's for a jig, or a tale of bawdry, or he sleeps'. As the private theatres got going, writers were optimistic at first: Marston hoped for 'judicious' appreciation from 'calm attention of choice audience' at Paul's, and Jonson (though 'doubtful') for 'sweet attention,/Quick sight, and quicker apprehension,/ (The lights of judgement's throne)', which shone—if 'any where'—at Blackfriars.[19] But very quickly, hope gave way to complaint, whichever type of playhouse was in question. In general, Ben Jonson took much the same line as Hamlet: on the one hand, he insisted that the common spectator was seduced by 'the concupiscence of dances and antics' and by that 'excellent vice of judgement' in play-writing that preferred dash and volubility to the exercise of 'election and a mean'; on the other hand, he attacked the arrogance of those who, for instance, would misjudge his unsuccessful *Catiline* on the strength of 'some pieces' of

---

[19] Marston, *Antonio's Revenge*, Prologue and epilogue (1600); Jonson, *Cynthia's Revels*, Prologue (1601).

Cicero conned at school.[20] In only one of his many statements on the subject—the prologue to *The Silent Woman* (at Blackfriars)—does Jonson say, as Marston had said in *What You Will*, that

> of old the art of making plays
> Was to content the people; and their praise
> Was to the poet money, wine, and bays—

as opposed to 'the sect of writers', in 'this age',

> That, only, for particular likings care,
> And will taste nothing that is popular;

everywhere else, he steps forward as a moral and cultural instructor, correcting an unenlightened and recalcitrant public. Similarly, Webster blamed 'the uncapable multitude' and the undiscriminating thirst for novelty among the general run of playgoers at the Red Bull for his disappointments over *The White Devil*; while after the failures of *The Faithful Shepherdess* and *The Knight of the Burning Pestle*, Fletcher blamed 'the common prate/ Of common people', devoid of 'judgement', and in 1613 Beaumont's publisher was to blame 'want of judgement' in the public for not initially 'understanding the privy mark of *irony* about' his piece. Both of these works by as yet little-known authors had been produced at Blackfriars.

The dramatists would have liked, or said they would have liked, to write on the neo-classical lines Sir Philip Sidney had advocated. Like the courtly writers of closet drama from Sidney's circle, Jonson, Webster and Chapman wished to model their tragedies on those of Seneca, compact in plot and unremittingly stately and sententious in language. But the public thwarted this ambition. When Jonson published *Sejanus* in 1605, he confessed that he had broken 'the strict Laws of *Time*' and had failed to provide 'a proper *Chorus*', because it was impossible 'to observe the old state, and splendour of *Dramatic Poems*, with preservation of any popular delight'. However, he defended his inclusion of footnotes from Latin sources for learned readers and maintained that he had kept the essentials of tragedy, namely 'truth of Argument, dignity of Persons, gravity and height of Elocution, [and] fulness and frequency of Sentence'. Webster followed suit in 1612 with *The White Devil*, while complaining that 'the uncapable multitude'

[20] See Jonson, *Volpone*, Dedication to the Universities (1607); *Catiline*, Dedication to William, Earl of Pembroke (1611); *The Alchemist*, Epistle to the Reader (1612): cf. Jonas A. Barish, 'Jonson and the Loathèd Stage', in William Blisset *et al.* (eds), *A Celebration of Ben Jonson* (Toronto, 1973).

would have choked off 'the most sententious tragedy that ever was written, observing all the critical laws, as height of style, and gravity of person', even if it was 'enriched' with a 'sententious *Chorus*' and with the 'divine rapture' of a 'passionate and weighty' Messenger speech. Chapman asserted that the 'soul' of 'an authentical tragedy' was 'material instruction' (though not literal truth) and 'elegant and sententious excitation to virtue'; and in dedicating his *Revenge of Bussy d'Ambois* in 1613 to the eminent courtier, Sir Thomas Howard, he pointed out that such works were patronized by 'the greatest Princes of Italy' and claimed that 'in the scenical presentation' (at Whitefriars) his own tragedy had 'passed with approbation of more worthy judgements', although admittedly it had also encountered 'some maligners'.[21] In a similar vein, Fletcher professed to dispel popular 'errors' for readers of *The Faithful Shepherdess* by summarizing the correct laws of tragicomedy, which he had absorbed from Guarini.

Uneducated prejudice was not the only ground for complaint. Although organized opposition to the stage seems to have dropped for a time after 1600, writers sniped at abiding puritan enemies; and they feared the malice of informers, not without cause. They mocked the swagger of be-feathered gallants on the stage, and suspected the influence of claques.[22] Above all, they hit out at 'maligners' in the theatrical world itself. Jonson furnished *Poetaster* with 'An armed *Prologue*' so as to quash the opening speaker, who is the monster, Envy; and Envy loomed large in other plays, especially for the private theatres. Among thirty-three plays from the private theatres issued with prologues or prefaces between 1599 and 1608, while sixteen appeal to the audience's 'judgement', no less than twelve, often the same plays, lash out at malicious or envious detractors. No doubt a playwright could sometimes find envy a convenient scapegoat. But it was not necessarily a myth. In the expanding London of around 1605 there were three public and three private theatres in regular use—an exceptionally large market for plays (especially when we consider that throughout the last third of the seventeenth century an even more populous London could only sustain two theatres

[21] Webster, *The White Devil*, To the Reader (1612); Chapman, *The Revenge of Bussy d'Ambois*, Dedication (1613), in Thomas Marc Parrott (ed.), *The Tragedies of George Chapman* (1910).

[22] See Day, *The Isle of Gulls*, Induction (referring to 'a prepared company of gallants, to applaud his [the author's] jests, and grace out his play'), ed. G. B. Harrison (1936), sig. A2; Dekker, *The Gull's Hornbook*, Chap. 6 (on the behaviour of gallants on the stage).

and, much of the time, only one). But the inner ring of frequent and most influential Jacobean playgoers—courtiers and law students, writers and gallants—must have composed, not a coterie but a small world, where jealousy and animosity were potentially explosive.

There was no settled code of manners or ideas prevailing in this small world surrounding the theatres. When Jonson published the Folio of his *Works* in 1616, he dedicated *Every Man out of his Humour* to his friends at the Inns of Court, 'as being born the judges of these studies'; but the lawyers only formed a single, though prominent, social group. Towards that time, we hear of meetings of scholarly gentlemen at the Mermaid, perhaps foreshadowing the clubs of Addison's day, but hardly constituting a nucleus of literary opinion.[23] The gentry who flocked to London in pursuit of pleasure and fashion as well as marriage-treaties or business made the prosperity of the private theatres possible. More than that, the influx of landed heirs, with their adventures and misadventures among the money-lenders, gallants and sharks of the capital, provided the central thread of social comedies, from Jonson's 'humour' plays onwards. But most of these gentlemen were lodgers, not residents; they were regarded (by the King, for instance) as social nuisances, neglecting their estates and duties in the shires; and they had little or no focus for social life, except perhaps in the taverns or in the theatres themselves.[24] Hence the importance of 'humours' and the social pretensions they imply, in comedy and satire, and in tragedy as well. In a number of plays about 1600 the central figure is a scholar or moralist, an aloof, caustic observer of the confusion of social values; for instance, Jonson's Macilente in *Every Man out of his Humour*, or Marston's Malcontent, or, in a sense, Hamlet or the Duke in *Measure for Measure*. Or else the theme of city comedies is a battle of wits over sex or money. *Volpone* is a supreme example, set at the aesthetic distance of Venice; but most plays with this theme have a topical, London setting, like *The Alchemist*. A characteristic example is Middleton's *A Trick to Catch the Old One*, produced at Paul's about 1605 and then at Blackfriars, where the hero is a bankrupt but sobered prodigal who resolves, in effect, to live up to his name, Witgood:

---

[23] I. A. Shapiro, 'The "Mermaid Club"', *Modern Language Review*, **45** (1950).
[24] Cf. Butler, *Theatre and Crisis* (n. 7, above), Chap. 6.

Well, how should a man live now, that has no living; hum? Why, are there not a million of men in the world, that only sojourn upon their brain, and make their wits their mercers; and am I not one amongst that million and cannot thrive upon't? Any trick, out of the compass of law, now would come happily to me.   [I.i]

Witgood's and similar tricks hinge on social pretensions, but it is the battle of wits that gives the comedies their drive, not definition of status; as the editor of another Middleton play observes, 'no meaningful code of "manners" is established to distinguish the pretender from the gentleman'.[25] Emrys Jones has recently described *The Silent Woman* as the first West End comedy,[26] and some of Fletcher's plays might be said to follow suit; but there was no *drawing-room* comedy of manners—or 'genteel' comedy, as it was originally called—before Shirley's plays under Charles I and then the plays of the Restoration. For Jacobean playwrights, the subject-matter of comedy was precisely the blurring of social boundaries in London and the mixture of classes. That was the image in the mirror they held up to their spectators.

Thinking of his own *salon*-centred audiences in Paris, Molière was to remark, 'C'est une étrange entreprise que celle de faire rire les honnêtes gens': making gentlefolk laugh was a funny business.[27] The task of writing for the market was, if anything, stranger still for the Jacobeans, in view of the mixed composition of their total public. As we have seen, both John Day and Francis Beaumont stressed the incompatibility of different playgoers' demands. They were not the first; a few years earlier, for instance, Heywood expected, in the epilogue to his domestic tragedy, *A Woman Killed with Kindness*, that 'some [would] judge [his play] too trivial, some too grave'. Diverse tastes in the theatre and changing standards constituted a problem. On the other hand, however, it was also a spur to writers to assert their independence. And here, I think, they gained a positive strength from the social mixture of their

[25] Richard Levin (ed.), Middleton, *Michaelmas Term*, Introduction (1966), p. xvii. For general studies of social topics in this body of plays, see L. C. Knights, *Drama and Society in the Age of Jonson* (1937), and the more recent work of Alexander Leggatt, *Citizen Comedy in the Age of Shakespeare* (Toronto, 1973), and Brian Gibbons, *Jacobean City Comedy* (2nd edn, 1980).

[26] Emrys Jones, 'The First West End Comedy', *Proceedings of the British Academy*, **68** (1983).

[27] Molière, *La Critique de L'École des femmes*, scene vi (1663): see Erich Auerbach, '"La Cour et la Ville"' (1951), in *Scenes from the Drama of European Literature* (New York, 1959); W. D. Howarth, *Molière: a Playwright and his Audience* (Cambridge, 1982).

public, envisaged as a whole. Although drama was gravitating towards the leisured and wealthy, no one class among playgoers was yet in a position to take over and monopolize the dramatist's point of view. On the contrary, the dramatist-as-entertainer had to reckon with the multitude, like it or not; while the dramatist-as-preacher kept in mind the ideal of an inclusive social order, with a place for clowns as well as princes, country as well as city, the poor as well as the rich. Variety of moods, of settings, of points of view was still common in Jacobean plays, as in an Elizabethan 'mingle-mangle'. And the basis of dramatic language was still the idiom of common speech, vigorously employed. There was an extra degree of literary artifice, which went along with the writers' appeal to educated 'judgement'. But it was precisely the inter-action, the felt tension, between literary artifice and common idiom that made for vitality in the language of the Jacobean stage.

Sir Philip Sidney had emphasized the neo-classical rules of unity in time and place, as observed (for their own type of picture-stage) by the Italians. In practice, of course, English playwrights ignored the rules, like their counterparts in Spain; most flagrantly, in dramatizations of history or legend for the public theatres. However, Shakespeare uses a choric speaker or presenter to supply gaps in the narrative and compensate for the physical limitations of the stage by urging spectators to 'work' their 'imaginary forces' so as to picture unstageable battle scenes or distant voyages, such as the transfer of Henry V's army to and fro across the Channel. Similarly, in *Old Fortunatus*, in the same year as *Henry V* (1599), Dekker follows Shakespeare's example, by pointing out through his Prologue that 'this small Circumference must stand,/ For the imagined Surface of much land', and begging the audience's 'thoughts to help poor Art', by allowing the speaker to interpose periodically as 'Chorus' to the action, 'Not when the laws of Poesy do call,/But as the story needs'.[28] Other plays likewise specify through a Chorus-speaker that the audience should 'imagine' sea-changes for the characters. This convention in radically unclassical plays was an indirect conces-sion to the classical 'laws of Poesy'.

[28] Dekker, *Old Fortunatus*, in *Dramatic Works*, Vol. 1; Shakespeare, *Henry V*, Prologue and Chorus II, III, IV, V; also *Pericles* (at the Globe, 1608; Chorus IV: 'Imagine Pericles arriv'd at Tyre ...'). Compare Anon., *Captain Thomas Stukeley* (Rose theatre, 1596/99?: Chorus, lines 2251 ff., 2296 ff., 2656ff.: 'imagination must supply' the full picture of the battle of Alcazar; Simpson [ed.], *School of Shakspere*, Vol. 1); Heywood (?), *2 Edward IV* (Derby's Men, *c.* 1599: Chorus relates King Edward's return from France and invites spectators to 'imagine'

More generally, one can trace a kind of zigzag through prologues or prefaces between the authors' uncertainty over public taste and confidence in their own professional skill. In his earliest plays, Marston, for instance, hopefully expected recognition for novelty—or freedom from 'mouldy fopperies of stale Poetry' and 'Unpossible dry musty Fictions'—and recognition for 'rare composed Scenes', adorned with 'purest elegance'; but when he published *Antonio and Mellida* soon afterwards, in 1602, he dedicated it to the 'only' discerning 'rewarder', namely, 'Nobody'.[29] And Chapman, in the prologue to his comedy, *All Fools*, in 1604, voiced 'amaze[ment]' over the inscrutable 'fortune' of the stage and the lordly presumption of spectators at Blackfriars, who '[scorned] to compose plays' but none the less pretended to 'judge better far' than the poets who '[made]' them. On the other side, Middleton was shrewder and more pragmatic. In his preface to *The Family of Love*, printed in 1608, he regretted that the lapse of several years since the comedy had been produced would deprive it of novelty for London gallants, so that it might now only be saleable for country audiences and to 'termers' (or visitors to London). But his preface to *The Roaring Girl*, written jointly with Dekker for the Fortune theatre and published in 1611, is a confident advertisement for the general appeal of the play, linked with a comment about fashion:[30]

Matthew Shore's oversea journeys; *Heywood's Dramatic Works*, Vol. 1, p. 119); Heywood, *Four Prentices* (Admiral's Men, *c.* 1600?; later at the Red Bull: Presenter, 'Imagine now ye see the air made thick/ With stormy tempests, that disturb the Main'; *Dramatic Works*, Vol. 2, p. 175); Anon., *Thomas, Lord Cromwell* (Chamberlain's Men [?], *c.* 1600: Chorus, opening Act II and at end of III.ii: 'imagines' Cromwell's travels abroad; William Hazlitt [ed.], *The Doubtful Plays of William Shakespeare*[1887]); Dekker, *The Magnificent Entertainment: Given to King James* (1604: the readers' 'imaginations' must 'suppose' part of the King's progress through London; *Dramatic Works*, Vol. 2, p. 264); Heywood, *2 If You Know Not Me You Know Nobody* (Queen Anne's Men, at the Curtain, 1605: Chorus, 'Imagine you now see them [the ships of the Armada] under sail'; *Dramatic Works*, Vol 1, p. 333); Day and others, *The Travels of Three English Brothers* (Queen Anne's Men at the Red Bull, 1607: Chorus asks spectators to imagine the Shirley brothers' far-flung journeys; A. H. Bullen [ed.], *The Works of John Day* [1881]).

[29] Marston, *Jack Drum's Entertainment*, Prologue (Paul's, 1600); *Antonio's Revenge*, epilogue (Paul's, 1600); Dedication (1602) to *Antonio and Mellida* (Paul's, 1599). Cf. Day, praising patronage of 'Signor No-Body' in preface (1608) to *Humour out of Breath* (Whitefriars, 1608).

[30] Middleton's signed preface (1611) to *The Roaring Girl* (ed. Bowers, in Dekker's *Dramatic Works*, Vol. 3).

The fashion of play-making, I can properly compare to nothing, so naturally, as the alteration in apparel: For in the time of the Great-crop-doublet, your huge bombasted plays, quilted with mighty words to lean purpose was only then in fashion. And as the doublet fell, neater inventions began to set up. Now in the time of spruceness, our plays follow the niceness of our Garments, single plots, quaint conceits, lecherous jests, dressed up in hanging sleeves, and those are fit for the Times, and the Termers: Such a kind of light-colour Summer stuff, mingled with diverse colours, you shall find this published Comedy. ...

'Neater inventions': Middleton's belief in stylistic improvements in play-making (reminding us today of our experience of changing techniques in films and television) was evidently shared by others. When Heywood dedicated his *Four Prentices of London* to the London apprentices of 1615, he felt bound to apologize for his fifteen-year-old piece in the light of 'these more exquisite and refined Times', 'more Censorious' now over 'accurateness both in Plot and Style'. And Webster, while regretting the impossibility of composing *The White Devil* as a 'sententious' classical tragedy, asked the reader of 1612 to measure it by the work of Chapman and Jonson, Beaumont and Fletcher, and Shakespeare, Dekker and Heywood—the contemporaries he admired 'in the strength of [his] own judgement'. Again, when commending his *Devil's Law Case* to 'the Judicious Reader', in 1623, Webster pressed for recognition of his own literary skill, while also paying tribute to the work of the actors:

A great part of the grace of this (I confess) lay in action; yet can no action ever be gracious, where the decency of the language, and ingenious structure of the scene, arrive not to make up a perfect harmony.

'Decency' (that is, appropriateness) of language and the 'ingenious structure of the scene' are much the same criteria as Jonson had consistently advocated and Marston had hoped to be judged by.

To return briefly to Middleton: one prologue of his is worth quoting in full because it is typical of his view of his audiences (though exceptional in its jaunty metre). It was probably written for a public theatre about 1612, and it takes account both of those 'above' (the better-off spectators in the galleries) and of those 'below' (the supposedly slower-witted groundlings):[31]

[31] Middleton, *No Wit, No Help Like a Woman's*, in Bullen (ed.), *Works*, Vol. 4. On the prologue, cf. H. S. Bennett, 'Shakespeare's Audience', *Proceedings of the British Academy*, **30** (1944), p. 76. There is a commentary on this play in George E. Rowe, Jr., *Thomas Middleton and the New Comedy Tradition* (University of Nebraska Press, 1979), pp. 114–29.

How is't possible to suffice
So many ears, so many eyes?
Some in wit, some in shows
Take delight, and some in clothes:
Some for mirth they chiefly come,
Some for passion—for both some;
Some for lascivious meetings, that's their errand—
Some to detract, and ignorance their warrant.
How is it possible to please
Opinion toss'd in such wild seas?
Yet I doubt not, if attention
Seize you above, and apprehension
You below, to take things quickly,
We shall both make you sad and tickle ye.

This prologue, with its frankly commercial ending, comes from *No Wit, No Help Like a Woman's*, a comedy in the style of quick-moving romantic complication that was beginning to make Fletcher successful, but which meant a new departure for Middleton. However, in *The Roaring Girl*, Middleton and Dekker had set out from the same view of many-headed Opinion to develop an independent standpoint. The girl of the title was a real Londoner of the day, the notorious Mary Frith, called 'mad Moll', who often dressed and behaved like a man. According to the preface, the play has deliberately defended her reputation. The prologue describes how, knowing the title, every spectator 'brings a play in's head' with his own idea of a Roaring Girl. The play shows Moll as a self-reliant, talented, generous character, street-wise and quick with her sword, a female Robin Hood, prompt to help lovers in distress but repeatedly obliged to free herself from the base expectations of the crooks and gallants she encounters. By the end, Sir Alexander Wengrave, her principal enemy, is forced to correct his opinion of her, based on prejudice and rumour; 'Forgive me, now I cast the world's eyes from me,/ And look upon thee freely with mine own' [V.ii.243]. The epilogue carries this moral further by telling the fable of the painter who, to please successive onlookers, altered every feature in a portrait in turn, until the portrait as a whole was ruined.[32]

---

[32] The parable of the painter in the Epilogue to *The Roaring Girl* was also used to illustrate a dramatist's difficulties with the public in Robert Daborne's Epilogue to *A Christian Turned Turk*, acted by the King's Men about 1610 and published in 1612. It is not clear which epilogue was written first but very likely both reflect common talk among theatrical writers at the time.

In this way, *The Roaring Girl* applies the idea of genuine judgement equally to the authors themselves, the spectators as critics and the characters within the play. The continuity between writer, spectators and characters, between judgement in dramatic literature and its counterpart with regard to social behaviour, was even more thoroughly worked out, a few years later, by Ben Jonson, in *Bartholomew Fair*. The Fair is represented as a place of popular holiday entertainment. But the induction at the Hope playhouse opens with a stage-hand, who confides to the audience that he has worked in theatres for thirty years (since 'Master Tarlton's time') and that, in his opinion, the self-important poet does not know his business, since he has omitted performing animals and the like time-honoured attractions. Then a Scrivener appears, to read out 'Articles of Agreement' between spectators and author, defining the spectators' right to 'their free-will of censure, to like or dislike at their own charge'. On the author's behalf, the Scrivener lists some of the attractions that will be provided, while ironically conceding that there will not be any 'drolleries' or 'monsters', 'to make Nature afraid', in the manner of *The Winter's Tale* or *The Tempest*. No informer should be 'so solemnly ridiculous' as to pick out any hidden political allusions. A stubbornly old-fashioned playgoer can be tolerated:

He that will swear *Jeronimo* [i.e. *The Spanish Tragedy*] or *Andronicus* are the best plays yet, shall pass unexcepted at here as a man whose judgement shews it is constant, and hath stood still these five and twenty or thirty years. Though it be an ignorance, it is a virtuous and staid ignorance; and next to truth, a confirmed error does well.

But above all, each spectator is to judge for himself—within the limits of his capacity:

the author having now departed with his right, it shall be lawful for any man to judge his six penn'orth, his twelve penn'orth, so to his eighteen pence, two shillings, half a crown, to the value of his place [presumably, inflated prices for the opening of a new playhouse]—provided always his place get not above his wit;

and provided, further, that he forms and stands by his own judgement, without copying his neighbour, be the latter 'never so first in the Commission of Wit'. Jonson's banter covers a serious inspection of the relations between writer and public under conditions of the market. The legal analogies he plays with were common and were bound to be prominent at the time in any reference to the mental process of 'judgement'. But Jonson traces trustworthy critical judgement more deeply, to self-knowledge on the part of the critic. He promises all the spectators of *Bartholomew Fair* 'sport' and 'delight'– 'provided they have either the wit or the honesty to think well of themselves'. Vanity and gloom are disqualifications.

The characters within the play are pleasure-seekers at the Fair, mostly naïve; or fairground operators, whose business it is to exploit them; or else self-appointed, censorious watchdogs. In other words, they cover the same spectrum of minds (in caricature) as those concerned with the London theatres. The censors prove no less gullible than the simpletons—notably, Adam Overdo, the minor magistrate who (like a real Lord Mayor of the day) disguises himself so as to detect 'enormities' with his own eyes. He first appears at the Fair in the dress of a local madman, congratulating himself that 'They may have seen many a fool in the habit of a Justice; but never till now a Justice in the habit of a fool' [II.i]. But he pedantically misinterprets the petty crimes he witnesses, while his officious interference earns him first a cudgelling and then a spell in the stocks. His first-hand judgement is absurd. However, neither Overdo nor the other victims of the Fair's topsy-turvydom are presented simply as farcical oddities. A prime impulse shared by watchdogs and pleasure-seekers alike is an interest in the Fair as spectators (or consumers). And the induction has provoked the real spectators in the playhouse to examine the same kinds of impulse in themselves.[33]

Unlike Jonson, of course, Shakespeare abstained from authorial criticism. The occasional prologues in his plays serve to introduce the story, and his epilogues mark the step, for the audience, back from fiction to ordinary life, while requesting their continued favour for his company: 'And we'll strive to please you every day'. Although Shakespeare refers very often to acting in his plays, he says nothing directly about his own function as a dramatist— probably because, as actor and sharer in the most successful company, he felt more sure of himself than other dramatists and more attuned to his audience. But that does not mean that he was left untouched by the critical ideas expressed by his contemporaries; only, that he reacted to them in his own way. For example, the Player scenes in *Hamlet* constitute, in effect, an induction within the play, dealing both with the actors' profession and with the responses of spectators who interest us as individuals.

---

[33] I have discussed *Bartholomew Fair* in more detail in an article for *Renaissance Drama*, **10** (n.s.) (1979), reprinted in *Dramatic Form in Shakespeare and the Jacobeans*.

And his development as a dramatist is strongly marked both by a growing attention to the human aspect of forming judgements and by a growing tendency towards reflectiveness, even sententiousness, on the part of his characters. In *The Merchant of Venice*, for instance, characters comment on one another and the climax is an exciting trial scene; but personal judgements barely affect the trial scene or the general course of the plot. But *Measure for Measure*, containing similar themes, turns on the way people judge one another, intimately and publicly. Again, in *Julius Caesar*, the conspiracy arises, is accomplished, and fails through the medium of personal judgements; and what brings this Roman history to life is precisely our impression of the main actors as patricians who have watched one another for years, an impression derived vividly from their terse incidental comments: 'He was quick mettle when he went to school', for instance; or, 'He thinks too much; such men are dangerous'. And in the major tragedies that followed, Shakespeare not only makes the action turn on the way characters evaluate their own or each other's motives, but repeatedly makes his speakers reflect and generalize, even in the course of passion; as (to quote one more example) when Macbeth's mind swerves to the moral consequence while he is steeling his will to the murder of Duncan:

> But in these cases
> We still have judgement here, that we but teach
> Bloody instructions, which, being taught, return
> To plague th' inventor.

This tendency gives an extra dimension to Shakespeare's speakers. It enhances their stage presence beyond personal character. It provides a choric commentary, sometimes an ironic overtone, enriching and complicating the flow of passion and the active will. And this tendency towards choric sententiousness was a tendency Shakespeare shared with the other Jacobeans, though as a rule his sententious passages are much more subtly keyed to the speaker and the occasion.

When Shakespeare's former colleagues, Hemings and Condell, published the First Folio of his plays in 1623, they cajoled the potential buyer in the tone of confident salesmen:

you will stand for your privileges we know: to read, and censure. Do so, but buy it first. ... Judge your six-penn'orth, your shilling's worth, your five shillings' worth at a time, or higher, so you rise to the just rates, and welcome. But, what ever you do, Buy. ...

The most likely buyers for such an expensive book would have been frequenters of the private theatres, whom the actor-editors greet without flattery:

And though you be a Magistrate of wit, and sit on the stage at *Blackfriars*, or the *Cockpit*, to arraign Plays daily, know, these Plays have had their trial already, and stood out all Appeals. ...

The editors strike a neat balance between artistic and business considerations, between reading plays and seeing them, and between the author's credentials and the rights of his critics. Their language, with its legal joking, recalls the induction to *Bartholomew Fair*; and they say they would rather have purchasers 'weighed' than 'numbered'—again, in the spirit of Ben Jonson, whose resonant poetic tribute to Shakespeare's memory they published over the page. To that extent, their edition seems like at least a qualified victory for the idea of judiciousness and whatever it stood for in the shape of discerning erudition and moral realism, sharpness, economy, dignity or restraint. Yet, with all that, Hemings' and Condell's preface is not addressed to 'the Judicious Reader' but, in the first place, '*To the Great Variety of Readers*. From the most able, to him that can but spell'. I imagine Shakespeare would have liked it that way.

INDEX

Note: page numbers *in italics* indicate illustrations. Footnotes are not indexed. Written works are listed under the names of their authors if known; anonymous works are listed under their titles.

absurdist drama, 15
acting: advice in *Hamlet*, 1, 10–13, 32, 231–2, 241, 251–2
Admiral's Men, 140, 160, 167
Aeschylus, 223
Ainger, Alfred, 192, 193, 210
Alexander, Peter, ix
Alleyn, Edward, 237
Ambales Saga, 223, 225
Anti-Jacobin Review, The, 189
Archenholz, J. W. von: *A Picture of England*, 52
Arcimboldo, 29
Arden, John, 14–15
Arden Shakespeare edition, xi, 26, 123, 136, 215
Aretino, Pietro: *Il Marescalco*, 74–5, 76
Aristotle, 1
Armada, Spanish, 148, 149
Arthur, Prince of Wales, 120
Ascham, Roger, 1
Ashcroft, Peggy, 206, 211
audiences, ix, x, xi, xii, 40, 165, 216, 231–53; and stage-illusion, 3–17, 33–5; as trial jury, 123–4, 127–30, 134
Augustine, Saint, 100

Bacon, Edmund, 136
Bakhtin, Mikhail, 219
Bancroft, Squire, 80
Bandello, Matteo, 150, 151–2
Barton, John, 150
Bate, Jonathan, 189
Beaumont, Francis, 84, 245, 248; *The Knight of the Burning Pestle*, 241, 242; 'Letter from the Country to Jonson', 56; *The Woman Hater*, 59, 60–3, 76, 240
bed-trick, 27–9, 32–6, 38, 39, 90
Behn, Aphra, 53
Bell, R. A., 210
Belleforest, 214
Bennett, H. S., xii
Berners, John Bourchier, 2nd Baron, 146
Betterton, Thomas, 162
Bevington, David, 167
Bible, 27, 101, 228
Blackfriars, 120, 124; Playhouse, 234, 238, 240, 241–2, 247; *Henry VIII* at, 123–4, 127–9, 133–5, 136
Blake, William: *The Sick Rose*, 25
Book of Sir Thomas More, The, x, 117, 162, 167–70, 178–9
Boucicault, Dion: *London Assurance*, 79; *Old Heads and Young Hearts*, 79–80
Bowdler, Henrietta Maria, 185, 187, 188

Bowdler, Thomas, 185
boy actors' companies, 59, 63, 70, 234, 238, 240
Brett Young, Francis, 204; *Hamlet* version 205–6, 211
British Academy: *Proceedings*, ix; Shakespeare lectures, ix, x, xi, 137, 214, 222–3
Brome, Richard: *The Court Beggar*, 46–7
Brontë, Charlotte: *Jane Eyre*, 80
Brook, Harold F., xi
Brook, Peter, 15
Brooke, William, Lord Cobham, 173
Brundage, Frances: illustration by, *184*
Buchan, John, 204, 205, 211
Buckman, Irene: *Twenty Tales from Shakespeare*, 206, 211
Bullen, Anne, 119, 121; in *Henry VIII*, 127–9, 131–2
Bulwer-Lytton, Edward, 42; *Not So Bad As We Seem*, 80
Burbage, Richard, 240; *Elegy* on, 3, 218
Burby, Cuthbert, 139, 160
'Burlington Bertie from Bow' (song), 81–2
Butler, Martin, x

Calais, 142, 143, 144, 145, 146, 149, 154
Camden, William, 234
Campeius, Cardinal, 119, 121; in *Henry VIII*, 129–31
Campion, Thomas, 122
Capell, Edward, 138–9, 144, 149, 161, 162
Cardenio, 162
Carey, George, 2nd Baron Hunsdon, 175
Carey, Henry, 1st Baron Hunsdon, 175
Carroll, Lewis: *Alice in Wonderland*, 191
Carter, Thomas, 203–4, 211
Casaubon, Isaac, 68
Cecil, Lord David, 190
censorship, 167, 179, 251
Chamberlain, John, 56, 234
Chambers, E. K., xi
Chapman, George, 59, 63, 116, 234, 238, 243, 248; *All Fools*, 247; *Revenge of Bussy d'Ambois*, 243; *The Widow's Tears*, 70
Charles V, King of France, 141
Children's Shakespeare, The, *184*, 200, 212
children's versions of Shakespeare, *184*, 185–216
Chorus, 246
Churchill, Winston, 204–5, 211
Chute, Marchette, 206, 211
Cicero, 1, 2, 10, 242
Clement VII, Pope, 121; in *Henry VIII*, 124, 129, 131
clowns, 23–6

Coghill, Nevill, 21
Coleridge, Samuel Taylor, 20, 189; on
 illusion, 6–7, 8, 14, 17
Collettivo di Parma, 180
Collins, Wilkie, 80
combat of cowards, 75
Condell, Henry, 252–3
Congreve, William, 66, 71, 77, 81; *Love for
 Love*, 42, 74; *The Way of the World*, 82
Conway, Viscount, 57
Cook, Ann Jennalie, x, 235
Copping, H., 194
Correggio, Antonio da, 132
Coward, Noel, 83, *Present Laughter*, 41–2
Coyne, William P., 195–6, 210
Craik, T. W., xi
Critical Review, 189, 190
Crosse, Henry, 235
Curtain theatre, 117, 140

Dane, Clemence, 204, 211
Daniel, Samuel, 238
Dante Alighieri, 228
Darwin, Erasmus, 5–6
David II, King of Scotland, 141, 156
Davies, Sir John, 237
Day, John, 245; *The Isle of Gulls*, 240
death, 227–8, 229
dedications, 241, 243, 247
Defoe, Daniel, 53
Dekker, Thomas, 234, 235, 238, 248; *Old
 Fortunatus*, 246; *Shoemaker's Holiday*, 42, 60;
 The Roaring Girl, 247–8, 249–50
Deloney, Thomas; *Jack of Newberry*, 28, 34
Denmark House, 66
Denny, Lady Honora, 122
Dent's Temple Classics for Young People,
 194, 210
Dickens, Charles, 80
Disraeli, Benjamin: *Tancred*, 80
Donatus, 1
Donne, John, 46, 71, 237; first Satire, 67–8
Donno, Elizabeth Story, 195, 211
Doran, Madeleine, 182
Dostoevsky, Fyodor, 219
Dover Wilson, John, 64, 173
Dowden, Edward, 202
Dryden, John, 69, 241; *Essay of Dramatic
 Poesy*, 43; translation of Persius, 68–9
Du Guernier: illustration by, 221
Duncombe's Miniature Library, 199
Dutch house libel, 169–70

Earl of Pembroke's Men, 140, 159–60
Edmund, Earl of Kent, 142
Edmund Ironside, x
Education Act, *1870*, 191
Edward III, King, 137, 138, 142–7; coins of
 his realm, 147–8
Edward, Prince of Wales (Black Prince), 143,
 148, 151
Edward III, see Reign of King Edward III, The

Edwards, Owen Dudley, 83–4
Edwards, Philip, 156, 215–16
El Greco: *View and Plan of Toledo*, 30, *31*, 34,
 39
Eliot, George, 114–15
Eliot, T. S., 20, 103; 'Gerontion', 179–80, 183
Elizabeth I, Queen, 117, 119, 121, 122; in
 Henry VIII, 132, 133–4
Elizabeth Stuart, Princess, 122, 123, 135
Empson, William, 216, 217–18, 220, 221,
 222, 227
endings, x; epilogues, 231, 232, 233, 245, 249,
 251; *Henry V*, 156–7
Etherege, Sir George: *The Man of Mode*, 42
Euripides, 223–4
Everyman's Library, 194
Exeter, 235–6

Family Shakespeare, The, 185
Famous Victories of Henry V, The, 142, 171–3,
 175, 176–7, 179
Farquhar, George, 4
Fawkes, Guy, 122
fiction, 16–17
film industry, 165–7
Finch, Henry, 170
First Folio of Shakespeare's plays, 161, 162,
 163, 252–3
First Part of Richard II, The, 171
Fisher, F. J., 49–50
Flather, J. L., 210
Fletcher, John, 3, 60, 135, 162, 242, 243, 248
Foakes, R. A., xi, 123, 136
Ford, John, 118
Foreman, Walter C., x
Fortune theatre, 238, 247
Foxe, John, 172–3
Foxon, David, 186
Frederick, Prince, Elector Palatine, 135
Freud, Sigmund, 221, 222
Frith, Mary, 249
Froissart, Jean, 144, 145, 146, 147, 150, 151,
 152, 154, 202
Fry, Christopher, 206
Furnivall, F. J., 193–4, 210, 211

Gabrieli, Vittorio, 167
Gardiner, Alfonzo, 195, 210
Garfield, Leon: *Shakespeare Stories*, 208–9, 211
Garrick, David, 197
genre, xi, 19–40; histories, 178–83
Gentleman's Review, The, 190
gentlemen, town: 17C., 56–9, 161, 236–7,
 244–5; later tradition, 78–84
George, Saint, 137
Gilbert, Sir John, 194, 210
Gilbert, Sir William: *Engaged*, 81
Globe theatre, 123, 124, 136, 238
Godwin, Mary Jane, 186
Godwin, William, 186
Goff, Thomas: *The Careless Shepherdess*, 139
Gosson, Stephen, 3

Granville-Barker, Harley, 14
Graves, Joseph, 199, 211–12
Greek drama, 214, 222–7
Green, Roger Lancelyn, 206–7, 212
Greene, Robert, 151
Greenwich theatre, 152
Guarini, 243: *Compendio*, 32
Gunkel, Hermann, 228
Gunpowder plot, 119, 122
Gurr, Andrew, x, 237

Hall, Edward, 142, 178
Hall, Joseph, 67
Hammond, Gertrude Demain, 211
Harbage, Alfred, x, 238–9, 241
Hardison, O. B., 195, 211
Harington, Sir John: *Orlando Furioso*, 30
Harpsfield, Nicholas, 172–3
Harrison, G. B.: *New Tales*, 206, 212
Harvey, Gabriel, 238
Hattaway, Michael, x
Hay, Lord, 122
Hazlitt, William, 209
Heminges, John, 252–3
Henry IV, King, 138
Henry VII, King, 117–18, 122
Henry VIII, King, 118, 119, 120, 121
Henry of Navarre, 149, 157
Henry Stuart, Prince of Wales, 122, 123, 135
Henslowe, Philip, 166
Herne, Hieronimus, 132
Heywood, Thomas, 139, 166, 233–4, 235, 248; *Apology for Actors*, 1, 141; *The Brazen Age*, 233; *Edward IV*, 139; *The Four Prentices of London*, 240, 248; *The Golden Age*, 232, 233; *The Silver Age*, 232; *A Woman Killed with Kindness*, 245
histories: remade, 165–83
Hoffman, Alice Spencer, 203, 212
Holinshed, Raphael, 109, 139, 146, 147, 168, 177
Holland, Sir Thomas, 151
Hollar, Wenceslaus: drawing of London, 45–6
Hollow Crown, The, 150
Homer, 220; *Odyssey*, 226
Honigmann, Ernst, 172
Hope theatre, 241, 250
Horace, 1, 67, 68
Howes: *Annales*, 66
Hoy, Cyrus, 152
Hudson, R., 203, 212
Hufford, Lois Grosvenor, 203, 212

Ibsen, Henrik: *Peer Gynt*, 98
illusion, stage, ix, xi, 3–17, 33–5, 112–14
imitation, 1–18
Inns of Court, 45, 46, 58–9, 61, 63, 67, 234, 235
Irving, Henry, 203
Isabelle, Queen, 142–3, 144

Iser, Wolfgang, 16

Jackson, MacDonald, 159
Jaggard, William, 185
James I, King, 109, 117, 118, 119, 121–3, 161, 238
James, Henry, 78, 87
Jenkins, Harold, 176, 215–16
Jermyn, Henry, Earl of St Albans, 51
Joan, 'Fair Maid of Kent', 151
Joan of Arc, 201
John II, King of France, 146
John of Gaunt, Duke of Lancaster, 143
Johnson, Dr Samuel, 4–5, 6, 20, 22, 29, 50, 81; *Rasselas*, 215
Jones, Emrys, x, 137, 245
Jones, Ernest, 223
Jones, Gemma, 197
Jones, Inigo, 48, 50–1
Jones, John, 223
Jonson, Ben, 19, 20, 51, 84, 234, 238, 248; *The Alchemist*, 69; *Bartholomew Fair*, 241, 250–1, 253; *Catiline*, 241; *Cynthia's Revels*, 231, 241; *Epicoene, or The Silent Woman*, 42–3, 44, 47, 48, 56, 58–60, 62, 66–7, 69–78, 242, 245; *Every Man In His Humour*, 64, 69, 77; *Every Man Out Of His Humour*, 1 60, 63, 231, 232, 234, 244, (dedication, 244), (induction, 239); 'Mortimer his Fall', 143; *The New Inn*, 69; *Poetaster*, 67, 69, 231–2, 243; *Sejanus*, 38, 143, 242; *Volpone*, 69, 77, 237, 244
Joyce, James: *Ulysses*, 178, 183
'judicious' and judgement, ix, 231–53
Juvenal, 67, 68

Kames, Henry Home, Lord, 5–6
Katherine of Aragon, Queen, 118, 119–24, 120, 134–5; in *Henry VIII*, 125–33
Kelso, Ruth, 58
Kemp, Will, 173
Kenrick, William, 5
Kent, Joan, Countess of, 151
Kermode, Frank, x
Keynes, John Maynard, 50
King's Men, 117, 123, 135, 136, 238
Kirk, M. L., 211
Knack to Know a Knave, A, 151
Knight, Charles, 192
Knights, Lionel, 177–8, 219–20
Kott, Jan, 99
Kyd, Thomas, 19, 170; *The Spanish Tragedy*, 37, 38, 214, 218, 232, 250

Lamb, Charles, 81, 185–6, 190, 194, 196–7; letter to Coleridge, 189–90; *Tales from Shakespeare*, 185–97, 204, 206, 208, (editions listed, 210–11)
Lamb, Mary, 185–97, 202; see also *Tales from Shakespeare above*
Lang, Andrew, 193
Lang, Mrs Andrew, 194, 211

Laughton, J. K., 148
le Bel, Jean, 146, 151, 152
Lee, Sidney, 202
levee scenes: 17C., 41–3, 67–72; later
  tradition, 78–84
Lewis, C. S., 214, 227
liars and lying, 85–116; puns on, 25–6, 85–6;
  stage-illusion, 3–17
Lisle Letters, The, 66
Literary Panorama, 189
Lloyd, Marie, 81
Lodge, Thomas, 214
London, 49–50; Belgravia, 53; City, 42, 44–6,
  53, 140; Covent Garden, 48, 50, 53; East
  End, 52–4, 66, 81; Lincoln's Inn, 46, 237,
  (Fields, 51); New Exchange, 48; Pall Mall
  Field, 51; Piccadilly, 44; Savoy, 46; St
  James's Square, 51; St Paul's, 50; wages,
  236; West End, 41–84; Westminster, 44–5,
  54; see also Inns of Court; playhouses and
  theatres; Strand, the
Lord Chamberlain's Men, 160, 166, 171, 173,
  175, 180
Lord Hunsdon's Men, 175
Lord Mayor of London: attacks theatre, 3
Lord Strange's Men, 140, 160
Lorkin, Thomas, 136
'Loving Mad Tom' (poem), 228–9
Lyly, John: Campaspe, 151; Midas, 232, 233

Macauley, Elizabeth Wright: Tales of the
  Drama, 198, 212
Mackail, J. W., ix
Macleod, Mary: Shakespeare Story-Book, 202–3,
  212
Malory, Sir Thomas: Morte d'Arthur, 27–8,
  202
Mannerists, 29–30, 32, 132
Manny, Sir Walter, 144, 146
Marlow, Christopher, 19; Dr Faustus, 63–4,
  232, 237; Edward II, 139, 143; The Jew of
  Malta, 37, 63–4; Tamburlaine, 1, 144, 149,
  232, 237
Marston, John, 63, 67, 232, 234, 237, 238,
  239, 241, 242–3, 247; Antonio and Mellida,
  240, 247; The Insatiate Countess, 28; The
  Malcontent, 37, 38, 240, 244; What You Will,
  70, 240, 242
Mary I, Queen, 119, 143
Mary Queen of Scots, 119, 122
mass media, 165–7
Maugham, W. Somerset, 42; Lady Frederick,
  82–3
Maxwell, Caroline: The Juvenile Shakespeare,
  198–9, 212
McMillin, Scott, 159
Melchiori, Giorgio, x, xi
Meredith, George, 26
Meres, Francis, 161, 237
Mermaid club, 244
metaphor, 114–15
Middleton, Thomas, 232, 234; A Chaste Maid

in Cheapside, 47; The Family of Love, 247;
  Father Hubburd's Tale, 46, 54; No Wit, No
  Help Like a Woman's, 248–9; The Roaring
  Girl, 247–8, 249–50; A Trick to Catch the Old
  One, 244–5
Miles, Bernard, 208, 212
mingling and mixing, 19–40
Molière, 245
Mond, Frida, ix
Montacute, Alice, 151
Montacute, Edward, 151
Montacute, William, Earl of Salisbury, 143
Montacute, William, junior, 151
Montaigne, Michel, essays, 87, 116, 215; 'Of
  the force of Imagination', 109–10; 'Of
  giving the lie', 94, 105, 109; 'Of Liars', 85
Montfort, John de, 144
More, Sir Thomas, 172; Utopia, 170
Morris, Harrison S., 192–3, 210
Mortimer, Roger, Earl of March, 142–3, 144
Muir, Kenneth, ix, 160, 161
Mumford, Lewis: The City in History, 65–6
Munday, Anthony, 96–7, 168
Munro, John, 118–19
Murray, Gilbert, 223–6
Murrillo, Bartolomé, 132
music-hall, 81

Nashe, Thomas: Pierce Penniless, 141–2
Neill, Michael, 232
Nesbit, Edith: The Children's Shakespeare, 184,
  200, 212
New Age Shakespeare edition, xi
New Cambridge Shakespeare edition, xi,
  215–16
New Variorum Shakespeare edition, 193
Nisbet, R. G. M., 69
Nottingham Playhouse, 152
Nuttall, A. D., xi

O'Casey, Sean, 21, 23; Juno and the Paycock,
  21
Ockham, William of, 222
Oedipus, 222, 227
Old Vic theatre, 152
Oldcastle, Sir John, Lord Cobham, 172–3,
  175
opening scenes, x, 63; inductions, 239–41;
  levees, 41–3, 64, 67–72, 78–84; prologues,
  123, 232–5, 239–40, 242, 243, 247
Order of the Garter, 137–8
Orestes, 222–7
Osborne, John, 54
Oxford, 109
Oxford Shakespeare editions, x, xi

Packe, Michael, 151
Painter, William: Palace of Pleasure, 149–50
paintings: Mannerist, 29–30
Partridge, Edward B., 73
Patterson, Annabel, x
Paul, Henry N., 109

Peacham, Henry, 19; *Complete Gentleman*, 57
Perrers, Alice, 143, 152
Perrin, J. B.,: *Contes Moraux*, 197–8, 199, 212
Persius, 67, 68–9, 71, 72
Petty, Sir William: *Treatise of Taxation*, 52
Philip II, King of Spain, 119
Philip VI, King of France, 146
Philippa of Hainault, 143, 152
Pickering, Sir Henry, 136
Pinciss, G. M., 160
Pinero, Sir Arthur, 79
Plautus, 237
playhouses and theatres, 50, 159–60, 165;
    private and public, 234–51; stage-illusion,
    3–17; Strand, 41; War of the, 234; West
    End, 44, 48, 83; *see also* audiences; *names of
    theatres*
plays: printed versions, 139–40, 160, 165–6,
    171; First Folio, 161, 162, 163, 252–3; *see
    also under names of authors*
Plutarch, 24–5, 181, 225
Poel, William: *The King and the Countess*, 152
Poitiers, 143, 144–5, 146, 148–9
Pontormo, Jacopo da: *Joseph in Egypt*, 29–30
prologues, 123, 232–5, 239–40, 242, 243, 247
prose/verse proportions, 181–2
Proudfoot, Richard, x
Pudsey, Edward, 237–8
Punchard, C. D., 210
puritans, 243
Puttenham, George: *The Arte of English Poesie*,
    114

Queen's Men, 140, 160, 171
Quiller-Couch, A. T.: *Historical Tales from
    Shakespeare*, 200–2, 212

Rackham, Arthur: illustrations by, 194, 210
Rainolds, John, 3–4
Red Bull theatre, 233, 235, 238, 242
Reign of King Edward III, The, x, 137–64, 174;
    images, 156; productions, 152; published
    texts, 139–40, 160; Shakespeare's plays,
    contacts, 158–9; visual effects, 154; themes,
    154–6
re-makes: histories, 165–83; *see also* Ur-*Hamlet*
Reni, Guido, 132
Restoration, 44, 49; comedy, 42, 43, 44,
    53–6, 59, 70, 78, 245
Richard II, King, 138, 143, 151
Robertson, J. M., 163
Robertson, T. W., 78; *Society*, 80–1
Robinson, W. Heath, 194, 210
Rochester, John Wilmot, Earl of, 80
Rome, 67–8
Rose theatre, 140, 160
Rossiter, A. P., 147
Rowe, Nicholas, 221
Rowley, Samuel, 118

S., W.: *A Funerall Elegye*, x
Salingar, Leo, x, xi–xii

Salisbury, Countesses of, 150–2
Sampson, George, 194, 211
satire, 59–60, 67–9
Saxo Grammaticus, 214, 223, 224, 225
Scarlet, Thomas, 139
schools' editions of Shakespeare tales, xi,
    195–7
Seneca, 11, 237, 242
sequels, 166
Serpieri, Alessandro, 182
Serraillier, Ian: *The Enchanted Island*, 207–8,
    212
Seymour, Mary: *Shakespeare's Stories Simply
    Told*, 199, 212
Shakespeare, William: birthday, 137, 138;
    authorship disputed, x; author of *The Reign
    of King Edward III?*, 137–8, 161–3, 174;
    authorial criticism, 251–2:
    WORKS: First Folio, 161, 162, 163, 252–3;
    prose versions, 185–212; *All's Well that Ends
    Well*, 34, 88, 186, 188, 189; *Antony and
    Cleopatra*, 115–16, ('asp' scene, 24–6, 86);
    As You Like It, 114, 188; *The Comedy of
    Errors*, 206–7; *Coriolanus*, 88, 214, 225,
    (Buchan's version, 205, 206); *Cymbeline*,
    87–8, 117, 188; *Hamlet*, 60, 87, 91, 96, 97,
    102, 134, 186, 202, 205–6, 209, 238,
    (conversations with the dead, 213–29),
    (grave-digging scene, 23–4, 86), (player
    scenes, 1, 10–13, 32, 231–2, 241, 251–2),
    ('To be or not to be', 22); *Henry IV*, 64–5,
    88–9, 171–81; *Henry V*, 7, 20, 117, 171,
    177, 180–1, (and *Edward III*, 158, 159, 160,
    161), (ending, 156–7); *Henry VI*, 159, 163,
    201; *Henry VIII*, x, xi, 78, 117–35, 181,
    (chronology, 135–6); *Julius Caesar*, 33, 115,
    252, (Churchill's version, 205); *King John*,
    158, 198; *King Lear*, x, 20, 85, 91, 98–102,
    103, 187, 189, 199, 204, 205, 206, 207;
    Love's Labour's Lost, 102, 112, 115; *Macbeth*,
    13, 19, 20, 91, 108–10, 182, 192, 203, 207,
    252, ('My husband!', 23), (porter, 24, 33);
    Measure for Measure, 19, 21, 32–40, 88,
    89–91, 188, 189, 193–4, 195, 199, 204, 252,
    (bed-trick, 27–9, 32–6, 90), (Duke 35–9,
    182, 244), (and *Edward III*, 158, 159, 160,
    189, 193–4, 195); *The Merchant of Venice*,
    91, 187, 198, 202–3, 204, 207, 208, 252; *A
    Midsummer Night's Dream*, 7–10, 15, 91–2,
    111–12, 187–8, 199, 203; *Much Ado about
    Nothing*, 91, 92, 95–6, 102, 106, 112–14;
    Othello, 86, 92, 94–5, 96, 97, 102, 103–6,
    111, (Iago's language, 182), ('My
    husband!', 23); *Pericles*, 89, 101, 162, 192;
    The Rape of Lucrece, 2, 160; *Richard II*, 175,
    179, 180, 199); *Richard III*, 106, 117, 118,
    170–1; *Romeo and Juliet*, 202; *Sonnets*, 85–6,
    95, 159; *The Taming of the Shrew*,
    (children's illustration, *184*), (prose
    version, 208); *The Tempest*, 97, 112, 188,
    198; *Timon of Athens*, 2, 87, 114, 229; *Titus
    Andronicus*, 19, 163, 193, 194–5, 197; *Troilus*

Shakespeare, William—*contd*
  and *Cressida*, 106–7; *Twelfth Night*, 75,
  102–3, 192, (prose version, 207); *Two
  Gentlemen of Verona*, 64, 92–4; *Two Noble
  Kinsmen*, 162; *Venus and Adonis*, 2; *The
  Winter's Tale*, 2, 15, 21, 33, 34, 91, 95, 96,
  102, 110–11, 117, 129, 188, 197, 198, 207
Shakespeare Tales for Boys and Girls, 204, 211
'Shall I die?' (poem), x
Shaw, George Bernard, 79, 201, 239
Shields, Ella, 81–2
Shirley, James, 245
Sidney, Sir Philip, 1, 19, 238, 239, 242, 246;
  An Apology for Poetry, 29, 97, 113; *Arcadia*,
  75–6
Sim, Adelaide C. Gordon: *Phoebe's Shakespeare*,
  200, 212
Simnel, Lambert, 118
*Sir Thomas More see Book of Sir Thomas More,
  The*
Six Stories from Shakespeare, 204–6, 211
Sluys, battle of, 144, 148, 149
Smidt, Kristian, 174
Smith, Sir Thomas, 57
Snowden, Viscount, 205, 211
Sophocles, 224
Spectator, The, 203
Spenser, Edmund, 202, 215; *The Faerie
  Queene*, 29
Spevack, Marvin: *Concordance*, 180–1, 182
Spilsbury, A. T., 211
St George's Day, 138
St Paul's, 60; playhouse, 232, 238, 240, 241,
  244
St Paul's cathedral, 120
St Paul's church, 50
Stafford, Simon, 140
Stationers' Register, 139, 160
Steele, Richard: *Town-Talk*, 55
Stoddart, Sarah, 186
Stoicism, 215
Stokes, Winston, 194, 211
Stoppard, Tom, 229
Stow, John, 146–7
Strand, the, 41, 45–8, 78, 81, 83; fish in, 66;
  theatres, 41
Strand magazine, 83
Strindberg, Johan August, 16, 103
Summerson, Sir John, 48
Swift, Jonathan, 74
Swinburn, A. C., 139–40, 161–2

Tales from Shakespeare (Lamb), 185–97, 204,
  206, 208, (editions, 190–7, *listed* 210–11)
Tarlton, Richard, 171, 250
teaching methods, xi, 195–7
Tennyson, Alfred: *Mariana*, 34–5
Thackeray, William Makepeace, 42, 83
Theatre (Shoreditch), 140

theatres *see* playhouses and theatres; *names of
  theatres*
Theobald, Lewis: *Double Falsehood*, 162
Thompson, A. Hamilton, 190, 191–2
Tilley, M. J., 58
Tilley, Vesta, 81
Tillyard, E. M. W., 173
Tofte, Robert, 237
Tree, Beerbohm, 202
Trewin, J. C., 195, 211
Trousdale, Marion, 157
True Tragedy, 167
Tuck, Raphael, 193

Ubaldino, Petruccio, 148
unities, 4–5
Unton, Sir Henry: portrait, *18*, 30
Ur-*Hamlet*, 167, 216, 218, 225

Vergil, Polydore, 137
Virgil: *Aeneid*, 220
Vivat Rex (radio series), 152

wages, 236
Walker, J. A., 211
Walpole, Horace, 56
Walpole, Hugh, 204, 205
War of the Theatres, 234
Warbeck, Perkin, 118
Ward, A. C., 197
Warning for Fair Women, A, 239–40
Webster, John, 234, 240, 242; *Devil's Law
  Case*, 58, 248; *A Monumental Column*, 147;
  The White Devil, 242, 248
Weeks, Richard, 136
Weever, John, 237
Wells, Stanley, xi, 166
Wentersdorf, K. P., 148
West End comedy: early, 41–78; later
  tradition, 78–84
Westminster, 44; Abbey, 121, 122; Great
  Hall, 45
Whitefriars, 238, 243
Wickham, Glynne, x, xii, 137
Wilde, Oscar, 42, 79; *The Importance of Being
  Earnest*, 81
Williams, Clifford, 206
Wilton, Marie, 80
wit, 232
Wittgenstein, Ludwig, 227, 228, 229
Wodehouse, P. G., 83
Wolsey, Cardinal Thomas, 119; in *Henry
  VIII*, 121, 124–32
Wood, Stanley, 211
Woodstock, 171, 179
Wordsworth, William, 186, 189; *The Prelude*,
  187
Wotton, Sir Henry, 136
Wroughton, Richard, 199
Wycherley, William: *The Country Wife*, 53